Contents

Foreword

Ken Dvorak

As this anthology demonstrates, steampunk presents the popular culture scholar with a multitude of venues from which to investigate this science fiction and fantasy subgenre. Ray Browne (1922–2009), the founder of the academic study of popular culture in America, wrote that popular culture "is the everyday world around us: the mass media, entertainments, and diversions. It is our heroes, icons, rituals, everyday actions, psychology, and religion—our total life picture. It is the way of living we inherit, practice and modify as we please, and how we do it. It is the dreams we dream while asleep."[1] And what if these dreams are steampunk influenced? Steampunk turns upside down the world of science fiction and fantasy. Reimagining both the past and the future, often through a neo-Victorian lens, steampunk also allows us to debate serious social, economic, political, and cultural issues relevant to our present lives.

Since the 1980s steampunk has witnessed the emergence of a global community of followers whose interest has moved beyond its Victorian literary foundations, and the genre has split into a mash-up of creative influences. A new generation of tinkerers and entrepreneurs make and sell steampunk-themed products, including home décor items; laptops retrofitted with gears, brass, and knobs; and fashion designs with such "must haves" as goggles, corsets, and skin art. Steampunk has crossed over into feature films, fandom groups, video games, and music (e.g., steampunk fair headliners Abney Park and Professor Elemental). One can even fantasize with steam-powered vibrators (beware, you need to wear welding gloves because the vibrator gets "hot," according to one inventor!).[2]

Steampunk's admirers and critics alike have grappled with its exact "meaning." Katherine Wilson observes "what makes Steampunk tricky to peg down is its amorphous nature."[3] She notes that steampunk, for the most part, has a decided Victorian influence but it may just as easily fit into other "clothes," such as Edwardian or perhaps psychedelic, but with steampunk it is what you choose for the masquerade ball. Fan blog sites provide additional examples of steampunk's accessibility to the general public. The Weird Tales blog has published Stephen H. Segal's "Five Thoughts on the Popularity of Steampunk," pointing out that for those who once were part of the Goth movement, some have drifted along with their parents to steampunk finding that "It's not just cool because it is trendy—it's cool because it is inspirational."[4]

Putting this levity aside for a moment, steampunk does provoke serious political and social debate—much of it self-reflective. Is it merely a nostalgia-driven fad or an actual "movement" with an ideology and agenda? Rebecca Onion, whose path-breaking chapter is cited throughout this collection, observes that "a social movement based around an aesthetic seems particularly vulnerable to imitation and misinterpretation."[5] In sync with Browne's call to explore the multiple manifestations of "popular culture," Onion acknowledges the heart of steampunk culture is best defined by "the object-based work of its fans" but cautions that "misinterpretation of an aesthetic movement as simple aesthetics leaves the deeper relationship between human and object unexamined."[6] One example of steampunk as more than mere "aesthetic" can be seen in its "radical" endeavors; bloggers James Schafer and Kate Franklin of Parliament & Wake, in their discussion "Why Steampunk (Still) Matters," describe steampunk as a counterculture movement aligned with those objecting to global corporate greed and the increasing disparities between the "haves" and "have nots"—themes familiar to those found in the Occupy Wall Street protests (OWS).[7] "Radical" steampunks envision a future far different from today, with political/economic/social power structures reversed, leaving its proponents asking "Why not?" and demanding greater accountability from the ruling political/corporate classes.

If we return to just the literary origins of steampunk, we see how it has moved beyond its sci-fi roots, fracturing into such subgenres as steampunk erotica and "paranormal steampunk." Popular culture scholars are presented with an interesting challenge: how to define this movement without assigning it a homogenizing identity. Steampunk devotees are well aware of previous anthologies—Ann and Jeff VanderMeer's essential *Steampunk* (2008) immediately comes to mind—that showcase the literature that has been inspired by Verne and Wells and seem to best epitomize the "steampunk" label. The chapters included in *Steaming into a Victorian Future* offer critical explorations of such fiction, as well as the other equally important manifestations of steampunk, from music to DIY websites. Hopefully this anthology will be a catalyst for further scholarly debate as steampunk becomes an even greater presence in popular culture.

Notes

1. "Conversations with Scholars in American Popular Culture: Ray B. Browne," *Americana: The Journal of American Popular Culture 1900 to Present* 1, no. 2 (2002), n.p., www.americanpopularculture.com/journal/articles/fall_2002/browne.htm (1 April 2012).

2. Ani Niows, inventor, cited in Katherine Wilson, "Steampunk," *Meanjin Quarterly* 69, no. 2 (2010): 26.

3. Wilson, "Steampunk," 24.

4. Stephen H. Segal, "Five Thoughts on the Popularity of Steampunk," in *Weird Tales: The Original Magazine of the Unique, Fantastic & Bizarre* (2008), http://weirdtales.net/wordpress/2008/09/17/five-thoughts-on-the-popularity-of-steampunk (1 April 2012).

5. Rebecca Onion, "Reclaiming the Machine: An Introductory Look at Steampunk in Everyday Practice," *Neo-Victorian Studies* 1, no. 1 (2008): 155, www.neovictorianstudies.com (1 April 2012).

6. Onion, "Reclaiming the Machine," 139.

7. James Schafer and Kate Franklin, "Why Steampunk (Still) Matters" (2011), http://parliamentandwake.com/veil/whysteampunkmatters/whysteampunkmatters.html (1 April 2012).

Bibliography

"Conversations with Scholars of American Popular Culture: Ray B. Browne." *Americana: The Journal of American Popular Culture 1900 to Present* 1, no. 2 (2002), n.p. www.americanpopularculture.com/journal/articles/fall_2002/browne.htm (1 April 2012).

Onion, Rebecca. "*Reclaiming the Machine: An Introductory Look at Steampunk in Everyday Practice.*" *Neo-Victorian Studies* 1, no. 1 (2008): 138–163. www.neovictorianstudies.com (1 April 2012).

Schafer, James, and Kate Franklin. "Why Steampunk (Still) Matters." (2011). http://parliamentandwake.com/veil/whysteampunkmatters/whysteampunkmatters.html (1 April 2012).

Segal, Stephen H. "Five Thoughts on the Popularity of Steampunk." (2008). http://weirdtales.net/wordpress/2008/09/17/five-thoughts-on-the-popularity-of-steampunk (1 April 2012).

VanderMeer, Jeff, and Ann VanderMeer. *Steampunk.* San Francisco: Tachyon Publications, 2008.

Wilson, Katherine. "Steampunk." *Meanjin Quarterly* 69, no. 2 (2010): 22–33.

Acknowledgments

This project owes a great debt to the vision, insight, and support of many, from the intellectual and creative influences of colleagues whose work laid the foundation for the chapters herein, to the patience and encouragement of friends and loved ones. First and foremost, we would like to extend our heartfelt thanks to Ken Dvorak, who conceived this project and infused it with his great enthusiasm for steampunk as a cultural phenomenon. We would also like to offer our thanks and admiration to our artists—Jody Steel, Ashley Norfleet, Brian Kesinger, and John Tibbetts—for generously sharing their time and talent to create the illustrations that appear on the cover and throughout the chapters. Thanks also to Jeff VanderMeer for providing the volume's afterword, and to Stephen Ryan, for his unwavering support of the project, from its earliest moments through completion. And finally, to the thirteen fine scholars whose contributions have brought depth and richness to this anthology, thank you, one and all.

Perils of the future. *Copyright Jody Steel*

Introduction

Cynthia J. Miller and Julie Anne Taddeo

Imagine a Victorian world where colorful flying contraptions crawl across the skies, rockets propel wrought-iron velocipedes, and clockwork men clamber about in mechanical bodies. Jules Verne and H. G. Wells brought these "different engines" into their contemporary world, calling forth both gods and monsters in the machine and, in the process, creating the building blocks for countless alternate universes. These are the worlds of steampunk, where spectacle intrudes into ordinary nineteenth-century settings, carrying with it timeless fears and fantasies.[1]

Originally coined in the late 1980s, the term *steampunk* was "retrofitted," if you will, to describe a group of nineteenth-century-inspired technofantasies[2]—darkly atmospheric novels of a time that never was—ranging from K. W. Jeter's *Morlock Night* (1979) and *Infernal Devices* (1987), James P. Blaylock's *Homonculus* (1986), and Tim Powers's *The Anubis Gates* (1983), which were becoming increasingly popular with readers of science fiction and fantasy, to the much earlier works of Verne and Wells. It is an uncommon hybrid of a term, describing even more uncommon tales of historical science fiction infused with Victorian visions of wildly anachronistic technologies. Here, in a London darker and wilder than anything imagined by Dickens, scientists and magicians, philosophers and poets, time travelers and clockwork humans animate worlds inspired by Gothic romances, where extraordinary inventions are seamlessly integrated into everyday life.[3]

In the decades since steampunk's formal inclusion in the literary and cinematic imagination, even more novels, short stories, and films have brought the genre's whirring gears and gleaming gadgetry to the far corners of the world. As a result, a complex global subculture and fandom have emerged, drawing together literature, film, music, art, fashion, and both material and digital cultures, along with institutions of preservation and display, creating what Rebecca Onion terms "a multi-textual aesthetic."[4] The constellations of meaning associated with steampunk have evolved and expanded beyond mere technofantasy, to signal innovation, creativity, unconventionality, and resistance—both imaginative and political.

While many well-known steampunk works, such as Brian Aldiss's trio of writings that began with *Frankenstein Unbound* (1973), William Gibson and Bruce Sterling's novel *The Difference Engine* (1991), and Alan Moore's graphic-novel series *The League of Extraordinary Gentlemen* (1999), stay close to their Victorian roots,[5] others range farther afield: Philip Pullman's young adult trilogy, *His Dark Materials* (2005), begins in an otherworldly version of Oxford that is a blend of nineteenth-century settings and mind-boggling technologies (including a truth-detecting alethiometer). Cherie Priest's *Boneshaker* (2009) and its sequels, *Dreadnought* (2010) and *Clementine* (2010), inject airship pirates, deadly gasses, and the titular "Incredible Bone-Shaking Drill Engine" into a Civil War–era United States. Joe R. Lansdale's *Zeppelins West* (2001) transports the performers of Buffalo Bill's Wild West show to Japan via zeppelin. Led by Cody, whose head is kept alive in a Mason jar, mounted atop a steam-powered man, the tale borrows characters and narrative devices from Shelley's *Frankenstein* (1818), Stoker's *Dracula* (1897), Verne's *20,000 Leagues Under the Sea* (1869), and even Baum's *The Wonderful Wizard of Oz* (1900), along the way.

As steampunk made its way from the page to the screen, it made itself at home in other locales, such as the American frontier in the television series *The Wild, Wild West* (CBS, 1965–1969). The series and its feature-film remake (1999) followed the James Bond–style adventures of two gadget-laden Secret Service agents who battled an assortment of diabolical inventors and their super-weapons in the late 1860s and early 1870s. Later, the unconventional Western heroes of *The Adventures of Brisco County, Jr.* (Fox, 1993–1994) and the short-lived series *Legend* (UPN, 1995)—a lawyer-turned-bounty-hunter and a dime-novelist-turned-adventurer—met similar opponents in the 1890s, defeating them with the help of eccentric inventor partners who equipped them with advanced technology of their own. In motion pictures, films such as *Van Helsing* (2004), *The Golden Compass* (2007), and *Jonah Hex* (2010) deepened the fantastic tones of their source material with steampunk imagery that helped define the subgenre's cinematic niche.

While the diversity of steampunk's formats, characters, and inventions is breathtaking, taken together, all of them work to place steampunk—with its collision of past and future and its dissonance of form and function—squarely in the visual foreground as a commentary on the relationship between human and machine. Nineteenth-century science and technology were often characterized by this ongoing conflict of wonder versus horror—the balance between the irrational and the rational, fantasy and realism—the two existing side by side in continual tension as the world around them grappled with notions of progress.[6] And while the continued advancement of technology pushed back the boundaries of the magical, the era's highly advanced technology often seemed—as science fiction writer Arthur C. Clarke famously observed—indistinguishable from magic. The fantastic machines it created stood for our ability to tame the most fearsome creations, with the Victorian inventor playing a role that was half scientist, half magus.[7]

And it is that magic, breathtaking and terrifying at the same time, that steampunk confers on the genres and contexts in which it appears. The introduction of Victorian technologies inflects even the most traditional of narratives with glimmers of spectacle, horror, and futuristic realism—the powers exhibited by its extraordinary machines are beyond comprehension. They defy gravity, annihilate distance, reshape the landscape with the pull of a lever, and obliterate entire cities with the push of a button. The disjuncture of their appearance focuses audiences' attention on *meaning*—not only of historical time, space, and capacity but also of the stability of the present as its ongoing extension. It releases our unspoken fears about the inherent moral qualities of technology and the politics of progress, at the same time reminding us of the fragility of our historically grounded cultural identities.[8] "Steampunk is fantasy made real," proclaimed an editorial in a recent issue of *SteamPunk Magazine*, "filtered through the brass sieve of nostalgia, vehemence, curiosity, wonderment, and apprehension. It is inherently political, . . . it is anti-establishment. It is dangerous to pluck our dreams from muddy scribblings and coax them into existence."[9]

The Scope of the Book

While often considered solely through the lens of literature—science fiction, in particular—steampunk is, in fact, a complex phenomenon that also affects, transforms, and unites a wide range of disciplines and the individuals and communities that create, interpret, and consume them. This volume expands and extends existing scholarship on steampunk in order to explore previously unconsidered questions about cultural creativity, social networking, fandom, appropriation, and the creation of meaning.[10] The following chapters examine the many and varied manifestations of steampunk, both separately and in relation to each other, in order to better understand the steampunk subculture and its effect on—and interrelationship with—popular culture and the wider society.

In a recent article for *Neo-Victorian Studies*, Christine Ferguson encouraged scholars to pay "more attention both to mass-market steampunk fiction and to the subculture's rich micro-media—to zines, blogs, and discussion board postings, music lyrics, artist's statements, manufactured objects, and costumes"; in doing so, we can move beyond the aesthetic, in order to appreciate the often competing "practices and political identifications" of steampunk.[11] As just one example of neo-Victorianism,[12] steampunk reflects the possibilities for subversion; it is not a mere nostalgia for corsets or fantasies of goggles and dirigibles, but another lens through which to examine the racial, class, and gender politics of both the past and present.

Part I of this collection is especially concerned with the social messages of the steampunk narrative, whether expressed through the medium of the novel or, in the case of "chap-hop" artist Professor Elemental, music. Despite their differences, the examples of steampunk presented in this section reflect not only the timelessness of Victorianism but also, as Rachel Bowser and Brian Croxall suggest, how we are the "Other Victorians."[13] We look to the Victorians—so familiar yet strange—not necessarily to escape the mundane of the present or to romanticize the past, but to understand and negotiate contemporary problems.

While Jules Verne and H. G. Wells clearly influence the technological fantasies and aesthetic of steampunk, Catherine Siemann suggests an even earlier Victorian influence: the social problem novel. Mastered by the likes of Charles Dickens, Wilkie Collins, and Elizabeth Gaskell, this genre of fiction exposed the cruelties of the Industrial Revolution as it wreaked havoc on the lives of the English working class. In her chapter, "Some Notes on the Steampunk Social Problem Novel," Siemann uses a diverse range of fiction, from William Gibson and Bruce Sterling's *The Difference Engine* (1991) to more recent works like China Miéville's *Perdido Street Station* (2000) and Cherie Priest's *Boneshaker* (2009) to explore how steampunk echoes the themes and reformist agenda of the Victorian "novel of purpose." Steampunk authors are less concerned with re-creating the "gaslamp" atmosphere of the past than they are with redressing such social issues as prostitution, voting inequalities, pollution, and crime, which dominated Victorian discourse and still speak to contemporary audiences.

One issue in particular links steampunk to its nineteenth-century roots: what the Victorians called the "Woman Question"—in other words, what can/should a woman do? In his chapter, "Useful Troublemakers: Social Retrofuturism in the Steampunk Novels of Gail Carriger and Cherie Priest," Mike Perschon addresses how these two steampunk writers reimagine the New Woman, whose rational dress and suffrage campaigns threatened society with "sexual anarchy," but who, in retrospect, was more often a literary construction than actual danger to Victorian convention. Carriger's *Parasol Protectorate* series and Priest's *Clockwork Century* series offer modern readers independent, strong female characters (what Perschon calls "damsels without distress") who challenge Victorian tropes of fallen women, mannish old maids, and rescued maidens, and in the process, illustrate steampunk's potential to investigate not just technological but social possibilities as well.

Perschon bemusedly observes that while many Victorian New Women longed to get *out* of a corset, the hope of many steampunk women seems to be to get *into* one. The social implications of steampunk's love affair with the corset are explored further in Julie Anne Taddeo's chapter, "Corsets of Steel: Steampunk's Reimagining of Victorian Femininity." What some Victorian New Women and twentieth-century feminists critiqued as a "straitjacket" of femininity, contemporary writers of steampunk romance and erotic fiction now envision as a garment of liberation and transgression. In the steampunk universe, corsets act as body armor, empower hearts with their clockwork technology, and, last but not least, facilitate sexual pleasure. In the process, these entertaining stories of corseted heroines defending Victoria's empire or coping with their own cyborged selves expose the social limitations that confronted their historical counterparts for whom the corset was often more restricting than liberating.

Since Janice Radway's groundbreaking 1984 study, *Reading the Romance*, other academics have recognized the romance genre's potential for social criticism and feminist commentary alongside the expected narratives of burgeoning love and passion. As Dru Pagliassotti (herself a writer of steampunk romance) notes in her chapter, "Love and the Machine: Technology and Human Relationships in Steampunk Romance and Erotica," steampunk romance and erotica have an additional special attraction as they promise that anyone can find love or sexual fulfillment even in a complex world increasingly shaped by technology. Like much contemporary neo-Victorian romance, steampunk romance and erotica call upon social restrictions on gender roles, cross-class and cross-race relationships, and same-sex relationships, using them to present obstacles to the protagonists' romantic and/or sexual fulfillment. However, when technology is a significant part of the plot, it is typically depicted as a means by which the characters may break down those restrictions. At the same time, these stories emphasize that although technology may aid or enhance human abilities and relationships, it is ultimately incapable of satisfactorily replacing them.

Our relationship to technology, and its often disastrous results, is the theme not just of steampunk fiction but of its music as well, as described in Jamieson Ridenhour's chapter, "'Anything Is Possible for a Man in a Top Hat with a Monkey with a Monocle': Remixing Steampunk in Professor Elemental's *The Indifference Engine*." Professor Elemental's 2010 album is in many ways an anthology of steampunk stories in rhyme set to a beat. The character, an explorer/inventor/tea afficionado who has a surgically altered orangutan butler and wears jodhpurs and a pith helmet, is revealed through the narratives in the raps, and like other steampunk works, many of Professor Elemental's songs use Victorian sensation literature as a jumping-off point. As hip-hop, Elemental's music also reflects how steampunk culture in general represents a "remix," a reverential nod to older works and ideas accomplished by combining them with new interpretations, new politics, and new technologies.

In "Animal Magic," Professor Elemental, in his mad scientist role, sings about his "home-made zoo," playfully prompting us to consider the ethics of "playing God." Part II of this collection looks at this more familiar manifestation of steampunk—science fiction—with its Victorian roots and contemporary concerns. The following chapters in this section also represent how steampunk itself has evolved, from the page to the screen, and now as a "real life" and virtual community, reflecting in the process steampunk's complicated embrace and repudiation of technology.

As an early example of the genre, Jacques Tardi's 1974 graphic novel, *The Arctic Marauder*, calls attention to the destructive potential of Victorian scientific ambition, and explores the moral consequences of the technologies that have come to exemplify steampunk narratives. In her chapter, "'In Sum, Evil Has Prevailed': The Moral Morass of Science and Exploration in Jacques Tardi's *The Arctic Marauder*," Erika Behrisch Elce describes how Tardi captures the spirit of Victorian polar exploration, but the main purpose of the novel is social critique; the idealism of scientific discovery for the benefit of humanity is replaced with the scientists' delight in destruction. At the end of Tardi's story of mad scientists and the evils they create, the narrator reassures us: "let not your heart be troubled, such individuals do not exist, they will never exist, and inventions of this ilk are impossible to build," but as Elce reminds us, readers of steampunk know that at the start of the twenty-first century, Tardi's narrator is, unfortunately, tragically wrong.

In "'Fulminations and Fulgurators': Jules Verne, Karel Zeman, and Steampunk Cinema," John C. Tibbetts introduces us to another example of proto-steampunk: the 1958 film *The Fabulous World of Jules Verne*. Based on one of Verne's later novels, *Face au drapeau* ("Facing the Flag"), Czech filmmaker Karel Zeman's production is a Victorian-era retrovision, imagining for the nineteenth century such wildly anachronistic technologies as submarines, air travel, and rocket missiles. Like Tardi's *Arctic Marauder*, Verne's story, and Zeman's film, echo both Victorians' and steampunks' ambivalence regarding the benefits of science, as the mad scientist Roch experiments with the "Roch Fulgurator," a sort of auto-propulsive engine charged with an explosive compound. Curiously, unlike his contemporary H. G. Wells, Verne displayed little, if any, awareness of early motion picture technology and its visual effects. As Tibbetts concludes, it was up to Zeman not just to *adapt* Verne's story, but to *create* a proto-steampunk vision of his own.

Not all of steampunk science fiction imagines technology as immoral and threatening. The iconic image of the dirigible graces the covers of innumerable steampunk novels and announces the joyful potential of human invention. In "Airships East, Zeppelins West: Steampunk's Fantastic Frontiers," Cynthia J. Miller describes how airships embody steampunk's imaginative power, even as they reference present-day nostalgia for the early years of flight. Miller looks at the history of the airship in popular culture, from the proto-steampunk novels of Jules Verne to more contemporary films like *Wild Wild West* (1999) as well as the historical origins (and disasters) of early airship travel. Despite such horrors as the Hindenburg explosion, the airship signifies, according to Miller, the possibility of magic and the magic of possibility as steampunk adventurers explore and redefine the frontier.

Similarly, for Suzanne Barber and Matt Hale, steampunk represents a proclivity toward a positivistic and reconstructive mentality as opposed to a nihilistic, deconstructive schema. In their chapter, "Enacting the Never-Was: Upcycling the Past, Present, and Future in Steampunk," they second Miller's notion of the magical and playful aspects of steampunk culture. Conducting their own ethnographic research with attendees at the Alternate History Track at Dragon*Con 2010 in Atlanta, Georgia, Barber and Hale prompt us to expand our reading of "texts" to include the expressive behaviors of those who identify themselves as steampunk. Participants in the "History Interactive!" panel were given a variety of historical scenarios to reconstruct and subsequently perform for one another with the aid of contemporary, historical, and steampunk-themed props. Panel attendees created skits that centered around the "what ifs" of history, creating, for example, an alternate, steampunked version of the Civil War or a Viking Thanksgiving. In the process, the participants engaged in what Barber and Hale call "upcycling" time—the past not only becomes the building blocks of an alternate history, it also presents new possibilities for shaping an alternate present and future.

Diana M. Pho in her chapter, "Objectified and Politicized: The Dynamics of Ideology and Consumerism in Steampunk Subculture," expands this analysis of the steampunk community to the virtual realm. Pho notes the strange irony that despite its admiration for preindustrial technologies, steampunk cannot thrive without the aid of social media platforms like Facebook, Tumblr, and Twitter; interpreting personal websites and blogs as "objects," she ponders how steampunk's postmodern, mediatized identity serves both in conjunction with and in reaction against anticonsumerist stances. Her comparison of two very different politically biased texts, the more "radical" *SteamPunk Magazine* and the "conservative" online comic *Steampunk Palin*, for example, illustrates how steampunk accounts for dynamic viewpoints (and engenders a great deal of controversy among its practitioners and fans).

While Pho broadens our understanding of the steampunk "object," Part III of our collection returns to a more traditional notion of steampunk "things"—and the individuals (both "real" and fictional) who make, collect, sell, use, and/or curate them. In the examples of science fiction discussed by our contributors, the fulgurators and airships would not be possible without the genius of the inventor, but steampunk, with its do-it-yourself ethic, has an "Everyman" (and woman) appeal, encouraging aficionados to retrofit a home computer or design jewelry out of old clock bits and pieces.

In "'Love the Machine, Hate the Factory': Steampunk Design and the Vision of a Victorian Future," Sally-Anne Huxtable considers the ways in which online marketplaces such as Etsy.com and Folksy.co.uk have facilitated the emergence of this DIY culture of art, craft, fashion, and design. Huxtable also suggests that the political activism and utopianism of the nineteenth-century arts and crafts movement are reimagined in steampunk design as an expression of resistance against the perceived uniformity and blandness of contemporary consumer culture. Inspired by *SteamPunk Magazine*'s motto, "Love the machine, hate the factory," Huxtable's chapter explores the ways in which steampunk offers a vision of an alternative future in which factory-made, mass-produced, and homogenous design is abandoned in favor of an aesthetic that celebrates the beauty of machines, the materiality of objects and dress, and the importance of the quality of individuality and the act of artistic creation itself.

Many steampunks, as Amy Sue Bix argues, portray the Victorian era as the last refuge of fine craftsmanship, as they express nostalgia for the look and feel of older technologies and ornamental objects made of brass, iron, levers, and glass. Bix's chapter, "Steve Jobs versus the Victorians: Steampunk, Design, and the History of Technology in Society," however, reminds us that Victorians themselves grappled with the aesthetics of their new technologies and strove to make them less ugly and terrifying by, for example, shrouding steam engines with Doric temples and laurel wreaths. Not only have Victorian anxieties become our own, but Bix provocatively suggests that one of the most iconic symbols of our modern age—the Apple computer—has in its origins, mission, and evolving design a kinship to the steampunk agenda. Like some of the steampunk artists discussed in this collection, Steve Jobs was a self-taught "tinkerer" who positioned his design and quest for minimalism as a conscious reaction against the trends he detested among other modern technology creators. Whether or not adherents of steampunk will recognize these connections is less relevant than how both sides illustrate the primacy of design choices and what they signify about technology's creators, users, and the cultures in which they are embedded.

As Bix adds, Jobs's death in 2011 has led to much postmortem mythologizing, not all of it positive, reflecting the contested position the inventor occupies in popular culture. A. Bowdoin Van Riper, in his chapter "Remaking the World: The Steampunk Inventor on Page and Screen," observes that steampunk novels and films, in particular, depict the inventor in morally ambiguous terms, tempering an uncritical Victorian-style embrace of engineers as a class with a sadder-but-wiser awareness of individual engineers' ulterior motives and ethical lapses. Exploring the fictional men (and in a few cases, the women) who design the fantastic machines that have become synonymous with steampunk—and their various roles as heroes, villains, sidekicks, and tragic victims of their own ingenuity—Van Riper traces how our attitudes toward technology, and those who create it, have evolved since the nineteenth century.

What began as a purely literary movement has expanded to encompass a range of art forms and cultural practices, including film and television, fashion, social media, music, and material culture. Just as it draws from and reimagines the past, steampunk has its own history and artifacts that are worthy of interpretation and display. But as Jeanette Atkinson argues in her chapter, "Steampunk's Legacy: Collecting and Exhibiting the Future of Yesterday," curating steampunk's material culture poses some unique challenges to Western museums. Atkinson analyzes steampunk exhibitions held in the United Kingdom in recent years to understand how museums engage with steampunk communities and provide a forum for their created identities and constructed realities. Steampunk artists may struggle with the implications of having their work collected and exhibited, resisting, for instance, the mainstreaming of their efforts; also, the museum's original Victorian mission to act as an "agent of civilization" may seem anathema to steampunk's anti-establishment stance. Nevertheless, the success, for example, of the 2011 exhibit held by the League of Victorian Imagineers in Oamaru, New Zealand, illustrates how museums can showcase and give a voice to steampunk culture.

The following chapters all highlight how steampunk—as subgenre, culture, and multitextual aesthetic—resists easy definition. This anthology, then, does not seek to construct one, but rather, maps the intellectual, social, and creative terrain that has been shaped and reconfigured by steampunk's influence, even as that terrain continues to shift and evolve. Scholarly explorations of steampunk, still in their infancy, are also evolving, and the chapters here engage with those conversations in ways that illustrate the dynamic impact of steampunk on our cultural, political, philosophical, and creative worlds.

Notes

1. Peter Nicholls, "Steampunk," *The Encyclopedia of Science Fiction*, ed. John Clute and Peter Nicholls (New York: St. Martin's, 1995), 1161.

2. Author James P. Blaylock has referred to steampunk as "Technofantasy in a neo-Victorian Retrofuture." For more, see Blaylock's blog, "Steampunk Scholar" at www.steampunkscholar.blogspot.com.

3. See also, works by nineteenth-century writer Albert Robida, such as *Le Vingtième siècle* (1883), *La Guerre au vingtième siècle* (1887), and *Le Vingtième siècle: la vie électrique* (1890), for earlier examples of what is now known as steampunk.

4. Rebecca Onion, "Reclaiming the Machine: An Introductory Look at Steampunk in Everyday Practice," *Neo-Victorian Studies* 1, no. 1 (Autumn 2008): 138–163, www.neovictorianstudies.com/past.../NVS%201–1%201–Onion.pdf (10 October 2011).

5. Nader Elhefnawy, "Of Alternate Nineteenth Centuries," *Internet Review of Science Fiction* (July 2009), www.irosf.com/q/zine/article/10562, n.p. (26 October 2010).

6. Martin Willis, *Mesmerists, Monsters, and Machines: Science Fiction and the Cultures of Science in the Nineteenth Century* (Kent, OH: Kent State University Press, 2006), 4–11.

7. Willis, *Mesmerists*, 5.

8. Shawn James Rosenheim, *The Cryptographic Imagination: Secret Writing from Edgar Allen Poe to the Internet* (Baltimore: Johns Hopkins University Press, 1997), 206.

9. Libby Bulloff, "Our Lives as Fantastic as Any Fiction!" *SteamPunk Magazine*, no. 4 (2008), www.steampunkmagazine.com (10 October 2010).

10. We are inspired by Rachel Bowser and Brian Croxall's special issue on steampunk for *Neo-Victorian Studies*. In their introduction, they aptly observe that steampunk is "more about instability than any other single characteristic. It resists fixedness by unsettling the categories from which it cribs." See Rachel A. Bowser and Brian Croxall, "Introduction: Industrial Evolution," *Neo-Victorian Studies* 3, no. 1 (2010): 6, www.neovictorianstudies.com (2 May 2012).

11. Christine Ferguson, "Surface Tensions: Steampunk, Subculture, and the Ideology of Style," *Neo-Victorian Studies* 4, no. 2 (2011): 66–67, www.neovictorianstudies .com (20 April 2012).

12. Ann Heilmann and Mark Llewellyn remind us that there is no single, all-encompassing definition of neo-Victorianism which is often used as "short-hand for any post-1901 text or film that happens to have a Victorian setting or re-write a Victorian text or a Victorian character." What truly designates a text as neo-Victorian is its "metahistoric and metacultural ramifications of such historical engagement." See Heilmann and Llewellyn, *Neo-Victorianism: The Victorians in the Twenty-First Century, 1999–2009* (Basingstoke and New York: Palgrave Macmillan, 2010), 6.

13. Bowser and Croxall, "Introduction," 30.

Bibliography

Blaylock, James P. "Steampunk Scholar." www.steampunkscholar.blogspot.com.

Bowser, Rachel A., and Brian Croxall. "Introduction: Industrial Evolution." *Neo-Victorian Studies* 3, no. 1 (2010): 1–45. www.neovictorianstudies.com (2 May 2012).

Bulloff, Libby. "Our Lives as Fantastic as Any Fiction!" *SteamPunk Magazine*, no. 4 (2008). www.steampunkmagazine.com (10 October 2010).

Elhefnawy, Nader. "Of Alternate Nineteenth Centuries." *Internet Review of Science Fiction* (July 2009). www.irosf.com/q/zine/article/10562, n.p. (26 October 2010).

Ferguson, Christine. "Surface Tensions: Steampunk, Subculture, and the Ideology of Style." *Neo-Victorian Studies* 4, no. 2 (2011): 66–90. www.neovictorianstudies .com (20 April 2012).

Heilmann, Ann, and Mark Llewellyn. *Neo-Victorianism: The Victorians in the Twenty-First Century, 1999–2009*. Basingstoke and New York: Palgrave Macmillan, 2010.

Nicholls, Peter. "Steampunk." 1161 in *The Encyclopedia of Science Fiction*, ed. John Clute and Peter Nicholls. New York: St. Martin's, 1995.

Onion, Rebecca. "Reclaiming the Machine: An Introductory Look at Steampunk in Everyday Practice," *Neo-Victorian Studies* 1, no. 1 (Autumn 2008): 138–163. www.neovictorianstudies.com/past.../NVS%201–1%201–Onion.pdf (10 October 2011).

Radway, Janice. *Reading the Romance: Women, Patriarchy, and Popular Literature.* Chapel Hill: University of North Carolina Press, 1984.

Rosenheim, Shawn James. *The Cryptographic Imagination: Secret Writing from Edgar Allan Poe to the Internet.* Baltimore: Johns Hopkins University Press, 1997.

Willis, Martin. *Mesmerists, Monsters, and Machines: Science Fiction and the Cultures of Science in the Nineteenth Century.* Kent, OH: Kent State University Press, 2006.

PART I

REIMAGINING CHARACTERS/ RECONFIGURING RELATIONSHIPS

Victorian London's working poor. *Copyright Jody Steel*

CHAPTER ONE

Some Notes on the Steampunk Social Problem Novel

Catherine Siemann

In Victorian Britain, as novelists struggled with the relative lack of respect afforded to their genre, the social problem novel helped to establish that prose fiction could have a serious purpose. As steampunk similarly finds itself dismissed as the latest fad, many of its most interesting manifestations to date can productively be categorized as steampunk social problem novels. In considering texts ranging from Gibson and Sterling's foundational *The Difference Engine* (1991), through China Miéville's *Perdido Street Station* (2000), to recent works by Stephen Hunt, Cherie Priest, and N. K. Jemisin, I will consider the elements that these disparate works have in common, and how these traits define the steampunk social problem novel. Steampunk's examination or rewriting of nineteenth-century social issues speaks to contemporary audiences, who see in them a reflection of our own concerns. Through its combination of history and speculative fiction, steampunk is uniquely positioned to explore ideas that have their roots in our past, and to consider and critique social and technological solutions of past, present, and future alike.

Steampunk novels, at least those set in the nineteenth century or its fictional analogues, may be considered neo-Victorian, engaging with both the same issues that might have concerned Dickens's audience and those the Victorians would have found puzzling or unfamiliar. Ann Heilmann and Mark Llewellyn contend that the neo-Victorian is "in some respect . . . self-consciously engaged with the act of (re)interpretation, (re)discovery and (re)vision concerning the Victorians."[1] The steampunk social problem novel examines issues of poverty and social inequality, as does its Victorian counterpart, but from a perspective of considered distance. At the same time, in critiquing colonialism, or examining the environmental impact of technology, it revises the boundaries of the social problem genre to incorporate a present-day perspective on the Victorians and their legacy.

The Social Problem Novel

What is the social problem novel? In many nineteenth-century novels, social injustices are foregrounded, featured prominently in the text so that both the issue itself and perhaps a call for its reform are inescapably brought to the reader's attention. In his classic study, *The Spirit of Reform*, Patrick Brantlinger suggests that "Victorian writers never tire of repeating . . . that literature is or can be an instrument of social amelioration, at the same time that it is shaped by social events."[2] In the United States, most famously, Harriet Beecher Stowe's *Uncle Tom's Cabin* (1852) popularized the antislavery cause. In Britain, the social problem novel is associated first and foremost with Charles Dickens.

Despite reforms made to many of Dickens's specific targets, such as the Chancery system, the debtors' prison, and the New Poor Law of 1834 (and the workhouses it created), new manifestations of those same issues—access to justice, bureaucracy, and protections for the poverty stricken and the elderly—have retained their currency. Dickens's Court of Chancery in *Bleak House* (1853) and his Bureau of Circumlocution in *Little Dorrit* (1857) rival Kafka's imagery in the public imagination as emblems of a dysfunctional society. Other Victorian novelists were known for their issue-driven novels, such as Elizabeth Gaskell, who focused on the conditions of the working poor in the Industrial North of England (*North and South* [1855], *Mary Barton* [1848]), and Wilkie Collins, who moved from his early sensation novels to issue-driven works engaging with the rights of illegitimate children (*No Name* [1862]), animal vivisection (*Heart and Science* [1883]), and assorted legal questions (*The Law and the Lady* [1875], *Man and Wife* [1870], *Armadale* [1866]).[3]

Dealing with social issues was a way for nineteenth-century novelists, seeking recognition for their prose fiction narratives as a "serious" form of writing, to achieve respectability. But in addition, they saw their works as communicating important ideas. Amanda Claybaugh, in her study of what she terms the "novel of purpose," says nineteenth-century novelists "thought of novels not as self-contained aesthetic objects but rather as active interventions into social and political life. They thought of novels as performative."[4] For the Victorians, therefore, writing fiction was not divorced from a commitment to social reform; it was a form of action in support of political or moral conviction.

There is a thread running through steampunk fiction that engages with this same tradition, as well as the commonly (and justly) cited Wells-and-Verne ancestry. Among the many steampunk books described as "Dickensian" in their jacket copy, at least some were so termed because the copywriters were reminded of Dickens's social critique, and not just because of their atmospheric re-creations of gaslamp London. Moreover, the steampunk community itself, or some portion of it, does not lack in serious purpose, engaging with issues like imperialism, racism, workers' rights, and so forth.[5] A more important question might be: Since steampunk histories are inherently alternate, what social issues do they engage with? Like all speculative fiction, of course, steampunk looks at alternative futures, or pasts, as a way of engaging with issues that are present for us now.[6] Further, the performativity that Claybaugh describes is manifested in steampunk by the representation of problems in new and proactive ways. The steampunk social problem novel is at its best when it engages with issues that resonate not only with the history it reflects, but with those uncomfortably familiar to its contemporary audience, as well.

Gibson, Sterling, and the Origins of the Steampunk Social Problem Novel

Tim Powers is quoted in *The Steampunk Bible* as saying that when he, K. W. Jeter, and James Blaylock wrote the first self-defined "steampunk" in the late 1980s, they used Henry Mayhew's *London Labour and the London Poor* (1851–1882) as inspiration;[7] in Powers's *The Anubis Gates* (1983), passages from Mayhew are dramatized in the misadventures of a time-traveling twentieth-century scholar in Coleridge's London. Despite their interest in Mayhew, however, Powers, Jeter, and Blaylock wrote essentially playful works, featuring time-traveling Morlocks and Romantic poets, and a Pickwick Club–style society of inventors.[8] It took an infusion of cyberpunk,[9] with its dystopian and often *noir* sensibility, to create the steampunk social problem novel.

William Gibson and Bruce Sterling's *The Difference Engine* (1991) first brought steampunk to a broader audience. Their book was widely reviewed in the mainstream press,[10] in part because of the phenomenon of their earlier work, particularly Gibson's *Neuromancer* trilogy, with its then-startling predictions of our cybernetic future. Set in 1855, *The Difference Engine* examines the consequences of an alternate history where Charles Babbage has successfully constructed his analytical engines (early computers), looking at their impact on science, political and social history, empire, and poverty. The authors telegraph their text's association with the novel of purpose by reappropriating characters from *Sybil: or the Two Nations* (1845), Benjamin Disraeli's politically idiosyncratic social problem novel about Chartism and the plight of the working poor.[11] The ways in which Gibson and Sterling rewrite Disraeli, transforming Sybil Gerard from an impossibly pure Victorian heroine (regularly described as "nun-like," despite her status as romantic protagonist) to a pragmatic prostitute, for example, and her father from a Chartist to a Luddite leader, create a fascinating dialogue between nineteenth- and twentieth-century interpretations.[12] The shift of Walter Gerard's priorities, from crusader for the political rights of the workers to anti-technologist, suggests that survival-based concerns about automation-generated unemployment overshadow the movement for political inclusion. Conversely, Disraeli's young factory worker Dandy Mick Radley has here risen in status to become the private secretary of deposed Texan president Sam Houston, through his talents with kinoscopy, a punch-card program form of pixelated display that is a precursor of cinema (and that also claims a middle-aged John Keats as a devotee).

The Difference Engine mirrors the Victorian novel in being dense and multi-plotted, although it shifts from viewpoint character to viewpoint character by section (as in Collins's *The Moonstone*) rather than moving back and forth between narratives (as in Dickens or George Eliot). Various issues are touched on, including the ecological catastrophe of London's Great Stink,[13] when the overwhelmed Thames, filled with too much human waste as a result of the newly invented flush toilets, resulted in such foul conditions that better-off Londoners have left town, while the working classes are forced to survive as best they can.[14] Sybil Gerard exemplifies the plight of women with no other resources who are forced to turn to prostitution; while she clearly maintains her self-respect despite her "fall," her status is not romanticized.[15] Her late father's role as Luddite leader is reprised in the Stink-generated riots by Captain Swing (whom Sterling has identified as being none other than Wilkie Collins himself[16]).

Though Walter Gerard retains the heroic status of a martyr, Swing is perceived by viewpoint character Edward Mallory as a "racetrack dandy" and a "tout";[17] he is presented as a criminal mastermind who is ultimately defeated by Mallory and his companions, which Jay Clayton calls a "triumphalist conclusion [that] contradicts the novel's larger critique of society."[18] This does not disqualify the text as a social problem novel; Patrick Brantlinger has pointed out that not all Victorian social problem novelists supported large-scale social change. Some, like Dickens, decry injustice but see in "benevolent middle-class industrialism" the best chance for reform.[19] Too much agency on the part of the working class causes anxiety even for many Victorian reformers. But Swing's critiques, though florid, are not unwarranted. In his manifesto, An Appeal to the People, he calls the people the "free Lords of Earth" and implores them to "kneel no more before the vampyre capitalist and the idiot savantry" and to "destroy the Moloch Steam."[20] Despite the upward mobility of Whitechapel under the Rad Lords and the exchange of the hereditary elite for an industrial meritocracy, The Difference Engine, in fact, shows that technological progress makes no substantial improvement in the lives of the many.

Moreover, the analytical engines have created a new surveillance society. Though Herbert Sussman, in his early reading of this novel, sees a utopian future here,[21] subsequent critics have seen a Foucauldian nightmare, a "full-blown information order, complete with massive databases on citizens, surveillance apparatus . . . and scientific societies that serve as unofficial intelligence arms of the military,"[22] ultimately leading to "surveillance and panoptic discipline, and eugenics" under the sponsorship of Lord Galton.[23] This ultimately accelerates until, in a few pages at the end of the novel, we discover that Babbage's invention has led us full circle from steampunk back to cyberpunk. The All-Seeing Eye, a cybernetically based consciousness, has achieved the status of "I" at the cost of human individuality, "human faces that are borrowed masks and lenses for a peering Eye."[24] Gibson and Sterling have taken the Foucauldian analysis of critical works on Victorian literature, like D. A. Miller's landmark The Novel and the Police,[25] and made it manifest in the fictional reality of their work.

Miéville's Steampunk Social Critique

Surprisingly, considering the attention it garnered, Gibson and Sterling's novel did not lead to a flurry of imitators; neither did its authors return to the same ground. Although steampunk continued to be written and published, the current resurgence did not occur until the middle of the first decade of the new century; VanderMeer and Chambers refer to the period from 1991 to 2007 as "a kind of Steampunk interregnum."[26] During this intermediate period, China Miéville published Perdido Street Station, in 2000. Although Miéville has never been associated with steampunk as a movement, Perdido Street Station and the succeeding novels in his Bas-Lag series are often identified as steampunk.[27] It is a social problem novel, equal parts Dickens and Marx, set in the fictional city of New Crobuzon, which parallels Victorian London on many levels. The range of political issues echoes the reality of nineteenth-century Britain: laborers' strikes, ruthless military actions against working-class unrest, press censorship, voting inequities, and a deeply class-biased government.

The government, with its towers above the novel's eponymous Perdido Street Station, again has the Foucauldian Panoptical feel so popular among critics of Victorian literature; its surveillance continues with disguised soldiers and agents scattered among the population. "The New Crobuzon militia did not like to be seen."[28] While the central plot, having to do with the unwitting release of the hallucination-causing slake-moths into the city by protagonist Isaac Dan der Grimnebulin, is an adventure scenario, it is played out against the background of the government's desire to continue milking the slake-moths for the drug dreamshit, which they use to control a segment of the population. Christopher Palmer has suggested that in the novel, "drug addiction [serves] as archetype of commodity capitalism; capitalism as making zombies,"[29] and the government is deeply invested in maintaining that status.

In New Crobuzon, the illusion of democracy is created by a lottery in which a certain number of ordinary citizens get the vote each year. The working-class editor of the radical newspaper *Runagate Rampant*, Benjamin Flex, recalls his one experience as a voter; when he asks his comparatively posh ally Derkhan Blueday if she automatically qualifies, she is appalled that he would imagine she had enough money. Nor is there a free press; *Runagate Rampant*'s offices are concealed beneath an abattoir in the poor industrial area of Dog Fenn, and both its editorial practices and its circulation are surreptitious. "In the oscillating, violent, disingenuous and repressive political atmosphere . . . the writers for *Runagate Rampant* did not meet. That way the chances of infiltration by the militia was minimized."[30] When Flex is captured by the government, in the midst of the unrest surrounding the dockworkers' strike, he is tortured for information; a government official tosses off casually that they had been aware of the paper's location but hadn't found it important enough to pursue, again suggesting the extent of surveillance in the city.[31]

The various neighborhoods of New Crobuzon, especially the slums, are vividly drawn, often decaying and squalid but filled with the persistence and determination of the inhabitants who make of them a home. Similar scenes of middle-class characters visiting poor neighborhoods occur in Dickens, Gaskell, and even Disraeli. Dog Fenn, where Benjamin Flex operates *Runagate Rampant*, is straight out of *London Labour and the London Poor*, filled with barrows of street merchants of food (onions, whelks, and broth, just as in Mayhew), as well as streetwalkers, not all of whom have the relative agency of Sybil in *The Difference Engine*. They include "children who played with little paper dolls and wooden quoits when no one watched them, pouted lasciviously and tongued the air whenever a man walked by."[32] The khepri ghetto of Creekside is one of New Crobuzon's most dismal places. "It had been a tumbledown slum for humans a hundred years ago, a rookery of found architecture . . . petrif[ied] forever on the point of collapse. The denizens of Creekside were . . . disreputable and hungry. They worked in the factories and in the sewers, sold themselves to whoever would buy."[33] The desperation of these streets, similar to the poverty-stricken districts of Victorian London, highlights one of the most prevalent subjects of the social problem novel, the plight of the poor.

While the New Crobuzon equivalents of the nineteenth-century London slums are a vivid part of Miéville's imagined landscape, the centerpiece of the novel from a social problem standpoint (though incidental to the main plot) is the Kelltree dockworkers' strike (parallel to the London dockworkers' strike of 1889), in which humans and the aquatic vodyanoi join together, presenting the government with an unexpectedly united front. Some humans counterdemonstrate, claiming the vodyanoi would drive down wages for humans, and the event is marked by a vociferous free exchange of ideas, in which the undecided human dockworkers are presented with both opinions (and *Runagate Rampant* flyers urging human cooperation with the vodyanoi circulate). Violence comes in with the arrival of government airships, sent to quell the "riots," which occasion much destruction of property and loss of life.[34] Notably, there is no panic generated by working-class unrest here, unlike the overt middle-class anxiety in Dickens's *Barnaby Rudge* (1841) or Charlotte Brontë's *Shirley* (1849), or even to that caused by Swing's unruly minions in *The Difference Engine*. Rather, it is clear that the disruption is caused by the government itself. In a *Locus* interview, Miéville stated: "Some of the political stuff in *PSS* is drawn from experience, most particularly the scene where there's a strike in the docks and it gets put down. And then from those people who weren't there, somebody mentions having read about the riots in the docks that the militia managed to stop."[35]

The Social Problem Novel and Steampunk's Second Wave

Around the same time Miéville was writing, steampunk was evolving and approaching its present state. The "maker" movement,[36] *SteamPunk Magazine* with its anachro-anarchist sensibility, and a gradually emerging subculture and aesthetic involving design and costume were transforming steampunk from a half-forgotten science fictional cul-de-sac to a cultural phenomenon. Among the current second wave of steampunk, we see a diversification of the genre. As its commercial appeal has grown, we see not only steampunk firmly grounded in its science fictional roots, but an expansion into fantasy-tinged steampunk, steampunk murder mysteries, and a burgeoning subgenre of steampunk ro-

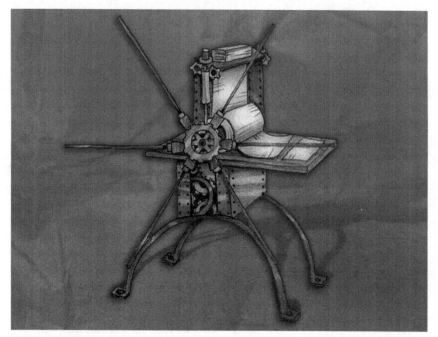

The printing press: a tool to comfort the afflicted and afflict the comfortable. *Copyright Jody Steel*

mance and erotica. Some of these works deal overtly with the consequences of a steampunked Industrial Revolution, with poverty and social problems, with racism and the legacy of colonialism, and with the position of women, although their approaches and philosophies vary. In examining the steampunk social problem novel at present, I have chosen several recent works, by Stephen Hunt, Cherie Priest, and N. K. Jemisin, each of which contains social problem elements but engages often similar themes in very different ways.

Stephen Hunt's *The Court of the Air* (2007) is on the more conservative end of the social problem novel spectrum. The text concerns itself with the plight of the poor, particularly in its opening chapters. Though it ultimately comes down on the side of benevolent capitalism (as, indeed, do many of its Victorian social problem counterparts), in the form of Jackelian (British) society, it recognizes the situation's complexities and features a broad canvas, a large cast, and a range of sociopolitical questions. Hunt's novel, though set in another world, reflects Victorian, and specifically Dickensian, England very strongly, which is emphasized by the many names derived from Dickens sprinkled throughout the text, including Oliver, Jarndyce, Meagles, and the engineering firm of Doyce and Clennam. But though Hunt begins by focusing on the trials of the poor and outcast, he shifts toward the invasion of

Jackals. The England analogue in Hunt's imagined world, Jackals is a "nation of shopkeepers," mimicking Adam Smith's famous phrase about the British, though it is unlike Victorian Britain in having no interest in conquest and little in international trade.[37]

The book opens with young Molly Templar, housed in an orphanage, poorly fed and clothed, and sent to hazardous and ill-paid jobs as a chimney sweep, a laundress, and an apprentice prostitute.[38] Molly is accused of Carlism, the novel's Marxism analogue, when she complains pointedly about the exploitation to which the orphanage's director has subjected its inhabitants. But the text soon shifts its focus, first to an underground Carlist dystopia, run by Tzlayloc,[39] formerly Jacob Walwyn and one of Benjamin Carl's star pupils, and later to the battle against invasion by neighboring Quatérshift, a Carlist nation that has brought itself to the brink of disaster by Cultural Revolution–type practices. A refugee Quatérshiftian nobleman-turned-mercenary points out that "the best way to evade famine is not to seize the breadbasket of the continent, leave her fields unharvested for two years of revolution, then fire a bolt through the neck of every disfavoured soul who knows anything about agriculture."[40]

Jackelian democracy is unlike that of New Crobuzon with its voting lottery; here there is universal adult suffrage, and Molly herself is just a year away from voting rights. The text valorizes the existing system. However, after being thoroughly discredited in practice, even the theory of Carlism/Marxism gets a partial vindication, in the person of the aged Benjamin Carl himself, who contends that neither his enemies nor his supposed followers have actually read or understood his *Community and the Commons* correctly. At the end of the novel, socialism and capitalist democracy seem to be reconciled enough to at least work together. The once-fugitive Carl, having reemerged during the conflict, plans to stand for Parliament and to begin his political life anew. However, for a novel that begins by focusing on the plight of the poor orphan, *The Court of the Air* makes a determined shift. It is not clear that the poor as a class are any better off at the end of the novel, though Molly personally is, due to her individual actions; that aspect of the text has faded away, replaced by a celebration of Jackelian political freedom. This places Molly squarely within the Victorian tradition of Samuel Smiles's *Self-Help* (1859) and the notion of rising in society through one's own hard work and diligence; Molly, though she is fortunate in being at the right place at the right time, is a bourgeois individualist heroine.

Cherie Priest's *Boneshaker* (2009) is one of the breakout steampunk novels, having been recently optioned by Hollywood.[41] It is a highly cinematic text, both visually and in its action-adventure structure; at the same time, it contains several social problem novel elements: the struggles of the working class, the destruction of the environment, and social manipulation through the drug trade. The novel's zombie-infested underground Seattle is the re-sult of a major environmental catastrophe, triggered by the titular device, a powerful drilling machine that has tapped into a subterranean gas that causes all who breathe it to become zombie-like "rotters." This serves as an amplification of the increasingly toxic environments created by the unregu-lated wastes of the Industrial Revolution, and it parallels our current fears of environmental catastrophe, as seen in contemporary concerns about global warming, toxins released by underground hydrofracking, and other disasters.

Priest's alternate 1880 envisions a walled city, condemned as unsafe for human habitation, as the toxic gas continues to pour out of the ruptured underground. The city is now inhabited by working-class survivors who have learned to adapt to their contaminated environs, wearing gas masks to keep from breathing in the toxins, except when safe inside sealed chambers, and adapting sunken buildings from the original city to their needs. The novel is full of steampunk tropes like airships, mad scientists (the Seattle underground is dominated by Dr. Minnericht, an inventor who always covers his face and is rumored to be none other than Leviticus Blue, inventor of the Boneshaker drill, himself), and the ubiquitous gas masks. But the heart of the story is the mostly working-class survivors who have chosen to stay, eking out a living in the hostile environment. Many of them, mostly male and mostly social cast-offs, congregate at Maynard's, an underground saloon that serves as a gathering place and support system. The underground is perilous (they lose a drunken member of their group when forced to flee the saloon due to an attack by rot-ters; his gas mask slips and he is transformed in a matter of minutes), but the inhabitants accept it. There is also a group of Chinese immigrants, segregated and keeping the furnaces and other mechanisms of the city going, reflecting the real-life situation of Chinese workers during the late-nineteenth century.[42]

Minnericht's empire is dependent less on his plethora of inventions (in-cluding special helmet-like gas masks, a gun called the Doozy Dazer, and the elaborate mechanical arm belonging to Maynard's owner Lucy O'Gunning, all of which echo maker-built steampunk constructions)[43] than on his manu-facturing and distribution of lemon sap, a highly addictive drug manufactured from the Blight itself (and leading ultimately to the zombification of its users, which does surprisingly little to harm its market). Most of the traffic into and out of the city is based on this drug trade; the profit motive suggests the untrammeled and unregulated commerce of the Gilded Age. "What changed was, people figured out that you could make good money off the Blight gas, if you turned it into lemon sap."[44] Minnericht's deliberate introduction of this dangerous drug into the general population is reminiscent of the British importation of opium into China as a means of both profit and social control; this parallel is made clear by the fact that Minnericht had tested it on the

Chinese, who he thought would "treat it like opium"; instead, it caused the deaths of several members of the community and cost him their allegiance.[45]

N. K. Jemisin's short story "The Effluent Engine" (2010) similarly deals with an environmental catastrophe, as well as with race and gender issues. It is also the one work I consider that engages with postcolonial issues, an issue of increasing concern in the steampunk community,[46] in this case, Haiti, in the wake of its anticolonial revolution. The story envisions a nation, both egalitarian and struggling, that is in the process of developing a system of methane extraction, reusing the waste from rum production to provide itself with a clean power source as an economic base for its postrevolutionary society. This is crucial, because rum and sugar production is Haiti's most significant industry, and the waste is devastating the countryside; additionally, the fuel is needed to power Haiti's airships to keep the country safe from invasion by the French, anxious to retake their liberated former colony.

The action of the story is set in New Orleans, where Jessaline, a Haitian agent, is sent to engage the Creole engineer Norbert Rillieux to work on perfecting this process of reclaiming waste into fuel. There, Jessaline finds a sharp contrast to her homeland, encountering multiple layers of prejudice as her dark skin marks her as less than equal to both whites and the mixed-blood free Creole community, which includes Rillieux and his sister Eugenie. As a woman, Jessaline is subject to social restrictions and unwanted sexual advances. Eugenie's higher social standing does not prevent her from being subject to limitations of both race and gender, either. She is a self-educated scientist because the Parisian schools where Norbert was educated would not admit her, and she is perceived as merely his helpmate and assistant, although she is the superior engineer, the one who readily perceives the solution to the Haitians' problem.

Postrevolutionary Haiti, despite its poverty and the constant threats of attack from France, promises Eugenie an environment in which her talents will be recognized. "In my land," says Jessaline, "men and women of *all* shades are free. I will not pretend that this makes us perfect; I have gone hungry many times in my life. Yet there, a woman such as yourself may be more than the coddled sister of a prominent scientist, or the mistress of a white man."[47] This differs from historical reality, which was similar to the social structure depicted in New Orleans; the mixed-race illegitimate children of the deposed white planters, having more access to education and power, became the new ruling class. But in Jemisin's Haiti, the combination of new technologies (Haiti has become a leader in the building and operation of airships) and the depopulation consequent to extended warfare creates a society with new social possibilities, regardless of race or gender. There is no bias against dark-skinned Haitians like Jessaline, and women fill many social positions traditionally belonging to men. "So many men died in the Revolution that women fill the ranks now as dirigible-pilots and gunners. We run factories and farms too, and are highly placed in government. Even the houngans are mostly women now—you have vodoun here too, yes? So we are important."[48] At the end of the story, Jessaline and Eugenie prepare to depart for Haiti, where Eugenie's technological knowledge can be fully appreciated, and where they will share a life together, in a society where they will be able to live openly in a same-sex marriage.

Conclusion

Taken as a whole, the steampunk social problem novel uses an alternative past to examine the problems of the present, as well as their historical antecedents. Like its Victorian original, the steampunk social problem novel does not center around one unitary political viewpoint; rather, it ranges from Hunt's very Victorian celebration of democracy and bourgeois individualism, to Miéville's and Priest's more radical engagement with the working classes and Jemisin's critique of race, class, and gender. There are certain issues, not considered by their Victorian social problem predecessors, that are reiterated among multiple texts: Miéville and Priest consider drug trafficking, Priest and Jemisin ecological catastrophe, and Gibson and Sterling, as well as Miéville, a surveillance society. Their placement in the past (or its analogue) suggests their origins, the deeply rooted nature of these issues, which becomes part of the critique.

Like most of their Victorian social problem predecessors, these steampunk novels do not suggest solutions so much as raise issues—only Jemisin's text provides a better alternative, postrevolutionary Haiti, and even Jessaline, its representative, freely recognizes its flaws. But, similar to the performativity that Amanda Claybaugh sees as characteristic of the self-perception of the Victorian novelists of purpose, these stories, too, may have a performative function, educating their readers about the historical antecedents of contemporary social issues, and through the alternative history of steampunk, considering other possibilities, other places we might have been, or other routes to where we are now. This is not to say they are philosophical novels; most of them contain villains, crises, and chase scenes, just like less overtly issue-driven steampunk. However, they also provide a thoughtful reading experience, demonstrating steampunk's potential as a medium of social critique and engagement. While it is to be hoped that steampunk's current popularity is not merely a Warholian fifteen minutes of fame, the steampunk social problem novel proposes one path for the genre's continued relevance and vitality.

Notes

1. Ann Heilmann and Mark Llewellyn, *Neo-Victorianism: The Victorians in the Twenty-First Century, 1999–2009* (Houndmills, Basingstoke, UK: Palgrave MacMillan, 2010).

2. Patrick Brantlinger, *The Spirit of Reform: British Literature and Politics, 1832–1867* (Cambridge: Harvard University Press, 1977), 1.

3. Not everyone approved of Collins's turn from his early sensation novels and prototypical detective fiction. Algernon Swinburne famously quipped, "What brought good Wilkie's genius near perdition? Some demon whispered—'Wilkie, have a mission.'"

4. Amanda Claybaugh, *The Novel of Purpose: Literature and Social Reform in the Anglo-American World* (Ithaca: Cornell University Press, 2007), 36.

5. Here I will refer briefly to politically engaged publications like *SteamPunk Magazine*, postcolonial steampunk blogs (*Beyond Victoriana, Silver Goggles*), and steampunk performance by Professor Elemental, Steampunk Emma Goldman, Painless Parker, and others. Diana Pho has addressed this subject in more detail in her contribution to this collection.

6. Bruce Sterling, coauthor of *The Difference Engine*, has said, "Yeah, *The Difference Engine* is about the 1990s, let's face it. . . . It's our disease projected onto a lab animal of the 19th century." Daniel Fischlin, Veronica Hollinger, and Andrew Taylor, "The Charisma Leak: A Conversation with William Gibson and Bruce Sterling," *Science-Fiction Studies* 19 (1992), 6.

7. Jeff VanderMeer and S. J. Chambers, *The Steampunk Bible* (New York: Abrams Image, 2011), 48.

8. In Jeter's *Morlock Nights*, Powers's *The Anubis Gates*, and Blaylock's *Homunculus*, respectively.

9. Cyberpunk, which rose to popularity in the 1980s, is a subgenre of science fiction. "The 'cyber' part of the word relates to cybernetics: to a future where industrial and political blocs may be global . . . rather than national, and controlled through information networks, a future in which machine augmentations of the human body are commonplace, as are mind and body changes brought about by drugs and biological engineering. . . . The 'punk' part of the word comes from the rock 'n' roll terminology of the 1970s, 'punk' meaning in this context young, streetwise, aggressive, alienated and offensive to the Establishment." John Clute and Peter Nicholls, *The Encyclopedia of Science Fiction* (New York: St. Martin's Griffin, 1995), 288. In response to cyberpunk's popularity, the term *steampunk* was coined by K. W. Jeter in a letter to the editors of *Locus* in April 1987. Bruce Sterling, "Historypunk and Futuritypunk," *Locus* 65, no. 3 (September 2010): 32.

10. Among others, by Thomas M. Disch, "Queen Victoria's Computers," *New York Times*, 10 March 1991, www.nytimes.com/books/98/08/09/specials/disch-gibson .html (7 January 2012).

11. *Sybil* was written to support Disraeli's own Young England political movement. He proposed an odd strain of Romantic Tory radicalism, wherein the working class and the aristocracy were seen as natural allies against the rising industrial middle class.

12. Critics who have considered this include Herbert Sussman and Jay Clayton. See Herbert Sussman, "Cyberpunk Meets Charles Babbage," *Victorian Studies* 38, no. 1 (Autumn 1994): 7–11; Jay Clayton, "Hacking the Nineteenth Century," in *Victorian Afterlife: Postmodern Culture Rewrites the Nineteenth Century*, ed. John Kucich and Dianne F. Sadoff (Minneapolis: University of Minnesota Press, 2000), 197.

13. Historically, of 1858, but here moved up to 1855.

14. Steven Johnson, *The Ghost Map: The Story of London's Most Terrifying Epidemic—and How It Changed Science, Cities, and the Modern World* (New York: Riverhead Books, 2006), 207.

15. This is made particularly clear in an extended episode detailing her erstwhile neighbor Hetty's tryst with protagonist Edward Mallory, which is neither brutalized nor romanticized but depicted as a slightly grubby exchange of cash for services.

16. Fischlin, Hollinger, and Taylor, "The Charisma Leak," 9.

17. William Gibson and Bruce Sterling, *The Difference Engine* (New York: Bantam, 1991), 89, 91, 262.

18. Clayton, "Hacking the Nineteenth Century," 198.

19. Brantlinger, *The Spirit of Reform*, 196.

20. Gibson and Sterling, *The Difference Engine*, 273.

21. Sussman, "Cyberpunk Meets Charles Babbage," 14.

22. Clayton, "Hacking the Nineteenth Century," 190.

23. Nicholas Spencer, "Rethinking Ambivalence: Technopolitics and the Luddites in William Gibson and Bruce Sterling's 'The Difference Engine,'" *Contemporary Literature* 40, no. 3 (Autumn 1999): 419; see generally Patrick Jagoda, "Clacking Control Societies: Steampunk, History, and the Difference Engine of Escape," *Neo-Victorian Studies* 3, no. 1 (2010): 46–71, www.neovictorianstudies.com (6 January 2012).

24. Gibson and Sterling, *The Difference Engine*, 428–429.

25. Miller's argument, that the Victorian novel is implicated in the larger cultural function of enforcing disciplinary power, draws on Foucault's *Discipline and Punish: The Birth of the Prison*, 1975, trans. Alan Sheridan (New York: Vintage Books, 1995); see D. A. Miller, *The Novel and the Police* (Berkeley: University of California Press, 1988), 17–18. Highly influential, it was part of a larger trend of Foucauldian readings of nineteenth-century texts.

26. VanderMeer and Chambers, *The Steampunk Bible*, 58.

27. Christopher Kendrick, "Monster Realism and Uneven Development in China Miéville's *The Scar*," *Extrapolation* 50, no. 2 (Summer 2009): 259–260; Jessica Langer, *Postcolonialism and Science Fiction* (Houndmills, Basingstoke, UK: Palgrave Macmillan, 2011), 120; Mike Perschon, "Perdido Street Station by China Mieville," *The Steampunk Scholar*, http://steampunkscholar.blogspot.com/search/label/China%20Mi%C3%A9ville (28 January 2012).

28. China Miéville, *Perdido Street Station* (New York: Del Rey, 2000), 267.

29. Christopher Palmer, "Saving the City in China Miéville's Bas-Lag Novels," *Extrapolation* 50, no. 2 (Summer 2009): 228.

30. Miéville, *Perdido Street Station*, 137.

31. Miéville, *Perdido Street Station*, 322.

32. Miéville, *Perdido Street Station*, 131.

33. Miéville, *Perdido Street Station*, 214.

34. Miéville, *Perdido Street Station*, 299–302.

35. Miéville, "Messing with Fantasy," *Locus* 48, no. 3 (March 2002): 75.

36. The "maker movement" is discussed but never defined in *The Steampunk Bible*, although the differences and overlaps between steampunk "makers" and steampunk "artists" is considered. Jeff VanderMeer and S. J. Chambers, *The Steampunk Bible* (New York: Abrams Image, 2011), 96. T. J. McCue, blogging for *Forbes* magazine, describes makers as "the people who create, build, design, tinker, modify, hack, invent, or simply make something. . . . people who invent and build and make things have the power to change the world. People who 'remix' something or hack a better way." T. J. McCue, "Moving the Economy: The Future of the Maker Movement," Forbes.com, 26 October 2011, www.forbes.com/sites/tjmccue/2011/10/26/moving -the-economy-the-future-of-the-maker-movement (23 February 2012).

37. Stephen Hunt, *The Court of the Air* (New York: Harper Voyager, 2007), 9.

38. This one promises to be more remunerative than the others; however, Molly's contract has been bought out without her consent. Her career as a sex worker ends before it has actually begun, as her first potential client turns out to be an assassin sent to kill her because she is the possessor of a rare blood disorder, which, as it turns out, suggests supernatural abilities and direct descent from Jackals's legendary founder.

39. It is difficult not to read this as a play on early steampunk writer James Blaylock's surname.

40. Hunt, *The Court of the Air*, 115.

41. Specifically, Cross Creek Pictures and Exclusive Media Group, with a screenplay by John Hilary Sheperd. See Pamela McClintock, "Cherie Priest's Novel 'Boneshaker' Headed for Big Screen," *Hollywood Reporter*, 30 November 2011, www .hollywoodreporter.com/news/boneshaker-cherie-priest-267568 (28 January 2012).

42. At this time, the Chinese Exclusion Acts, halting immigration, were in effect, and the absence of Chinese women in the underground city mirrors their relative absence as members of a community essentially of guest workers.

43. See generally, Art Donovan, *The Art of Steampunk* (East Petersburg, Pa.: Fox Chapel Publishing, 2011); Thomas Willeford, *Steampunk: Gears, Gadgets, and Gizmos* (New York: McGraw-Hill, 2012).

44. Cherie Priest, *Boneshaker* (New York: Tor, 2009), 267.

45. Priest, *Boneshaker*, 267.

46. In response to the critique that steampunk too often fell into "white, straight, male imperialist fantasies," the editor of the collection in which Jemisin's story appears, JoSelle Vanderhooft, deliberately sought out diverse and often politically engaged stories, taking place in a wide variety of countries and cultures. JoSelle Vanderhooft, "Introduction: Build a Better Engine," in *Steam-Powered: Lesbian Steampunk Stories*, ed. JoSelle Vanderhooft (Round Rock, Tex.: Torquere Press, 2010), 9–12. Steampunk engagement with postcolonial issues is the focus of the blogs Beyond Victoriana and Silver Goggles.

47. N. K. Jemisin, "The Effluent Engine," in *Steam-Powered: Lesbian Steampunk Stories*, ed. JoSelle Vanderhooft, 32.

48. Jemisin, "The Effluent Engine," 32.

Bibliography

Brantlinger, Patrick. *The Spirit of Reform: British Literature and Politics, 1832–1867.* Cambridge: Harvard University Press, 1977.

Brontë, Charlotte. *Shirley.* 1849. London: Penguin Books, 1974.

Claybaugh, Amanda. *The Novel of Purpose: Literature and Social Reform in the Anglo-American World.* Ithaca: Cornell University Press, 2007.

Clayton, Jay. "Hacking the Nineteenth Century." 186–210 in *Victorian Afterlife: Postmodern Culture Rewrites the Nineteenth Century,* ed. John Kucich and Dianne F. Sadoff. Minneapolis: University of Minnesota Press, 2000.

Clute, John, and Peter Nicholls. *The Encyclopedia of Science Fiction.* New York: St. Martin's Griffin, 1995.

Collins, Wilkie. *Armadale.* 1866. Oxford: Oxford University Press, 1989.

———. *Heart and Science.* 1883. Peterborough, Ont.: Broadview Press, 1997.

———. *Man and Wife.* 1870. Oxford: Oxford University Press, 1995.

———. *No Name.* 1862. London: Penguin Books, 1994.

———. *The Law and the Lady.* 1875. London: Penguin Books, 1998.

Dickens, Charles. *Barnaby Rudge.* 1841. Harmondsworth, Middlesex, UK: Penguin Books, 1973.

———. *Bleak House.* 1853. London: Penguin Books, 2003.

———. *Little Dorrit.* 1857. Oxford: Oxford University Press, 1989.

Disch, Thomas M. "Queen Victoria's Computers." *New York Times,* 10 March 1991. www.nytimes.com/books/98/08/09/specials/disch-gibson.html (7 January 2012).

Disraeli, Benjamin. *Sybil.* 1845. London: Penguin, 1985.

Donovan, Art. *The Art of Steampunk.* East Petersburg, Pa.: Fox Chapel Publishing, 2011.

Fischlin, Daniel, Veronica Hollinger, and Andrew Taylor. "The Charisma Leak: A Conversation with William Gibson and Bruce Sterling." *Science Fiction Studies* 19 (1992): 1–16.

Foucault, Michel. *Discipline & Punish: The Birth of the Prison.* 1975. Trans. Alan Sheridan. New York: Vintage Books, 1995.

Gaskell, Elizabeth. *Mary Barton.* 1848. London: Penguin Books, 1996.

———. *North and South.* 1855. Oxford: Oxford University Press, 1986.

Gibson, William, and Bruce Sterling. *The Difference Engine.* New York: Bantam, 1991.

Heilmann, Ann, and Mark Llewellyn. *Neo-Victorianism: The Victorians in the Twenty-First Century, 1999–2009.* Houndmills, Basingstoke, UK: Palgrave MacMillan, 2010.

Hunt, Steven. *The Court of the Air.* New York: Harper Voyager, 2007.

Jagoda, Patrick. "Clacking Control Societies: Steampunk, History, and the Difference Engine of Escape." *Neo-Victorian Studies* 3, no. 1 (2010): 46–71. www.neovictorianstudies.com (6 January 2012).

Jemisin, N. K. "The Effluent Engine." 13–48 in *Steam-Powered: Lesbian Steampunk Stories,* ed. JoSelle Vanderhooft. Round Rock, Tex.: Torquere Press, 2010.

Johnson, Steven. *The Ghost Map: The Story of London's Most Terrifying Epidemic—and How It Changed Science, Cities, and the Modern World.* New York: Riverhead Books, 2006.

Kendrick, Christopher. "Monster Realism and Uneven Development in China Miéville's *The Scar*." *Extrapolation* 50, no. 2 (Summer 2009): 258–275.

Langer, Jessica. *Postcolonialism and Science Fiction*. Houndmills, Basingstoke, UK: Palgrave Macmillan, 2011.

Mayhew, Henry. *London Labour and the London Poor*. 1851–1852. London: Penguin Books, 1985.

McClintock, Pamela. "Cherie Priest's Novel 'Boneshaker' Headed for Big Screen." 30 November 2011. www.hollywoodreporter.com/news/boneshaker-cherie-priest -267568 (28 January 2012).

McCue, T. J. "Moving the Economy: The Future of the Maker Movement." Forbes .com, 26 October 2011. www.forbes.com/sites/tjmccue/2011/10/26/moving-the -economy-the-future-of-the-maker-movement (23 February 2012).

Miéville, China. *Iron Council*. New York: Del Rey, 2004.

———. *Perdido Street Station*. New York: Del Rey, 2000.

———. *The Scar*. New York: Del Rey, 2002.

———. "Messing with Fantasy" (interview). *Locus* 48, no. 3 (March 2002): 4–5, 75–76.

Miller, D. A. *The Novel and the Police*. Berkeley: University of California Press, 1988.

Palmer, Christopher. "Saving the City in China Miéville's Bas-Lag Novels." *Extrapolation* 50, no. 2 (Summer 2009): 224–238.

Perschon, Mike. "Perdido Street Station by China Miéville." 17 October 2009. *The Steampunk Scholar*, http://steampunkscholar.blogspot.com/search/label/China%20 Mi%C3%A9ville (28 January 2012).

Powers, Tim. *The Anubis Gates*. New York: Ace, 1983.

Priest, Cherie. *Boneshaker*. New York: Tor, 2009.

———. *Dreadnought*. New York: Tor, 2010.

———. *Ganymede*. New York: Tor, 2011.

Spencer, Nicholas. "Rethinking Ambivalence: Technopolitics and the Luddites in William Gibson and Bruce Sterling's *The Difference Engine*." *Contemporary Literature* 40, no. 3 (Autumn 1999): 403–429.

Sterling, Bruce. "Historypunk and Futuritypunk." *Locus* 65, no. 3 (September 2010): 32.

Stowe, Harriet Beecher. *Uncle Tom's Cabin*. 1852. London: Penguin Books, 1986.

Sussman, Herbert. "Cyberpunk Meets Charles Babbage: *The Difference Engine* as Alternative Victorian History." *Victorian Studies* 38, no. 1 (Autumn 1994): 1–23.

Vanderhooft, JoSelle. "Introduction: Build a Better Engine." 9–12 in *Steam-Powered: Lesbian Steampunk Stories*, ed. JoSelle Vanderhooft. Round Rock, Tex.: Torquere, 2010.

VanderMeer, Jeff, and S. J. Chambers. *The Steampunk Bible: An Illustrated Guide to the World of Imaginary Airships, Corsets and Goggles, Mad Scientists, and Strange Literature*. New York: Abrams Image, 2011.

Willeford, Thomas. *Steampunk: Gears, Gadgets, and Gizmos*. New York: McGraw-Hill, 2012.

The Victorian New Woman. *Copyright Jody Steel*

CHAPTER TWO

Useful Troublemakers: Social Retrofuturism in the Steampunk Novels of Gail Carriger and Cherie Priest

Mike Perschon

Introduction: Beyond the Retro-Techno Discussion

In relation to steampunk, the term *retrofuturism* likely conjures up images of antiquated technology, dirigibles and ornithopters, Harper Goff's *Nautilus*, or Datamancer's brass-worked keyboards. Discussions concerning retrofuturism at conventions or online forums are often couched in a technological framework. A quick Google search for retrofuturism links to pages like the *Web Urbanist*'s "Steampunk Styling: Victorian Retrofuturism at Home" or *Smashing Magazine*'s "Retro Futurism at Its Best: Designs and Tutorials." In both cases, the art and photography reveal a myopic conflation of the term retrofuturism with technological objects, such as steampunk-style motorcycles or interior decor.

Consequently, steampunk's backward gaze becomes uniformly associated with technology. The nostalgia and regret Rob Latham identifies as "typical retrofuturist emotions"[1] are likewise often associated with the retrofuturism of steampunk art and literature. Rebecca Onion, echoing a number of steampunk artists, states that "steampunks see modern technology as offensively impermeable to the everyday person, and desire to return to an age when, they believe, machines were visible, human, fallible, and above all, accessible."[2] Onion speaks mainly of steampunk "object-based work," which she perceives as attempts at reclaiming a "human connection" with a "perceived 'lost' mechanical world."³ In his review of the special issue of *Neo-Victorian Studies* devoted to steampunk, Jess Nevins calls such interpretations of steampunk artworks "programmatic intent" and suggests critical approaches need to move beyond materiality as an essential feature of steampunk.⁴ I agree: while technology is undeniably foundational to the steampunk aesthetic, discussions of steampunk retrofuturism should encompass more than technofantastic anachronisms, automatons, and airships; the ambitions of late-Victorian progressives were more concerned with medical advancements and human rights than with sky dreadnoughts and phlogiston-powered ray guns.

Filippo Tommaso Marinetti and the Italian futurists were unabashed technophiles of the machines they used and praised in their *avant-garde* art, but they were also interested in the social change such art would produce. Likewise, steampunk retrofuturism is arguably much more than just nostalgia for hands-on approaches to technology; it is not, as it is sometimes understood, simply how the past imagined the future. There is little about steampunk retrofuturism that realizes the historical aspirations of the nineteenth century. Rather, it is the way *we* imagine the past seeing the future. While these imaginings often take the shape of dirigibles and clockwork beings, they can also reimagine the social spaces of the past.

Consider the *fin-de-siècle* phenomenon of the New Woman, that "Protean figure" to whom Wilhelmina Murray compared herself while seated at a typewriter in Bram Stoker's *Dracula* (1897). One of the expressions of the New Woman phenomenon was the Rational Dress campaign, "which rejected the physically confining clothes deemed suitable for 'respectable' women,"⁵ specifically recommending abandoning corsets.⁶ It is interesting to consider the hope of many real Victorian-era women was to get *out* of a corset, while if the number of booths at steampunk conventions selling corsets are any indication, the hope of many steampunk women is to get *into* one.

George Parsons Lathrop's "In the Deep of Time" (1897) is an excellent example of the distance between late-Victorian aspirations and steampunk retrofuturism. Lathrop's Time Traveler, sent forward by the Society of Futurity, finds a decidedly un-Victorian future. Where steampunk nostalgically revisits the fashion of the nineteenth century, Lathrop's Time Traveler summarily rejects it. Contrasting Eva Pryor, his love interest from the nineteenth century, and Electra, a modern woman, the Time Traveler is clearly attracted to Electra's futurist fashion, which seems pulled from the set of Michael Anderson's *Logan's Run* (1976):

Charming though Eva was in her way, she had perhaps placed herself at a dis-advantage by having insisted on keeping her nineteenth-century costume. The angular slope and spread of her skirt, her unnatural wasp waist, the swollen sleeves, and the stiff, ungainly bulge of her corsage had a grotesque and even offensive effect. The extraordinary tangle, also, of artificial flowers, wings, and other rubbish that she had carried on her head—for she still wore her hat—was as barbaric or savage as the head-dress of some early Norse warrior or Red Indian chief. To all this Electra presented a refreshing contrast of harmony, with grace and dignity and style of dress modern, yet classic, womanly, yet sug-gesting the robes of a goddess.[7]

This is only one of several such rejections in this story of the very style and aesthetic that steampunk currently embraces. This lighthearted example reinforces the idea that steampunk retrofuturism is a present-day roman-tic vision of how the past viewed the future, since the temporal spaces of steampunk are rarely concerned with precise historical accuracy. Steampunk evokes a sense of the past, rather than slavishly replicating it. Further, the past steampunk evokes may be far more literary than historical. Steampunk isn't as interested in history so much as the history of Victorian and Edward-ian literature:

> The mix of the historical and the literary have been the game of steampunk since its inception. . . . Steampunk offerings continue to utilize a mix of histori-cal figures whose lives have become legend, and fictional heroes whose stories have become truth in the minds of their readers, carrying on the tradition of blurring the lines between fiction as history, and history as fiction.[8]

Istvan Csicsery-Ronay Jr. also sees steampunk works as "not so much coun-terfactual, as, to use Matt Hills's term, counterfictional." He clarifies by using Sterling and Gibson's London in *The Difference Engine* (1991):

> Their focus is not on what might have been historically possible, which would presuppose the discourse of historical realism. Instead, they focus on the imaginatively possible, a dialectical mesh of fantasies of the Victorians' social, political, and cultural institutions, as both the Victorians themselves and the fin de millennium U.S. techno-bohemians might imagine them.[9]

The Difference Engine is an excellent example of how a technological focus in a discussion of retrofuturism might prove detrimental to significant analysis; the actual Difference Engine is seen only briefly in the novel. Instead, Gibson and Sterling spend most of the book working through the social, political, and

Imagining possibilities. *Copyright John C. Tibbetts*

cultural ramifications of the Difference Engine as counterfictional novum: "a stone thrown into the pool of social existence, and the ripples that ensue."[10] The focus of retrofuturistic speculation shouldn't simply be the stone, but the ripples.

The steampunk novels of Cherie Priest and Gail Carriger deal with these ripples, what I call the *social retrofuturism* of their counterfictions. This chapter follows in the footsteps of LeeAnne Richardson in her study on New Women in colonial adventure fiction, where she states, "The relationship between the women who imaginatively ventured into the territory of feminine emancipation cannot be studied separately from the men who imaginatively adventured into the outreaches of empire."[11] Steampunk literature, arguably due to its antecedent roots in such adventure stories, often blends these two journeys, as evidenced in Emilie P. Bush's *Chenda and the Airship Brofman* (2009), where a young woman is cut loose from the domestic sphere by her wealthy husband's death, but her considerable inheritance permits a journey of exploration and adventure. Other notable examples of blending feminine emancipation with steampunk adventure include *The Glass Books of the Dream Eaters* by Gordon Dahlquist (2006), *All Men of Genius* by Lev AC Rosen (2011), the *Leviathan* trilogy by Scott Westerfeld (2009–2011), and *The Innocent's Progress* by Peter Tupper (2010).

One particular scene in Ora Le Brocq's *Steampunk Erotica* (2010) echoes the distance between steampunk fashion and the Rational Dress movement in which many New Women participated. In a kinky striptease, the protagonist sheds both clothing and the trappings of the society in which she has been raised. Clothing herself afterward in steampunk attire, the heroine is effectively reborn: transformation of self is visualized symbolically through steampunk fashion.[12] Despite other works' contributions to the discussion of steampunk and the New Woman, the most popular stories mixing feminine identity with high Victorian-era adventure would be Carriger's and Priest's series. My hope is that this approach inspires others to investigate the political and cultural retrofuturism in steampunk, or other works engaged in making the past in our own image.

Carriger's humorous *Parasol Protectorate* series (2009–2012) features protagonist Alexia Tarabotti, later Lady Maccon, a spinster-turned-aristocrat whose lack of soul renders her a *preternatural*, the opposite of the *supernatural* werewolves, vampires, and ghosts. Preternaturals negate the supernatural, posing a potential threat to members of those societies, or an aid to those who need to govern them. The series mixes comedy, horror, adventure, and romance; while the novels contain episodic plotlines, the series is primarily character based, relying on readers' investment in Alexia's relationships with supporting characters, primarily the werewolf agent of the Crown, Lord Maccon, to keep interest.

By contrast, Priest's *Clockwork Century* (2009–2011) is a gritty alternate reality where the American Civil War has ground on into the 1880s. Unlike Carriger's, Priest's series does not feature a single character as protagonist throughout but maintains a thread of continuity with the spread of a zombie plague. Minor characters from one novel become major characters in the next: major events from one story become distant news in another. Yet consistently, all of Priest's steampunk novels feature strong female protagonists: in *Boneshaker* (2009), it is Briar Wilkes, a factory-working mother who pursues her son into walled Seattle to rescue him; in *Dreadnought* (2010), it is Mercy Lynch, a wartime nurse who travels across the United States to see her dying father a final time; in *Clementine* (2010), it is Maria Isabella Boyd, actor-turned–Pinkerton Agent; and in *Ganymede* (2011), it is mixed-race prostitute Josephine Early successfully rescuing a submersible prototype to sway the balance of the war.

Carriger's and Priest's novels are counterfictions, "exercises in pastiche and homage that work through a detailed appropriation of their originating texts' structures, literary devices, and fictional worlds."[13] Admittedly, neither author works from a single canonical or authoritative text as Kim Newman does with Stoker's *Dracula* in *Anno Dracula* (1992), but Carriger's playful engagement with the intertextual canon of vampire texts spawned by Stoker's is undeniable. The world of Alexia Tarabotti owes much to other fictional universes, from the nineteenth-century novels of Jane Austen to the cinematic franchise of *Underworld* (2003). Priest plays on the mythos of the Wild West and the American Civil War, blending these with zombie fiction. And in both cases, intentionally or not, the series act as intertexts for the New Woman.

The Parasol Protectorate:
"I would so like something useful to do."

In the first chapter of *Soulless* (2009), book one of the *Parasol Protectorate* series, Alexia Tarabotti confronts Lord Maccon, a werewolf and head of the Bureau of Unnatural Registries (BUR), a sort of Victorian X-Files, about his tendency to dismiss her: "Do you realize I could be useful to you?"[14] Alexia's desire for "something useful to do"[15] echoes the words of Mary Wollstonecraft in *A Vindication of the Rights of Woman*:

> How many women thus waste life away the prey of discontent, when they might have practiced as physicians, regulated a farm, managed a shop, and stood erect, supported by their own industry, instead of hanging their heads surcharged with the dew of sensibility?[16]

Alexia's need to be useful to the BUR, and later the British Empire, provides a character arc that parallels the aspirations of the New Woman. Instead of wasting life away "the prey of discontent," Alexia transforms from a twenty-five-year-old bluestocking spinster into an adventurer, "a lady who scurried about whacking at automatons and climbing into ornithopters."[17]

Granted, Alexia does not self-identify as a New Woman. Arguably, she has no need to; by the end of the first book, she is one of three members on Queen Victoria's advisory Shadow Council. In response to her vacuous sister's involvement in the suffragette movement, Alexia considers how her own vote "counted a good deal more than any popular ballot might."[18] Besides, as Lyn Pykett notes, "the extent to which women in the 1890s self-identified as New Women is difficult to quantify."[19] Instead of creating a nineteenth-century suffragette, Carriger has created a character who has been granted the sort of agency necessary for her to appeal to twenty-first-century readers who are used to female protagonists portrayed by Sigourney Weaver as Ellen Ripley in the *Alien* film franchise (1979–1997), Sarah Michelle Gellar in the *Buffy the Vampire Slayer* television series (1997–2003), or Trinity from *The Matrix* (1999). Alexia embodies new forms of femininity, even for the radically different society of Carriger's London. She enjoys reading and pursues scientific knowledge at a time when "education in itself was generally thought deleterious to female health."[20] And while she enjoys the attention of her husband, she does not need him in order to survive, or to some degree, even thrive in Carriger's neo-Victorian alternate world.

Consequently, when this steampunk New Woman is mistakenly accused of being a Fallen Woman, another fictional staple of the Victorian era, she does not, like Gaskell's *Ruth* (1853), resort to self-destruction or self-loathing. Alexia is the antithesis of the "innocent young victim" or the "fallen Madonna" Ruth represents.[21] At the close of the second book, *Changeless* (2010), Alexia discovers she is pregnant; her husband Lord Maccon believes the child must be the result of infidelity, as popular opinion holds that a supernatural, arguably being dead, cannot produce natural offspring. In a rage, he casts her out. The third book, *Blameless* (2011), finds Alexia in the role of Fallen Woman, rejected by Lord Maccon for assumed adultery, newly with child, and firmly at the center of "The Scandal of the Century."[22] Her subsequent altercation with upper-class London's gossip mongers demonstrates how "Lady Alexia Maccon was the type of woman who, if thrown into a briar patch, would start to tidy it up by stripping off all of the thorns,"[23] deflecting a society busybody's invective with sharp wit:

> "Lady Maccon, how dare you show your face here? Taking tea in such an obvious manner . . . in a respectable establishment, frequented by honest, decent

women of good character and social standing. Why, you should be ashamed! Ashamed to even walk among us . . . you should have hidden your shame from the world. Imagine dragging your poor family into the mire with you. . . . Why, you might have done them a favor by casting yourself into the Thames."

Alexia whispered back, as if it were a dire secret, "I can swim, Lady Blingchester. Rather well, actually."[24]

It is essential that we note Alexia's combative response to Lady Blingchester and her ilk, lest we be tempted to misinterpret Alexia's later actions in *Blameless* as flight. Alexia's response to her husband's dismissal of society's gossip and reproach is not retreat: despite becoming the Fallen Woman, she ignores the dirty laundry, leaves London, and goes on a quest. Admittedly, some motivation is derived from an attempted assas-

"Lemongrass": Taking matters into her own hands. *Copyright Brian Kesinger*

sination by ballistic ladybug automata, but seeking a solution without her husband's assistance further supports my notion of steampunk women as *damsels without distress*.[25] That isn't to say there won't be crisis after page-turning crisis once Alexia crosses the English Channel, but she and her steampunk sisterhood do not require the rescue of a Prince Charming to deal with these situations. They have inherited the Earth prepared by the likes of Xena and Lara Croft.

Yet this passage is noteworthy for another reason. Perhaps more than any crisis Alexia faces over the course of her adventures, her pregnancy provides further points of intersection between steampunk retrofuturism and the New Woman. I am appropriating the "unifying vision of the New Woman as a figure who privileged independence over family and who rejected social and sexual roles predicated on a politics of sexual difference,"[26] since this is arguably the popular understanding of the New Woman, and as such the one most likely to inhabit steampunk narratives. It is Alexia's rejection of sexual and social roles over the course of her pregnancy that is of interest to this inquiry, both in the sex act that leads to the pregnancy and the way Alexia deals with her so-called delicate condition.

Critics of steampunk, such as fantasy writer Catherynne M. Valente,[27] have decried the lack of historical accuracy, calling for greater attention to be paid to the darker side of Eurocentric colonialism and hegemonic patriarchy. I suppose there are some who would say Carriger has ignored the popular Victorian ethics inherent in Gaskell's *Ruth*, which held that "the fallen woman was a stain on society and had to be punished, either by the intolerable pangs of conscience or by death, preferably both."[28] After all, Alexia doesn't end up in a work house or as a prostitute after Lord Maccon casts her off. Alexia's path may lack the pathos and gravitas of nineteenth-century Fallen Woman narratives, but her journey nevertheless challenges Victorian ideas about feminine roles.

In *The Victorian Woman Question in Contemporary Feminist Fiction*, Jeannette King identifies two ideologically influential images that divide the Victorian woman into "polarized extremes": the Madonna and the Magdalene. These Biblical allusions "played an important part in the popular imagination. . . . Images of the Madonna and of angels therefore contribute to the formation of the Victorian feminine ideal."[29] Alexia is the inversion of that ideal: she is a sensualist, disinclined toward chastity, lacking the requisite soul for a spiritual life. By contrast, imitation of the Madonna produced "a highly idealized picture of a woman as disembodied, spiritual, and, above all, chaste."[30] Alexia is Magdalene insofar as appearances of the day go—she is sexually forward with Lord Maccon before they are married, and she enjoys sex with him after they are married. Both actions are scandalous within a nineteenth-century context:

> Chastity, moreover, meant for many not only a lack of sexual experience, but a lack of sexual feeling, or 'passionlessness'. Associated with the rise of evangelical religion between the 1790s and 1830s, the ideology of passionlessness made it possible for women to attain the apparently impossible goal of emulating the virgin mother: mothers were able to remain sexless, 'virgin' in a sense, because they remained sexually unaroused.[31]

Alexia not only explores sexual passion but is so prone to being given over to it that she and Lord Maccon engage in a moment of lovemaking while both are trapped and in danger:

> When Alexia finally dropped back, they were both panting again.
> "This has got to stop," she insisted. "We are in danger, remember? You know, ruination and tragedy? Calamity just beyond that door." She pointed behind him. "Any moment now, evil scientists may come charging in."[32]

It is this more wanton side of Alexia's character that alerted me to the connections between Carriger's books and the New Woman. *Dracula*'s Lucy Westenra, for example, shares an affinity with Alexia, who encompasses both Lucy's prevampire Madonna and postvampire Magdalene personas. In her excellent article on the New Woman and *Dracula*, Carol Senf identifies Stoker's scene between Jonathan Harker and the three vampire women as a "reversal of sexual roles, a characteristic frequently associated with the New Woman."[33] Alexia engages in such a reversal twice in *Soulless*, initiating the first liaison with these brazen words: "I am going to take advantage of you."[34] Yet ultimately it is Alexia's Magdalene nature that produces Prudence at the end of *Blameless*, a miraculous child able to temporarily steal a supernatural's powers through touch.

Even in childbirth, Carriger's humor conveys the strong sense of agency her heroine possesses. Once again, Alexia flouts conventional wisdom in a manner akin to the hyperbolic action of epic heroes. Alexia doesn't just remain active during her pregnancy. She investigates a potential threat on Queen Victoria's life. While in labor, she evades a clockwork automaton, stages a retaliatory attack upon it, and negotiates the sensitive politics between werewolves and vampires before finally giving birth to a baby daughter. All this, in direct rejection of the wisdom of the Victorian mind-set: "Discussions of the female reproductive system also tended to take a pathologised view of the female body as a whole, seeing women as semi-permanent invalids. A standard American work on female diseases, published in 1843, stated that women were liable to twice as much sickness as men, most of it stemming from the womb."[35] After all her exertions, Alexia realizes a young werewolf is in danger and endeavors to venture forth to save him. One of her servants objects, reminding her, "But my lady, you're about to, well, uh, give birth!" To which Alexia replies, "Oh that's not important. That can wait."[36]

Cherie Priest's *Clockwork Century*

Dreadnought begins with an epigraph of author Louisa May Alcott's statement, "I want something to do," when she announced "her intention to serve as a nurse at the Washington Hospital during the Civil War."[37] Later in the same novel, fictional nurse Mercy Lynch asks, "What about me, Captain? Where can you use me?" in the middle of a firefight between two armored trains.[38] Priest's heroines are clearly as interested in being "useful" as Alexia is, but the grittier tone of Cherie Priest's *Clockwork Century* series is the least of contrasts to Carriger's *Parasol Protectorate* books. We might say that Carriger gives us a steampunk New Woman from polite society, whereas Priest provides us with ones from the fringes of civilization. Unlike Alexia, Priest's heroines move from the domestic spaces of matrimony and maternity into the wild blue yonder. *Boneshaker*'s Briar Wilkes is admittedly a mother, but one who abandons all to find her lost son in a walled Seattle peopled with outlaws and zombie revenants. While Mercy Lynch of *Dreadnought* is certainly returning home to see her dying father, the journey there is perilous and violent, a steampunked *Planes, Trains, and Automobiles* (1987) as imagined by Quentin Tarantino. Maria Isabella Boyd of *Clementine* is likewise a woman entirely apart from the domestic sphere, having left a trail of ex-husbands in her wake. All of Priest's female protagonists are largely unconcerned with liaisons with the opposite sex.

Priest imagines her heroines this way in defiance of the expectation that all female leads need a romantic interest, instead filling the lives of these women with epic challenges common to the male action hero. In *Clementine*, after being told to stay out of the way and be quiet while the male crew of an airship engage in aerial combat, Maria Isabella Boyd demands the captain make her useful by putting her "where I can make the most trouble."[39] Her request finds her operating a Gatling-gun turret: in order to get into the chamber, she is forced to divest herself of her bulky undergarments. In a gunfight, petticoats can only get in the way; it seems likely that unlike Alexia Tarabotti, Priest's heroines prefer Rational Dress to Victorian finery.

Priest's retrofuturism is tied to the intricate matrix of race and gender in the nineteenth century. Her trump card is strong female characters transcending nineteenth-century gender stereotypes and limitations, without oversimplification. Her setting of America permits her to posit spaces where equality of gender and race isn't sidetracked until the suffragette or African American civil rights movement, but finds purchase on the frontier of a nation still in the process of becoming. This isn't to say her heroines have it easy. Unlike many steampunk writers, Priest doesn't cut corners laying the tracks for her alternate history: while her heroines are strong women, they don't live in a world of egalitarian emancipation.

While Priest is clearly neither sexist nor racist, many of her characters are. Priest hasn't just researched the events of nineteenth-century America, she understands how people thought at the time. Her characters live and breathe in the complex web of post-abolition laws and pre-abolition prejudices. When Mercy Lynch attends to an injury in the "colored car," her fellow white passengers cast disparaging glances, which results in the following epiphany: "Before long, she came to the conclusion that she was not much more out of place in the colored car than in the rich car, where her fellow passengers were high-class ladies who'd never worked a day in their lives, with their trussed up offspring and turned-up noses."[40] Not long after, Mercy faces the stigma of being a "woman traveling alone,"[41] which nearly costs her a place to stay for the night. In *Ganymede* when a well-intentioned soldier awkwardly inquires if one of Josephine Early's girls is a prostitute, Josephine replies, "We are what we are, and we use the tools at our disposal." When the soldier gallantly states, "But she shouldn't have to," Josephine upbraids him by saying, "She *chooses* to."[42] The proliferation of steampunk heroines who are prostitutes is not incidental. It is rooted in history, if books like Henry Mayhew's *London Labour and the London Poor* (1851) are any indication. Priest does not valorize the profession of prostitution, but rather concedes its existence, creating round characters who make hard choices to survive in a hard world.

Here we see Priest subverting the adventure novel's justification of the "subaltern's subordinated status"[43] through the steampunk New Woman's point of view. LeeAnne Richardson notes that New Women fictions focalize their narratives from the subordinated perspective, "interrogating the inequities of a system that assumes and asserts the very things adventure novels champion: male superiority, the right to dominate and rule others, paternalistic ideology."[44] By giving subordinated ethnicities and women a voice, steampunk retrofuturism creates a space for remembering history in the way Nietzsche "located the problem of the worth of history . . . in the problem of the value or need which it serves."[45] Steampunk writers choose to "remember" and "forget" the past in ways that "sculpture the past" into "the kind of image" these authors impose upon it, as preparation for "launching [themselves] into the future."[46] This is problematic when such an approach whitewashes or ignores historical atrocity, but also powerful when used to highlight inequities or injustices.

Priest has openly stated similar intentions in writing the *Clockwork Century* books. In a personal epigraph to *Ganymede*, Priest dedicates the book "to everyone who didn't make it into the history books . . . but should have."[47] She makes her intentions abundantly clear at her website:

> When mainstream society members don't see people who are different from them (in pop culture, in history books, in their neighborhoods), they get the impression that those people don't exist . . . or if these Others do exist, then they aren't very important. But with its time-travel/history-altering underpinnings, steampunk has the capacity to un-write some of the rules that created the Other in the first place. It offers a voice to those who were marginalized, allowing them to stand up and say, "I was here. And I absolutely, defiantly reject the implication that I wasn't." It's open to everyone—including those whose historical representation got left out, written out, or killed out of hand.[48]

Priest gives voice to women who never existed, and by doing so, gives voice to those who still do: "Historical fiction by women is part of the wider project, pioneered by second wave feminism, of rewriting history from a female perspective, and recovering the lives of women who have been excluded or marginalized."[49] While some might decry the exaggerated spaces of adventure in which these voices find utterance, I am not alone in underscoring the importance of strong, independent female heroines: "To the extent that media images and role models have an impact on what we deem acceptable or desirable, it is important to construct alternatives to media images and role models that perpetuate oppression."[50]

Priest constructs these alternatives in each book, and inasmuch as the focus of this inquiry is the New Woman, it is notable how many marginalized ethnicities Priest places in the thick of the action, not simply as tokenism but as viable characters with agency. Consider Josephine Early, mixed-race madam, who orchestrates the subterfuge of hiding a prototype submersible in the thick of a battleground, before arranging for a crew to sail it out of hiding to safety. When compatriot Andan Cly asks why she didn't "stay home where it's warm and dry and . . . safe?" Josephine replies:

> I've worked entirely too hard these last few months, planning and plotting, and buying every favor I can scare up to get this damn thing out to the admiral. I'm not going to sit someplace warm and dry and safe while the last of the work gets done. I intend to hand this craft over myself, and shake the admiral's hand when I do so. This was *my* operation, Andan. *Mine.* And I'll see it through to the finish.[51]

Repeatedly, Priest's heroines have to inform their male counterparts they "want something to do." They are not interested in being sidelined, left behind, or told to mind the kitchen, the children, or their manners. Priest's heroines cuss and shoot as well as any man, but this is not their defining trait. They are not simply "gals with guns," an image that—popular interpretations aside—does not embody emancipation or empowerment. Mercy Lynch can wield pistols, but she is most useful as a healer. Despite being cast in a somewhat traditional role as a nurse, she ultimately undoes the machinations of *Dreadnought*'s primary villain, who lays the blame for his failure firmly at Mercy's feet. Briar Wilkes becomes the first female sheriff in the Wild West but is still romantically attracted to airship pirate Andan Cly. They are more than just the Angel in the House or the Fallen Woman. Like Alexia Tarabotti, they are the mix of beatific and bitch, the complex combination that makes a character recognizable as human, which is the source of their retrofuturistic vision. The New Woman of history always had to choose between career and love: the desire for female emancipation produced by late-nineteenth-century realities was both a "condition of possibility as well as its condition of impossibility."[52] By contrast, the romanticized New Woman of steampunk can have career and family, and do it all while foiling an assassination plot on the queen or delivering a high-tech prototype of underwater vessel to Union forces.

Conclusion

The idea of the New Woman can be understood as the *hope* for social regeneration, a striving toward a future through the conception of "new, or newly perceived, forms of femininity which were brought to public attention in the last two decades of the nineteenth century."[53] Gail Carriger and Cherie Priest have created female characters who act as intersection points for the concept of the New Woman, as historical reality and fictional imaginary. These examples initially may seem too playful for a serious study of the New Woman, but they are, in fact, amplified expressions of subtler ideas. At the very least, they are an indication that the singular focus of steampunk toward technology is missing an opportunity to investigate social possibilities, not just technological ones. If the Industrial Era proved anything, it was that massive technological change results in massive social change. And while neither Carriger nor Priest are as fastidious in their investigations into the ramifications of the fantastic upon their alternate worlds as Bruce Sterling or William Gibson were in *The Difference Engine*, they are certainly more attentive to their leading ladies.

These counterfictional works are concerned not with the counterfactual inquiry of "What would have happened to the suffragette movement if . . . ?" but in the case of Carriger, "What would it be like if the New Woman had a relationship with a werewolf, a being possessing social standing while simultaneously being the object of social derision?" Likewise, Priest doesn't seem interested in knowing the actual historical ramifications of an extended American Civil War so much as asking, "What would the New Woman do if she ended up working as a Pinkerton?" Nevertheless, these counterfictions have a value to them. Gail Cunningham notes how quickly the New Woman disappeared from fiction but that the latent effect of those fictions upon reality could still be seen:

> The old stereotypes of the female character, with the strict moral divisions into what Charlotte Brontë had defined as "angel" and "fiend", were gone forever as female sexuality became a legitimate study for the novelist. . . . Feminist demands for freedom of expression, for smashing of taboos, had helped to drag the English novel out of its cocoon of stifling respectability and behaviour which had previously been denied it.[54]

Despite those latent effects, Cunningham highlights the speed with which "women were . . . packed off back to the home; ideas about free motherhood, sexual liberation or self-fulfillment through work were condemned to lie dormant for more than a half a century before sprouting once more in the modern Women's movement."[55] She then wonders whether the same thing has happened to the modern woman, if they have been presented with, in the words of H. G. Wells, "a sham emancipation."[56]

That was in 1978.

In 2005, Jeannette King's ruminations on the Victorian woman in contemporary fiction seem to indicate that the New Woman may still have some useful trouble to stir up:

> Gender is as politically charged an issue now as it was at the end of the nineteenth century, and continues to be debated in both the popular and the academic press. If we are in the middle of another shift in what we know and think about gender, in the "post-feminist" mood that prevails at the beginning of the twenty-first century, we need to know how our beliefs came about, and how much has been excluded or forgotten in what we know.[57]

The steampunk New Woman can do this in ways the Victorian New Woman never could. Neo-Victorian writers will be able to write only about *what was*, or in the rare case when their characters seek to break convention, their tales will likely end in tragedy. The steampunk New Woman, however, is not the New Woman as she was imagined in the nineteenth century, or even reimagined by neo-Victorian writers in the twentieth and twenty-first centuries: she has far more agency than those women and is given the option to have her proverbial cake and eat it too. The New Woman of the nineteenth century "was (and remains) a shifting and contested term . . . a mobile and contradictory figure or signifier,"[58] and so it seems that the steampunk New Woman further stirs these already muddied waters: she can be the Madonna and the Magdalene, the Angel and the Fiend: useful to have around but a handful of "trouble" as well. As Angeline, the enigmatic cross-dressing Native princess from *Boneshaker* states, "We don't have too many women down here inside the walls, but I sure wouldn't mess with the ones we've got."[59]

Notes

1. Rob Latham, "Our Jaded Tomorrows," *Science Fiction Studies* 36, no. 2 (2009): 341.

2. Rebecca Onion, "Reclaiming the Machine: An Introductory Look at Steampunk in Everyday Practice," *Neo-Victorian Studies* 1, no. 1 (2008): 145, www.neovictorianstudies.com/past_issues/Autumn2008/NVS%201–1%20R-Onion.pdf (10 March 2012).

3. Onion, "Reclaiming the Machine," 138–139.

4. Jess Nevins, "Prescriptivists vs. Descriptivists: Defining Steampunk," *Science Fiction Studies* 38, no. 3 (November, 2011): 516.

5. Sally Ledger, "Ibsen, the New Woman, and the Actress," in *The New Woman in Fiction and in Fact: Fin-de-Siècle Feminisms*, ed. Angelique Richardson and Chris Willis (New York: Palgrave, 2002), 82.

6. Joan Perkin, *Victorian Women* (New York: New York University Press, 1995), 97.

7. George Parsons Lathrop, "In the Deep of Time," in *Steampunk Prime: A Vintage Steampunk Reader*, ed. Mike Ashley (New York: Non-Stop Press, 2010), 99.

8. Mike Perschon, "Fictional Histories and Historical Fictions: Collisions of the Real and Imaginary in Steampunk," *Locus* 65, no. 3 (September 2010): 40.

9. Istvan Csicsery-Ronay Jr., *The Seven Beauties of Science Fiction* (Middletown, Conn.: Wesleyan University Press, 2008), 108–109.

10. Csicsery-Ronay Jr., *The Seven Beauties of Science Fiction*, 59.

11. LeeAnne M. Richardson, *New Woman and Colonial Adventure Fiction in Victorian Britain* (Gainesville: University Press of Florida, 2006), 3–4.

12. Ora Le Brocq, *Steampunk Erotica* (Squamish, BC: eXtasy Books), 126–131.

13. Matt Hills, "Counterfiction in the Work of Kim Newman: Rewriting Gothic SF as 'Alternate-Story Stories,'" *Science Fiction Studies* 30, no. 3 (2003): 451.

14. Gail Carriger, *Soulless: The Parasol Protectorate: Book the First* (New York: Orbit Books, 2009), 21.

15. Carriger, *Soulless*, 22.

16. Mary Wollstonecraft, *A Vindication of the Rights of Woman*, ed. Carol H. Poston (New York: Norton 1988), 149.

17. Gail Carriger, *Heartless: The Parasol Protectorate: Book the Fourth* (New York: Orbit Books, 2011), 60.

18. Carriger, *Heartless*, 44.

19. Lyn Pykett, foreword to *The New Woman in Fiction and in Fact: Fin-de-Siècle Feminisms*, ed. Angelique Richardson and Chris Willis, xi.

20. Jeannette King, *The Victorian Woman Question in Contemporary Feminist Fiction* (New York: Palgrave MacMillan, 2005), 18.

21. George Watt, *The Fallen Woman in the 19th Century English Novel* (Totowa, N.J.: Barnes and Noble, 1984), 19–21.

22. Gail Carriger, *Blameless: The Parasol Protectorate: Book the Third* (New York: Orbit Books, 2010), 10.

23. Carriger, *Blameless*, 8.

24. Carriger, *Blameless*, 57.

25. Mike Perschon, "Steam Wars," *Neo-Victorian Studies* 3, no. 1 (2010): 159, www.neovictorianstudies.com/past_issues/3–1%202010/NVS%203–1–5%20M-Perschon.pdf (10 March 2012).

26. Angelique Richardson, *Love and Eugenics in the Late Nineteenth Century* (Oxford: Oxford University Press, 2003), 8.

27. See especially her article under username yuki-onna: Catherynne M. Valente, "Here I Stand, with Steam Coming Out of My Ears," *Rules for Anchorites*, 3 November 2010, http://yuki-onna.livejournal.com/616832.html (13 February 2012).

28. Gail Cunningham, *The New Woman and the Victorian Novel* (London: Mac-Millan, 1978), 21.

29. Jeannette King, *The Victorian Woman Question in Contemporary Feminist Fiction* (New York: Palgrave MacMillan, 2005), 10.

30. King, *The Victorian Woman Question in Contemporary Feminist Fiction*, 10.

31. King, *The Victorian Woman Question in Contemporary Feminist Fiction*, 11.

32. Carriger, *Soulless*, 292.

33. Carol A. Senf, "'Dracula': Stoker's Response to the New Woman," *Victorian Studies* 26, no. 1 (September 1982): 40.

34. Carriger, *Soulless*, 164.

35. King, *The Victorian Woman Question in Contemporary Feminist Fiction*, 17.

36. Carriger, *Heartless*, 350.

37. Cherie Priest, *Dreadnought* (New York: Tor, 2010), 9.

38. Priest, *Dreadnought*, 345.

39. Cherie Priest, *Clementine* (Burton: Subterranean Press, 2010), 123.

40. Priest, *Dreadnought*, 125.

41. Priest, *Dreadnought*, 113.

42. Cherie Priest, *Ganymede* (New York: Tor, 2011), 112.

43. Richardson, *New Woman and Colonial Adventure Fiction*, 1.

44. Richardson, *New Woman and Colonial Adventure Fiction*, 1.

45. Hayden White, *Metahistory: The Historical Imagination in Nineteenth Century Europe* (Baltimore: Johns Hopkins University Press, 1990), 348.

46. White, *Metahistory*, 349.

47. Priest, *Ganymede*, 5.

48. Cherie Priest, "Steampunk: What It Is, Why I Came to Like It, and Why I Think It'll Stick Around," *The Clockwork Century*, 8 August 2009, http://the clockworkcentury.com/?p=165 (22 February 2012).

49. King, *The Victorian Woman Question in Contemporary Feminist Fiction*, 4.

50. Mimi Marinucci, "Feminism and the Ethics of Violence," in *Buffy the Vampire Slayer and Philosophy: Fear and Trembling in Sunnydale*, ed. James B. South (Chicago: Open Court, 2003), 75.

51. Priest, *Ganymede*, 282.

52. Patricia Comitini, "A Feminist Fantasy: Conflicting Ideologies in *The Odd Women*," *Studies in the Novel* 27, no. 4 (December, 1995): 530.

53. Angelique Richardson and Chris Willis, introduction to *The New Woman in Fiction and in Fact: Fin-de-Siècle Feminisms*, 1.

54. Cunningham, *The New Woman and the Victorian Novel*, 156.

55. Cunningham, *The New Woman and the Victorian Novel*, 156.

56. H. G. Wells, *Marriage* (1912), quoted in Gail Cunningham, *The New Woman and the Victorian Novel*, 157.

57. King, *The Victorian Woman Question in Contemporary Feminist Fiction*, 6.

58. Lyn Pykett, foreword to *The New Woman in Fiction and in Fact*, xi.

59. Cherie Priest, *Boneshaker* (New York: Tor, 2009), 382.

Bibliography

Bush, Emilie P. *Chenda and the Airship Brofman*. Norcross: EmitoneB Books, 2009.

Carriger, Gail. *Blameless: The Parasol Protectorate: Book the Third*. New York: Orbit Books, 2010.

———. *Heartless: The Parasol Protectorate: Book the Fourth*. New York: Orbit Books, 2011.

———. *Soulless: The Parasol Protectorate: Book the First*. New York: Orbit Books, 2009.

Colwell, C. Carter. "Primitivism in the Movies of Ridley Scott." 124–131 in *Retrofitting Blade Runner*, ed. Judith B. Kerman. Madison: University of Wisconsin Press, 1997.

Comitini, Patricia. "A Feminist Fantasy: Conflicting Ideologies in *The Odd Women*." *Studies in the Novel* 27, no. 4 (1995): 529–543.

Csicsery-Ronay Jr., Istvan. *The Seven Beauties of Science Fiction*. Middletown, Conn.: Wesleyan University Press, 2008.

Cunningham, Gail. *The New Woman and the Victorian Novel*. London: MacMillan, 1978.

Dahlquist, Gordon. *The Glass Books of the Dream Eaters*. New York: Bantam Dell, 2006.

Gaskell, Elizabeth. *Ruth*. 1853. Oxford edition. Ed. Alan Shelston. Oxford: Oxford University Press, 1985.

Gibson, William, and Bruce Sterling. *The Difference Engine*. New York: Bantam Books, 1992.

Hills, Matt. "Counterfiction in the Work of Kim Newman: Rewriting Gothic SF as 'Alternate-Story Stories.'" *Science Fiction Studies* 30, no. 3 (2003): 436–455.

King, Jeannette. *The Victorian Woman Question in Contemporary Feminist Fiction*. New York: Palgrave MacMillan, 2005.

Latham, Rob. "Our Jaded Tomorrows." *Science Fiction Studies* 36, no. 2 (2009): 339–349.

Lathrop, George Parsons. "In the Deep of Time." 89–128 in *Steampunk Prime: A Vintage Steampunk Reader*, ed. Mike Ashley. New York: Non-Stop Press, 2010.

Le Brocq, Ora. *Steampunk Erotica*. Squamish, BC: eXtasy Books, 2010.

Ledger, Sally. "Ibsen, the New Woman, and the Actress." 79–93 in *The New Woman in Fiction and in Fact: Fin-de-Siècle Feminisms*, ed. Angelique Richardson and Chris Willis. New York: Palgrave, 2002.

Marinucci, Mimi. "Feminism and the Ethics of Violence." 61–75 in *Buffy the Vampire Slayer and Philosophy: Fear and Trembling in Sunnydale*, ed. James B. South. Chicago: Open Court, 2003.

Mayhew, Henry. *London Labour and the London Poor*. Ed. Victor Neuburg. London: Penguin Classics, 1985.

Nevins, Jess. "Prescriptivists vs. Descriptivists: Defining Steampunk." *Science Fiction Studies* 38, no. 3 (November, 2011): 513–518.

Newman, Kim. *Anno Dracula*. London: Titan Books, 2011.

Onion, Rebecca. "Reclaiming the Machine: An Introductory Look at Steampunk in Everyday Practice." *Neo-Victorian Studies* 1, no. 1 (2008): 138–163. www .neovictorianstudies.com/past_issues/Autumn2008/NVS%201–1%20R-Onion. pdf (10 February 2012).

Perkin, Joan. *Victorian Women*. New York: New York University Press, 1995.

Perschon, Mike. "Fictional Histories and Historical Fictions: Collisions of the Real and Imaginary in Steampunk." *Locus* 65, no. 3 (September 2010): 40.

———. "Steam Wars." *Neo-Victorian Studies* 3, no. 1 (2010): 127–166. www.neovictor ianstudies.com/past_issues/3–1%202010/NVS%203–1–5%20M-Perschon.pdf.

Priest, Cherie. *Boneshaker*. New York: Tor, 2009.

———. *Clementine*. Burton: Subterranean Press, 2010.

———. *Dreadnought*. New York: Tor, 2010.

———. *Ganymede*. New York: Tor, 2011.

———. "Steampunk: What It Is, Why I Came to Like It, and Why I Think It'll Stick Around." *The Clockwork Century*, 8 August 2009. http://theclockworkcentury .com/?p=65 (22 February 2012).

Pykett, Lyn. "Foreword." xi–xii in *The New Woman in Fiction and in Fact: Fin-de-Siècle Feminisms*, ed. Angelique Richardson and Chris Willis. New York: Palgrave, 2002.

Richardson, Angelique. *Love and Eugenics in the Late Nineteenth Century: Rational Reproduction and the New Woman*. Oxford: Oxford University Press, 2003.

Richardson, Angelique, and Chris Willis. Introduction. 1–38 in *The New Woman in Fiction and in Fact: Fin-de-Siècle Feminisms*, ed. Angelique Richardson and Chris Willis. New York: Palgrave, 2002.

Richardson, LeeAnne. *New Woman and Colonial Adventure Fiction in Victorian Britain*. Gainesville: University Press of Florida, 2006.

Rosen, Lev AC. *All Men of Genius*. New York: Tor, 2011.

Ross, Sharon. "Retro Futurism at Its Best: Designs and Tutorials." *Smashing Magazine*. 8 June 2009. www.smashingmagazine.com/2009/06/08/retro-futurism-at-its-best -designs-and-tutorials (8 March 2012).

Senf, Carol A. "'Dracula': Stoker's Response to the New Woman." *Victorian Studies* 26, no. 1 (September 1982): 33–49.

"Steampunk Styling: Victorian Retrofuturism at Home." Weburbanist. http:// weburbanist.com/2010/10/26/steampunk-styling-victorian-retrofuturism-at-home (8 March 2012).

Stoker, Bram. *Dracula*. 1897. Norton Critical Edition. Ed. Nina Auerbach and David J. Skal. New York: Norton, 1997.

Tupper, Peter. *The Innocent's Progress and Other Stories*. Cambridge, Mass.: Circlet Press, 2010.

Valente, Catherynne M. "Here I Stand, with Steam Coming Out of My Ears." *Rules for Anchorites*. 3 November 2010. http://yuki-onna.livejournal.com/616832.html (13 February 2012).

Von Busack, Richard. "Boiling Point." *Metroactive*. 29 October 2008. www.metro active.com/metro/10.29.08/cover-steampunk-0844.html (27 December 2008).

Watt, George. *The Fallen Woman in the 19th Century English Novel*. Totowa, N.J.: Barnes and Noble, 1984.

Westerfeld, Scott. *Behemoth*. New York: Simon Pulse, 2010.

———. *Goliath*. New York: Simon Pulse, 2011.

———. *Leviathan*. New York: Simon Pulse, 2009.

White, Hayden. *Metahistory: The Historical Imagination in Nineteenth Century Europe*. Baltimore: Johns Hopkins University Press, 1990.

Wollstonecraft, Mary. *A Vindication of the Rights of Woman*. Ed. Carol H. Poston. New York: Norton, 1988.

A new kind of femininity. *Copyright Jody Steel*

CHAPTER THREE

Corsets of Steel: Steampunk's Reimagining of Victorian Femininity

Julie Anne Taddeo

> There was a side of Finley that saw the corset as a little frightening, but it was beautiful. Another side couldn't wait to put it on. It was protection—armor. A normal girl shouldn't need armor, but a girl who often courted trouble, who wanted to protect herself and her friends, loved it.
>
> —Kady Cross, *The Girl in the Steel Corset* (2011)

Feminist scholars typically have regarded the corset as a metaphor for the "straitjacket of femininity."[1] Once a unisexed article of clothing, by the early nineteenth century the corset represented the larger Enlightenment shift in gender roles and the Rousseauian belief in female weakness, maternity, and virtue; a corset "impressed apparently natural virtues upon the shape of a woman's body, qualities that somehow she lacked without the garment."[2] Made of whale bone and reinforced with steel, the corset dramatically altered a woman's figure and restricted movement and breathing, thus making the fainting heroine of Victorian novels recognizable to many readers. Late Victorian dress reformers criticized the corset's harmful effects on the spine and potential to puncture internal organs, and *fin de siècle* New Women, in their pursuit of athletics and as a statement of emancipation, joyfully shed the garment. Despite such obvious drawbacks to the corset, Wendy Johnson suggests that we focus not only on "what corsets did *to* women—but also perhaps *for* them."[3] Ignoring warnings about moral and health risks, a woman "might find that wearing a corset actually made her a lady of leisure. With it she fit not only a tiny-waisted bosomy dress but also a social ideal of women with position and power."[4] Johnson adds that for Victorian women, corsets, like writing, "became disciplines that women put on in order to test the limits of feminine roles proscribed for them."[5] Of course, such an interpretation ignores working-class women who often performed heavy labor wearing corsets, and the pressures put on all women by the growing fashion industry to conform to a specific physical ideal. Nonetheless, Johnson's notion of resistance offers us a way to interpret steampunk's love affair with the Victorian corset.

Feminist scholarship over the last thirty years has both solidified and contested the stereotype of the Victorian "Angel in the House," restricted to the private domestic sphere and denied access to the same sexual and intellectual privileges of men.[6] Novels, poetry, art, domestic manuals, and religious sermons of the era may have heralded women as "princesses" and the "queens of the garden," but as Mary Poovey has demonstrated, Victorian gender ideology from the start was "uneven" and "fissured," with women maneuvering and undermining separate sphere ideology long before the "sexual anarchy" of the New Women of the 1890s.[7] Nothing demonstrated this tension between the image of the submissive, confined female and her quest for agency better than the corset. As historian Leigh Summers notes, the corset truly marked the female body as "a political object par excellence."[8] While some contemporary critics warned that corsets prohibited a true equality of the sexes, Victorian women themselves knew the subtleties and contradictions of corsetry; the corset created a space in which women could be sexually "innocent yet dangerous, chaste yet breathless with anticipation."[9] Corsets not only aided in the creation of a "refined" appearance (which also helped working-class women attract suitors from a better class) but also allowed women to conceal (and even miscarry) pregnancies and to transgress prevailing moral restrictions.[10] Rather than an instrument of torture and disempowerment, the corset enabled women to manipulate and define their own femininity.

In his introduction to the 2008 anthology, *Steampunk*, Jess Nevins notes the "attraction of the surface elements of the Victorians" to modern writers who use the period's ambience and garb to "portray contemporary issues" as well as critique the social inequalities of the past.[11] As a genre, steampunk reflects not only the continuing historical relevance and accessibility of the Victorian period but also its "dangerous edginess" and "possibilities for subversion."[12] The corset-clad steampunk heroine may look "dashing" and "fascinating,"[13] but more importantly, she facilitates the interrogation of gender issues that connect the past and present. Of course, the nostalgia that infuses the fiction and websites that market a steampunk lifestyle (and/or fantasy) may sometimes seem at odds with, and indeed obscure or trivialize, the subversive potential of the genre as a whole,[14] but as Linda Hutcheon reminds us, "the act of adaptation always involves both (re)interpretation and then (re)creation."[15] Sahara Kelly's romance, *Letting Off Steam* (2011), for example, makes a nod to Hutcheon's notion of textual appropriation and the pleasure it affords readers who long for a "world of mad scientists, corsets, flying dirigibles and searingly hot sex." Preparing for a steampunk-themed party, Kelly's heroine dons her corset and muses, "It's a chance to dress up and do something different."[16] Steampunk, then, is not just about borrowing what Nevins calls "the trappings and visual style" of the nineteenth century, but creating a neo-Victorian[17] world in which its inhabitants, particularly women, safely and triumphantly play with and transgress its boundaries.

The Corset as Neo-Victorian Fashion Statement

On any steampunk-themed website, at conventions, at fairs, and of course, on the jackets of romance novels, the corseted female—also outfitted in the obligatory goggles, perhaps a pistol at her waist—makes her appearance. The steampunk corset, worn *outside* rather than underneath the weighty Victorian-styled clothes, rejects any notion of the garment as "straitjacket." Nor is the steampunk corset intended simply as a "Victoria's Secret" type of "sexy little thing."[18] This is not to deny the erotic potential of the corset, but for writers and fans of steampunk romance, the corset reflects a larger "ideology of style"[19] that showcases female empowerment above all else. In the novel *Steamed* (2010) by Katie MacAlister, Octavia Pye's time-traveling lover convinces her to wear her corset on the outside of her blouse, telling her, "Don't you think it gives you a kind of dashing look? Somewhat devil-may-care? Something that says you're not a slave to convention, that you set your own trends? . . . All the steampunk ladies I met wore their corsets outside their clothes. I never once saw one hide hers."[20] In short, the steampunk corset is an announcement of a woman's place in the public sphere, clad for battle alongside, or against, men and cyborgs.

Steampunk couture websites are especially adept at showcasing the corset as the gateway to romance and adventure for those who purchase this garment. On steampunkemporium.com, entire ensembles are marketed with a backstory and an accompanying image of a neo-Victorian persona (or "steamsona") "inspired by the whimsical, inventive and adventurous spirit of the Age of Steam." For example, "Stella Maguire—Reformist," according to her product description, "has a rough yet undeniably charismatic edge that the other reformists in her women's rights group just can't hold a candle to." That she exposes her corset under her velvet jacket is further proof of "her mysterious past. . . . Where was she from and how did she come by her immense fortune? No one knows and Stella isn't saying." Another lady of mystery, "Narcissa Von Trapp,

Beguiling Horticulturalist," is more demurely attired in hoop skirts and Evangeline blouse, but the "brass inspectors" hint at her knowledge of "cultivating both plants and relationships." Actual Victorian personages are occasionally paid homage to on clockworkcouture.com, with the Mary Kingsley explorer vest, pith helmet, and safari skirt, but the centerpieces of this site seem to be the steampunk harness (underbust) and "Good Girl/Bad Girl" bodice: "Innocent and dangerous at the same time, wear over one of our blouses or over bare skin. Will attract artists and mechanics alike." The steampunk shopper is offered the accoutrements for "a touch of elegance, a dash of daring." And, if the cost of a corset is too prohibitive (prices range from $100 to $300), you can create a corset-clad avatar on such role-playing games as Cogs and Corsets, where "people live everyday lives in a world of wonder and steam."[21]

In "The Case for Steampunk Romance," blogger Heather Massey declares, "Let's face it, Victorian fashion may have been stiff and uncomfortable, but it sure looks amazing."[22] YouTube videos of steampunk couture fashion shows reinforce Massey's observation, as young, hip, long-haired beauties wander through the woods in laced boots, ripped tights, exposed crinolines, and, of course, clockwork corsets; for the grand finale: a "white steam" wedding dress, sealing the connection between steampunk and romance.[23] Steampunkemporium.com also offers a steam bridal gown, accompanied with a mini top hat and the "naughty but nice" white corset and bustle skirt, "for brides traditional and non." Blurring the Victorian binary of angel/whore, companies like Harlots and Angels custom-make corsets "for all your corset needs," from proms and weddings to steampunk events and bondage balls, reflecting the corset's multiple meanings.

For any woman who has qualms about donning this restrictive garment, there are plenty of reassurances from fellow corset devotees. Self-described "Resident Steampunk Gal" for tasteslikecomics.com, Calen Spindler argues that since steampunk is built on "an alternate history, corset fanciers can enjoy cinching our waists while still enjoying our liberty since we lace up by choice." A steampunk heroine may have to cope with zombie invasions and cyborg attacks, "but she will do it while sporting a 20 inch waist. If that does not illustrate the power of women, then I don't know what does."[24] Of course, the quest for such a tiny waist may seem the exact opposite of empowerment, but this particular example illustrates yet again the contradictions inherent in the corset's design and function. By the late nineteenth century, the aesthetic ideal of the "hand-span waist" (the term derived from the ability, and desire, of men to completely encircle the corseted female waist with their two hands) compelled women to lace themselves into dangerously tight proportions.[25] Steampunkemporium.com wistfully compares the feeling incited by

"Couture": not the typical Victorian woman. *Copyright Brian Kesinger*

its velvet corset to that of a "well-worn glove," transforming its wearer into a "19th century buxom beauty" who requires the "sumptuous" support of the "fainting couch in the Victorian boudoir." Evocations of such images, while intending to assert the corset as a signifier of sexual emancipation ("this amazing garment sustains a slight feeling of arousal if properly tightened, no wonder we steampunkers are such a happy lot," Spindler muses), also underscore the waist as an enduring "site of sexual objectification."[26]

In his study *Consuming History*, Jerome de Groot describes the varied ways in which we reenact history, often transforming the past into a "romantic fantasy" with the aid of role-playing games and period costumes. The danger, however, is that a true understanding of the past and its inequalities, especially for women, the poor, and racial minorities, sometimes takes a backseat to the thrill of dressing up. Nevertheless, appropriating such pieces as the corset can allow for the "construction and re-construction of the self" as well as an exploration of "the gap between then and now."[27] Steampunk writers, like romance novelist Kady Cross (shown on her blog in corset and goggles), readily admit that they enjoy appearing at conventions for their fans, who expect to see them in their Victorian accoutrements. In an interview for CNN, several steampunk writers, including Cross, Cherie Priest, and Gail Carriger, describe how steampunks try on various identities and, in the process, critique and rewrite history and women's place in it; as Cross succinctly puts it, "in a steampunk world, women can be anything."[28] Still, there is the potential for disappointment when fantasy and reality collide, as romance writer Olivia M. Grey describes in her poem "Steampunk Fantasy":

> Tight corset, fluffy bustle,
> Victorian demure.
> Red hair and lips to match,
> Mysterious for sure.
> A woman of their dreams;
> Lady with great allure.
> Until the wig comes off
> And the corset's undone....
> When they truly see me,
> They're no longer so keen.
> I become too plain.
> I become too real. [29]

The Corset's Hidden Mysteries

Grey suggests the disappointment that arises when the dress-up fantasy of the past collides with the dreary reality of modernity, but for the most part, steampunk fiction perpetuates the notion of the mysteries that lie beneath (or are a very part of) the corset. The unlacing of the steampunk corset, a scene that appears in almost every steampunk romance, obviously denotes a sexual act, but unlacing also works to undermine the "gendered nature of secrecy."[30] As Ludmilla Jordanova observes in her study of Victorian medicine, the "unveiling" of the female body on the vivisectionist's table signified men's privileged relationship to Truth and to Nature as doctors sought the "mysteries" of the female body.[31] In some steampunk stories, the corset functions much like a veil, harboring the secret mechanism that literally makes the heroine tick and that men are determined (often without success) to control. Lesley Livingston's short story "Rude Mechanicals" describes Jewel's corset as "a housing for machinery . . . a series of rivets and intricate brass buckling. . . . What Quint had taken to be nothing more than the stays of Jewel's corsetry was actual piping; thin pneumatic tubing that ribbed her garment in vertical stripes like whalebone." Jewel, an "Actromaton," has been specially designed for Quint's theatrical company; hardwired with the ability to simulate human movements and feelings so genuine, her performance of "Juliet" convinces Quint, in the role of "Romeo" (and as her overbearing director), to nearly commit suicide.[32]

On first encountering the Actromaton, Quint "felt as though he should have been repulsed. She wasn't real. She was a mockery. A machine." But the more he considers Jewel's lifelike face and slender hands, the more he realizes that he "was far more rudely mechanical"—after all, he asks himself, "What else are you Quint, but a biological machine? You're not so different. Just muscles and tendons instead of gears and pulleys."[33] Steampunk's fascination, like that of the Victorians, with human anatomy and physiology, has its roots in the Enlightenment debate on "man-machine"[34] and the scientific quest to create/control life, but Frankenstein's monster, when feminized with a corset, is more beautiful than frightening. When machined cogs are added to the garment's design, the corset becomes more than empowering—it is an actual *power source*. In Adrienne Kress's "The Clockwork Corset," for example, the corset is a "circulatory pump" keeping its owner alive. For Imogen, the corset had always been "a hateful thing," representing only the restrictions of womanhood. When she is shot in the heart during wartime, her inventor lover saves her life by outfitting her with what is not "just an ordinary corset. It was made of a tough leather and covered in moving pieces, winches and wheels, and leather straps holding it together. And over [her] heart was a forest of tiny gears in constant motion." The corset has become for Imogen "a moving work of art" and her "permanent fashion statement."[35]

The ending of "The Clockwork Corset" seals the connection between human and machine, since Imogen is dependent not only on the corset for her life but also on its inventor, Rafe, who becomes her husband and "personal clock winder." What is intended as a romantic conclusion, or what the narrator describes as "being there for each other," also hints at the potential power (both literal and figurative) dynamics of such a relationship. When steampunk takes on the classic Pygmalion tale, the master's creation, as Quint discovers when his "Juliet" has been "taught too well," often achieves a satisfying revenge. "The Perfect Girl," in Jay Lawrence's short story of the same title, is revealed to be the steam-powered creation of "Professor Higgins . . . that geezer who lured a poor defenseless flower seller from her pitch at Covent Garden and tried to turn her into a duchess. Mad as a hatter." When the "girl" lets out a "terrible hiss," Higgins yells, "They always spoil *everything* when they talk."[36] And in Paul di Filippo's "Victoria," twenty-five-year-old Cosmo Cowperthwaite is already so disillusioned with "real" women that he creates a life-sized newt that somehow, thanks to a good corset and wig, resembles the young queen and exists only for his sexual pleasure. When Prime Minister Melbourne desires the newt, a tug of war between the two men ensues, leaving Victoria temporarily damaged. Victoria's ability to regenerate her limbs should ensure a happy ending for Cowperthwaite, but as he watches her "snap a passing fly from the air," he shudders with the realization that he will have to live out the rest of his life with his "creation."[37]

Romancing the Corset

The previously mentioned stories, "Rude Mechanicals" and "The Clockwork Corset," appear in the anthology *Corsets and Clockwork*, whose editor, Trisha Telep, reminds readers "yearn[ing] for the infernal devices" that it is really "the heroine" in "her too tight corset" that makes steampunk "romantic." Beneath that corset beats "the heart of a true pioneer adventurer" with an "optimistic desire for love."[38] Scott Westerfeld explains, "In many steampunk works, history is rewritten in a very positive way, with women . . . given roles and powers beyond their historical station. It's a way of reclaiming history, and rewriting the roots of our modern world."[39] Steampunk's feminist agenda mirrors the changes that the romance genre as a whole has undergone in recent years. Since Janice Radway's oft-cited 1984 study of women readers' engagement with popular romance fiction, more scholars have recognized that such narratives no longer rely on fairy-tale endings and the "patriarchal dependence of women on men."[40] Writers of steampunk romances especially are keen to subvert the "bourgeois representation" of "'ladylike' behaviors of waiting and passivity,"[41] and while her love for a wounded (in many cases, half-cyborg) hero is a common theme, the heroine's own struggle to refashion her identity takes center stage.

When we first meet Finley Jayne in Kady Cross's *The Girl in the Steel Corset* (2011), she is a sixteen-year-old domestic servant fending off the advances of her employer's sadistic son. The two engage in a knock-down, drag-out fight, with Finley "victorious and self-satisfied. . . . Lord Felix had promised to teach her a lesson but he was the one who had been schooled."[42] Her corset bears her employer's family crest, but Finley's social and sexual vulnerability is counterbalanced by the "thing inside her"—an uncontrollable urge to "act in a way that was far from civilized."[43] A more kindly aristocrat, the orphaned duke Griffin King, rescues Finley from her newly unemployed status (and the possibility of a life on the streets); he enlists her in his band of misfits to defend Queen Victoria's empire from the Machinist and his army of automatons. In return, Griffin promises to help Finley balance her Jekyll/Hyde selves but recognizes the latter is what makes her so intriguing (and useful). Finley's internal struggle is not only between her "civilized" and "darker" halves but also between what she has been taught to believe are "respectable" and "unladylike" feelings about men. Her sexual attraction to "the devil" Jack Dandy, a cockney gang leader of London's underworld, clashes with her loyalty and growing affection for Griffin, whose social class she believes puts him beyond her "sphere." Interestingly, neither man is threatened by this "Amazon warrior" whose "heels of her black leather boots looked sturdy enough to grind a man's bones to dust."[44]

Cross's novel borrows from Victorian journalists' and ethnographers' descriptions to re-create 1897 London, especially Whitechapel—"a great unwashed area that only showed itself under the cover of darkness"[45]—and the familiar site of Jack the Ripper's crimes less than a decade earlier that prompted many at the time to decry the East End as a "murderland." But Cross's London is also distinctly steampunk—with velocycles and dirigibles as the modes of transport, and mechanized villains who make the Ripper seem like an amateur. Into this environment "a pretty girl with a full set of teeth and not a pockmark to be seen" confidently roams the nighttime streets; after all, Finley wonders, "why shouldn't she go wherever she wanted?"[46] For insurance, though, Finley dons her new steel corset of the novel's title, intricately designed to fend off "bullets and most blades" and "break a knuckle or two."[47]

Finley's corset is the creation of Emily, the Irish red-headed teen genius whose workshop resembles a "macabre toy shop . . . All around her were parts of automatons, bits of gears and machinery."[48] In the Doctor Frankenstein role usually reserved for male characters, Emily, who looks "so delicate and fragile," does more than corset design (though she is always clad in her own "grungy leather corset" and short trousers); she also brings the dead back to life, replacing the damaged face, limbs, and heart of Sam (Griffin's loyal sidekick) with mechanical parts. Unfortunately, Sam's new "mandroid" status only makes him feel like "an abomination"—the very evil he has been trained to kill—and he wonders "was it a lie when he saw Emily and the thing in his chest began to beat a little faster?"[49] Sam's uncontrollable rages over what he sees as his loss of humanity means that Griffin must rely on Finley's strength and Emily's intelligence to foil the Machinist's plot; Cross's heroines clearly do not belong to what the Victorians deemed "the weaker sex."

Tilda Booth's *Stealing Utopia* (2010) is yet another example of how steampunk romance uses the revisionist lens of contemporary feminism to create an alternative Victorian universe for women. Part of Samhain Publishing's *Silk, Steel and Steam* e-novella series, Booth's story features some familiar steampunk faces—H. G. Wells and Tesla—and a deep-pink-corseted heroine who carries a two-shot Derringer inside her reticule and an etheric force transmitter in her bustle! Initially part of a scheme to kidnap Wells, "Jane" becomes his rescuer (and lover), in the process saving Prime Minister Huxley's government from Tesla's treasonous actions. In the epilogue we see the happily married couple and their three children, ready for takeoff in an airship, armed for their next battle. Only near the story's end do we learn the true identity of Jane—Amy Catherine Robbins—the name of the woman who did become the real Wells's second (and much cheated on) wife. Robbins was already reimagined in the 1979 film *Time after Time* as a "liberated" American woman whom Wells must rescue when Jack the Ripper steals his time machine and escapes to late-twentieth-century San Francisco. In Booth's novel, she is a welcome change from the "doll-like" women Wells has previously known, and she prompts him to rethink some of his own less than utopian views. In a side plot, Jane conceals the fact that she has a younger, mentally challenged half-sister, afraid that the government's desire to create a utopia of supermen will lead to the killing of "undesirables" like Lizzie. Booth not only transforms the bespectacled Wells into the "hard-bodied" lover of romance fantasy but (armed with the hindsight of history) also prompts him to reject what today would be seen as his less than progressive support of eugenics, or what he had once called the necessary "sterilization of failure."[50] Jane must remind Wells that "sometimes the greatest evils are done by good men in the name of a good cause."[51]

The Corset as Pornographic Icon

As Jane and Finley learn, their corseted bodies are just as effective at concealing weapons and distracting the enemy as they are in winning their men. However, since many of these stories, like Cross's, are marketed to a young adult audience, the "steaminess" of the romances tends to be tame (Finley only imagines what it would be like to kiss both men), but there is another subgenre, steampunk erotica, that illustrates the corset's enduring status as "pornographic icon."[52] Victorian pornography often showcased the corseted woman, hair loosened, breasts partially exposed, arms raised in seductive pose, on its book covers and postcards. Victorian critics of the corset expressed anxiety over its role as an "agent of sexualization," and the fashion of low-cut ball gowns and *décolletage* that aided young women competing on the "marriage market" appeared "immodest" and "unchaste" to some.[53]

Such responses feed into the enduring stereotype in popular culture of the Victorians as asexual or repressed, even though scholars since Foucault have challenged this image of stuffy prudes compelled to cover up not only their bodies but the legs of their pianos! As Foucault observed in his first volume of *The History of Sexuality*:

> For a long time, the story goes, we supported a Victorian regime, and we continue to be dominated by it even today. Thus the image of the imperial prude is emblazoned on our restrained, mute, and hypocritical sexuality.[54]

Instead, Foucault countered that in the nineteenth century there was a multiplication of discourse concerning sex (a "discursive explosion"), as well as

> an institutional incitement to speak about it, and to do so more and more; a determination on the part of the agencies of power to hear it spoken about, and to cause it to speak through explicit articulation and endlessly accumulated detail.[55]

Laws such as the Contagious Diseases Acts of the 1860s that sought to curb prostitution and the spread of syphilis, as well as the burgeoning field of Victorian gynecology, for example, may have tried to repress and regulate female sexuality,[56] but, as Foucault concludes, they also made the discussion of sex more open and available to the lay public.

Steampunk erotica simultaneously reinforces the myth of repression even as it seeks to expose the "sexual undercurrents of the Victorian era."[57] In the earlier-mentioned story "Victoria," the real queen (not the newt imposter) has gone into hiding on the eve of her coronation. Taking refuge in a brothel, she gains "self-confidence . . . not to mention the tricks I've learned that will certainly please my darling Albert when we've married."[58] Di Filippo's story turns the eighteen-year-old Victoria (who reportedly vowed upon becoming queen, "I will be good," setting a moral example for a nation tired of aristocratic debauchery) into a sex-crazed teenager. Di Filippo gives new meaning to that infamous advice (incorrectly attributed to Victoria) to "lie back and think of England."

In her introduction to *Carnal Machines* (2011), an anthology of steampunk erotica, D. L. King muses, "But what about those corsets? Oh, yes, corsets, tightly laced carnality."[59] The stories that follow feature Victorian heroines who hide beneath their "voluminous skirts and breath-stealing corset[s]" their "irresistible desire," ultimately satisfied by machines that run on steam and electricity. For example, Delilah Devlin's account of "Dr. Mullaley's Cure" and "the lengths he went to please his patients" parodies Victorian medicine and its treatment of women's bodies. In particular, the most-quoted opinion on female "passionlessness"—Dr. William Acton's 1857 treatise that argued "the majority of women (happily for them) are not very much troubled with sexual feeling of any kind"[60]—is turned upside down in this story. In agreement with Acton's theory, gynecologist Isaac Baker Brown, in the 1860s, performed hundreds of clitoridectomies (or what he called his "usual cure") as treatment and prevention of female hysteria believed to be caused by "perverse" female sexual desire.[61] Mullaley is no Baker Brown, however, and his nurse finds that fitting in so many patients eager for his "cure" was "akin to cinching in the waist of a corset. There was only so much ribbon one could pull before something gave."[62] Hydrotherapy, used by Victorian doctors to calm "shattered nerves," is employed here by Mullaley to stimulate female genitalia, and mechanical "pelvic massages" alleviate "the many illnesses of the mind and body that occurred when a woman didn't release the noxious poisons boiling inside her."[63] The widowed scientist in Teresa Roberts's story "Human Powered" knows all too well the harmful effects of culturally mandated abstinence for unmarried women; she invents a small device that stores the energy from sexual frustration and converts it to enough electricity to power a home![64]

As a companion to such fiction, websites like Lady Clankington's Cabinet of Carnal Curiosities sell steampunk-themed "adult novelties." Attired in a bosom-revealing corset, pith helmet, and goggles, the website's buxom model wields the most popular vibrator, the "deathray." The website also sells a larger fantasy to those who purchase the wares designed by "Lady Clankington . . . heiress and adventuress." Providing her backstory, the website describes "a lust for life so insatiable" that compelled Lady Clankington to commission "the mad Dr. Visbaun to construct infernal devices to appease her appetite." Her biography is like that of the daring characters whose outfits are for sale on the much tamer site, steampunkemporium.com; in addition to her sexual appetite, Lady Clankington possesses a great love of "reading, exploring foreign lands, and perusing the international network of communications." But by far the most entertaining part of the site are the testimonials from the "Lords" and "Dames" who have purchased these "pieces of fine hand artillery" for their voltaic cell-fueled "duels."[65]

Victorian pornography, according to Steven Marcus, was itself subversive, an alternative language (or "pornotopia"[66]) made necessary by the strict

"Earl Grey": destined for so much more. *Copyright Brian Kesinger*

codes of respectability the culture imposed on itself. But while it championed the claims of "impulse, nature, and pleasure," Victorian pornography was also obsessed with the themes of female submission and disgrace. The "carnal machine" is always the penis, described in countless stories as an "instrument" or "wind-up clock" that never runs down and "reek[s] with the blood of virginity."[67] Steampunk erotica continues this notion of the body as machine but often replaces the human male organ with a mechanical one; more importantly, the "carnal machine" is now controlled by the woman and used to stimulate her own body and those of other women and men. In the steampunk pornotopia, no one is raped or punished with venereal disease (which the Contagious Diseases Acts miserably failed to curb) or warned against the debilitating illnesses and hysteria that result from excessive masturbation; in short, steampunk erotica promises "a lush and fantastical world of women-centered stories and romantic scenarios."[68]

Conclusion

In their study of neo-Victorian forms of popular culture, Ann Heilmann and Mark Llewellyn remind us that it is not enough to set a story in nineteenth-century London or dress its characters in crinolines and bustles; neo-Victorian texts must self-consciously engage with the acts of reinterpretation and revision.[69] Steampunk's use of the corset—in fiction, on websites, and for role-playing—not only fulfills this definition of neo-Victorianism but also demonstrates the garment's "lasting iconic power."[70] Nevins adds that "the attire of [Britain's] empire" (and this certainly includes the corset) is never free of meaning, "even if we wish it to be."[71] When a steampunk puts on a corset, she (or he) does so by choice—making a "fashion statement"—as the owner of the "Clockwork Corset" declares—but more importantly, the corset (to borrow from Fields) functions as a "resource of resistance," critiquing and reimagining Victorian gender norms and roles.

I will end with one final example that aptly illustrates the corset's multiple functions and meanings. In Sahara Kelly's *Flavia's Flying Corset* (2010), the heroine of the title reflects on her youth spent as the sexually naïve, obedient daughter and then submissive wife expected of her culture. The e-novella, also part of the *Silk, Steel, and Steam* series, hints at the darker side of the Victorian notion of "home sweet home" (a myth feminist scholars since the 1980s have aptly debunked[72]) as Flavia recalls the beatings she endured at the hands of her first husband. "It's apparently all part of being wed. Husbands are allowed to do such things, as long as they don't leave any obvious evidence."[73] Indeed, the common law of coverture in Victorian Britain allowed a husband to

> give his wife moderate correction. For, as he is to answer for her misbehaviour, the law thought it reasonable to intrust him with this power of restraining her, by domestic chastisement, in the same moderation that a man is allowed to correct his apprentices or children.[74]

Although Victorian campaigns against wife beating tended to focus on working-class "kicking districts," the much publicized case of Caroline Norton, for example, revealed that even aristocratic women were not immune from domestic abuse.[75]

With divorce a socially damaging solution for an upper-class woman, Flavia's escape from her unhappy marriage is not only very convenient but also quite steampunkish—a dirigible accident disposes of her brute of a husband—and now she is free to live alone: "It's my choice and my pleasure." Her widowhood also has freed her to focus on "women's matters, attempting to use the advances her father had made to better the condition of her sex." There is one small problem, however: how to put on a corset unaided by servants or spouse? Well-schooled by her years at her father's side in the laboratory, she designs a corset that laces up the front, as well as a small magnesium flare that can easily be hidden within the corset, to afford her greater protection when she ventures out unchaperoned. Admiring how unlike most "fragile creatures" Flavia is, Harland (a rival scientist, soon to be her lover) comments: "We don't do very much to prepare women for the dangers the world has to offer on occasion."[76]

Rejecting the Victorian dictate of female passionlessness, Flavia finally decides to take charge of her sexuality (her husband had no concern for her pleasure, and she endured five years of lonely widowhood). She readily engages in multiple acts of passion with Harland, who, with her consent, tests his mechanical devices on her. Her emotional and sexual transformation is accentuated by each new corset she puts on, displaying her "womanly curves" but also endowing her with certain powers. She excitedly welcomes Harland's gift—the flying corset of the book's title—which runs on the "Icarus compound" Flavia created. As a romance, the story inevitably allows for a "happy ending" for the two like-minded and sexually compatible scientists. But Flavia will accept Harland's marriage proposal only if *he* accepts that she's "quite likely to disappear into the laboratory for days on end."[77]

The corset—a garment so pivotal to constructing nineteenth-century femininity—also symbolizes just how malleable and central to modern popular culture Victorianism has become. In trying to pinpoint certain traits as "Victorian" we run the inevitable risk of imposing a homogenizing identity that ignores the complexities of the era and its people; the image of sexual repression and female submissiveness, for example, was often more myth than reality and challenged by the Victorians themselves. The corset may have imposed a degree of conformity (and certainly a lot of discomfort) on Victorian women, but it did provide opportunities for sexual transgression and self-expression. Likewise, the relationship between steampunk and the corset is not a uniform one, and its power lies in its ability to "accommodate a diversity of polemical positions."[78] Steampunk may at times look to the past through nostalgic-colored glasses, but more often it highlights some of the very real legal, social, and sexual inequalities that dominated late-Victorian and Edwardian discourse and politics; in doing so, it offers an alternative world for women that steampunk's hero, H. G. Wells, would have applauded. In one of his essays concerning the advancement of women, Wells aligned himself with "those who sanely and healthily await the changes taking place in woman's status and activity at the present day [and] are hoping for honest comradeship with no false sentiment, no mystery, and no repression, mental or physical."[79] On steampunk commercial websites and in romance stories and erotica, the corset promises its wearer just such a life of social and sexual transgression. Equally important, and not to be ignored, however, is the pure joy of fantasy when women like Flavia Winters "settled her skirts, adjusted her corset more comfortably and walked out of reality into a dream late one Thursday afternoon."[80]

Notes

1. Elaine Showalter, *The English Malady: Women, Madness, and English Culture, 1830–1980* (New York: Viking Penguin, 1987), 98.
2. Wendy Dasler Johnson, "Cultural Rhetorics of Women's Corsets," *Rhetoric Review* 20, no. 3/4 (Autumn 2011): 204.
3. Johnson, "Cultural Rhetorics of Women's Corsets," 213.
4. Johnson, "Cultural Rhetorics of Women's Corsets," 217–218.
5. Johnson, "Cultural Rhetorics of Women's Corsets," 225.
6. For a detailed discussion of the origins of Victorian gender ideology, see Lenore Davidoff and Catherine Hall, *Family Fortunes: Men and Women of the English Middle Class, 1780–1850*. Revised edition (New York: Routledge, 2003), and Chapter 1, "The Ideal of Domesticity," in John Tosh, *A Man's Place: Masculinity and the Middle-Class Home in Victorian England* (New Haven: Yale University Press, 2007).
7. See Mary Poovey, *Uneven Developments: The Ideological Work of Gender in Mid-Victorian England* (University of Chicago Press, 1988), ix.
8. Leigh Summers, *Bound to Please: A History of the Victorian Corset* (Oxford: Berg, 2001), 129.
9. Summers, *Bound to Please*, 142.
10. Summers, *Bound to Please*, 213.
11. See Nevins's introduction in *Steampunk*, ed. Ann and Jeff VanderMeer (San Francisco: Tachyon Publications, 2008), 8.
12. Ann Heilmann and Mark Llewellyn, eds. *Neo-Victorianism: The Victorians in the Twenty-First Century, 1999–2009* (Basingstoke and New York: Palgrave Macmillan, 2010), 4.
13. The heroine's description on the dust jacket of Nathalie Gray's *Full Steam Ahead* (Seminole, Fla.: Red Sage Presents, 2010), Kindle edition, n.p.
14. Justin Bieber's 2011 music video for "Santa Claus Is Coming to Town" (for the *Arthur Christmas* movie) clearly upset those who define themselves as "true" steampunkers, with bloggers declaring, "steampunk has jumped the shark" and "it's over!"
15. Linda Hutcheon, *A Theory of Adaptation* (New York and London: Routledge, 2006), 8.
16. Sahara Kelly, *Letting Off Steam* (CreateSpace, 2011), dustjacket.
17. Heilmann and Llewellyn admit that trying to define "neo-Victorianism" is just as difficult a task as defining what Henry James called "the baggy monster" of Victorianism. But in its broadest sense, the term signifies "aspects of contemporary culture

which embrace historical settings" and "involve themselves . . . in the self-analytic drive." See *Neo-Victorianism*, 5.

18. Victoria's Secret online description of its trademarked line of "Sexy Little Things" corsets that offer "one for every sexy you," www.victoriassecret.com/ss/Satel lite?ProductID=1265724350962&c=Page&cid=1327029210133&pagename=vsdWr apper&search=true (10 January 2012).

19. Christine Ferguson, "Surface Tensions: Steampunk, Subculture, and the Ideology of Style," *Neo-Victorian Studies* 4, no. 2 (2011): 66–90, www.neovictorian studies.com (28 January 2012).

20. Katie MacAlister, *Steamed: A Steampunk Romance* (New York: Penguin, 2010), 178.

21. *Cogs and Corsets* is just one steampunk RP Game. See http://support.proboards .com/index.cgi?board=adroleplay&action=display&thread=386492.

22. Heather Massey, "The Case for Steampunk Romance," *Dear Author*, 1 September 2009, http://dearauthor.com/features/letters-of-opinion/guest-op-the-case-for-steampunk-romance (5 January 2012).

23. See Steampunk Couture's Spring 2011 Collection video fashion show at http://support.proboards.com/index.cgi?board=adroleplay&action=display&thr ead=386492.

24. Calen Spindler, "Well Cinch Me Up: Steampunk & Corsets," *Tastes Like Comics*, 19 April 2011, www.tasteslikecomics.com/2011/04/well-cinch-me-up -steampunk corsets (15 January 2012).

25. Summers, *Bound to Please*, 210.

26. Summers, *Bound to Please*, 210.

27. Jerome de Groot, *Consuming History: Historians and Heritage in Contemporary Popular Culture* (London and New York: Routledge, 2009), 139.

28. For the full interview with Cross and other steampunk romance writers, see "Steampunk Powers Female Characters Forward," http://geekout.blogs.cnn.com/ 2011/11/16/steampunk-powers-female-characters-forward.

29. See Grey's website at http://omgrey.wordpress.com/2011/07/22/steampunk -fantasy. She notes that while she enjoys promoting a Victorian-styled image at conventions and online, she's troubled by the response from men who "want a fantasy, not a real person."

30. Ludmilla Jordanova, *Sexual Visions: Images of Gender in Science and Medicine Between the Eighteenth and Twentieth Centuries* (Madison: University of Wisconsin Press, 1993), 93.

31. Jordanova, *Sexual Visions*, 94.

32. Lesley Livingston, "Rude Mechanicals," in *Corsets and Clockwork: 13 Steampunk Romances*, ed. Trisha Telep (London: Mammoth, 2011), Kindle edition, n.p.

33. Livingston, "Rude Mechanicals," n.p.

34. Jordanova, *Sexual Visions*, 121.

35. Adrienne Kress, "The Clockwork Corset," in *Corsets and Clockwork*, Kindle edition, n.p.

36. Jay Lawrence, "The Perfect Girl," in *Carnal Machines*, ed. D. L. King (Berkeley, Calif.: Cleis Press, 2011), 78–79.

37. Paul di Filippo, "Victoria," in *Steampunk*, eds. Ann and Jeff VanderMeer, 293–294.

38. Trisha Telep, Introduction, in *Corsets and Clockwork*, Kindle edition, n.p.

39. Westerfeld, quoted in "Steampunk Powers Female Characters Forward."

40. For a discussion of how women readers respond to and use romance fiction, see Janice Radway, *Reading the Romance: Women, Patriarchy, and Popular Literature* (University of North Carolina Press, 1984), and Bridget Fowler, *The Alienated Reader: Women and Romantic Literature in the Twentieth Century* (London: Harvester Wheatsheaf, 1991).

41. Judy Giles, "'You Meet 'em and That's It': Working Class Women's Refusal of Romance Between the Wars in Britain," in *Romance Revisited*, ed. Lynne Pearce and Jackie Stacey (New York: New York University Press, 1995), 279–292.

42. Kady Cross, *The Girl in the Steel Corset* (Don Mills, Ont.: Harlequin Teen, 2011), 17.

43. Kady Cross, *The Girl in the Steel Corset*, 17.

44. Kady Cross, *The Girl in the Steel Corset*, 287.

45. Kady Cross, *The Girl in the Steel Corset*, 92.

46. Kady Cross, *The Girl in the Steel Corset*, 92.

47. Kady Cross, *The Girl in the Steel Corset*, 210.

48. Kady Cross, *The Girl in the Steel Corset*, 275.

49. Kady Cross, *The Girl in the Steel Corset*, 79.

50. David M. Levy and Sandra J. Peart, "Eugenics Rides a Time Machine: H. G. Wells' Outline of Genocide," *Reason Magazine*, 26 March 2002, http://reason.com/archives/2002/03/26/eugenics-rides-a-time-machine (18 January 2012).

51. Tilda Booth, *Stealing Utopia: A Silk, Steel, and Steam Story* (Cincinnati: Samhain Publishing, 2010), Kindle edition, n.p.

52. Summers, *Bound to Please*, 210.

53. Summers, *Bound to Please*, 275.

54. Michel Foucault, *A History of Sexuality, Volume 1: An Introduction*, trans. Robert Hurley (New York: Vintage Books, 1990), 3.

55. Foucault, *A History of Sexuality*, 17–18.

56. For a discussion of the CD Acts, see Judith Walkowitz, *Prostitution and Victorian Society: Women, Class, and the State* (Cambridge: Cambridge University Press, 1982).

57. Heilmann and Llewellyn, *Neo-Victorianism*, 21.

58. Paul Di Filippo, "Victoria," 291.

59. D. L. King, ed., *Carnal Machines*, vii–viii.

60. Dr. William Acton, cited in John Tosh, *A Man's Place*, 44.

61. For a discussion of Dr. Baker Brown's "cure," see Showalter, *The Female Malady*, 76–78.

62. Delilah Devlin, "Dr. Mullaley's Cure," in *Carnal Machines*, 81.

63. Delilah Devlin, "Dr. Mullaley's Cure," 85.

64. Teresa Noelle Roberts, "Human Powered," in *Carnal Machines*, ed. D. L. King, 1–15.

65. Here is one such "testimonial" that reads like a steampunk erotic short story:

"While attending the 104th Sussex Manservant Rally, Lady Stotescrue and I cheered on our favorites as they pulled their wagons around the second bend. At about this time, Lady Stotescrue pulled out a tiny, practically limp little weapon and complained that she was having the most dreadful time achieving any kind of satisfaction in her duels. She was in absolute distress and I just had to introduce her to my Little Death Ray. After going behind the refreshment tent and firing it just once, I was forced to attempt to wrest it from the veritable death grip she had on it. I don't dare let it out of my site again!"—Dame Edith Weesleshague

See http://littledeathray.com/infernal-devices (15 January 2012).
66. Marcus defines "pornotopia" as an imaginary world in which men are "infinitely Potent. . . . Everyone is always ready for anything. . . . One gets the distinct impression, after reading a good deal of this literature, that it could only have been written by men who at some point in their lives had been starved." Steven Marcus, *The Other Victorians: A Study of Sexuality and Pornography in Mid-Nineteenth Century England* (New Brunswick, N.J., and London: Transaction Publishers, 2009), 273.
67. Steven Marcus, *The Other Victorians*, 210–214.
68. Product description for Kristina Wright and Meljean Brook, eds., *Steamlust: Steampunk Erotic Romance* (Berkeley, Calif.: Cleis Press, 2011).
69. Heilmann and Llewellyn, *Neo-Victorianism*, 5–6.
70. Jill Fields, "'Fighting the Corsetless Evil': Shaping Corsets and Culture, 1900–1930," *Journal of Social History* 33, no. 2 (Winter 1999): 66.
71. Nevins, cited in Christine Ferguson, "Surface Tensions," 77.
72. See, for example, Mary Lyndon Shanley, *Feminism, Marriage and the Law in Victorian England, 1850–1895* (Princeton: Princeton University Press, 1993).
73. Sahara Kelly, *Flavia's Flying Corset: A Silk, Steel, and Steam Story* (Cincinnati: Samhain Publishing, Ltd, 2010), Kindle edition, n.p.
74. William Blackstone's *Commentaries on the Laws of England: A Facsimile of the First Edition of 1765–1769*, Vol. 1 (Chicago: University of Chicago Press, 1979).
75. See Poovey, *Uneven Developments*, chapter 3 on Caroline Norton's case.
76. Sahara Kelly, *Flavia's Flying Corset*, n.p.
77. Sahara Kelly, *Flavia's Flying Corset*, n.p.
78. Christine Ferguson, "Surface Tensions," 81.
79. H. G. Wells, "*Woman and Primitive Culture*," *Saturday Review* 79 (22 June 1895): 815.
80. Sahara Kelly, *Flavia's Flying Corset*, n.p.

Bibliography

Anon. "Steampunk Powers Female Characters Forward." *Geek Out!* 16 November 2011. http://geekout.blogs.cnn.com/2011/11/16/steampunk-powers-female-characters-forward (20 January 2012).

Beschizza, Rob. "Justin Bieber's Steampunk Christmas Video." *Boingboing*. 7 December 2011. http://boingboing.net/2011/12/07/justin-biebers-steampunk-chr.html (6 January 2012).

Blackstone, William. *Commentaries on the Laws of England: A Facsimile of the First Edition of 1765–1769*. Vol. 1. Chicago: University of Chicago Press, 1979.

Booth, Tilda. *Stealing Utopia: A Silk, Steel, and Steam Story*. Cincinnati: Samhain Publishing, 2010, Kindle edition.

"Clockwork Couture." www.clockworkcouture.com/ladies (15 December 2011).

"Cogs and Corsets." http://cogsandcorsets.proboards.com (16 December 2011).

Cross, Kady. *The Girl in the Steel Corset*. Don Mills, Ont.: Harlequin Teen, 2011.

———. *History, Twisted*. www.kadycross.com (10 January 2012).

Davidoff, Leonore, and Catherine Hall. *Family Fortunes: Men and Women of the English Middle Class, 1780–1850*. Revised edition. New York: Routledge, 2003.

Devlin, Delilah. "Dr. Mullaley's Cure." 80–96 in *Carnal Machines: Steampunk Erotica*, ed. D. L. King. Berkeley, Calif.: Cleis Press, 2011.

De Groot, Jerome. *Consuming History: Historians and Heritage in Contemporary Popular Culture*. London and New York: Routledge, 2009.

Di Filippo, Paul. "Victoria." 241–294 in *Steampunk*, ed. Ann and Jeff VanderMeer. San Francisco: Tachyon Publications, 2008.

Ferguson, Christine. "Surface Tensions: Steampunk, Subculture, and the Ideology of Style." *Neo-Victorian Studies* 4, no. 2 (2011): 66–90. www.neovictorianstudies.com (28 January 2012).

Fields, Jill. "'Fighting the Corsetless Evil': Shaping Corsets and Culture, 1900–1930." *Journal of Social History* 33, no. 2 (Winter 1999): 355–384.

Foucault, Michel. *A History of Sexuality, Volume I: An Introduction*. Trans. Robert Hurley. New York: Vintage Books, 1990.

Fowler, Bridget. *The Alienated Reader: Women and Romantic Literature in the Twentieth Century*. London: Harvester Wheatsheaf, 1991.

Gray, Nathalie. *Full Steam Ahead*. Seminole, Fla: Red Sage Presents, 2010.

Grey, O. M. "Caught in the Cogs." http://omgrey.wordpress.com/2011/07/22/steampunk-fantasy (6 January 2012).

"Harlots and Angels Steampunk, Corsetry & Haberdashery." www.harlotsandangels.co.uk/catalog (26 January 2012).

Johnson, Wendy Dasler. "Cultural Rhetorics of Women's Corsets." *Rhetoric Review* 20, no. 3/4 (Autumn 2001): 203–233.

Jordanova, Ludmilla. *Sexual Visions: Images of Gender in Science and Medicine Between the Eighteenth and Twentieth Centuries*. Madison: University of Wisconsin Press, 1993.

Kelly, Sahara. *Flavia's Flying Corset: A Silk, Steel, and Steam Story*. Cincinnati: Samhain Publishing, 2010, Kindle edition.

———. *Letting Off Steam*. CreateSpace, 2011, Kindle edition.

Lawrence, Jay. "The Perfect Girl." 71–79 in *Carnal Machines: Steampunk Erotica*, ed. D. L. King. Berkeley, Calif.: Cleis Press, 2011.

Levy, David M., and Sandra J. Peart. "Eugenics Rides a Time Machine: H. G. Wells' Outline of Genocide." *Reason Magazine*. 26 March 2002. http://reason.com/archives/2002/03/26/eugenics-rides-a-time-machine (18 January 2012).

Livingston, Lesley. "Rude Mechanicals," in *Corsets and Clockwork: 13 Steampunk Romances*, ed. Trisha Telep. London: Mammoth, 2011. Kindle edition, n.p.

MacAlister, Katie. *Steamed: A Steampunk Romance*. New York: Signet, 2010.

Marcus, Steven. *The Other Victorians: A Study of Sexuality and Pornography in Mid-Nineteenth-Century England*. New Brunswick and London: Transaction Publishers, 2009.

Massey, Heather. "The Case for Steampunk Romance." *Dear Author*. 1 September 2009. http://dearauthor.com/features/letters-of-opinion/guest-op-the-case-for-steampunk-romance (5 January 2012).

Poovey, Mary. *Uneven Developments: The Ideological Work of Gender in Mid-Victorian England*. Chicago: University of Chicago Press, 1988.

Radway, Janice. *Reading the Romance: Women, Patriarchy, and Popular Literature*. Chapel Hill: University of North Carolina Press, 1991.

Shanley, Mary Lyndon. *Feminism, Marriage and the Law in Victorian England, 1850–1895*. Princeton: Princeton University Press, 1993.

Showalter, Elaine. *The Female Malady: Women, Madness, and English Culture, 1830–1980*. New York: Penguin Books, 1985.

Spindler, Calen. "Well Cinch Me Up: Steampunk and Corsets." *Tastes Like Comics*. 19 April 2011. www.tasteslikecomics.com/2011/04/well-cinch-me-up-steampunk-corsets (15 January 2012).

"Steampunk Couture Spring 2011 Collection." www.youtube.com/watch?v=C7qbvuizl94 (12 January 2012).

"Steampunk Emporium." www.steampunkemporium.com/store/steam_ladies (10 December 2011).

Summers, Leigh. *Bound to Please: A History of the Victorian Corset*. Oxford: Berg, 2001.

Telep, Trisha, ed. *Corsets and Clockwork: 13 Steampunk Romances*. London: Mammoth, 2011. Kindle edition.

Time After Time, directed by Nicholas Meyer, 1979.

Tosh, John. *A Man's Place: Masculinity and the Middle-Class Home in Victorian England*. New Haven: Yale University Press, 2007.

VanderMeer, Ann, and Jeff VanderMeer, eds. *Steampunk*. San Francisco: Tachyon Publications, 2008.

"Victoria's Secret." Online catalog description of corsets. www.victoriassecret.com/ss/Satellite?ProductID=1265724350962&c=Page&cid=1327029210133&pagename=vsdWrapper&search=true (10 January 2012).

Walkowitz, Judith. *Prostitution and Victorian Society: Women, Class and the State*. Cambridge: Cambridge University Press, 1982.

Wells, H. G. "Woman and Primitive Culture." *Saturday Review* 79 (22 June 1895): 815.

Wright, Kristina, and Meljean Brook, eds. *Steamlust: Steampunk Erotic Romance*. Berkeley, Calif.: Cleis Press, 2011.

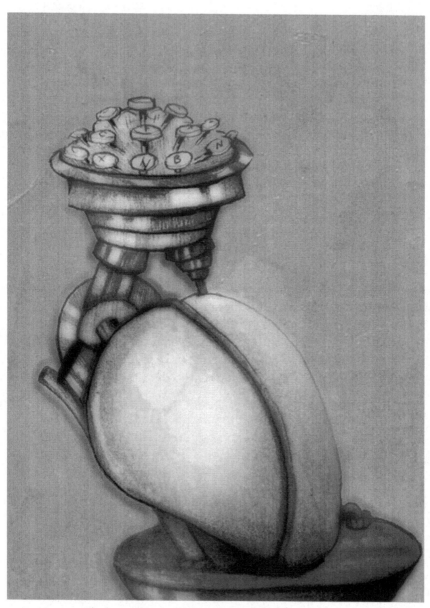

The heart of steampunk romance. *Copyright Jody Steel*

CHAPTER FOUR

Love and the Machine: Technology and Human Relationships in Steampunk Romance and Erotica

Dru Pagliassotti

Steampunk literary research has concentrated on what have been character-ized as the first and second generation of steampunk novels, those written in the 1990s, most notably Gibson and Sterling's first-generation *The Difference Engine* (1991) and Di Filippo's second-generation *The Steampunk Trilogy* (1995).[1] Most, if not all, early steampunk was written by men and revolved around male protagonists. But things have changed in what might be called the third generation of steampunk, works written in the early 2000s. How-ever, little research has addressed these newer, more diverse works, leaving scholars with a limited view of steampunk's scope and promise.

Female authors and protagonists entered the genre in the early 2000s, notably with the comic *Girl Genius*, even though comic coauthor Kaja Foglio described it as "gaslamp fantasy" because "we have no punk, and we have more than just steam."[2] In 2007 and 2008, female novelists, including this author, broke into the scene with steampunk romance.[3] Now, steampunk of all types is written by both men and women, although its rapid spread to multiple subgenres has raised questions over its adherence to the punk ideol-ogy. What many critics have forgotten, however, is that K. W. Jeter's use of "punk" was intended to be more facetious than foundational:

> My coining back in 1987 of the word steampunk originally might have been more of a humorous jab at a tendency going around those days, of labeling any two genre writers with more in common than bipedal locomotion as the "[insert word here]punk" movement.[4]

Nevertheless, practitioners' descriptions of the genre typically emphasize its punk component, such as the Catastrophone Orchestra and Arts Collective's manifesto published in the first issue of *SteamPunk Magazine*:

> Too much of what passes as steampunk denies the punk, in all of its guises. Punk—the fuse used for lighting cannons. Punk—the downtrodden and dirty. Punk—the aggressive, do-it-yourself ethic. We stand on the shaky shoulders of opium-addicts, aesthete dandies, inventors of perpetual motion machines, mutineers, hucksters, gamblers, explorers, madmen and bluestockings.[5]

Jess Nevins's later analysis of the genre condemned most second-generation steampunk as "steam sci-fi" or "gaslight romance": "This abandonment of ideology is an evolution (or, less charitably, an emasculation) that is inevitable once a subgenre becomes established."[6]

The use of "emasculation" is provocative, given the sexist nature of those earliest works of steampunk. Although *Infernal Devices* (1987) by K. W. Jeter is primarily populated by male characters, the most prominent female character, Miss McThane, is sexually brazen but ultimately subordinate to her male partner, and the other notable female in the novel, Mrs. Augustina Trabble, is simultaneously the termagant leader of the Ladies Union for the Suppression of Carnal Vice and a corrupt bawd running a sexual slavery ring. Gibson and Sterling's *The Difference Engine*, called by Nevins "the finest expression of the genre yet written,"[7] has only two central female characters, the prostitute Sybil Gerard and inventor Ada Brown, both of whom are portrayed as perpetually under male surveillance and subject to sexual slurs.[8] Di Filippo's *The Steampunk Trilogy*'s first story features a young Queen Victoria who shamefully runs away from her duties and is replaced with a cloned and sexually insatiable newt. Its second story depicts a racist protagonist who, over the course of the story, mistakes a Hottentot woman for an ape and constantly denigrates her and her marriage to a white man. Its third story shows Emily Dickinson losing her virginity to Walt Whitman, and her brother consulting Madam Selavy, who claims to ooze "ideoplasm" from her breasts, so that he can communicate with his two aborted babies. In short, the "masculine," oft-analyzed steampunk classics offered readers few, if any, strong, independent, and sympathetic female protagonists. By contrast, the later, "emasculated" steampunk has discarded gender stereotypes, retrieved marginalized voices, and embraced popular genres. Rather than dismissing its diversity and popularity as an abandonment of ideology, it could be regarded as manifesting steampunk's "punk" ethic of renewing, recycling, and reinventing. Just because it doesn't look like classic steampunk doesn't mean it's not steampunk.

One of steampunk's defining attributes is its description of the human/machine relationship. According to the COA's manifesto, "The technology of steampunk is natural; it moves, lives, ages and even dies."[9] Steampunk scholars have consistently pointed to the presence of technology and/or the Industrial Revolution as a key component of the genre,[10] even though steampunk machines in literature and film are often anachronistic, fantastic, and even magical in their operation.[11] Machines are as integral to steampunk as horses, revolvers, and wide-open spaces are to the Western. This may be why third-generation steampunk has so easily shaken off the nineteenth-century alternate history that early scholars identified as a key component of the genre;[12] it is the technological aesthetic, rather than any historical fidelity, that has emerged as symbolically central to the genre.

Steampunk also has been called utopian,[13] preferring individual craftsmanship and physically accessible workings to modern, mass-produced, bland designs that hide technology's inner operation. It exhibits technonostalgia in its romantic longing for nineteenth-century technologies that are unique, man-made, homely, personal, and easier to understand.[14] These tendencies can be seen in the numerous articles in *SteamPunk Magazine* that refer to the importance of the DIY ethic and in Cory Doctorow's introduction to the 2011 edition of *The Difference Engine*, which reiterates that "steampunk venerates the artisan, celebrates an abundance of technology, and still damns the factory that destroyed the former's livelihood to create the latter."[15] Machines, in the steampunk worldview, should be subject to human control, rather than a means of human control. The inventor, tinkerer, and engineer who are typical steampunk heroes use their mastery of technology to master their own fates, and "in utopic steampunk conceptions, part of the effect of this expanded capacity for mastery is that technological knowledge is available to the disempowered: women, children, and members of the working class."[16]

To suggest that technology offers a means for the disenfranchised to claim power echoes Donna Haraway's 1985 "A Cyborg Manifesto: Science, Technology, and Socialist-Feminism in the Late Twentieth Century." The cyborged woman relies on any number of technologies, from contraception to prosthetics to digital representation, to construct and empower herself on a physical, social, and conceptual level.[17] Steampunk romance draws this conception of the cyborged woman back in time. That is, at their most ideological, steampunk romance and erotica offer writers and readers an opportunity to imagine the ways in which technology has been, or could have been, used to define, restrict, or resist those socially constructed categories of sexuality, gender, and ethnicity that have stood in the way of human intimacy.

For the analysis in this chapter, fourteen volumes of steampunk romance and erotica were examined in terms of the role technology played in the romantic narrative. Seven of the volumes were written by single authors, and seven were edited collections of short stories by multiple authors. The works were written by male and female authors and encompass male/female, male/male, and female/female romantic relationships, plus a few that confounded gender classification entirely. Stories that appeared in more than one collection were analyzed only once, for a total of eighty-five individual works of fiction (either story or novel) in the data set.

The Western romantic formula typically includes a definition of society, a meeting, a barrier, an attraction, a declaration, a point of ritual death, a recognition, and a betrothal.[18] The barrier, or obstacles to the romance, may include the romantic protagonists' understanding and control over their own sexuality, their ability to defeat a villain and resolve a mystery, or their ability to triumph over sociohistorical constraints on their gender.[19] Erotica may follow the romantic formula but include a series of sexually explicit passages, or it may simplify the romantic formula by focusing on the characters' meeting, attraction, declaration of desire, and "betrothal"—a mutually satisfactory sexual encounter. Neither steampunk romance nor steampunk erotica deviates significantly from these formulae, although the plot of many such works is structured as much around the protagonists' physical adventures as their emotional transformations.

In this analysis, technology was found to serve one of three functions within the steampunk romance: (1) it may be a part of the background aesthetic, ultimately irrelevant to the overall romantic/sexual relationship; (2) it may play a significant role in the development of a romantic/sexual relationship by serving as the shared interest that connects the romantic protagonists, helping the romantic protagonists overcome an obstacle to their relationship, and/or acting as the obstacle that must be overcome; or (3) it may replace a human in the romantic/sexual relationship, either disappointingly or successfully. It's worth noting that when technology becomes significant to the romantic narrative, as in second and third cases, the narrative ends up addressing two types of relationships: the relationships humans experience with each other and the relationships humans experience with their machines. In this postmodern, posthuman world, relationships with people may rely upon relationships with technology, and relationships with technology may be as emotionally laden as relationships with people. Steampunk romance acknowledges both possibilities.

Technology as Aesthetic

Twenty-eight of the individual works of fiction analyzed here fell into the first category; the technology within the story was described sufficiently to create a steampunk aesthetic but was not integral to the development of the romantic or sexual relationship. Technology was not the reason that the characters met or cooperated, and it did not offer a substitute for a romantic or sexual relationship. For example, in Nathalie Gray's male/female romance novel *Full Steam Ahead*, steampunk technology is ubiquitous—the heroine, Laurel, is rescued from the ocean by an airship that is soon engaged in midair combat with other flying ships. However, it is not Laurel's interest in airships or any other form of technology that causes her to meet and bond with the airship captain, Phineas, nor does the airship or any other form of technology in the story aid, impede, or replace their romantic relationship. Laurel's ability to sail a ship eventually leads to her capture by enemies, but her skill doesn't help her fight her captors or win her freedom.

Similarly, in J. T. Whitehall's male/male romance novella *Surface Tension*, U.S. Naval officer Geoffrey is rescued from a beached submersible by the English inventor Sheldon. Sheldon is intrigued by Geoffrey and the submersible, but at no point is the submersible integral to the development of their relationship; it is simply a prop that permitted the two to meet, functioning as a horse, chariot, or spaceship might in another genre. Along the same lines, in Frewin Jones's male/female story "The Cannibal Fiend of Rotherhithe," the half-mer Silka takes a road train to London and encounters technologies such as Teslagraphs and vorpal lances, but the development of her relationship with Toby has nothing to do with technology, and ultimately it is her biological skill at swimming that allows her and Toby to escape imprisonment. In Mary Louise Eklund's male/female story "Cassandra's Kiss," the presence of dirigibles, a multiomaton butler, and a mechanically controlled greenhouse is ultimately irrelevant to the attraction between the two main characters, which instead relies on their history of shared experiences. Georgina Bruce's female/female story "Brilliant" shows Hamida meeting Brilliant on a train and later escaping pursuit on a zeppelin, but the technology remains a background element unimportant to the developing attraction between the two characters.

The relative unimportance of technology to the romance in these stories should not be taken to suggest that they are devoid of any "punk" value. Although some of the stories seem to call on steampunk only as an aesthetic rather than as an ideological frame for social critique, others offer messages that would likely be considered sufficiently punk for those policing the genre's boundaries. In the previously mentioned "Brilliant," Hamida defies traditional gender roles by using a stolen ticket to take *The Vanquisher* through Africa to escape her husband. She notes on the way,

> They can make a railroad from one end of the continent to the other, but women are still not supposed to wear trousers. I find, however, that the holder of a thousand dollar ticket to Cape Town can wear whatever the hell she wants.[20]

Later she muses, "I could become shadowy-thin, like my mother, who never laughed and rarely even smiled if my father was in the house. I could have stepped into the waiting straitjacket called 'duty' and 'good wife.'"[21] The story is "punk" inasmuch as it critiques women's oppression and points out the privileges of class, but because its plot did not include an interaction between technology and romance, it fell outside the scope of this thematic analysis.

Technology Significant to the Relationship

In forty of the analyzed works, technology played a significant role in the development of the protagonists' relationships. In twelve stories, a shared interest in technology brought or kept the characters together; in twenty-five, technology helped the protagonists overcome an obstacle to the relationship or achieve a personal goal; and in three, technology itself was the obstacle.

In some works, the characters' interaction with prosthetic or enhancement technologies sparks and enables the development of their romance. In Christine Danse's male/male novel *Island of Icarus*, the Englishman Jonathan's ungainly clockwork arm leads to his journey to the Galapagos Islands; along the way, he is swept off deck during a storm and lands on a remote island. There, the solitary American inventor Marcus replaces his clunky arm with a streamlined version. Marcus's work on, and acceptance of, Jonathan's prosthetic arm helps build the romantic tension between them. In turn, Jonathan aids Marcus in his attempts to invent a set of mechanical wings, finally offering Marcus the insight that leads to success.

The creation or modification of a prosthetic as a sign of love also appears in Jody Lynn Nye's male/female short story "Clockworks." In this story, an inventor uses the creation of a miniature version of a young lady's giant gas-powered mechanical heart regulator as an excuse to visit her. Similarly, in Adrienne Kress's male/female story "The Clockwork Corset," an inventor creates a clockwork corset to regulate his girlfriend's heartbeat after she is shot in the chest defending him from enemy soldiers. In both of these stories, the woman entrusts the care of her heart regulator to her loved one as a sign of continuing commitment.

The theme is also seen in two female/female stories. In Beth Wodzinski's "Suffer Water," the cyborged bounty hunter Annie's mechanical limbs are replaced by nanoengineered flesh by her target and former lover, Phoebe, although this ostensible gesture of love fails to keep Annie from turning her over to the authorities. In Rachel Manija Brown's "Steel Rider," abused or damaged women who escape into the desert are, sometimes, mysteriously interfaced with mechanical, artificially intelligent "steeds" to become steel riders, or seminomadic duelists-for-hire. In the story, the experienced rider

Corazon teams up with a new rider she calls Tirzah. Tirzah suffers daily amnesia, and Corazon's care of her includes reminding her how to use her "prosthetic," the steed with which she's bonded.

Although romantic protagonists with disabilities are not unknown in mainstream romantic fiction,[22] this minor theme of prosthetic creation and care as a sign of love is particularly steampunk in its emphasis on the construction and acceptance of a cyborged body. On the other hand, it is worth noting that the two male/female stories reiterated traditional gender dynamics rather than transforming the cyborged women into symbols of resistance and disruption, even though the heroine of "The Clockwork Corset" demonstrates resistance when she disguises herself as a male and joins the army to protect her love interest. Only "Steel Rider" suggests that cyborging may free women from an oppressive existence, giving them a freedom traditionally reserved for the male protagonist of a Western.

Prosthetics are not the only technologies that may bring or keep a couple together. In Cari Z's male/male story "Nothing Ventured," aeronautical engineer Sean and pilot Nicholas must work together to build a ship capable of winning an international altitude competition. In N. K. Jemisin's female/female story "The Effluent Engine," Jessaline seeks a way to convert the gases produced by Haiti's sugar industry into methane in order to power the free blacks' airships and save them from reenslavement by France. Her quest leads her to meet and fall in love with the chemist Eugenie, who can help her achieve her goal. In Meredith Holmes's female/female story "Love in the Time of Airships," wealthy Anouk falls in love with aether tube technician Olympe and is inspired to use the aether tube technology to reveal her husband's treachery to authorities and escape to a new life with her lover. In Kiersten White's male/female story "Tick, Tick, Boom," Catherine secretly manufactures explosives for unionists fighting oppressive factory conditions, leading her to meet and fall in love with another secret rebel.

These stories, and others in this category, use technology as the point of attraction in the romantic formula. They emphasize the importance of technological mastery, and in the majority of cases, they suggest a level of equality between the two technologically savvy protagonists that is not always seen in the classic romantic formula, wherein the romantic protagonist "rarely initiates any part of the story or even carries the action along. . . . The heroine wins the love of the hero by no other means than by being lovable."[23] If the classic romantic heroine is less powerful than the hero as a result of patriarchy, and steampunk suggests technology is an important means of social empowerment, then it makes sense that steampunk's romantic protagonist masters technology and finds a partner with whom she or he can be intellectually, if not always socially, equal.

"Chamomile": a different sort of romance for a different sort of reader. *Copyright Brian Kesinger*

Technology Overcomes or Acts as an Obstacle

The romantic formula requires the presence of an obstacle or barrier, internal or external, that hinders the relationship. As romance scholar Pamela Regis explains, "removal of the barrier usually involves the heroine's freedom from societal, civic, or even religious strictures that prevented the union between her and the hero. This release is an important source of the happiness in the romance novel's happy ending."[24] In twenty-five of the works analyzed, technology helped the romantic protagonists overcome such an obstacle and achieve their "happily ever after."

For example, Stephen D. Sullivan's male/female story "Automata Futura" depicts the inventor Victor choosing the automated shell that holds his dead wife's soul over the admiring assistant Zoe with whom he's been sleeping. In this story, technology plays two roles: for the inventor, it permits him to overcome the obstacle of his wife's death, but for the inventor's assistant, it becomes the obstacle that ends her romantic relationship. In Donald J. Bingle's "Dashed Hopes," a steam-powered voice communication device allows Genevieve to marry and consummate her marriage from afar with her beloved Trevor, who is trapped in a mining collapse and certain to die.

Some obstacles to romance are political or social. In Ross Baxter's male/male story "Spoils of War," Valmont obtains a confiscated Confederate dirigible in order to create a floating brothel dedicated to masculine love, because state laws prohibiting male/male physical intimacy don't apply to airspace. In Ariel Tachna's male/male romance novel *The Inventor's Companion*, perfecting a personal flying machine provides the inventor Gabriel with the funds he needs to purchase the freedom of his true love, the pleasure-caste worker Lucio.

Other obstacles may be psychological or physiological. In steampunk erotica especially, technology is often described as necessary to spark the protagonists' sexual intimacy or permit its successful consummation. For example, in Vanessa Vaughn's male/male story "In the Flask," the accidental creation of a lust-inducing gas gives assistant Nicholas the freedom to "act as shameless and wanton" as he likes with his mentor, Dr. Aubrey: "I could always claim I was under the influence of those mysterious chemicals. And, who knows, perhaps I was."[25]

Multiple stories in the collection *Carnal Machines* show technology enhancing the sexual pleasure between two characters—it improves sexual satisfaction in Teresa Noelle Roberts's "Human Powered" and Tracey Shellito's "Lucifer Einstein and the Curious Case of the Carnal Contraption" and helps a husband win back his estranged wife in Renee Michaels's "Sleight of Hand":

"Will you come back to me?" He looked away, fearing a rejection.
"Well, now, that all depends," Cassie purred.
His head jerked up. "On what?" His heart pounded.
"On the other toys you plan to make."[26]

Not all of the technology being used in these stories was invented as a sex machine, however. In Roxy Katt's f/phallogyne story "The Zeppelin Raider," in *Like a Corset Undone*, a magnetized zeppelin suit that freezes its wearer in place permits the young protagonist to take advantage of the hermaphroditic ship captain with whom she's been flirting. Similarly, in Vinnie Tesla's *The Erotofluidic Age*, the Ontological Engine, which was created as an experiment in the transformation of reality but is powered by sexual energy, is the excuse for a variety of erotic encounters that occur while the protagonist and his assistants conduct their experiments.

Technology may also function as the obstacle to the romantic relationship, in which case it must be overcome. However, this category was the smallest in the sample, with only three examples found. For example, in Ann Aguirre's male/female story "Wild Magic," a scientifically minded regime has appropriated magic and strictly controls it. The protagonist, Pearl, is drawn into a magical resistance movement by her love interest, Pick, who needs her skills and knowledge to break into a technologically protected vault. In this case it's the technologically savvy, magic-controlling society that poses the primary obstacle to a romantic relationship between Pearl and Pick, although the prejudices of Pick's own culture also act as an obstacle to be overcome, and both must defeat technological guardians to obtain the magical texts they need to reshape society.

Technology is even more central in Tobias S. Buckell's male/female story "Love Comes to Abyssal City," where artificially intelligent cities control their populaces and regulate marriages. When the ambassador Tia falls in love with the foreigner Riun, he initially rejects her: "Your city has computed the best possible match already for you. I will not endanger that."[27] However, her questioning of the city's judgment leads the city to issue an order for her quarantine, and in the end Riun invites her to flee the city with him. Although not itself artificially intelligent, the domed city of Teresa Wymore's female/female story "Under the Dome" seems equally oppressive. Within this city, a factory system in which impoverished workers are grafted with animal DNA leads shark-grafted Alice to stray from her lover and assert her humanity by doing things that proved that "the blood of murderers and rapists flowed through me, though the dome had tried to domesticate my people, had tried to dilute our humanity, and had turned every relationship into a transaction."[28] Unlike Tia, Alice cannot escape the system and does not look forward to a happily-ever-after ending; the technology of her oppression has been made a part of her.

In all three of these stories, technology serves the ruling class of a city or society as a tool of control and colonization. Given their dystopic view of technology and society, these stories seem likely to satisfy purists looking for ideological critique in steampunk fiction, but they are unusual within the subgenre of steampunk romance. Instead, the steampunk movement's more utopian, positive view of the human/machine relationship is reflected within steampunk romance, so that when the subgenre incorporates technology as a significant part of the plot, it is most likely to present it as a means of the protagonists' salvation rather than subjugation.

Technology Replaces Humans

The most thought provoking of the categories in steampunk romance are those in which technology replaces a human. Of the works examined for this anthology, seven stories and one novel showed machines being used as better-than-nothing replacements for human companionship, and seven stories suggested that machines could be better companions than humans.

As might be expected, *Carnal Machines* featured the most stories showing machines replacing humans. In the majority of these works, sex machines are used for physical pleasure, but human assistance is required to reach orgasm. For example, in Janine Ashbless's male/female "The Servant Question," Delilah Devlin's male/female "Dr. Mullaley's Cure," Kathleen Bradean's male/female "Lair of the Red Countess," and Elias A. St. James's male/male "Infernal Machine," machines fail to bring their users to fulfillment until a human intervenes. Similarly, in Clancy Nacht's male/male novel *A Certain Pressure in the Pipes*, Conrad creates a sex machine to keep himself satisfied, but when he uses it in front of Ezhno, the man he loves, he can reach orgasm only after abandoning the machine in favor of his lover. In all of these cases the machines are essentially mindless sex toys.

By contrast, in Elizabeth Schechter's male/female-mechanical "The Succubus," a room-sized artificial intelligence controls a clockwork female avatar that provides clients with sexual satisfaction, but the experience is so terrifying that they never return—a combination of both categories. The concept of a frightening mechanical lover is also seen in Lesley Livingston's male/female-mechanical "Rude Mechanicals," where a man falls in love with a beautiful actromaton that loves him back—but, trained as Juliet and failing to differentiate script from reality, she attempts to poison him. The machine is taken away, and the protagonist returns to humans for companionship.

On the other hand, Marc Tassin's female/male-mechanical/female-mechanical story "For the Love of Copper" describes the unrequited love of an automaton for a human. Christopher, the automaton, doesn't know what he is when he creates an automaton, Ellie, for his beloved human Eleanor. He realizes his nature only when he is abandoned, along with Ellie. Looking at the copper under his flesh, he laments that his artificial nature will make him unlovable. Ellie, however, protests that she loves him. Christopher, still shaken with his new self-knowledge, looks at the automaton he'd made and notes her beauty and the smile that "reflected the love of her creator."

> "You'll stay with me?" Christopher asked.
> "Of course, Christopher," Ellie answered.
> Together, hand in hand, they disappeared into the darkness.[29]

In this twist on Pygmalion, instead of a human loving his own creation and then bringing it to life, a creation loves a human and brings another creation to life for her . . . and then accepts the creation as a substitute for the original. It's not clear whether Christopher is in love with Ellie or merely accepting her as a substitute for his lost Eleanor. His final question suggests that it is his fear of being abandoned a second time, rather than love, that leads him to accept her offer of companionship.

Although some steampunk stories argued that humans can't be replaced by machines, about an equal number suggested that humans *can*. In several of these works, the machines are merely sex toys; for example, Kannan Feng's female-mechanical "Deviant Devices" features a sex machine that satisfies both the woman strapped into it and the voyeur who is watching her. However, in others, the machine is an automaton; for example, in Jay Lawrence's male/female/female-mechanical "The Perfect Girl," Professor Higgins prefers his mechanical—and mute—automaton Victoria to the human prostitute who is with them. Robert E. Vardeman's male/female-mechanical story "Her Faith Is Fixt" features a man who falls in love with an automaton and is loved in return; in this case, the automaton destroys herself to save his life. Shira Lipkin's female/female-mechanical "Truth and Life" describes an inventor who creates an automaton of her childhood beloved, who had rejected her; the implication is that the automaton will be an ideal and accepting version of the girl she'd admired. In Shweta Narayan's female/female-mechanical "The Padishah Begum's Reflections," the ruling mechanical Jahanara loves and wins the love of weaver and inventor Maitresse Vaucanson.

Steampunk romance's general consensus on sex toys seems to be that they are not satisfying unless another human is present; even in the one story in which the sex machine was satisfying, a human operator was present. However, the verdict on automata is less clear. Only the mysterious and powerful Padishah Begum is independent and free-thinking, and the story leaves the reader uncertain whether her people were originally built by humans or were created in some other fashion entirely. Of the remaining human-manufactured automata, some are dangerous while others are desirable—but the desirable automata were specifically built to be loyal and uncomplaining. Christopher, for example, is in love with his human master's daughter and heartbroken when she is evacuated and he is left behind, but there is no suggestion that this cavalier treatment by humanity will lead him to rebel against his master. He seems resigned to his fate. Even the intimidating Succubus is subject to the human brothel madam's control. Since steampunk seeks a return to controllable, understandable technologies, this raises the question of whether these stories suggest that relationships with machines might be easier and preferable to relationships with humans. This question is very much a part of contemporary discourse about the future of humans and technology.

Loving and Fearing the Machine

New genres reflect the concerns and tensions of the historical moment in which they are created, and steampunk is no exception. Steampunk's adoption of quasi-Victorian settings permits it to serve as a metaphor for this historical moment, which has so often been referred to as neo-Victorian. Neo-Victorianism proposes "a series of metatextual and metahistorical conjunctions as they interact within the fields of exchange and adaptation between the Victorian and the contemporary"[30]—that is, that the Victorians' literature, scholarship, politics, and technologies significantly shaped, and continue to shape, contemporary Western social and political imagination.[31] Steampunk regularly addresses these conjunctions. For example, when the dieselpunk/steampunk magazine *Gatehouse Gazette* ran a "Victorientalism" issue in March 2010, it sparked a widespread debate over the historical and contemporary uses of Orientalism and imperialism, with critics arguing that steampunk's writers cannot use such terms innocently or apolitically.[32] Thus, the various ways in which steampunk frames questions of technology, power, and change reflect the ways in which contemporary society frames those questions.

Is technology enhancing the abilities of humans to create and maintain relationships over distance, or is it putting distance between them by providing multiple ways to avoid face-to-face interaction? Will Facebook "friends" and cybersex replace face-to-face friendships and physical contact, or will human contact endure? Although there is a strong undercurrent of fear in the contemporary discourse about technology's effect on human relationships, research has not borne out society's misgivings. Multiple studies of Internet usage indicate that "rather than being an isolating, personally and socially maladaptive activity, communicating with others over the Internet not only helps to maintain close ties with one's family and friends, but also, if the individual is so inclined, facilitates the formation of close and meaningful new relationships within a relatively safe environment."[33] An overview of online relationships notes that the Internet may support familial relationships and facilitate romantic and (cyber)sexual contact between individuals but warns that although the Web "can facilitate disembodied forms of knowing, loving, caring, and sex, this is not always a substitute for the physical intimacy of a parental hug or a lover's caress."[34]

This warning is reiterated in Sherry Turkle's *Alone Together*, a book that expresses the central concerns of social technology's critics:

> We expect more from technology and less from each other. This puts us at the still center of a perfect storm. Overwhelmed, we have been drawn to connections that seem low risk and always at hand: Facebook friends, avatars, IRC chat partners. If convenience and control continue to be our priorities, we shall be tempted by sociable robots, where, like gamblers at their slot machines, we are promised excitement programmed in, just enough to keep us in the game. At the robotic moment, we have to be concerned that the simplification and reduction of relationship is no longer something we complain about. It may become what we expect, even desire.[35]

These are the fears that steampunk romance and erotica must address when they make the interaction between humans and technology a significant part of their plot. How can the two be reconciled? Will automata become better than humans at providing companionship? The solution that steampunk romance and erotica offer to that question is one of three explanations that can be proposed for the rapidity of steampunk romance's rise and the growth of its popularity.

The first reason for its popularity may be that romance (male/female and female/female romance, at least) has been one of the very few genres in which women are reliably depicted as strong, active, and autonomous agents and in which a happy ending is all but guaranteed. Since early steampunk novels were dominated by male authors writing about male protagonists, often in a way that ignored, if not denigrated, women, it's not surprising that women were quick to embrace manifestations of the genre that promised relief from gender invisibility or oppression. Although strong female protagonists have since appeared in nonromantic steampunk fiction,[36] romance novels seem to have been instrumental in breaking the barrier. The same may be said for the presence of gay and lesbian characters in steampunk. Despite the fact that most first- and second-generation steampunk featured male protagonists, few if any of them indicated same-sex desire until male/male steampunk romance hit the market, and the same may be said for lesbian steampunk protagonists.

The second reason may be that steampunk's nineteenth-century-inspired settings and their attendant rules of comportment and propriety pose convenient, ready-made obstacles for a romantic plot. Although the romantic formula requires overcoming a serious obstacle to the relationship, "a problem facing lovers today is the almost complete absence of impediments, with the ironic consequence that romance itself is socially inconsequential and distinctly unromantic."[37] Thus, while romantic comedies may thrive, romantic dramas are on the decline, except when they are situated within a historical context that preserves some element of social taboo for the lovers to overcome. Steampunk offers the romantic genre a new, quasi-Victorian setting free from the restrictive trappings of historical accuracy, and writers and readers may be eager to explore its possibilities. What remains to be seen is whether steampunk romance will result in romantic protagonists, especially heroines, who successfully resist patriarchy and oppression in a way that critics have said heroines in traditional romance have not.[38]

Finally, and of particular relevance to this analysis, the third reason that the genre may be so popular at this time is that steampunk romance and erotica operate on an ideological level to soothe contemporary fears that technology is replacing human relationships. Western romance and erotica provide readers with happy endings that affirm that anyone can find love or sexual fulfillment. Steampunk romance and erotica go a step further by providing readers with happy endings that affirm that anyone can find love or sexual fulfillment *in a society increasingly shaped and mediated by technology.* The protagonists of the steampunk romance have mastered technology without sacrificing their emotional and physical connections with each other; on the contrary, that mastery often helps them forge emotional and physical connections. Technology, rather than replacing humans, strengthens and empowers them, and in the majority of the stories analyzed here, it is depicted as a tool that aids, supports, or liberates human passion. Steampunk romance and erotica, despite being set in quasi-Victorian societies, offer readers a message of hope about the power of human relationships in a world that so often threatens to plunge them into a technologically divided and emotionally estranged future.

Notes

1. Jess Nevins, "The Nineteenth Century Roots of Steampunk," *The New York Review of Science Fiction* 245 (January 2009): 1, 4–5.

2. Kaja Foglio, "Dirt, Collection Vol. 5, Furniture and Gaslamp Fantasy," *Kaja's Monster Table*, 24 April 2006, http://kajafoglio.livejournal.com/60562.html (30 December 2011).

3. In the Juno Books e-newsletter of 30 June 2007, editor Paula Guran wrote, "THE CLOCKWORK HEART is a steampunkish romantic fantasy (are we launching a new subgenre?)." She and I consistently struggled with the question of how to market a type of fiction nobody recognized. Wikipedia's "List of Steampunk Works" suggests that Ginn Hale's *Wicked Gentlemen* may have been the first published steampunk romance, predating *Clockwork Heart* by a year. *Wicked Gentlemen* may be the first male/male steampunk romance, and *Clockwork Heart* the first male/female

steampunk romance. Note that my analysis of the steampunk genre is limited to English-language books; it's possible that earlier female-authored steampunk novels appeared in other languages.

4. K. W. Jeter, *Infernal Devices* (Nottingham: Angry Robot, 2011), "Introduction: On Steampunk and 'Steampunk,'" Kindle edition, n.p.

5. Catastrophone Orchestra and Arts Collective, "What, Then, Is Steampunk? Colonizing the Past So We Can Dream the Future," *SteamPunk Magazine* 1 (March 2007): 5, www.steampunkmagazine.com/downloads (3 January 2012). For an extended discussion about the role of ideology in steampunk, albeit with particular attention paid to costume, see Christine Ferguson, "Surface Tensions: Steampunk, Subculture, and the Ideology of Style," *Neo-Victorian Studies* 4, no. 2 (2011): 66–90, www.neovictorianstudies.com (27 March 2012).

6. Nevins, "The Nineteenth Century Roots of Steampunk," 5.

7. Nevins, "The Nineteenth Century Roots of Steampunk," 1.

8. See Jay Clayton, *Charles Dickens in Cyberspace: The Afterlife of the Nineteenth Century in Postmodern Culture* (Oxford: Oxford University Press, 2003), 111–112, for discussion.

9. Catastrophone Orchestra and Arts Collective, "What, Then, Is Steampunk?," 4.

10. See, for example, Stefania Forlini, "Technology and Morality: The Stuff of Steampunk," *Neo-Victorian Studies* 3, no. 1 (2010): 72–98, www.neovictorian studies.com (3 January 2012); Margaret Rose, "Extraordinary Pasts: Steampunk as a Mode of Historical Representation," *Journal of the Fantastic in the Arts* 20, no. 3 (2009): 319–333; Jess Nevins, "The Nineteenth Century Roots of Steampunk," 1, 4–5; Mike Perschon, "Steam Wars," *Neo-Victorian Studies* 3, no. 1 (2010): 127–166, www.neovictorianstudies.com (3 January 2012); and Michaela Sakamoto, "The Transcendent Steam Engine: Industry, Nostalgia, and the Romance of Steampunk," in *The Image of Technology in Literature, Media, and Society: Proceedings From the 2009 Conference of the Society for the Interdisciplinary Study of Social Imagery*, ed. Will Wright and Steven Kaplan (Pueblo: Society for the Interdisciplinary Study of Social Imagery, Colorado State University–Pueblo, 2009), 124–131.

11. Lavie Tidhar, "Steampunk," *The Internet Review of Science Fiction* 2, no. 1 (February 2005), www.irosf.com/q/zine/article/10114 (3 January 2012); Perschon, "Steam Wars."

12. For example, Steffan Hantke, "Difference Engines and Other Infernal Devices: History According to Steampunk," *Extrapolation* 40, no. 3 (1999): 244–254; Margaret Rose, "Extraordinary Pasts: Steampunk as a Mode of Historical Representation," *Journal of the Fantastic in the Arts* 20, no. 3 (2009): 319–333.

13. Rebecca Onion, "Reclaiming the Machine: An Introductory Look at Steampunk in Everyday Practice," *Neo-Victorian Studies* 1, no. 1 (2008): 138–163, www .neovictorianstudies.com (4 January 2012).

14. Alice R. Bell, "The Anachronistic Fantastic: Science, Progress and the Child in 'Post-Nostalgic' Culture," *International Journal of Cultural Studies* 12, no. 1 (2009): 5–22.

15. Cory Doctorow, "The Difference Engine: A Generation Later," in William Gibson and Bruce Sterling, *The Difference Engine: 20th Anniversary Edition* (New York: Ballantine Books, 2011), Kindle edition, n.p.

16. Onion, "Reclaiming the Machine," 152.

17. Donna Haraway, "A Cyborg Manifesto: Science, Technology, and Socialist-Feminism in the Late Twentieth Century," www.stanford.edu/dept/HPS/Haraway/CyborgManifesto.html (2 January 2012).

18. Pamela Regis, *A Natural History of the Romance Novel* (Philadelphia: University of Pennsylvania Press, 2003).

19. Kay Mussell, *Fantasy and Reconciliation: Contemporary Formulas of Women's Romance Fiction* (Westport, Conn.: Greenwood Press, 1984). Although Regis's and Mussell's romantic conventions were originally identified in heterosexual romance novels, they remain consistent in same-sex romance novels; for a discussion of them in the context of male/male romance, see Dru Pagliassotti, "Better Than Romance? Japanese BL Manga and the Subgenre of Male/Male Romantic Fiction," in *Boys' Love Manga: Essays on the Sexual Ambiguity and Cross-Cultural Fandom of the Genre*, ed. Antonia Levi, Mark McHarry, and Dru Pagliassotti (Jefferson, N.C.: McFarland, 2010), 64.

20. Georgina Bruce, "Brilliant," in *Steam-Powered: Lesbian Steampunk Stories*, ed. JoSelle Vanderhooft (Round Rock, Tex.: Torquere Press, 2011), 50.

21. Bruce, "Brilliant," 59–60.

22. An emotionally or physically wounded romantic interest (traditionally the hero) offers the romantic protagonist (traditionally the heroine) an opportunity to offer transformative protection, comfort, and love, passing the "domestic test," as Mussell describes it. In this analysis, however, the formula surrounding the wounded hero falters. Only in two stories, one male/male and one female/female, does the traditional formula play out as expected, with the wound offering the other a chance to provide comfort, reassurance, and assistance. In the two stories about heterosexual couples, the women are wounded and the men prove themselves capable nurturers by using technology to resolve a life-threatening condition, perhaps, ideologically, an acceptably "masculine" form of nurture. Finally, in the second story about a female couple, the woman offering nurture is rejected and taken captive by the woman whose physical, but not emotional, wounds she treats. Although Heinecken notes that depictions of a wounded hero may also serve to contain the threat of male power, that function doesn't seem to be played by the wounded hero(in)es in these works. See Mussell, *Fantasy and Reconciliation*, especially chapter 5, and Dawn Heinecken, "Changing Ideologies in Romance Fiction," in *Romantic Conventions*, ed. Anne K. Kaler and Rosemary E. Johnson-Kurek (Bowling Green, Ohio: Bowling Green University Popular Press, 1999), 164.

23. Mairead Owen, "Re-Inventing Romance: Reading Popular Romantic Fiction," *Women's Studies International Forum* 20, no. 4 (1997): 543.

24. Regis, *A Natural History of the Romance Novel*, 33.

25. Vanessa Vaughn, "In the Flask," in *Like a Wisp of Steam: Steampunk Erotica*, ed. C. Tan and J. Blackmore (Cambridge, Mass.: Circlet Press, 2008), Kindle edition, n.p.

82 ～ Dru Pagliassotti

26. Renee Michaels, "Sleight of Hand," in *Carnal Machines: Steampunk Erotica*, ed. D. L. King (Berkeley, Calif.: Cleis Press, 2011), Kindle edition, n.p.

27. Tobias S. Buckell, "Love Comes to Abyssal City," in *Hot and Steamy: Tales of Steampunk Romance*, ed. Jean Rabe and Martin H. Greenberg (New York: Daw Books, 2011), Kindle edition, n.p.

28. Teresa Wymore, "Under the Dome," in *Steam-Powered: Lesbian Steampunk Stories*, ed. JoSelle Vanderhooft (Round Rock, Tex.: Torquere Press, 2011), 244.

29. Marc Tassin, "For the Love of Copper," in *Hot and Steamy: Tales of Steampunk Romance*, ed. Jean Rabe and Martin H. Greenberg (New York: Daw Books, 2011), Kindle edition, n.p.

30. Ann Heilmann and Mark Llewellyn, "Neo-Victorianism and Post-Authenticity: On the Ethics and Aesthetics of Appropriation," in *Neo-Victorianism: The Victorians in the Twenty-First Century, 1999–2009*, ed. Ann Heilmann and Mark Llewellyn (Basingstoke, Hampshire: Palgrave MacMillan, 2010), 4.

31. Rohan McWilliam, "Victorian Sensations, Neo-Victorian Romances: A Response," *Victorian Studies* 52, no. 1 (2009): 106–113.

32. *Gatehouse Gazette*, 11 March 2010, www.ottens.co.uk/gatehouse/gazette-11 (29 January 2012). For an influential critique of the issue, see Diana M. Pho (Ayleen the Peacemaker), "The Semantics of Words & the Antics of Fashion: Addressing 'Victorientalism,'" *Beyond Victoriana*, 7 March 2010, http://beyondvictoriana .com/2010/03/07/beyond-victoriana-17the-semantics-of-words-the-antics-of-fashion -addressing-victorientalism (29 January 2012).

33. John A. Bargh and Katelyn Y. A. McKenna, "The Internet and Social Life," *Annual Review of Psychology* 55 (2004): 582.

34. Gill Valentine, "Globalizing Intimacy: The Role of Information and Communication Technologies in Maintaining and Creating Relationships," *Women's Studies Quarterly* 34, no. 1/2 (2006): 388.

35. Sherry Turkle, *Alone Together: Why We Expect More from Technology and Less from Each Other* (New York: Basic Books, 2010), 295.

36. For example, the mechanic Briar Wilkes in Cherie Priest's *Boneshaker* and the airship middie Deryn Sharp of Scott Westerfeld's Leviathan series.

37. James Dowd and Nicole R. Pallotta, "The End of Romance: The Demystification of Love in the Postmodern Age," *Sociological Perspectives* 43, no. 4 (2000): 553.

38. Many scholars have argued that romances and romantic heroines do not oppose patriarchy so much as offer temporary escape from it or a means of coping with it. For example, Modleski suggests that "romances to some extent 'inoculate' against the major evils of sexist society" such as the cruel or bullying man, and writes that "romances not only reflect the 'hysterical' state, but actually, to some extent, induce it." Owen argues that romances cloak a patriarchal reality and "writers and readers subvert the ideology with a message of how to survive that society"—survive, not defeat. Mussell argues that although romances do not threaten patriarchy, they at least allow women to write their own dramas within that patriarchal framework. Regis notes that the heroine of a romance, like the hero of a comedy, achieves freedom

at the end of the romance, although "she does not so much throw off the threat of an overbearing parent in competition for the same goal as she rejects various encumbrances imposed by the old society to arrive at a place where society stops hindering her." This freedom, she notes, is limited in scope. See Tania Modleski, *Loving with a Vengeance: Mass-Produced Fantasies for Women* (Hamden, Conn.: Archon Books, 1982), 42, 57; Owen, "Re-Inventing Romance: Reading Popular Romantic Fiction," 545; Mussell, *Fantasy and Reconciliation*, 186; and Regis, *A Natural History of the Romance Novel*, 30.

Bibliography

Aguirre, Ann. "Wild Magic." 72–111 in *Corsets & Clockwork: 13 Steampunk Romances*, ed. Trisha Telep. London: Constable & Robinson, 2011.

Ashbless, Janine. "The Servant Question." In *Carnal Machines: Steampunk Erotica*, ed. D. L. King. Berkeley, Calif.: Cleis Press, 2011. Kindle edition.

Bargh, John A., and Katelyn Y. A. McKenna. "The Internet and Social Life." *Annual Review of Psychology* 55 (2004): 573–590.

Baxter, Ross. "Spoils of War." In *Silver Wings: An Anthology of Homoerotic Steampunk Adventures*, ed. Leigh Ellwood. Cincinnati: Phaze Books, 2011. Kindle edition.

Bell, Alice R. "The Anachronistic Fantastic: Science, Progress and the Child in 'Post-Nostalgic' Culture." *International Journal of Cultural Studies* 12, no. 1 (2009): 5–22.

Bingle, Donald J. "Dashed Hopes." In *Hot and Steamy: Tales of Steampunk Romance*, ed. Jean Rabe and Martin H. Greenberg. New York: Daw Books, 2011. Kindle edition.

Blackmore, J., ed. *Like a Corset Undone: Steampunk Erotica*. Cambridge, Mass.: Circlet Press, 2009. Kindle edition.

Bradean, Kathleen. "Lair of the Red Countess." In *Carnal Machines: Steampunk Erotica*, ed. D. L. King. Berkeley, Calif.: Cleis Press, 2011. Kindle edition.

Brown, Rachel Manija. "Steel Rider." 139–160 in *Steam-Powered: Lesbian Steampunk Stories*, ed. JoSelle Vanderhooft. Round Rock, Tex.: Torquere Press, 2011.

Bruce, Georgina. "Brilliant." 46–61 in *Steam-Powered: Lesbian Steampunk Stories*, ed. JoSelle Vanderhooft. Round Rock, Tex.: Torquere Press, 2011.

Buckell, Tobias S. "Love Comes to Abyssal City." In *Hot and Steamy: Tales of Steampunk Romance*, ed. Jean Rabe and Martin H. Greenberg. New York: Daw Books, 2011. Kindle edition.

Catastrophone Orchestra and Arts Collective. "What, Then, Is Steampunk? Colonizing the Past So We Can Dream the Future." *SteamPunk Magazine* 1 (March 2007): 4–5. www.steampunkmagazine.com/downloads (3 January 2012).

Clayton, Jay. *Charles Dickens in Cyberspace: The Afterlife of the Nineteenth Century in Postmodern Culture*. Oxford: Oxford University Press, 2003.

Danse, Christine. *Island of Icarus*. Carina Press, 2010. Kindle edition.

Devlin, Delilah. "Dr. Mullaley's Cure." In *Carnal Machines: Steampunk Erotica*, ed. D. L. King. Berkeley, Calif.: Cleis Press, 2011. Kindle edition.

Di Filippo, Paul. *Steampunk Trilogy*. New York: Four Walls Eight Windows, 1995.

Doctorow, Cory. "The Difference Engine: A Generation Later." In William Gibson and Bruce Sterling, *The Difference Engine: 20th Anniversary Edition*. New York: Ballantine Books, 2011. Kindle edition.

Dowd, James J., and Nicole R. Pallotta. "The End of Romance: The Demystification of Love in the Postmodern Age." *Sociological Perspectives* 43, no. 4 (2000): 549–580.

Eklund, Mary Louise. "Cassandra's Kiss." In *Hot and Steamy: Tales of Steampunk Romance*, ed. Jean Rabe and Martin H. Greenberg. New York: Daw Books, 2011. Kindle edition.

Ellwood, Leigh. *Silver Wings: An Anthology of Homoerotic Steampunk Adventures*. Cincinnati, Ohio: Phaze Books, 2011. Kindle edition.

Feng, Kannan. "Deviant Devices." In *Carnal Machines: Steampunk Erotica*, ed. D. L. King. Berkeley, Calif.: Cleis Press, 2011. Kindle edition.

Ferguson, Christine. "Surface Tensions: Steampunk, Subculture, and the Ideology of Style," *Neo-Victorian Studies* 4, no. 2 (2011): 66–90. www.neovictorianstudies .com (27 March 2012).

Foglio, Kaja. "Dirt, Collection Vol. 5, Furniture and Gaslamp Fantasy." *Kaja's Monster Table* (24 April 2006). http://kajafoglio.livejournal.com/60562.html (30 December 2011).

Foglio, Phil, and Kaja Foglio. "Girl Genius Online Comics." www.girlgeniusonline .com (3 February 2012).

Forlini, Stefania. "Technology and Morality: The Stuff of Steampunk." *Neo-Victorian Studies* 3, no. 1 (2010): 72–98. www.neovictorianstudies.com (3 January 2012).

Gatehouse Gazette. 11 March 2010. www.ottens.co.uk/gatehouse/gazette-11 (29 February 2012).

Gibson, William, and Bruce Sterling. *The Difference Engine: 20th Anniversary Edition*. New York: Ballantine Books, 2011. Kindle edition.

Gray, Nathalie. *Full Steam Ahead*. Seminole, Fla.: Red Sage Publishing, 2009. Kindle edition.

Hale, Ginn. *Wicked Gentlemen*. Bellingham, Wash.: Blind Eye Books, 2007.

Hantke, Steffen. "Difference Engines and Other Infernal Devices: History According to Steampunk." *Extrapolation* 40, no. 3 (1999): 244–254.

Haraway, Donna. "A Cyborg Manifesto: Science, Technology, and Socialist-Feminism in the Late Twentieth Century." www.stanford.edu/dept/HPS/Haraway/ CyborgManifesto.html (2 January 2012).

Heinecken, Dawn. "Changing Ideologies in Romance Fiction." 149–172 in *Romantic Conventions*, ed. Anne K. Kaler and Rosemary E. Johnson-Kurek. Bowling Green, Ohio: Bowling Green University Popular Press, 1999.

Heilmann, Ann, and Mark Llewellyn. "Neo-Victorianism and Post-Authenticity: On the Ethics and Aesthetics of Appropriation." 1–32 in *Neo-Victorianism: The*

Victorians in the Twenty-First Century, 1999–2009, ed. Ann Heilmann and Mark Llewellyn. Basingstoke, Hampshire: Palgrave MacMillan, 2010.

Holmes, Meredith. "Love in the Time of Airships." 189–223 in *Steam-Powered: Lesbian Steampunk Stories*, ed. JoSelle Vanderhooft. Round Rock, Tex.: Torquere Press, 2011.

Jemisin, N. K. "The Effluent Engine." 8–45 in *Steam-Powered: Lesbian Steampunk Stories*, ed. JoSelle Vanderhooft. Round Rock, Tex.: Torquere Press, 2011.

Jeter, K. W. *Infernal Devices*. Nottingham: Angry Robot. 2011. Kindle edition.

Jones, Frewin. "The Cannibal Fiend of Rotherhithe." 29–71 in *Corsets & Clockwork: 13 Steampunk Romances*, ed. Trisha Telep. London: Constable & Robinson, 2011.

Katt, Roxy. "The Zeppelin Raider." In *Like a Corset Undone: Steampunk Erotica*, ed. J. Blackmore. Cambridge, Mass.: Circlet Press, 2009. Kindle edition.

King, D. L., ed. *Carnal Machines: Steampunk Erotica*. Berkeley, Calif.: Cleis Press, 2011. Kindle edition.

Kress, Adrienne. "*The Clockwork Corset.*" 191–231 in *Corsets & Clockwork: 13 Steampunk Romances*, ed. Trisha Telep. London: Constable & Robinson, 2011.

Lawrence, Jay. "The Perfect Girl." In *Carnal Machines: Steampunk Erotica*, ed. D. L. King. Berkeley, Calif.: Cleis Press, 2011. Kindle edition.

Lipkin, Shira. "Truth and Life." 161–163 in *Steam-Powered: Lesbian Steampunk Stories*, ed. JoSelle Vanderhooft. Round Rock, Tex.: Torquere Press, 2011.

Livingston, Lesley. "Rude Mechanicals." 4–28 in *Corsets & Clockwork: 13 Steampunk Romances*, ed. Trisha Telep. London: Constable & Robinson, 2011.

McWilliam, Rohan. "Victorian Sensations, Neo-Victorian Romances: A Response." *Victorian Studies* 52, no. 1 (Autumn 2009): 106–113.

Michaels, Renee. "Sleight of Hand." In *Carnal Machines: Steampunk Erotica*, ed. D. L. King. Berkeley, Calif.: Cleis Press, 2011. Kindle edition.

Modleski, Tania. *Loving with a Vengeance: Mass-Produced Fantasies for Women*. Hamden, Conn.: Archon Books, 1982.

Mussell, Kay. *Fantasy and Reconciliation: Contemporary Formulas of Women's Romance Fiction*. Westport, Conn.: Greenwood Press, 1984.

Nacht, Clancy. *A Certain Pressure in the Pipes*. Atlanta, Ga.: Noble Romance Publishing, 2010. Kindle edition.

Narayan, Shweta. "The Padishah Begum's Reflections." 319–350 in *Steam-Powered: Lesbian Steampunk Stories*, ed. JoSelle Vanderhooft. Round Rock, Tex.: Torquere Press, 2011.

Nevins, Jess. "The Nineteenth Century Roots of Steampunk." *The New York Review of Science Fiction* 245 (January 2009): 1–5.

Nye, Jody Lynn. "Clockworks." In *Hot and Steamy: Tales of Steampunk Romance*, ed. Jean Rabe and Martin H. Greenberg. New York: Daw Books, 2011. Kindle edition.

Onion, Rebecca. "Reclaiming the Machine: An Introductory Look at Steampunk in Everyday Practice." *Neo-Victorian Studies* 1, no. 1 (2008): 138–163. www.neo victorianstudies.com (4 January 2012).

Owen, Mairead. "Re-Inventing Romance: Reading Popular Romantic Fiction." *Women's Studies International Forum* 20, no. 4 (1997): 537–546.

Pagliassotti, Dru. *Clockwork Heart*. Rockville, Md.: June Books, 2008.

———. "Better than Romance? Japanese BL Manga and the Subgenre of Male/Male Romantic Fiction." 59–83 in *Boys' Love Manga: Essays on the Sexual Ambiguity and Cross-Cultural Fandom of the Genre*, ed. Antonia Levi, Mark McHarry, and Dru Pagliassotti. Jefferson, N.C.: McFarland, 2010.

Perschon, Mike. "Steam Wars." *Neo-Victorian Studies* 3, no. 1 (2010): 127–166. www .neovictorianstudies.com (3 January 2012).

Pho, Diana M. (Ay-leen the Peacemaker). "The Semantics of Words & the Antics of Fashion: Addressing 'Victorientalism,'" *Beyond Victoriana* (7 March 2010), http:// beyondvictoriana.com/2010/03/07/beyond-victoriana-17the-semantics-of-words -the-antics-of-fashion-addressing-victorientalism (29 January 2012).

Priest, Cherie. *Boneshaker*. New York: Tor, 2009.

Rabe, Jean, and Martin H. Greenberg, eds. *Hot and Steamy: Tales of Steampunk Romance*. New York: Daw Books, 2011. Kindle edition.

Regis, Pamela. *A Natural History of the Romance Novel*. Philadelphia: University of Pennsylvania Press, 2003.

Roberts, Teresa Noelle. "Human Powered." In *Carnal Machines: Steampunk Erotica*, ed. D. L. King. Berkeley, Calif.: Cleis Press, 2011. Kindle edition.

Rose, Margaret. "Extraordinary Pasts: Steampunk as a Mode of Historical Representation." *Journal of the Fantastic in the Arts* 20, no. 3 (2009): 319–333.

Sakamoto, Michaela. "The Transcendent Steam Engine: Industry, Nostalgia, and the Romance of Steampunk." 124–131 in *The Image of Technology in Literature, Media, and Society: Proceedings from the 2009 Conference of the Society for the Interdisciplinary Study of Social Imagery*, ed. Will Wright and Steven Kaplan. Pueblo: Society for the Interdisciplinary Study of Social Imagery, Colorado State University–Pueblo, 2009.

Schechter, Elizabeth. "The Succubus." In *Carnal Machines: Steampunk Erotica*, ed. D. L. King. Berkeley, Calif.: Cleis Press, 2011. Kindle edition.

Shellito, Tracey. "Lucifer Einstein and the Curious Case of the Carnal Contraption." In *Carnal Machines: Steampunk Erotica*, ed. D. L. King. Berkeley, Calif.: Cleis Press, 2011. Kindle edition.

St. James, Elias A. "Infernal Machine." In *Carnal Machines: Steampunk Erotica*, ed. D. L. King. Berkeley, Calif.: Cleis Press, 2011. Kindle edition.

Sullivan, Stephen D. "Automata Futura." In *Hot and Steamy: Tales of Steampunk Romance*, ed. Jean Rabe and Martin H. Greenberg. New York: Daw Books, 2011. Kindle edition.

Tachna, Ariel. *The Inventor's Companion*. Frisco, Tex.: Dreamspinner Press, 2011. Kindle edition.

Tan, Cecelia, and J. Blackmore, eds. *Like a Wisp of Steam: Steampunk Erotica*. Cambridge, Mass.: Circlet Press, 2008. Kindle edition.

Tassin, Marc. "For the Love of Copper." In *Hot and Steamy: Tales of Steampunk Romance*, ed. Jean Rabe and Martin H. Greenberg. New York: Daw Books, 2011. Kindle edition.

Telep, Trisha, ed. *Corsets & Clockwork: 13 Steampunk Romances*. London: Constable & Robinson, 2011.

Tesla, Vinnie. *The Erotofluidic Age*. Cambridge, Mass.: Circlet Press, 2011. Kindle edition.

Tidhar, Lavie. "Steampunk." *The Internet Review of Science Fiction* 2, no. 1 (February 2005) www.irosf.com/q/zine/article/10114 (3 January 2012).

Tupper, Peter. *The Innocent's Progress and Other Stories*. Cambridge, Mass.: Circlet Press, 2010. Kindle edition.

Turkle, Sherry. *Alone Together: Why We Expect More from Technology and Less from Each Other*. New York: Basic Books, 2010.

Valentine, Gill. "Globalizing Intimacy: The Role of Information and Communication Technologies in Maintaining and Creating Relationships." *Women's Studies Quarterly* 34, no. 1/2 (2006): 365–393.

Vanderhooft, JoSelle, ed. *Steam-Powered: Lesbian Steampunk Stories*. Round Rock, Tex.: Torquere Press, 2011.

Vardeman, Robert E. "Her Faith Is Fixt." In *Hot and Steamy: Tales of Steampunk Romance*, ed. Jean Rabe and Martin H. Greenberg. New York: Daw Books, 2011. Kindle edition.

Vaughn, Vanessa. "In the Flask." In *Like a Wisp of Steam: Steampunk Erotica*, ed. Cecelia Tan and J. Blackmore. Cambridge, Mass.: Circlet Press, 2008. Kindle edition.

Westerfeld, Scott. *Leviathan*. New York: Simon & Schuster, 2009.

White, Kiersten. "Tick, Tick Boom." 405–430 in *Corsets & Clockwork: 13 Steampunk Romances*, ed. Trisha Telep. London: Constable & Robinson, 2011.

Whitehall, J. T. *Surface Tension*. Cincinnati, Ohio: DLP Books, 2011. Kindle edition.

Wodzinski, Beth. "Suffer Water." 125–139 in *Steam-Powered: Lesbian Steampunk Stories*, ed. JoSelle Vanderhooft. Round Rock, Tex.: Torquere Press, 2011.

Wymore, Teresa. "Under the Dome." 224–244 in *Steam-Powered: Lesbian Steampunk Stories*, ed. JoSelle Vanderhooft. Round Rock, Tex.: Torquere Press, 2011.

Z, Cari. "Nothing Ventured." In *Silver Wings: An Anthology of Homoerotic Steampunk Adventures*, ed. Leigh Ellwood. Cincinnati: Phaze Books, 2011. Kindle edition.

Professor Elemental, gentleman rhymer. *Copyright Jody Steel*

CHAPTER FIVE

"Anything Is Possible for a Man in a Top Hat with a Monkey with a Monocle": Remixing Steampunk in Professor Elemental's *The Indifference Engine*

Jamieson Ridenhour

In addition to being a literary mode, and a nexus for invention, art, and clothing, steampunk is reasonably well-established as a guiding principle for bands playing a wide variety of music. A listing on the Steampunk Wiki posits 125 bands as "steampunk" to some degree.[1] Even though some of those so listed (Amanda Palmer, for instance) might not conceive of themselves as strictly steampunk, a good portion of these groups self-consciously reproduce the literary and sartorial tropes of the culture: dashing be-goggled frontmen singing songs about airships, corseted keyboardists standing behind ornately brassed organ enclosures, dancers in striped stockings with tiny top hats perched among feathers and dreadlocks. There is an air of cabaret (which perhaps explains Ms. Palmer's inclusion) and fusion—of look, of culture, of temporality, of musical style. Jeff VanderMeer, writing about this music subculture in his *Steampunk Bible*, admits that, as with steampunk literature, "the definitions are vague and the boundaries fluid," before attempting to catalog common traits: "theatricality and performance, a Gothic or Victorian-inspired aesthetic, playfulness and spontaneity, grittiness and darkness, and narrative and storytelling."[2]

The "narrative and storytelling" element may be the common thread binding bands that collectively cover a diverse swath of musical terrain. There are bands who take the "punk" portion of the genre's name literally, such as the Men Who Will Not Be Blamed for Nothing. There are steampunk incarnations of electronica, Goth, and classic rock. But they are all telling stories, and often those stories spill out of the lyrics and inhabit the on-stage personas of the musicians themselves. Seattle-based Abney Park, perhaps the quintessential steampunk band, operates on the crest of a backstory casting the band as airship pirates, and their world-music-inflected tunes sport lyrics that flesh out this narrative. A role-playing game and forthcoming novel based on the band's tales are natural extensions. So if there is a communal element in "steampunk music" beyond the genre itself, it is that beneath the gypsy violins and leather waistcoats, these bands by and large are making narrative music. They are characters telling their own stories, and those stories are steampunk. Any style of music can become steampunk if the story is right. Thus the rise of a seemingly incongruous pairing: steampunk rap, or chap-hop.

"Chap-hop" is a relatively new subgenre of music that combines the beats and wordplay of hip-hop with late-nineteenth- and early-twentieth-century stereotypical upper-class British concerns. It is not strictly steampunk in its content, but it is quintessentially British in its concerns. A chap-hop performance may contain rapping about cricket, smoking a pipe, and taking high tea. The rapper's propensity for bragging self-glorification underpins the proceedings, and basic tracks are likely to be samples of earlier music.

The two best-known proponents of chap-hop are Jim Burke, who performs as Mr. B the Gentleman Rhymer, and Paul Alborough, who performs as Professor Elemental. Though having surface similarities and interacting together in performance and on recordings, these two personae take different approaches from the range of historical stereotypes available. Mr. B presents himself as a Bertie Wooster–type character who plays a banjolele and raps about the good life ("Straight Outta Surrey"). Paul Alborough, however, has developed Professor Elemental as a steampunk mad scientist with a complicated backstory and a cast of recurring characters that people his plot-driven hip-hop vignettes. His work has gained wide attention in the steampunk community (he recently headlined the 2011 Steampunk World's Fair) and in the mainstream media, via a feature on chap-hop in the *Wall Street Journal*.[3]

The professor's backstory, lyrical concerns, and stage persona are all obvious signifiers of Alborough's steampunk credentials. But as important to the effectiveness of his music, though not perhaps as immediately evident, are the correlations between hip-hop and steampunk as hybrid or "mash-up"—the merging of the past and present that underpins both genres. In short, Professor Elemental is steampunk on at least two levels: the level of convention, where Alborough self-consciously uses the outward trappings and symbols of steampunk, and the level of musical style, where we find the fabric of hip-hop woven from the same thematic thread as steampunk. Both elements are necessary to the final product, and we will consider them one at a time in this chapter.

"If You're All about Steam and Brass"

Professor Elemental's 2010 album *The Indifference Engine* is in many ways an anthology of steampunk stories in rhyme set to a beat. The character, an explorer/inventor/tea aficionado who employs a surgically altered orangutan as butler and wears jodhpurs and a pith helmet (at least one commentator has dubbed the music "pith-hop"), is revealed through the narratives in the raps, as well as spoken introductions to each song that are often presented as club conversations overheard by the listener. And like other steampunk works, many of Professor Elemental's songs use Victorian sensation literature as a jumping-off point. *Strange Case of Dr. Jekyll and Mr. Hyde* (1886), *Island of Doctor Moreau* (1896), and the imperial adventures of H. Rider Haggard are all evoked directly, and a host of other works are obliquely referenced. And of course, there is an airship.

The Indifference Engine's self-conscious steampunkery begins with its title, a deliberate mangling of the title of Bruce Sterling and William Gibson's seminal 1991 steampunk novel *The Difference Engine*. Individual tracks function as a sort of hip-hop tour of steampunk tropes: the mad inventor, the explorer, the Gothic monster, the time traveler, etc. Airships crash into Buckingham palace, twisted hybrid animals escape their cages and hunt their tuxedoed captors, expeditions are mounted to discover legendary artifacts. Much tea is drunk, much Battenberg is eaten. Gleefully leading the listener through this madcap soundscape is the good Professor himself: "Exotic dancer third, then scientist, but explorer first!"[4]

The Professor's character is fully fleshed out over the course of the album, beginning with the opening track, "Splendid," in which we learn that Professor Elemental lives in a castle surrounded by a tea-filled moat and that his is a happy and comfort-filled life to be envied:

> Woke up this morning feeling super
> Where's the butler?
> Pass me the butter
> My muffins are freshly baked
> Wake up then I stretch and shake
>
> My life well yes it's great
> Like I live on a slice of special cake
> With loads of ingredients
> If my home is my castle,

> That's most convenient
> Because my home is a castle
> And I laugh at the top of my turrets
>
> My drawbridge is over a moat filled with tea
> And I'm far above it
> I just love it
> This life of mine
> Life every day is a prize that shines
> Lighting my way through the unsightly times
> To the stage where I find that the mic is mine[5]

From this basic picture of a wealthy and eccentric inventor, Alborough builds a humorous larger-than-life character who embodies a plethora of steampunk "types." As mentioned already, he does this through narratives that pay homage to Victorian science and Gothic fiction, some by directly invoking the works that inspired them.

"Animal Magic" is a Moreau-esque tale of animal experimentation gone awry. In the song, Professor Elemental has invited a group of gentlemen to observe the fruits of his experiments in a "home-made zoo" featuring a host of surgically spliced creatures. The professor proudly displays the owltoise, badgermingo, and chimpangoat while admitting that there are some understandable shortcomings (the batraffes "fly into doors," for instance). As in Wells's *The Island of Dr. Moreau*, the obvious model for "Animal Magic," the mad scientist has been ostracized by the scientific establishment: "I'm currently avoiding arrest and detection / Expelled from the roll of clubs and societies / Been told I lack sanity—even sobriety." Moreau also displays his work to the (inadvertently) visiting Edward Prendick, but in Wells's novel the beast-men who inhabit Moreau's island prove ultimately impossible to control, and their revolutionary uprising forms the climax of the book. Likewise, Professor Elemental's hyphenated beasts mutiny and wreak revenge on their creator by attaching his head to a chicken's body. It's all very funny, the more so because of the familiarity of Dr. Moreau in particular and the Victorian mad scientist in general. The professor is even able to deliver a version of the accepted moral of all mad scientist stories in the song's final line: "In retrospect perhaps a mistake to play God."[6]

Victorian Gothic fiction finds expression on *The Indifference Engine* as well. "Elixir" is a confessional song in which the speaker reveals a secret vice to his increasingly horrified friend. The dark secret involves a double life—the speaker has been buying an illicit concoction (the elixir of the title) that transforms him into a savage criminal. The narrative is clearly a reworking of Stevenson's *Strange Case of Dr. Jekyll and Mr. Hyde*. Indeed, this is the only song on the album to reference the source material

An evening of chap-hop. *Courtesy of Professor Elemental*

directly—the name of the speaker's supplier is Mr. Hyde. The meeting between the speaker and his listening friend is reminiscent of Hyde's visit to Dr. Lanyon in Stevenson's novella, where the secret of Hyde's identity is first revealed. Whereas Stevenson has Hyde transform into Jekyll in front of the horror-struck Lanyon, Elemental reverses the process. His speaker becomes the monster, and the song dissolves into guttural smacking as the singer apparently kills and eats his interlocutor.

"Elixir" does more than simply retell the familiar Jekyll and Hyde story. Alborough's track engages with the thematic structure of Stevenson's story as well. *Jekyll and Hyde* is not lacking in scholarly analysis, and there are a myriad of interpretations that can be supported in varying degrees by the text. One of the most common of these interpretations is that the novella is about addiction—a respectable doctor transfigured into a criminal by ingesting a powder, who gradually loses his ability to control the transformation.[7] Alborough explicitly invokes this reading of Stevenson by having his speaker describe his vice in terms of intoxicants: "It's not whiskey or gin or puffed in a pipe / not opium or laudanum, a different high." He also highlights the seedy reverse side of the coin of Victorian respectability that Stevenson indicts. Professor Elemental's elixir is "for afterhours gentlemen" who "stride briskly to a risky life" down back streets "rife with bad atmosphere, a glimpse of crime." The speaker's story ends with a lie to his wife and a certainty that he will buy more elixir in the future. It is a brief vignette—at under two minutes it is the shortest song on *The Indifference Engine*—but in execution it is a complete distillation of Stevenson's narrative and themes.

No other songs on the album draw on specific works (though he plans future pieces based on *The War of the Worlds* and the legend of Spring-heeled Jack[8]) but instead reference general ideas and established tropes from Victorian literature and late-twentieth/early-twenty-first-century steampunk. The magnanimous lord of the manor providing an annual party for the locals ("A Fete Worse than Death"), the Allan Quatermain-like explorer on a quest for a famed object d'tribal art ("The Quest for the Golden Frog"), the pinky-raising tea aficionado ("Cup of Brown Joy"), all of these are recognizable "types" that Alborough employs to develop his mad emcee. The resulting character parodies the stereotypical aristocratic male in much the same way that music hall performers of the mid- to late Victorian era did.

These reworkings of Victoriana are enough to qualify Professor Elemental as a steampunk, but in case we want more solid ground, the good professor also makes explicit references to steampunk as a genre. Professor Elemental is the quintessential eccentric inventor ("Ideas? I've a headful / A one-man penny dreadful"[9]), the centerpiece of most steampunk narratives. The centrality of an airship to the song "Penny Dreadful" is another steampunk staple, as is the bioengineered manservant ("By brain-switching with my cranial cutter / I created my apish butler"[10]). And then there is "Steam Powered," which tries to accomplish that oft-attempted feat—the defining of the genre:

> If you're all about steam and brass
> And all you need to start is tea and a flask
> Sharp set of gears in a gleaming arc
> In the sky race heaving and screaming past
>
> If you're all about reaching far
> Seeking the past on secret charts
> Meeting in secret beneath the stars
> With a decent mask and a good moustache
>
> If you're really part of an army
> Marching armed for starting a party
> A special weapon so wondrous
> And a specially constructed blunderbuss
> So thunderous
> But don't come to fuss
> Got a wanderlust
> Then you're one of us[11]

As far as definitions go, it covers the basic ground in a fairly adept manner, encompassing the material trappings, questions of class, and passion for travel and invention that underpin steampunk in both literature and the wider subculture. "Steam Powered" grows from that subculture; Alborough says that the track is "directly inspired by the fantastic range of inventions witnessed at steampunk conventions."[12]

That is a clue to the professor's own origins, it turns out. Alborough admits that in the chicken-or-egg question of Professor Elemental's origins, the character predates the genre connections. "I had no knowledge at all about Steampunk before the Professor came along," writes Alborough. "The song 'Penny Dreadful' was the first one that we recorded and it was very much supposed to be a 'one off' for a Victorian themed variety show."[13] That show, called "Come into My Parlour" and featuring a number of other performers engaged in a sort of pseudo-Victorian cabaret show, was itself a very steampunkian affair, but Alborough came to it as an established emcee, taking on the Victorian persona only as part of the overall conceit of the evening. The popularity of the character led to more songs and eventually the full-blown characterizations of *The Indifference Engine*. Alborough admits, "It was a lucky coincidence that the professor persona fitted so neatly into Steampunk. Complete accident rather than design," but he goes on to say: "That said, [steampunk] has been a huge influence on subsequent songs and the shape of my current show. I am now much more inclined to write songs about outlandish inventions and airship adventures, safe in the knowledge that there is an audience that accepts and embraces these bizarre concepts."[14]

That audience consists of members of the steampunk subculture, who have received Professor Elemental with open cogs. Alborough is grateful for the welcome and acknowledges the appeal of steampunk, saying that "it's like live action role playing games, and comic books and movies, it's that escapism. You can take it in any different direction that you want to—spend a day as an airship captain or a sky pirate or an evil villain or whatever it is you might want to do. And you can change that from day to day as well."[15] But for Alborough, Professor Elemental's appeal allows the mixing of genres to go in both directions: "There is another side too, in that I now get to bring hip-hop music to an audience who might not have come across it before, or have certain preconceptions about what rap is usually like. My greatest pleasure is 'bridging the gap' to show listeners that rap can be for anyone."[16] This hip-hop proselytizing is the core of Professor Elemental's unique place in steampunk music. It is therefore worth noting that hip-hop's own characteristics have much in common with the professor's more esoteric subcultural ties. Hip-hop may in fact be the perfect vehicle for steampunk.

"I've Got Super Producers and Fans That Play Me"

Professor Elemental may be "explorer first," but Paul Alborough's first love is hip-hop. An emcee[17] on his own and as part of Special School (with whom

"Such pride in my creations." *Courtesy of Professor Elemental*

he still performs and records), Alborough is a committed aficionado of hip-hop and a knowledgeable historian of the form. When asked, he frames Professor Elemental's music not in terms of steampunk, but as hip-hop: "It's been named a number of things. Some call it steampunk rap, some call it chap-hop, but really it's good old-fashioned hip-hop served with scones and cream."[18] In the professor's hands, the two genres seem a natural fit. At first glance, a large measure of Professor Elemental's humor springs from the perceived incongruity of Victorian stereotypes being delivered in the language of rap. And over the course of the ten songs on *The Indifference Engine*, nearly every accepted and expected hip-hop trope is played out for the listener.

The bravado of the mad scientist, for instance, is in perfect keeping with the traditional bragging emcee, and Professor Elemental slips easily into this role. In hip-hop, this self-promotion often involves a celebration of wealth, and it is common to hear rappers talk about Rolls Royces, champagne, and mansions as evidence of material status. Professor Elemental similarly spends a great deal of time detailing the opulence of his lifestyle. As we saw earlier, "Splendid" is simply a litany of the comfort and ease of the professor's life, but the lavish party thrown in "A Fete Worse than Death" is also an exercise in braggadocio in both its scope and the magnanimous nature of its being offered. The Annual Village Fete features a DJ (you can "guess the weight of the break"), a "bling" tombola, and a cake "laced with herbs" all on offer for free ("there's no need to pay me").[19] The constant presence of a butler, albeit one bioengineered from a monkey, is also an indication of the professor's wealth and status.

This easy and excessive wealth—the moat around his castle is filled with tea—is a staple of hip-hop, where the fantasy of affluence is used as a counter to poverty, a myth of escape. That the most successful artists are able to achieve the fantasy merely reinforces the stereotype. Alborough's professor places this trope in the context of the British class system, performing clichés and ostentatious acts of generosity. His posh-come-lately professor is a Fresh Prince of Brighton, an awkward nouveau riche tutted and muttered over by the true aristocrats at the gentlemen's club.

The hip-hop propensity for references to drinking and drug use is also present in the professor's genteel reimagining of the genre. Subtle references, such as the herb-laced cake just mentioned (which will "knock you for six"), give way in places to overt declarations. In "The Quest for the Golden Frog," the professor spends week three of his expedition having "an absinthe party with the Munchkins of Oz" before indulging in "opium, tea, and mushrooms in Wonderland."[20] In "A Fete Worse than Death," he promises guests a "forty of Baileys."[21]

Likewise, there is a song focused on seducing a woman, or at least cajoling her into sex. "Sweet Cold Colation" couches the sexual banter in baking metaphors and innuendo but fairly represents the hip-hop obsession with sex. In the song, guest rapper Madame Faye has made a dress out of cake. The professor, home from an expedition ("nine years later, here I am"), is peck-ish: "If you cover my love with your truffles and dumplings / I'll cover you up with my custard and something / I'll spank you on the Battenberg." Though Madame Faye is coquettishly teasing ("I've whipped my eggs till custard, smeared it over my gentle frame / Floured, pale and lusty"), she ultimately refuses him. In a bizarre ending, perhaps parodying the misogynistic turn rap can unfortunately take at times, Professor Elemental takes the cake by force and uses his drill to remove Madame Faye's teeth.[22]

Most famously, Professor Elemental participates in the time-honored hip-hop tradition of the diss song, part of a rap beef, or feud, with chap-hop em-cee Mr. B. This rivalry, gleefully orchestrated by the two gentlemen rhymers, is the subject of the *Wall Street Journal* article mentioned earlier as well as the central focus of "Fighting Trousers," one of the more popular songs from *The Indifference Engine*. In the tradition of the Biggie/Tupac rivalry, among many others, Professor Elemental calls out Mr. B in rhyme: "I've got super produc-ers and fans that play me / You've got a granddad's mustache and a ukulele." The song, peppered with references to Mr. B's own persona and stage show as well as obscure pop culture allusions (ex-Blue Peter presenter Peter Duncan's five-minute cameo in the 1980 camp film *Flash Gordon*, for instance), is a perfect blend of Victorian chappiness and hip-hop. The professor challenges Mr. B to a boxing match, Queensbury rules, and warns him "set foot on my stage and get ruined again." Attacks on the rival rapper's sartorial choices are also evident: "I don't like your tweed, sir."[23] The idea of the rap beef is a staple of hip-hop culture. Here, as in traditional hip-hop, the rivalry both creates a tense drama for listeners and generates considerable publicity for both rappers: "'I really enjoy the beef,' says Mr. Alborough, who says he can't wait to take on Mr. Burke. 'NaS and Jay-Z had a big battle a few years ago; it was all a nonsense. They're friends again now. It's all ridiculous entertain-ment, and anyone who thinks otherwise is a banana.'"[24]

So the thematic content of *The Indifference Engine* is authentic hip-hop, despite the steampunk trappings. Similarly, the construction of the songs on the album reflects standard hip-hop practice. In particular, producer Tom Ca-ruana creates the basic tracks for Professor Elemental's songs by incorporating existing recordings into new mixes. The practice of sampling is a fundamental of hip-hop—the genre is to a large degree predicated on taking older tunes and reworking or adding to them. Caruana validates Professor Elemental's hip-hop credentials by sampling from a variety of songs from the early twentieth century. Thus, instead of using breaks from earlier rap music, *The Indifference Engine* features backing tracks such as Nat Gonella's 1938 recording of Slim Gail-lard's swing number "Flat Foot Floogie (with the Floy Floy)." This song, parts of which form the basic track of "A Fete Worse than Death," is included down to the scratchy sound of needle on vinyl, evoking both the Victrola on which it would have been originally played and the turntable mixing of 1980s and '90s hip-hop.[25] "Fighting Trousers" is underpinned by a slowed-down version of Raymond Scott's "Twilight in Turkey," and while not every track uses recognizable songs in their entirety, snatches of piano music and other brief melodies are in copious evidence. The result is somewhat reminiscent of the electro-swing music of the early 1990s but uniquely Elemental in its execution.

Conclusion

Ultimately, the tradition of the remix, so central to hip-hop music and culture, is the most important connective tissue between the genres in which Professor Elemental works. Alborough maintains that "hip-hop music and culture is largely based on recycling the old and turning it into something new," citing the sampling work of Prince Paul as an early example.[26] "Recycling the old and turning it into something new" is as good a working definition as any of steampunk, which is, in the words of Jeff VanderMeer, "simultaneously retro and forward-looking in nature."[27] Steampunk, both literature and subculture, is at a very basic level a "remix," a reverential nod to older works and ideas accomplished by combining them with new interpretations, new politics, new technology, new trajectories. And though it isn't absolutely necessary to be familiar with the works of H. G. Wells, Jules Verne, or Robert Louis Stevenson in order to enjoy steampunk, a knowledge of Victorian literature certainly deepens understanding of how the genre is constructed. Likewise hip-hop is, according to Alborough,

> relentlessly self-referential—constantly quoting other rap songs and making new versions of established tunes. Sometimes whole songs have been made up using quotes from previous classics. . . . You have to have "done your homework" on the past songs, as it were, to fully appreciate the new music.[28]

Hip-hop thus creates itself out of that which has gone before, a forward-thinking nostalgia that honors its ancestors while celebrating invention and novelty. It's all remix.

The flexibility of this idea—this reinvention using existing materials—may be a clue to the appeal of Professor Elemental. Chap-hop is, like steampunk, a specialized niche within the genres it blends. But unlike steampunk, chap-hop has not yet breached the mainstream. Whether or not steam-powered Victorian rap can ever transcend the small world of its relatively few practitioners is grounds for speculation, but Professor Elemental has garnered enough attention to suggest that it is possible. The Professor's music is well-loved by steampunks certainly, but he also enjoys the attention of a wide variety of audience "types."

Alborough cites a show in Manchester, UK, in which he looked out from the stage and discerned several different groups within the audience:

[The audience] was made up partly of steampunks, a few hip-hop heads, some Goth/fetish types and a few slightly confused looking "normal" people. That is my ideal audience. There definitely is a steampunk contingent, and some gigs are entirely just that—but increasingly I have found the further towards the edge of society my audience (for example the fetish, Goth, and transsexual crowd), the better my material goes down. Maybe it's because I am spending a lot of my time trying to show that it is ok to be yourself, even if yourself is very silly indeed.[29]

As subcultures grounded on individual expression and subversion of cultural (and/or literary) norms, steampunk and hip-hop have common ground. As Professor Elemental sings in "Splendid": "few are strangers in my fan bases."[30] Perhaps the "bridging" that Alborough refers to—the bringing of hip-hop to audiences that would not otherwise discover it—may work in both directions, and Professor Elemental's deftly woven steampunk/hip-hop remix may expand both its genres in directions neither could have gone alone. For a man in a top hat with a monkey with a monocle, that could just be possible.

Notes

1. "List of Steampunk Bands," *Steampunk Wiki*, n.d., http://steampunk.wikia.com/wiki/List_of_steampunk_bands (15 January 2012).

2. Jeff VanderMeer, "Steampunk Music," in *The Steampunk Bible* (New York: Abrams Image, 2011), 158.

3. Frances Robinson, "In 'Chap-Hop,' Gentlemen Rappers Bust Rhymes about Tea, Cricket," *Wall Street Journal*, 4 April 2011, http://online.wsj.com/article/SB10001424052748703716904576133674200088328.html (15 December 2011).

4. Professor Elemental in "The Quest for the Golden Frog," in *The Indifference Engine*, Tea Sea Records, 2010.

5. Elemental, "Splendid," in *The Indifference Engine*.

6. Elemental, "Animal Magic," in *The Indifference Engine*.

7. One such is Daniel Wright, "'The Prisonhouse of My Disposition': A Study of the Psychology of Addiction in Dr. Jekyll and Mr. Hyde," *Studies in the Novel* 26, no. 3 (Fall 1994): 254–267.

8. Paul Alborough, interview with the author, 16 January 2012.

9. Elemental, "Penny Dreadful," in *The Indifference Engine*.

10. Elemental, "Animal Magic," in *The Indifference Engine*.

11. Elemental, "Steam Powered," in *The Indifference Engine*.

12. Alborough, interview with the author, 16 January 2012.

13. Alborough, interview with the author, 16 January 2012. The members of Come Into My Parlour can be seen in the music video for Professor Elemental's "Cup of Brown Joy."

14. Alborough, interview with the author, 16 January 2012.

15. "Steampunk: Yesterday's Tomorrow," CBS *Sunday Morning*, 30 October 2011, www.cbsnews.com/8301–3445_162–20127610/steampunk-yesterdays-tomorrow.

16. Alborough, interview with the author, 16 January 2012.

17. "Emcee" or "MC" denotes the frontman or rapper in a hip-hop group. The emcee's job is to rap—to rhythmically speak rhymes or "flows" over the music (often sampled and mixed from other songs) provided by the DJ.

18. "Interview with Professor Elemental," *The Geek Show*, 18 September 2011, www.youtube.com/watch?v=LsD692SX-DU&feature=related (4 January 2012).

19. Elemental, "A Fete Worse than Death," in *The Indifference Engine*.

20. Elemental, "The Quest for the Golden Frog," in *The Indifference Engine*.

21. Elemental, "A Fete Worse than Death," in *The Indifference Engine*.

22. Elemental, "Sweet Cold Colation," in *The Indifference Engine*.

23. Elemental, "Fighting Trousers," in *The Indifference Engine*."

24. Robinson, "In 'Chap-Hop,' Gentlemen Rappers Bust Rhymes about Tea, Cricket."

25. Some chap-hop DJs, such as DJ Earl of Ealing, perform mixes using old Victrola gramophones, thus solidifying the crossover.

26. Alborough, interview with the author, 16 January 2012.

27. VanderMeer, "It's a Clockwork Universe, Victoria: Measuring the Critical Mass of Steampunk," in *The Steampunk Bible*, 9.

28. Alborough, interview with the author, 16 January 2012.

29. Alborough, interview with the author, 16 January 2012.

30. Elemental, "Splendid," in *The Indifference Engine*.

Bibliography

Alborough, Paul. Interview with the author. 16 January 2012.

Elemental, Professor. *The Indifference Engine*. Tea Sea Records, 2010.

"Interview with Professor Elemental." *The Geek Show*, 18 September 2011. www.youtube.com/watch?v=LsD692SX-DU&feature=related (4 January 2012).

"List of Steampunk Bands." *Steampunk Wiki*, n.d. http://steampunk.wikia.com/wiki/List_of_steampunk_bands (15 January 2012).

Robinson, Frances. "In 'Chap-Hop,' Gentlemen Rappers Bust Rhymes about Tea, Cricket." *Wall Street Journal*, 4 April 2011. http://online.wsj.com/article/SB10001424052748703716904576133674200088328.html (15 December 2011).

"Steampunk: Yesterday's Tomorrow." CBS *Sunday Morning*. 30 October 2011. www.cbsnews.com/8301–3445_162–20127610/steampunk-yesterdays-tomorrow.

VanderMeer, Jeff, and S. J. Chambers. "It's a Clockwork Universe, Victoria: Measuring the Critical Mass of Steampunk." 6–15 in *The Steampunk Bible*. New York: Abrams Image, 2011.

———. "Steampunk Music." 158–165 in *The Steampunk Bible*. New York: Abrams Image, 2011.

Wright, Daniel. "'The Prisonhouse of My Disposition': A Study of the Psychology of Addiction in Dr. Jekyll and Mr. Hyde." *Studies in the Novel* 26, no. 3 (Fall 1994): 254–267.

PART II

REFURBISHING TIME AND PLACE

At the foot of the Great Ice Barrier. *Copyright Jody Steel*

CHAPTER SIX

"In Sum, Evil Has Prevailed": The Moral Morass of Science and Exploration in Jacques Tardi's *The Arctic Marauder*

Erika Behrisch Elce

With its detailed descriptions of imaginary Victorian technological innovations and historically accurate illustrations, Jacques Tardi's 1974 graphic novel *Le Démon des glaces* (*The Arctic Marauder*) has been described not just as "proto-'steampunk'" but as "ur-steampunk—one of the works that laid the groundwork" for the genre.[1] *The Arctic Marauder* follows the unlikely journey of young Jérôme Plumier, a French medical student, from the modest berth of a mail steamship to the mysteriously abandoned home of his eccentric scientist uncle Louis-Ferdinand Chapoutier—"held in contempt by the rest of the family, but favored by Jérôme"—to the extravagant decks of the *Arctic Marauder*, a giant manufactured iceberg.[2] Built by Chapoutier and his comrade-in-arms, Carlo Gelati, and sailed by a crew "recruited . . . from the dregs of the ports," the *Marauder* is designed to float inconspicuously through the world's oceans, dispersing chemical bombs "containing the most horrible diseases known to mankind."[3] When the iceberg becomes battle-ready, the mad scientists torpedo unsuspecting ships, including two on which Plumier himself is a passenger, the steamship *Anjou*, and the scientific vessel *Jules Vernez*. Saved from the wreck of the *Jules Vernez*, Plumier is reunited with Chapoutier and joins the two scientists in their destructive plans. The book's narrative has two centers: the first, the men's intentions to annihilate the world as they are chased from the Pole to the Amazon by government agent Simone Pouffiot; the second, the anxiety of the narrator for the safety of the world: "Is there no one to thwart their wicked plans?"[4] A confection of fantastical 1889 technological wonders that include "really quite marvellous" torpedoes, "underwater lamps powered by electric batteries," and a personalized flying machine—the Motorized Ichthyornis—*The Arctic Marauder* includes both the aesthetic and narrative details that have come to define steampunk.[5] However, the book's content is not merely responsible for laying the groundwork for steampunk; it articulates what is missing from much of the genre: the destructive potential of Victorian scientific and technological ambition.

Certainly, many steampunk narratives follow similar trajectories to Tardi's, in which the ambition of a few powerful characters threatens global safety; as well, they exploit actual historical events to enhance their stories' realism. Looming over Alan Moore, Kevin O'Neill, Ben Dimagmaliw, and Bill Oakley's *League of Extraordinary Gentlemen* (1999), for example, is the threat of an "aerial bombardment" by a hostile foreign power; likewise, Stephen Baxter's *Anti-Ice* (1993) is a tale framed by cataclysmic explosions that end two pan-European wars.[6] Like Tardi's *Marauder*, the exploitation of science and technology in these tales is the central source of tension, but Tardi's use of real, not fictional, technology sets his narrative apart. For the heroes (and villains) of *League*, the fictional antigravity substance "cavorite" is the key to the weapons of mass destruction; in *Anti-Ice* the eponymous imaginary crystal is the remains of a meteorite embedded in the South Pole, while a fragment of it circles Earth as a "Little Moon."[7] Thus, whereas the threats themselves show science as a potentially dangerous pursuit, the narratives maintain a careful separation between fictional and real worlds. In contrast, Tardi's articulation of a steampunk ethic is expressed in his ironic inversion of such steampunk tropes: by ultimately collapsing the narrative distance between the world he creates and the world we live in, Tardi shows us the all-too-real consequences of separating science from citizenship.

Narrative Traditions of Science and Citizenship

Dubbed "icepunk" by Kim Thompson because of its polar setting, *The Arctic Marauder* overlays the romance of Victorian scientific exploration with a modern tale of cruelty and violence, drawing on the rich cultural tradition of well-known nineteenth-century fictional narratives of scientific hubris, most notably Jules Verne's *20,000 Leagues Under the Sea* (1869) and his polar series *The Adventures of Captain Hatteras* (1865), as well as Robert Louis Stevenson's *Strange Case Dr. Jekyll and Mr. Hyde* (1886).[8] Many of Tardi's plot devices are clear echoes of Verne and Stevenson: the narrative opens, for instance, as an unsuspecting ship is destroyed by an unseen force; escaping from the fast-sinking exploration vessel *Jules Vernez*, Plumier becomes

Jacques Tardi, *The Arctic Marauder*, plate 6.2. Copyright Casterman, courtesy of Fantagraphics

"The ice was all around." *Used with permission of Dover Editions*

caught "in the grip of a hideously tentacled sea monster" uncannily similar
to the same giant beast that tries to eat Verne's Captain Nemo in *20,000
Leagues*.[9] Physically, Chapoutier and Gelati resemble the well-known pair
Dr. Jekyll and Mr. Hyde from Stevenson's story of scientific idealism gone
awry. Tardi's graphics also tap into an aesthetic tradition associated with

Verne's fiction, and re-create the feel of nineteenth-century woodcuts from "old Jules Verne books" Tardi himself read "as a kid."[10] Tardi even intentionally used an anachronistic method of illustration—scratchboard—to lend authenticity to the book's visual narrative, and his images of ships surrounded by looming icebergs provide an important artistic connection to Gustave Doré's illustrations of Verne's novels as well as his 1876 illuminations of Samuel Taylor Coleridge's *The Rime of the Ancient Mariner*. Just as they invoke Verne's publications, these visual allusions make the *Ancient Mariner*'s own misadventures in the ice—the mariner's near death, his social isolation, his moral humbling—an important narrative shadow. For all its "rollicking adventures," *The Arctic Marauder* tackles the same essential moral question Coleridge's *Ancient Mariner* articulates about the human value of exploration and scientific ambition.[11] Indeed, while, as Glen Weldon notes, the book is both a "loving homage and a smart satire" of nineteenth-century science fiction, it also contains an important moral reflection: in the relationship it traces between social duty and personal ambition, the responsibilities of the scientist and the citizen appear profoundly at odds with each other.[12]

The distinction Tardi makes between the scientist and the citizen in *The Arctic Marauder* establishes a different moral direction than do the works from which he draws, and it calls attention to the ethical underpinnings of science as a social pursuit. Like Stevenson's Dr. Jekyll, Chapoutier is "a tall, fine build of a man," whereas Gelati, with several warts on his face, a prominent club foot, and decidedly greasy hair, is "more of a dwarf" exuding "a haunting sense of . . . deformity," closely resembling Stevenson's Mr. Hyde.[13] Significantly, however, Tardi refuses the possibility of scientific error that Stevenson offers his readers: while Dr. Jekyll becomes an unwilling victim of his own darker forces unleashed during his transformation into Mr. Hyde, Tardi's Chapoutier is a "comrade-in-arms and associate" of the mad Gelati, whose maniacal "HA! HA! HA!" reverberates throughout the halls of the *Marauder*. While Jekyll is horrified by the criminal pursuits of Hyde, Chapoutier and Gelati actively collaborate to accelerate the world's destruction. Humanity's relationship with nature is equally compromised, and the fertile submarine gardens Captain Nemo cultivates in *20,000 Leagues* are transformed in *The Arctic Marauder* into graveyards of sunken ships, from which Chapoutier and Gelati's crew members harvest "ill-gotten gains" to fund the scientists' continued violence, while the motivation for this violence remains both unjustified and uncontained.[14] As Pierre Macherey has argued, in Verne's narratives humanity and nature are linked in "perfect harmony" through human industry, but in Tardi nature is co-opted to become an instrument of death.[15] More significantly, whereas Verne's wild adventures remain rooted in what Adam Roberts terms "comforting social and cultural certainties" that ultimately preclude his protagonists from challenging the status quo, Tardi's characters exploit a shifting moral code that abandons social duty in favor of private satisfaction.[16]

In addition to its narrative engagement with nineteenth-century fictional accounts of scientific adventurism, the history of Victorian polar exploration equally enriches Tardi's tale, providing a realistic gloss to events and underscoring *The Arctic Marauder*'s value as a cautionary tale of scientific hubris. By setting his story near the Pole, Tardi engages with the very question that lay at the heart of the Victorian Arctic craze: his narrator asks, "What is this location whose very lack of distinguishing characteristics makes it even more mystifying?"[17] The *Marauder* includes important parallels to historical narratives of British polar exploration, and parts of its plotline are strikingly similar to the trajectory of Britain's lost Franklin expedition, the largest European Arctic disaster in history. Sent out in 1845 to discover a Northwest Passage with two ships, 129 men, and a surfeit of imperial optimism, Sir John Franklin was never seen alive again by Europeans. Franklin's fate was considered one of the greatest questions of the age, and it prompted a twelve-year-long, internationally organized search. Speculation about the expedition's fate, including a rumor of two ships seen frozen in an iceberg, abounded, and in the same way that Tardi's Plumier follows the mystery of the exploding ships in *Le Figaro*, Victorian readers followed the expanding narrative of the search for Franklin in the nation's newspapers.[18] The prophecy of one Victorian critic eventually proved correct—Franklin had indeed been sent "to form the nucleus of an iceberg"[19]—and the tragedy of his lost expedition enriches Tardi's reimagining of the Arctic ocean landscape, "littered with sinister wrecks" that have met their fate through the "mad, murderous peregrinations of the Arctic icebergs."[20]

Between 1847 and 1859, the main period of the Franklin search, eight ships were crushed or abandoned (including Franklin's own *Terror* and *Erebus*), with appalling loss of human life.[21] Published journals of these searching expeditions underscored the connection between human vulnerability against the elements and the heroism of exploration; as Leopold McClintock, captain of the 1857 expedition that finally discovered Franklin's fate, opined, "the less the [technological] means, . . . the more glorious . . . the success, the more honourable even the defeat."[22] According to Chauncey Loomis, the nineteenth-century Arctic was a moral testing ground "for the best of British manhood," and there existed a general belief that the polar explorer represented a cultural exemplar who survived by relying on an unquenchable sense of moral duty.[23] The morality of the explorer was the key to his success, and scientific triumph

was the expected result of moral superiority. As Sir Roderick Murchison proclaimed in 1859 upon McClintock's triumphant discovery of Franklin's fate,
Arctic adventure was "the best school for testing, by the severest trials, the skill
and endurance" of England's heroes.[24]

For Tardi, however, the Arctic is not the proving ground for moral for-
titude, but rather the geographical location of its disintegration. Though
his story draws on the British narrative tradition of perseverance and pluck,
Tardi counters the determined optimism of the nineteenth-century narrative
with one of inexorable moral decay. Whereas the Franklin search—and polar
exploration more generally—was peopled with men Sir John Barrow, Second
Secretary to the Admiralty from 1808 to 1848, described as "the ablest, the
most learned, and most respectable men of the times," Tardi's Arctic is dominated by two madmen exacting global revenge for a petty personal slight.[25]
This moral degeneration is first expressed in the series of Arctic shipwrecks,
an echo of the Franklin search but with a sinister twist: the rate of destruction in Tardi's Arctic is accelerated more than tenfold, and eight ships are
lost "in six months."[26] This apparent intentionality increases the sense of
foreboding that dominates the graphic novel. Whereas failure meant further
opportunity for heroism in historical explorations, for the characters in *The
Arctic Marauder* there is no romance: a sinking ship means only death.

Moreover, while Tardi initially seems to celebrate the compelling lure of
the Arctic as a place where the answers to questions fundamental to human
survival might be answered (as many Victorians believed), he transforms
the Arctic's destructive power from nature's indifference to human intention. Tardi's Arctic is the site for scientific breakthroughs, but those break-
throughs threaten humanity's existence. *The Arctic Marauder* thus reveals a
world dominated not by scientific optimism but by madmen bent on the destruction of all life. Indeed, while the men aboard the historical nineteenth-
century searching vessels battled icebergs, foul weather, and stormy seas, the
evil lurking in Tardi's Arctic is human, and thus all the more terrible.

The opening scenes of Verne's *Captain Hatteras* and McClintock's best-
selling 1859 journal, *The Voyage of the 'Fox,'* provide marked contrasts to the
start of *The Arctic Marauder* and illustrate the way Tardi revises the relationship between ambition, science, and social responsibility. Verne's *Hatteras*
opens with a jubilant air, with a large and varied crowd gathered dockside to
cheer "the *Forward*'s departure" for the north, while McClintock finds both
his crews and the public irrepressible, his expedition celebrated by "every
honest English heart."[27] In sharp contrast, Tardi's opening scene is one of danger and foreboding, with the threat of being crushed by ice weighing "heavily
upon the crew" of the French ship *Anjou*.[28] This sense of danger is heightened

by the identity of the ship: far from participating in the expansion of scientific knowledge, the *Anjou* is merely a "mail steamship" bound for Le Havre, traversing its regular route.[29] The purpose of the ship's presence in the Arctic is not to battle heroically with icebergs "for the advancement of science," to enjoy the frisson of scientific conquest, or to claim the triumph of penetrating "beyond the limits of the habitable world," but to deliver the mail, a task that ties it to the social, domestic world of human interaction rather than highlights its separation from it.[30] For all of its humble normalcy, however, the *Anjou* is not exempt from the dangers of Arctic travel; rather, it is surrounded by "sinister escorts," looming icebergs "who appear to be awaiting an unforeseeable signal to assail the ship."[31] The essential difference between the peril of the *Anjou* and that of historical expeditions is that, for the *Anjou*, the enemy is a manufactured iceberg, with human malevolence at its heart.

Initially, science and the social world are bound together in the text: like the scientists who sail on the *Jules Vernez*, the "hastily mounted scientific expedition" charged with "determining the cause of the mad, murderous peregrinations of the Arctic icebergs," young Plumier is on his own quest to "resolve the enigma that haunts him, and to find his 'late' uncle . . . at the voyage's end."[32] The *Jules Vernez* is sent out to "make a study of the currents . . . that are guiding these lethal icebergs," but the purpose of the expedition remains social: having lost men to the mysteries of the polar seas, it remains imperative to discover the source of the danger so that it may be avoided in future.[33] The men putting themselves in the path of the polar menace are thus not on a purely scientific mission, but one equally grounded in the empathetic concern for human welfare. For Plumier, the scientific enables the social, and the quest for his uncle is tinged with the possibility of both rescue and redemption: Plumier will rescue his uncle and redeem his character, while the scientists will keep ships—and sailors—safe in the far north. Science is thus put to use to improve human safety, not for the expansion of personal power or influence.

The relationship between science and ambition that comes to dominate the narrative, however, is far more sinister, and the nefarious activities of Chapoutier and Gelati demonstrate the consequences of pursuing scientific advancement without moral responsibility. When Plumier, searching out his uncle after his own near-death experience aboard the *Anjou*, explores Chapoutier's abandoned home in Paris, he finds his laboratory replete with jars of "abominations," the remains of vivisected animals preserved in formaldehyde, while a cupboard reveals a "startling and complex machine whose function eludes the intrigued visitor."[34] Ironically, it is this mysterious machine, which coats itself in ice, that frightens the nonscientific visitors most;

Plumier's reaction—"Dear God in Heaven, what could be the meaning of this?"—is mild compared to the housekeeper's: "Of course I'd seen the ice. It frightened me, that mechanical monstrosity from Hell, it surely did!"[35] The destroyed "animals glimpsed within the formaldehyde"—a more obvious source of revulsion—are nothing but a distraction from the object of greater terror, the manufactured ice.[36] Unlike experimenting on animals, the manufacture of ice is perhaps less understandable than is vivisection, and because its purpose is not immediately apparent, it takes on a more suspicious aspect.

Ultimately, of course, Plumier and the housekeeper are proven correct when the full scale of Chapoutier and Gelati's Marauder is revealed: resembling a normal (if enormous) iceberg in both appearance and behavior, the Marauder conceals twenty floors of Victorian architectural decadence loaded with "cannon-armed turrets," completely undetectable from the outside.[37] Whereas Verne's Nautilus (to which the Marauder is a "loving homage") represents "the conquest of nature by industry," the Marauder represents its moral co-option.[38] Nature itself remains indifferent, but the manufactured iceberg moves with deadly purpose. The ice itself, already a source of terror to northern mariners, is merely an expression of the machine's internal structure: at its core, it is "an immense death machine."[39]

Hearts of Ice

Though initially providing a neutral explanatory gloss to Plumier's character and his quest to find and help his uncle, as the adventure progresses the narrator comes to disagree with Plumier's decisions, and the two ultimately move along opposing moral trajectories. More specifically, as Plumier descends into madness, seduced by his uncle's "marvelous" plan of global annihilation, the narrator ascends into delusional idealism; though David Brothers calls his tone "mocking," it becomes tragic in its lamentation for a world devoid of empathy.[40] At the start of the narrative, Plumier expresses a strong sense of social responsibility, and as the tale begins he and the narrator inhabit the same moral position. Put simply, Plumier is eminently likable: a civilian passenger aboard the ill-fated Anjou, he exhibits admirable pluck when confronted with what he believes to be the ship's imminent destruction. As he pulls his buffalo coat over his disheveled suit and climbs on deck, the alarm bell sounding around him, Plumier's thoughts reveal him to be just the sort of person one would want on board a ship in distress, a cool-headed hero in possession of a stoic self-confidence: "We shall be sinking in short order, then . . . damn! In the middle of the night, and with this cold! What rotten luck."[41] When Plumier, a medical student, learns the true cause of the alarm—the discovery of a ship frozen to a nearby iceberg—his earnest request to accompany the hastily launched lifeboat establishes his good reputation.[42] Significantly, the *Anjou*'s captain identifies Plumier as a rare specimen of a dying social breed: "How comforting to know one may still encounter young men whose ardor burns with a hot flame in their chest."[43] Even at the end of the world and in imminent danger themselves, the *Anjou*'s crew members recognize the human responsibility, the "moral obligation," of providing succor where possible, and Plumier's polite request to help puts him firmly at the story's moral center.[44]

Ironically, Plumier's early attachment to the social world gives way with alarming rapidity in his quest for the missing Chapoutier, since it is Plumier's attachment to his mad scientist uncle that reveals to him the destructive potential—and, perversely, the allure—of polar scientific pursuit. After the sinking of the *Jules Vernez*, Plumier and Chapoutier's tearful reunion aboard the *Marauder* suggests that human empathy remains at the core of the narrative even in the midst of death and destruction, that the outcast uncle might once again be returned to the social fold through the earnest affection of the young nephew. However, the men's location, "at the heart of an iceberg," is more than geographical: though Chapoutier remains attached to his nephew and his scientific associate Gelati, he is a confirmed misanthrope and has withdrawn utterly from a world he considers "populated by fools."[45] Chapoutier's vision of the world as full of "idiots" contradicts the world already described in the book, in which captains of mail ships risk their lives to find survivors of other wrecks, housekeepers watch over the dead, and a nephew seeks out a disinherited uncle.[46] Chapoutier and Plumier thus appear to be fundamentally opposed, and upon discovery of Chapoutier's sinister calling, the narrator assumes that Plumier's "ardor" for life will effectively distance him from Chapoutier, the young man devastated that his "determined quest for his uncle merely turned up two bitter, vengeful madmen, two pitiable individuals of the most contemptible sort."[47] Plumier's reaction, however, to Chapoutier and Gelati's explanation—"MARVELOUS! THIS PROJECT IS MARVELOUS!"—reveals the narrator, in fact, to be the odd one out.[48] Indeed, when confronted with the details of his uncle's madness—the ship graveyard and the threat of biological warfare—Plumier puts up surprisingly little resistance. His initial mute surprise quickly gives way to enthusiasm, while his meek question, "Come to think of it, why sink all those ships?" is easily dismissed by Chapoutier's "deep sense of satisfaction we enjoy at this spectacle."[49] As the narrative continues, Plumier even adopts the mad scientists' disheveled look, representing his development into the next generation of malevolent ambition. Having initially approved of Plumier as a sympathetic character from the narrative's beginning, the

Armor to face the Arctic depths. *Copyright Jody Steel*

narrator laments the loss of the story's "gentle scholar," asking, "Why are we always disappointed in the ones we love?"[50]

Even the lone character in position "to thwart their wicked plans," rival scientist and government agent Simone Pouffiot, fails to be a source of optimism for readers.[51] Though she stands against Chapoutier and Gelati, Pouffiot's motives are equally selfish. In fact, her history with the two elder marauders is of long duration and complexity, for when they were young and "seeking happiness for humanity," she herself "desired to destroy the world."[52] Though now socially acceptable because of her quest to destroy Chapoutier and Gelati, her end goal compromises the purity of her redemption. When she believes she has her two rivals in her grasp, her first thought is of fame: "in a few days I will be a guest at L'Élysée!"[53] Far from the *Anjou* captain's simple "moral obligation" to rescue fellow sailors, the race between scientists is for individual fame, and no thought is given to its destructive consequences. The now outcast narrator can only lament, "Why must man always be tempted by evil?"[54]

Men and Machines

The technology used in *The Arctic Marauder* is historically accurate, and this technological fidelity (the machines are in fact not fantastical) brings the adventure closer to a historical narrative than the scientific imaginings of Verne or Stevenson, or the revised Victorian worlds of *League* or *Anti-Ice*. Inside the iceberg, Plumier finds all the accoutrements of traditional polar exploration expanded to sumptuous proportions: instead of the cramped reading lessons, amateur theater, and small printing presses of Victorian vintage, Chapoutier and Gelati supply "game rooms, lounge rooms and a gymnasium" to their crews on six expansive levels.[55] The cannons used to bombard unsuspecting ships are adapted Krupp weapons,[56] while the ice-producing machine in Chapoutier's closet might be modeled on Ferdinand Carré's ammonia refrigeration system, developed in 1859 in France.[57] The iceberg itself is moved by massive underwater paddle wheels; the only thing left unexplained is its fuel, though as Chapoutier tells Plumier, "Everything runs on electricity."[58] The ship is, in the narrator's words, "ultimate technical perfection."[59] Plumier's modest berth aboard the *Anjou* provides a striking contrast to the elaborate parlor in which he revives after abandoning the exploded *Jules Vernez*, but the architectural decadence of the *Marauder* is an early sign of its moral corruption. While the *Marauder* is both aesthetically pleasing and technologically impressive, morally it remains an object to be abhorred. With such technology at their command, the scientists' early idealism to work "for the good of humanity" is replaced by their delight in destruction.[60] Benign scientific instruments are replaced with weapons of mass destruction, and Chapoutier's malevolent iceberg-ship destroys all vessels—including those simply delivering the mail—that pass within range. Thus while the *Marauder* is "magnificent," it is also perverted, "symbolizing the excess of the nefarious ambitions of the two madmen . . . for all of its admirable qualities."[61] Unlike Plumier, who sighs in appreciation of the *Ma-*

rauder's scale, the narrator ensures that readers are not allowed to admire the technology, lamenting that Chapoutier and Gelati have not "devoted their energies to other pursuits."[62]

Rather than a source of optimism for the future, then, science in *The Arctic Marauder* represents the worst of human ambition, the manifestation of the worst in human behavior. Nineteenth-century exploration was crowded with scientific optimism, a belief that science and technology could and would lead to human triumph. As the *Penny Magazine* enthused in 1832, for example, "The progress of science enables us to overcome difficulties which could not be surmounted in a preceding age."[63] In the world of the *Marauder*, however, it is the opposite. Science is not, in Macherey's words, the "'equal sign' between the real and the imaginary," but the stuff of real-life nightmares.[64] Chapoutier and Gelati's most fantastical invention, the Motorized Ichthyornis, "capable of flight (propelled by twin motors atop its two giant bat-like wings), of underwater travel through a propeller at the rear, able to float like a boat and roll on solid ground," is not the savior of civilization but the machine that allows the menace—the scientists themselves—to survive: Chapoutier, Gelati, and the stubbled Plumier climb aboard and escape the crippled *Marauder*, which Gelati explodes with a "timed auto-destruction device, thus slaying their entire crew."[65] Upon their escape, Chapoutier and Gelati employ the same strategies of scientific information gathering that made the collection of data and specimens possible in the nineteenth century: they refuel their Ichthyornis "at relay posts installed around the world," not unlike the real cairns that dotted the Arctic landscape, left by explorers and filled with provisions and mapping information to aid future travelers.[66] Like their historical contemporaries, Chapoutier and Gelati make their grandest discoveries beyond the restrictions of society, and they revive their quest for world domination in a "virgin forest."[67] At the end of the tale, Gelati looms over a globe, anticipating that "the entire world may begin to tremble, and await the worst disasters"—specifically, biological weaponry that Gelati has developed, "stuffed to overflowing with a brew of bacterial cultures capable of contaminating whole cities."[68]

At the heart of the graphic novel's argument is the question of a scientist's moral contract: as a young scientist, Chapoutier was inspired to pursue scientific discovery "for the good of humanity" but, as his compatriot Gelati explains, "There are limits to how long one can work for humanity and be continually thwarted."[69] While rejection is an adequate reason for withdrawal from society, it is not enough to justify revenge. Chapoutier and Gelati claim to have wisely withdrawn "far from this abhorrent world . . . to pursue [their] respective areas of research," but their research suggests they remain far too invested in what they consider their reputations as scientists should be to engage in responsible science: they work solely on orchestrating the world's "destruction while causing it to pay dearly for its incapacity to recognize genuine great spirits"—that is, their own.[70] Their sense of injustice is profoundly selfish; while Verne's Captain Nemo's thirst for vengeance is a consequence of the loss of his family and country, Chapoutier and Gelati suffer academic humiliation, chafing under a sense of underappreciation and unwilling "to try to improve the lives of . . . idiots, indifferent . . . to [their] discoveries."[71] Their scientific quests, unsuccessful in the academy, are thus turned against the very establishments—staffed by "idiots," of course—from whom the scientists seek approval. Moreover, Chapoutier and Gelati appear to misunderstand the goals of society in their pursuits, for they imagine that "had we succeeded in our research on the world's destruction, we would have been showered with laurels."[72] Their delusions seem ridiculous, as Gelati opines that this research actually constitutes work "for the good of humanity," an attitude clearly at odds with the empathy established early in the narrative.[73] By inverting the empathetic social impulse that opens the tale, Chapoutier and Gelati call attention to *The Arctic Marauder*'s central message: the moral imperative to use technology responsibly. In Tardi's scientific world, there is no neutral ground between the "good of humanity" and the "annihilation" of "idiots."

Conclusion: Awaiting the Worst Disaster

Because of the pettiness of their disaffection, Chapoutier and Gelati's insistence that their "research on the world's destruction" should have brought them global accolades seems ridiculous, and the two men's joy at blowing up merchant as well as scientific vessels is nothing more than the perverse satisfaction of two mad scientists. That they are mad, however, does not mean we can merely dismiss them and return to our comfortable "social and cultural certainties." Specifically because Tardi frames it as a whimsical steampunk confection, *The Arctic Marauder*'s naturalization of violence is terrifying. Krupp's cannons, adapted for underwater use in an imaginary world that "will never exist," are just as real today as is the scientists' fantastical chemical weaponry, and Gelati's mad "HA! HA! HA!" that echoes throughout Tardi's imaginary 1889 world is not so funny today.[74] The technologies in *The Arctic Marauder*, in fact, are not alternative at all: all the steampunk-flavored innovations that Tardi includes in his narrative are real, from the cannons to the flying machines, the biological weapons and the "ocean floor littered with sinister wrecks" sunk by unseen enemies.[75] The narrator's penultimate statement, "Let not your heart be troubled, such individuals do not exist, they will never exist, and inventions of this ilk are impossible to build," imagines for readers a more innocent world; we know, at the start of the twenty-first century, that Tardi's narrator is dreadfully, tragically wrong.[76] Indeed, he is right only when he describes Chapoutier and Gelati's world as it is: "In sum, evil has prevailed."[77]

Tardi thus collapses the steampunk fantasy of the graphic novel, refusing the possibility of escape from Chapoutier and Gelati's destructive vision. The narrator's final comment, that "man carries in his heart the desire always to wield his scientific knowledge in service of the greater good," is thus all the more feeble; readers are not convinced by the narrator's "always" and "never," knowing as they do that the world is much more akin to Chapoutier and Gelati's fantasy than otherwise.[78] Ultimately, the narrator himself remains unconvinced; his timid "Ha! Ha! Ha! Ha! . . ."—the last words in the book—lack the force of Gelati's bold guffaw, and the final ellipsis suggests, in fact, a sustained sense of foreboding.[79] The narrator's moral rejection of *The Arctic Marauder*'s two madmen, who in the narrative we must agree are mad, makes us look at our own mad century more critically: if men who delight in the world's destruction are mad, what does that make us? Though the book ends with laughter, Tardi's inversion of steampunk to reflect our own "alternative" morality shows us there is really very little to laugh at.

Notes

1. Mike Baehr, "*The Arctic Marauder* by Jacques Tardi" (Seattle: Fantagraphics Books, 2011), www.fantagraphics.com/index.php?option=com_myblog&show=The-Arctic-Marauder-by-Jacques-Tardi---Previews-Pre-Order.html&Itemid=113 (5 January 2012); Glen Weldon, "*The Arctic Marauder*: A Mystery Wrapped in an Enigma Wrapped in ICY DEATH," www.npr.org/blogs/monkeysee/2011/04/07/135139790/the-arctic-marauder-a-mystery-wrapped-in-an-enigma-wrapped-in-icy-death npr.org (5 January 2012).

2. Jacques Tardi, *The Arctic Marauder*, 1972, trans. Kim Thompson (Seattle: Fantagraphics, 2011), 18.

3. Tardi, *The Arctic Marauder*, 44, 63.

4. Tardi, *The Arctic Marauder*, 54.

5. Tardi, *The Arctic Marauder*, 50, 53.

6. Alan Moore, Kevin O'Neill, Ben Dimagmaliw, and Bill Oakley, *The League of Extraordinary Gentlemen, Volume 1* (La Jolla, Calif.: Wildstorm Productions, 1999), 2: 47; Stephen Baxter, *Anti-Ice* (New York: HarperCollins, 1993).

7. Moore et al., *The League of Extraordinary Gentlemen*, 2: 46; Baxter, *Anti-Ice*, 279.

8. Kim Thompson, "Editor's Notes: Kim Thompson on *The Arctic Marauder*," www.fantagraphics.com/books/editors-notes-kim-thompson-on-the-arctic-marauder.html (5 January 2012).

9. Tardi, *The Arctic Marauder*, 38.

10. Thompson, "Editor's Notes."

11. Weldon, "A Mystery Wrapped in an Enigma."

12. Weldon, "A Mystery Wrapped in an Enigma."

13. Robert Louis Stevenson, "The Strange Case of Dr. Jekyll and Mr. Hyde" (1886), in *The Norton Anthology of English Literature*, 8th ed., Vol. E, ed. Carol T. Christ and Catherine Robson (New York: Norton, 2006), 1666, 1657.

14. Tardi, *The Arctic Marauder*, 53.

15. Pierre Macherey, *A Theory of Literary Production* (1966), trans. Geoffrey Wall (London: Routledge, 2006), 185.

16. Adam Roberts, *The History of Science Fiction* (New York: Palgrave, 2006), 130.

17. Tardi, *The Arctic Marauder*, 16.

18. Janice Cavell identifies the nineteenth-century British popular press as responsible for producing "a coherent metanarrative of Arctic exploration" that contributed to the construction of explorers as cultural exemplars. See Janice Cavell, *Tracing the Connected Narrative: Arctic Exploration in British Print Culture, 1818–1860* (Toronto: University of Toronto Press, 2008), 9.

19. Richard King, quoted in Fergus Fleming, *Barrow's Boys* (New York: Atlantic Monthly Press, 1998), 370.

20. Tardi, *The Arctic Marauder*, 50, 34.

21. For a record of searching expeditions, see Erika Behrisch Elce, ed., *As Affecting the Fate of My Absent Husband: Selected Letters of Lady Franklin Concerning the Search for the Lost Franklin Expedition, 1848–1860* (Kingston: McGill-Queen's University Press, 2009), or Alan Cooke and Clive Holland, *Exploration of Northern Canada: 500 to 1920* (Toronto: Arctic History Press, 1978), for a longer history of northern exploration in general.

22. Leopold McClintock, *In the Arctic Seas: A Narrative of the Discovery of the Fate of Sir John Franklin and His Companions* (Chicago: Winston, 1859), 11.

23. Chauncey Loomis, "The Arctic Sublime," in *Nature and the Victorian Imagination*, ed. U. C Knoepflmacher and G. B. Tennyson (Los Angeles: University of California Press, 1977), 95–112, 104.

24. Roderick Murchison, "Preface," in Leopold McClintock, *In the Arctic Seas*, xx.

25. John Barrow, *A Chronological History of Voyages into the Arctic Regions, Undertaken Chiefly for the Purpose of Discovering a North-East, North-West or Polar Passage between the Atlantic and Pacific* (1818) (New York: Barnes and Noble, 1971), 52.

26. Tardi, *The Arctic Marauder*, 24.

27. Jules Verne, *The Adventures of Captain Hatteras* (1865), trans. William Butcher (Oxford: Oxford World Classics, 2005), 5; McClintock, *In the Arctic Seas*, 10.

28. Tardi, *The Arctic Marauder*, 6.

29. Tardi, *The Arctic Marauder*, 6.

30. Barrow, *A Chronological History of Voyages*, 368; Anonymous, *Northern Regions: or, a Relation of Uncle Richard's Voyages for the Discovery of a North-west Passage* (1825) (New York: S. R. Publishers, 1970), 15.

31. Tardi, *The Arctic Marauder*, 6.

32. Tardi, *The Arctic Marauder*, 24, 34, 35.

33. Tardi, *The Arctic Marauder*, 24.

34. Tardi, *The Arctic Marauder*, 22.

35. Tardi, *The Arctic Marauder*, 22, 23.

36. Tardi, *The Arctic Marauder*, 24.

37. Tardi, *The Arctic Marauder*, 46.

38. Weldon, "A Mystery Wrapped in an Enigma"; Macherey, A *Theory of Literary Production*, 184.

39. Weldon, "A Mystery Wrapped in an Enigma."

40. David Brothers, "Jacques Tardi: Fantagraphics Helps a Legend Get His Due with an 'Icepunk' Graphic Novel," www.comicsalliance.com/2011/05/16/jacques-tardi (5 January 2012).

41. Tardi, *The Arctic Marauder*, 8.

42. Tardi, *The Arctic Marauder*, 10.

43. Tardi, *The Arctic Marauder*, 10.

44. Tardi, *The Arctic Marauder*, 10.

45. Tardi, *The Arctic Marauder*, 41, 42.

46. Tardi, *The Arctic Marauder*, 43.

47. Tardi, *The Arctic Marauder*, 10, 43.

48. Tardi, *The Arctic Marauder*, 43.

49. Tardi, *The Arctic Marauder*, 50.

50. Tardi, *The Arctic Marauder*, 43.

51. Tardi, *The Arctic Marauder*, 54.

52. Tardi, *The Arctic Marauder*, 45.

53. Tardi, *The Arctic Marauder*, 58.

54. Tardi, *The Arctic Marauder*, 43.

55. Tardi, *The Arctic Marauder*, 45.

56. Krupp was in fact the German manufacturer of the first *Unterseeboote* for World War I, including the U-18, designed to fire "monstrous torpedoes . . . with a range of 6,000 yards and a speed of 40 knots," with possible targets including "merchant ships," in William Manchester, *The Arms of Krupp, 1587–1968* (Boston: Little, Brown and Company, 1968), 258.

57. My thanks to Dr. Michael Bardon, professor emeritus of mechanical engineering at the Royal Military College of Canada, for this information.

58. Tardi, *The Arctic Marauder*, 47.

59. Tardi, *The Arctic Marauder*, 47.

60. Tardi, *The Arctic Marauder*, 43.

61. Tardi, *The Arctic Marauder*, 54.

62. Tardi, *The Arctic Marauder*, 54.

63. "Arctic Land Expedition," in *Monthly Supplement of the Penny Magazine* (12 December 1832): 387.

64. Macherey, A *Theory of Literary Production*, 188.

65. Tardi, *The Arctic Marauder*, 59, 61.
66. Tardi, *The Arctic Marauder*, 62.
67. Tardi, *The Arctic Marauder*, 62.
68. Tardi, *The Arctic Marauder*, 63, 56.
69. Tardi, *The Arctic Marauder*, 43.
70. Tardi, *The Arctic Marauder*, 43, 42, 43.
71. Tardi, *The Arctic Marauder*, 43.
72. Tardi, *The Arctic Marauder*, 43.
73. Tardi, *The Arctic Marauder*, 43.
74. Tardi, *The Arctic Marauder*, 63.
75. Tardi, *The Arctic Marauder*, 50.
76. Tardi, *The Arctic Marauder*, 63.
77. Tardi, *The Arctic Marauder*, 63.
78. Tardi, *The Arctic Marauder*, 63.
79. Tardi, *The Arctic Marauder*, 63.

Bibliography

"Arctic Land Expedition." *Monthly Supplement of the Penny Magazine* (12 December 1832): 386–389.

Baehr, Mike. "*The Arctic Marauder* by Jacques Tardi." www.fantagraphics.com/index.php?option=com_myblog&show=The-Arctic-Marauder-by-Jacques-Tardi---Previews-Pre-Order.html&Itemid=113 (5 January 2012).

Bardon, Michael. Personal interview with the author (4 January 2012).

Barrow, John. *A Chronological History of Voyages into the Arctic Regions, Undertaken Chiefly for the Purpose of Discovering a North-East, North-West or Polar Passage between the Atlantic and Pacific.* 1818. New York: Barnes and Noble, 1971.

Baxter, Stephen. *Anti-Ice.* New York: HarperCollins, 1993.

Behrisch Elce, Erika, ed. *As Affecting the Fate of My Absent Husband: Selected Letters of Lady Franklin Concerning the Search for the Lost Franklin Expedition, 1848–1860.* Kingston: McGill-Queen's University Press, 2009.

Brothers, David. "Jacques Tardi: Fantagraphics Helps a Legend Get His Due with an 'Icepunk' Graphic Novel." www.comicsalliance.com/2011/05/16/jacques-tardi (5 January 2012).

Cavell, Janice. *Tracing the Connected Narrative: Arctic Exploration in British Print Culture, 1818–1860.* Toronto: University of Toronto Press, 2008.

Cooke, Alan, and Clive Holland. *Exploration of Northern Canada: 500 to 1920.* Toronto: Arctic History Press, 1978.

Fleming, Fergus. *Barrow's Boys.* New York: Atlantic Monthly Press, 1998.

Loomis, Chauncey. "The Arctic Sublime." 95–112 in *Nature and the Victorian Imagination*, ed. U. C Knoepflmacher and G. B. Tennyson. Los Angeles: University of California Press, 1977.

Macherey, Pierre. *A Theory of Literary Production*. 1966. Trans. Geoffrey Wall. London: Routledge, 2006.

Manchester, William. *The Arms of Krupp, 1587–1968*. Boston: Little, Brown and Company, 1968.

McClintock, Leopold. *In the Arctic Seas: A Narrative of the Discovery of the Fate of Sir John Franklin and His Companions*. Chicago: Winston, 1859.

Moore, Alan, Kevin O'Neill, Ben Dimagmaliw, and Bill Oakley. *The League of Extraordinary Gentlemen, Volume 1*. La Jolla, Calif.: Wildstorm Productions, 1999.

Murchison, Roderick. "Preface." vii–xx in Leopold McClintock, *In the Arctic Seas*. *Northern Regions: or, a Relation of Uncle Richard's Voyages for the Discovery of a North-west Passage*. 1825. New York: S. R. Publishers, 1970.

Roberts, Adam. *The History of Science Fiction*. New York: Palgrave, 2006.

Stevenson, Robert Louis. "The Strange Case of Dr. Jekyll and Mr. Hyde." 1886. 1645–1685 in *The Norton Anthology of English Literature*, 8th ed., Vol. E, ed. Carol T. Christ and Catherine Robson. New York: Norton, 2006.

Tardi, Jacques. *The Arctic Marauder*. 1972. Trans. Kim Thompson. Seattle: Fantagraphics, 2011.

Thompson, Kim. "Editors Notes: Kim Thompson on *The Arctic Marauder*." www.fantagraphics.com/books/editors-notes-kim-thompson-on-the-arctic-marauder.html (5 January 2012).

Verne, Jules. *The Adventures of Captain Hatteras*. 1865. Trans. William Butcher. Oxford: Oxford World Classics, 2005.

Weldon, Glen. "*The Arctic Marauder*: A Mystery Wrapped in an Enigma Wrapped in ICY DEATH." www.npr.org/blogs/monkeysee/2011/04/07/135139790/the-arctic-marauder-a-mystery-wrapped-in-an-enigma-wrapped-in-icy-death npr.org (5 January 2012).

Jules Verne, who dressed the future in Victorian clothes. *Copyright Jody Steel*

CHAPTER SEVEN

"Fulminations and Fulgurators": Jules Verne, Karel Zeman, and Steampunk Cinema

John C. Tibbetts

However, one thing is certain, and that is that I have embarked upon an extraordinary adventure.

—Simon Hart in Jules Verne's *Facing the Flag* (1896)

If men go on inventing machinery they'll end by being swallowed up by their own inventions.

—Kennedy in Jules Verne's *Five Weeks in a Balloon* (1862)

Many of us who saw *The Fabulous World of Jules Verne* during its first release in 1961 never forgot it. As a Victorian-era retrovision, it pinned upon the map of the nineteenth century a series of wildly anachronistic technologies derived from Verne's fertile genius. People sailed the seas in submarines, flew the skies in bizarre machines, and waged war with rocket missiles. Live-action images mingled with animated steel engravings. It was like a quaint storybook for young and old whose "once-upon-a-time" quality was a blend of *never-was* and *might-have-been*. Now, after almost half a century's absence, *The Fabulous World of Jules Verne* (1958) is back in video and YouTube formats and delighting a new generation, while the older generation greets it with an old affection and a new respect. Moreover, we can recognize it now as a proto-steampunk movie—although the term would not be invented by K. W. Jeter for another thirty years after its release—since it matches the definition recently advanced by Jeff VanderMeer: "STEAMPUNK = Mad Scientist Inventor [invention (steam × airship or metal man/ baroque stylings) × (pseudo) Victorian setting] + adventure plot."[1]

125

Writer Howard Waldrop greeted the film's rerelease in 2004 with boyish enthusiasm:

> It is the ultimate Steampunk movie; the inventions here seem like 1890s projections of what planes, machine-pistols, and giant cannon might look like in an alternate history. . . . The Fabulous World of Jules Verne is of its time, about *another* time—you watch it now with a double-focus that wasn't there when 1958 was The Present.[2]

This whimsical mixture of satire and silliness, of science and speculation, of animation and live action, is as much a creation of the renowned Czech animator, Karel Zeman (1919–1989), as it is of Verne (1828–1905) himself. Working in the tradition of Georges Méliès, Zeman created in this and in his other Vernian films a unique vision of motion-picture technology wholly appropriate to Verne's time, even though, paradoxically, the novelist himself seems to have paid little attention to it. I will argue here that Zeman envisioned *the film apparatus* itself as a kind of steampunk machine, whose mechanism of intermittent movements, interlocking cogs, gears, and escapements, transforms through the agency of light and chemistry Verne's printed page into celluloid fantasies that *move* and *dream*.

Verne's Imagination, on Screen

Before Joseph E. Levine brought Zeman's film to America in 1960 in a dubbed version retitled *The Fabulous World of Jules Verne*, the Czech-produced film was known abroad as *Vynález Akazy* (*The Deadly Invention*).[3] It is based on one of Verne's later novels, *Face au drapeau* (*Facing the Flag*), part of Verne's *Voyages Extraordinaires* series.[4] After its premiere in Czechoslovakia on 22 August 1958, it appeared at Expo '58 in Brussels, where it won the Grand Prix at the International Film Festival. More awards in the following months included a Silver Sombrero at the First International Film Festival in Guadalajara, a Czechoslovak Film Critics Award, and a Crystal Star from the French Academy of Film. Critic Pauline Kael hailed it at the time as a "wonderful giddy science fantasy" that "creates the atmosphere of the Jules Verne books."[5]

Described as "the Czech Méliès," in recognition of the whimsies and innovative daring of his animation, Zeman was, with his countrymen Jiri Trynka and Bretislav Pojar, a leader in *cinema d'animation*, a French term designating techniques in hand-drawn, puppet, object, and photographic frame-by-frame exposure. Trained in France and his native Czechoslovakia, Zeman got his start in the 1940s with puppet films. Working at the Gottwaldov studios in the 1950s, his A *Journey to Prehistoric Times* began the series of fantastic, live-action/animated films for which he is best known, and which included his celebrated Vernian adaptations *Cesta do Pravĕka* (*Journey to the Center of the Earth*) in 1962, *Ukradena vzducholod* (*The Stolen Airship*) in 1967, and *Na kometě* (*Off on a Comet*) in 1970.[6] Even more ambitious than *Vynález Akazy*, in terms of budget, the use of color, and orchestral scores, they retain nonetheless Zeman's characteristic storybook charm and arsenal of artificial effects. *Na kometě* takes things further with animated sea monsters, land lizards, and dinosaurs. Although outside the immediate scope of this chapter, they are all marvelous adaptations of Verne and deserve extended study on their own.[7] According to Michaela Mertova, a historian at the National Archive in Prague, "[Zeman] was one filmmaker who was really able to capture the imagination of works by Jules Verne. In visual terms, there is no question the films continue to resonate with audiences even today." Even if viewers were aware they were seeing an artificial world, continues Mertova, "it was so alive, so natural, that audiences were never distracted by the tricks."[8] As part of a "rediscovery" of Zeman's works, a centenary program of Zeman's films was presented in 2010 at the Czech Centre in London.[9]

Verne's ambivalence regarding the benefits of science in *For the Flag* and other novels is typical of his times. He grew up precisely at a time in the nineteenth century when the cities of New York, Paris, and London were the epicenters of a vast technological upheaval. "There is no doubt," writes Mike Ashley, "that it was the opening up of the world through steam trains and the opportunities that steam power introduced that ushered in the Industrial Revolution and began the true scientific revolution that allowed science fiction to prosper."[10] New technologies were escaping the solitary inventor's laboratory and were becoming mass-produced commodities. Machines were replacing muscle, and the airwaves supplanted keen eyes and ears. As biographer Herbert R. Lottman says, "That so many things suddenly became possible suggested to the prescient that more and better inventions lay just around the corner."[11]

Based on the many explorers of the times penetrating jungles, traversing deserts, and mapping the skies, Verne's inventors deployed and expanded available technologies to build improbable propeller-driven, heavier-than-air flying machines to cruise the skies, electrically powered submarines to explore the ocean depths, and experimental weapons of war to threaten the security of the world. They imparted a romantic *frisson* to available science and technology. "[By giving] the ordinary a mysterious appearance," wrote the poet Novalis in his seminal romantic novel, *Henry von Ofterdingen* (published posthumously in 1802), "—the known the dignity of the unknown, the finite an infinite aura, I thus romanticize them."[12] Indeed, Verne's machines, notes cultural historian Cynthia Miller, seem like quasi-magical objects, the latest in a seemingly endless string of fresh technological wonders:

> We never see them being built or bought; they simply *are*. These fantastic machines highlight, by their very existence, the character archetypes, narrative tropes, and often, layers of meaning inherent in the storyline of steampunk

Verne's fantastic possibilities. *Copyright Jody Steel*

texts. Readers and viewers are instantly alert to the machines' potential to remake the social order, and to the damage those devices can do in the hands of the reckless or the ruthless."[13]

Speculations about these fantastic technologies place them squarely in the foreground as a commentary on technology and progress.

Many oft-cited examples attest to the remarkable degree to which some of Verne's "voyages" predicted the future. For example, *From the Earth to the Moon* (1865) and its sequel, *Around the Moon* (1870), predicted many details of the Apollo moon shots.[14] Less well known is the amazing accuracy of his vision of life closer to home in an early novel, *Paris in the Twentieth Century*, written in 1860 but unpublished in his lifetime. He looked ahead to urban life in 1960, where he forecast electrical street lighting, rapid transportation by elevated and underground urban-transit trains driven by compressed air, and gasoline-powered horseless carriages. In the home were mechanical elevators. In the office, a telegraph sent stock quotations around the world, and facsimile documents were transmitted by *telematiques photographique* devices.[15] The book was finally published in 1994, when it created a sensation and moved to the top of the best-seller lists. "I have always made a point in my romances," wrote Verne,

"of basing my so-called inventions upon a groundwork of actual fact, and of using in their construction methods and materials which are not entirely without
the pale of contemporary engineering skill and knowledge."[16]

Extraordinary Voyages

Verne himself was neither a scientist nor the first person to write science fiction—the term was not in use until the 1920s. But Isaac Asimov insists he was
the *first science fiction writer*, the first to *specialize* in the form and the first to
make a living at it. Beginning at midcentury, the success of his many novels,
his "extraordinary voyages," as he called them, proved "that the public was
hungry for adventures told from the new viewpoints that were made possible
by science in an age when optimism concerning the coming scientific advances
was at its height."[17] In his classic study of science fiction, *New Maps of Hell*,
Kingsley Amis pronounced Verne "the first great progenitor of modern science
fiction. . . . While usually wrong or implausible or simply boring in detail, his
themes foreshadow a great deal of contemporary thinking, both inside and
outside science fiction."[18] And Arthur C. Clarke wrote, "He was the first writer
to welcome change and to proclaim that scientific discovery could be the most
wonderful of all adventures. For this reason, he will never grow out-of-date."[19]

While researching *For the Flag*, the sixty-eight–year-old Verne, who was
living in Amiens at the time, acknowledged to his brother Paul that his character of the inventor Thomas Roch—whose invention of a new explosive, a
kind of "doomsday device," is rejected by the international market—was to be
based on the real-life French scientist Eugéne Turpin. Turpin, like his fictional
counterpart, had invented an explosive substance that had been spurned by
his country's military. Unlike Turpin, Roch was to be portrayed as a mentally
unstable and ruthlessly opportunistic visionary, venting his anger upon a world
that turned its back on him. (After the publication of *For the Flag*, Turpin
launched a suit against Verne for libel. Contrary to his earlier statements, Verne
now denied any such association. The court determined that Turpin had served
as inspiration but that Verne had not intended any harm. There could be no
libel without intention to harm.[20]) Perhaps Verne himself was laboring under
the increasing realization that his newest books were being overlooked by the
public and critics.[21] He may have seen in Roch's mental instabilities, writes biographer Peter Costello, signs of his own "neurotic symptoms" of "eccentricities
of character, melancholy, apathy," abetted by worries over the insanity of his
nephew; the death of his beloved publisher, Jules Hetzel; and his own increasing lameness and weakening sight: "Perhaps the only thing that stopped Verne
going mad was his very 'serious occupation,' his incessant work."[22] Moreover,
notes Brian Aldiss, the novel is among several at this time indicating Verne's

Professor Roch (Arnost Navartil): Genius or madman?

disillusionment at the promise of science and frustration at the triumph of what seemed to be a "machine mentality": "Even the brave scientists show signs of deterioration, eccentricity, blindness. The heroic age of the engine is done. Things fall apart, the centre will not hold."[23]

Thus, Roch emerges an ambivalent figure and joins the long list of Verne's troubled inventors and eccentrics, including most famously Captain Nemo and Robur and the lesser-known Professor Schultz (modeled after the German industrialist Alfred Krupp).[24] However, we can locate this skepticism about the energies of science and technology as early as 1854, in Verne's cautionary tale of scientific hubris and Gothic horror, "Master Zacharias."[25] The titular character is a master clockmaker who believes he has animated his clocks into living beings. Life, to him, is merely an "ingenious mechanism," and, as the narrator explains, "As [Zacharias] constructed his clocks, he fancied that he had discovered the secrets of the union of the soul with the body."[26] He demonstrates "that vanity of science which connects everything with itself, without rising to the infinite source whence first principles flow."[27]

Zacharias's legacy is passed on to his most famous counterpart, Robur. First seen as a benevolent hero in *Clipper of the Clouds* in 1886, Robur reappears as a destroyer in the 1904 sequel, *Master of the World*. Robur is not Satan; but in his pride he *is* satanic. Like a Miltonic Satan, he is cast down from heaven by bolts of lightning and falls to his death in the Gulf of Mexico. Robur could conquer the human race with his inventions; but when he arrogantly attempts to ignore the natural order itself, he is spectacularly defeated. Providence wins.

Since *For the Flag* is one of Verne's least-known novels, a brief synopsis is in order. Inventor Roch is experimenting with the "Roch Fulgurator," a "sort of auto-propulsive engine, of peculiar construction, charged with an explosive composed of new substances.[28] Maddened by the rejections of his work, Roch denounces the world, lapses into a state of mental confusion, and is hospitalized in a North Carolina institution, Healthful House. (We are reminded that Verne set twenty-three of his novels in America.[29]) "It was only too evident that he had lost all notion of things as far as the ordinary acts of life were concerned; but in regard to subjects demanding the exercise of his genius, his sanity was unimpaired and unassailable—a fact which demonstrates how true is the dictum that genius and madness are often allied."[30] When a French engineer, Simon Hart, arrives to guard and protect Roch, both men are kidnapped by one Count d'Artigas, who spirits them away in his schooner, *Ebba*. What follows is a series of adventures narrated in Hart's journal. The schooner is "incontestably propelled by some powerful machine . . . perhaps one of those turbines that have been spoken of lately.[31] Under the command of d'Artigas—actually the fierce pirate Karraje—the *Ebba* and a submarine operate in tandem to attack and destroy shipping. Inside Karraje's hideout,

Hart is kept prisoner while the vengeful Roch is put to work, happy to comply with Karraje's plans to use his explosives against the world.

Hart sends out a warning message. It is answered when an English naval officer, Lieutenant Davon, arrives in his small submarine, "Sword," to rescue Hart and Roch. But Karraje's submarine sinks it, and Hart and Roch are returned to the cavern. Now alerted that an invasion might be imminent, Karraje sets up a number of launching "trestles" about the island to hurl the explosives at approaching warships. "If warships approach within five or six miles," declares Karraje, "they will be sunk before they have had time to fire a single shot."[32] However, when Roch hears bugle calls from an approaching French ship and sees the French flag, his patriotism and his sanity are restored. Roch detonates explosives and destroys the entire mountain stronghold, perishing in the process and with him the secret of his inventions. Only Hart survives.

The Fabulous World of Jules Verne begins with an extended opening sequence depicting a fantastic succession of modern technologies in a graphic and whimsical manner that qualifies it as a classic example of what we now call steampunk cinema. "My adventures began when I booked passage on the *Savannah*," narrates Simon Hart (Lubor Tokos), gazing raptly at the skies above him and the seas below—at the propeller-driven flying boats, steam-powered ocean liners, and electrically driven submarines. His rhapsodic celebration of Victorian invention is intoxicating:

> It was the first steamship to cross the Atlantic. The sky was clear as we sailed proudly to her destination. And high in the clouds a prodigious sight. Man, who mastered the sea had tamed the land, was now set to challenge the very kingdom of the clouds. All the elements of earth were conquered and forced to yield their most precious secrets. Ah, what an age to live in when each new day brought science ever more glorious triumphs.

Hart continues overland by locomotive, and we see "the steel juggernaut which devoured every obstacle in its path, a machine of steam and steel so cunningly fashioned that it required only the most perfunctory attention from its driver." Then, most miraculous of all, a gigantic sky-boat sails above, a flying platform drawn by propeller engines and maintained aloft by smaller helicopter blades. "Look up there!" shouts Hart. "The *Albatross* [a reference to Robur's great airship]! A fantasy brought to life—the wildest dream of the centuries translated into a way of life by the indomitable genius of man, flying at heights that no human has before attained." It is indeed an age of wonders, he proclaims—"our century, the century of steam power, the age of that mysterious force, electricity, has overthrown tradition and tossed by the wayside old-fashioned ideas and outmoded ways of life."

After a series of adventures by boat and submarine, and kidnapped by Artigas's (Miroslav Holub) goons, Hart and scientist Roch (Arnost Navartil), find themselves in the castle-like battlements of Artigas's "retreat," an extinct volcano. The befuddled Roch seems unaware of Artigas's dastardly plans to use the Fulgurator to destroy the world. Nothing can stop him, privately declares Artigas: "Although they can bring to bear against us the guns of all the navies in the world, it is yet within our power to reduce them to rusting, burnt out hulks."

Hart sends out his warning message in a small balloon. It is answered by Lieutenant Davon, who arrives in a small submersible equipped with four oars that propel the machine. But Artigas's submarine destroys Davon's vehicle. Hart escapes back to the surface and immediately goes to warn the professor. Meanwhile, a great cannon is built that will launch the professor's explosive shells against a line of approaching warships. An observation balloon will send reports from men with "magnetic telephones" and breathing gear for the high altitude. The professor finally realizes the extent of Artigas's plans. Unobserved, he climbs aboard the cannon and looses a shell from its moorings. It tumbles down the mountain and blows the whole island to smithereens. Artigas's top hat flies up into the air and out the volcano's mouth, a whimsical footnote to the disaster.

Apart from *For the Flag*, *The Fabulous World of Jules Verne* is packed with references to the submarines, grotesque deep-sea creatures, giant cannons, and flying boats of other Vernian adventures. The gigantic cannon replacing Roch's "launching trestles" derives from *The Begum's Fortune*, whose villain, Professor Schultz, intends to use it to destroy entire cities. Other departures include the addition of a romantic interest for Hart (since Verne rarely allowed such trifles to interrupt his narratives). The most significant change involves the character of the inventor Roch. The greedy, opportunistic scientist on a vendetta against an uncaring world in the novel is here simply a scientist so immersed in his experiments he fails to divine the criminal agenda of Artigas. And while in Verne's novel Roch's patriotic instincts are awakened at the last minute, here Roch simply sabotages the cannon out of pique at the misuse of his experiments.

The Magic of Technology

More relevant to the purposes of this chapter, however, are Zeman's visual effects. Utilizing the motion picture animation techniques being developed in Verne's day, most of which were also available to Méliès—magic-lantern dissolves, stop-motion, pixilation, etc.—he translates the technological dreams of Verne's prose into their visual correlatives. He transcends as much as he embodies historical contingency. Oddly, Verne himself, in this and his other novels, displays little, if any, awareness of motion picture technology and its visual effects. As we will see, it is up to Méliès and Zeman not just to *adapt* Verne's story, but to *create* a proto-steampunk vision of their own.

Verne's seeming lack of interest in the developing motion picture tech-nology transpiring all around him at this time is astonishing, particularly in-asmuch as his rival, H. G. Wells, exploits its filmic effects vividly in his first novel, *The Time Machine*, published in 1895. The novel appeared precisely at the same time that Verne was working on *For the Flag*, and that news of exciting developments in motion picture technology was already attracting the public and scientists alike. Between 1895 and 1905 numerous inventors and filmmakers all across Europe and America were building and displaying their machines and their moving images. In America there was the Edison/ W. K. L. Dickson Kinetoscope and Vitascope; in France, the Lumiere Broth-ers' *Cinématographe*; in Germany, Maximilian Skladanowsky's Bioscope; and in England, Robert Paul's Theatograph. Wells took notice, even if Verne did not. Wells's "time machine" is obviously a metaphor for the action and effects of the film camera and projector.

Wells was only twenty when he wrote "The Chronic Argonauts" in 1888, the first of several drafts that resulted in the finished novel, *The Time Machine*. It postulated that a machine could be built that mastered time. At the flick of a switch the machine could move forward and backward in time, slowing and accelerating its perceived passage, by turns. Although the first draft contained no description of the actual workings and effects of time travel, it is significant that by 1895, with his growing awareness of filmic technology, Wells describes time travel in a manner, as historian Thomas C. Renzi notes, "that often imitates filmmaking techniques. Some famous examples occur in *The Time Machine*, where the inventor's journey describes the fast-forward and reverse-action modes of film." There are even "additional suggestions of sound dubbing and fade-in and fade-out effects with accelerated movement, reverse-action, stop-motion, and slow-motion."[33]

Indeed, the novel not only alludes to those effects, but it may have *an-ticipated* the commercial exploitation of the medium itself. Certainly British inventor and film pioneer Robert Paul thought so. "In this story," explained historian Terry Ramsaye, "Paul saw an opportunity to use the special proper-ties of the motion picture in a new and perhaps especially effective method of narration. . . . the evidence is such that if [Wells's] story was not evolved directly from the experience of seeing the Kinetoscope, it was indeed an amazing coincidence."[34] At any rate, on 24 October 1895, shortly after the publication of his book, Wells and Paul obtained a provisional patent for a viewing apparatus—a kind of movie theater—wherein viewers would be seated in a compartment, rather like a train car, whose seats would vibrate slightly to impart the illusion of motion. Writing in *The Era* magazine, Paul noted that the spectator would have the sensation of "voyaging upon a machine through time," viewing through the windows a series of rear-projected films, scenes "which are supposed to occur in the future or past."[35]

Amid all this, one naturally assumes that Verne, ever on the alert for new technologies, would not only know about these theories and developments in the mechanical manipulation of time and space—an "extraordinary voyage" with a machine rivaling anything he had hitherto envisioned—but would incorporate them into his own stories and pursue their incarnations in the movies. Indeed, years before, in 1854, Verne's short story, the aforementioned "Master Zacharias," anticipated Wells's *The Time Machine* in its plot about an inventor's attempts to master time.[36] But Verne never followed up "Master Zacharias." Moreover, extant research suggests that either Verne was oblivious to the motion picture or he chose to ignore it altogether. Science fiction writer John Taine flatly declares, "When these things were new, they offered as imaginative a mind as Verne's an opportunity to surpass the Arabian Nights. Yet Verne, to whom they were accessible had he looked in the right places, missed them."[37] Or did he? It is apparent that further research needs to be done on this question.

Meanwhile, former magician/filmmaker Georges Méliès was the first to bring Verne and Wells to the screen. In 1897 Méliès made a short film based on Verne's *The Adventures of Captain Hatteras*. Unfortunately, it is lost. More importantly, in 1902, his *Trip to the Moon* based the first half of its story on Verne's *From the Earth to the Moon* and the second half on Wells's *First Men on the Moon* (which had been initially serialized in *Cosmopolitan Magazine* in 1900–1901).[38] It was Méliès's most elaborate and longest film to date, with its eighteen settings amounting to a total cost of ten thousand francs. It ran for several months at the Olympia Theater and was soon seen all over Europe and America. Méliès later declared that *A Trip to the Moon* was "a film that people will talk about after thirty years. It made a deep impression, being the first of its kind."[39] Lunar spectacles were already a favorite fairground entertainment at the end of the century. Nicholas Camille Flammarion, who founded the French Astronomical Society in 1887 and had written a novel in the 1870s about interstellar travel, *Masters of Time and Space*, was likely the prototype for President Barbenfouillis. Verne knew Flammarion, and his *Off on a Comet* (1877) was a fictional counterpart to the more sober works of the man.[40]

The iconic image in *Trip to the Moon* of the rocket shell penetrating the eye of the Man in the Moon was Méliès's own contribution. Today's moviegoers know it as the guiding image of Martin Scorsese's *Hugo* (2011). For historian Lynda Nead, that image represents "a symbolic vision of the end of an astronomical science based on the transcription of the observation of the eye and the triumph of a new astronomy based on the superior gaze and representational capacities of the camera lens." Images like this "disturbed

What did the inventor of the extraordinary think of motion pictures? *Copyright John C. Tibbetts*

the idea of a fixed viewing position, [creating] a dynamic, kinetic viewer whose point of view was just as likely to be that of the Lunarian or Martian as that of an inhabitant of earth." It epitomizes, continues Nead, "the fusion of scientific investigation and fantasy . . . to look at a photographic image of the moon was to detach oneself from the everyday things of the earth and to embark on the first stage of an endless celestial voyage."[41] In words that could be applied to Verne himself, John Frazer notes, in his study of Méliès, "In treading the line between parody and prediction Méliès captured the ambivalence felt by people at the turn of the century as they attempted to accommodate to the forward rush of science."[42]

Two years later Méliès produced another Vernian property, this time derived from the 1882 Verne/d'Ennery stage production of *The Impossible Voyage*, at the Théâtre de la Gaîté. While the stage adventure featured a trip to the center of the Earth, the film ventured further and explored the interior of the sun. The trip is mounted by the Institute of Incoherent Geography. An engineer unveils his remarkable vehicles, an automobile, a dirigible, a submarine. The train travels through the heavens, past stars and comets, and flies into the yawning, open mouth of the sun. Again, turning to John Frazer: "Méliès predicted the technological wonders of our time with a sense of humor that retains the human dimension. . . . Living at a period of rapid social change, in the climate resulting from the accomplishments of the industrial revolution, Méliès employed the resources of technology to express emerging perceptions about the future."[43]

In their retro vision of Jules Verne, Méliès and Zeman achieved a disorienting *strangeness* of effect that, to me, is an essential element of steampunk in general. They reveled in their antique artifice, they gloried in it, no matter how crude or primitive it may seem in comparison to the glossier, more sophisticated adaptations to come later from Hollywood. Beginning in the 1950s and 1960s, *20,000 Leagues Under the Sea* (1954), *Journey to the Center of the Earth* (1959), *The Mysterious Island* (1961), and *Master of the World* (1961) tended to mute the *verfremdung* effect so essential to steampunk, emphasizing instead the *realism* of the machines and the effects of the monsters. The more real, the less fantastic. Conversely, the more surreal, the more an *independent reality* is achieved. Similarly, compare the relative clunkiness of television's *Wild, Wild West* (1965–1969) with its smoother, more sophisticated recent 1999 film version. Only the first version seems to derive naturally—or, unnaturally—from the mid-nineteenth-century era from which it properly springs.

Thus, when Zeman decides to add to Verne's story a cinematic device, he deliberately chooses a clumsy nineteenth-century magic lantern apparatus: Artigas returns from one of his criminal errands and brings with him "a new invention which causes pictures to move on a screen." He mounts a kind of Zoetrope device with flat, circular discs with images around the rim to a magic lantern, and he rotates them by crank in front of a magic lantern beam. The flickering, animated slide show is a kind of illustrated newspaper, featuring a story that reveals a move against Artigas's island by infantry and a submarine. The effect is engagingly clumsy, yet wholly consistent with the rest of the film's artifice.

Similarly, Zeman's quaint deployment of effects—stop-motion, paper cutouts, drawings, animation, painted backdrops and foregrounds, dissolves, miniatures and models, double exposures, still images, and traveling and stationary mattes—inflects the live action and renders it . . . *unfamiliar*. A meticulous craftsman, Zeman carefully contrives a *faux* crudity of these effects. Coming to life are the steel engravings so popular with Victorian illustrators and familiar to Verne's readers—in this case the celebrated illustrations by Verne's favorite illustrator, Leon Bennet (1873–1910), who illustrated twenty-five of the *Voyages Extraordinaires*. The striations of Bennet's images are cleverly duplicated on screen by inscribing on the characters' clothing and the sets imitations of the engraved line patterns and double-exposing live-action footage with striped screens. Thus, moving waves of *real* water take on the appearance of *engraved lines*. All the while, as we watch, we are caught up in the wonder of the artifice, which suspends us between the reality of live action and the fantasy of an animated dream. "The variety of tricks and superimpositions seems infinite," reported Pauline Kael in her aforementioned review. "As soon as you have one effect figured out another image appears to baffle you." One of several examples she cites is a scene of Artigas's sailors in their rowboat on the stormy seas: "The sailors in their little striped outfits are foreshortened by what appears to be the hand of a primitive artist. Then the waves move, the boat rises on the water, and when it lands, the little sailors—who are live actors—walk off, *still foreshortened* [my italics]."[44]

Historian Harriet R. Polt, writing in 1964, provides some on-site glimpses into Zeman's working methods:

> While I was at Gottwaldov last summer, Zeman was just shooting an exterior on the hill above the studio. The camera was set on a platform on which Zeman, his cameraman, and a couple of assistants, all in shirt-sleeves or shirtless, worked. . . . Erected on a rather flimsy scaffolding in front of the camera was an enlarged photograph of a drawing of a castle, with two wing-like projections (representing the sides of a road leading to the castle) coming out of its gates.[45]

He then combines photographed backgrounds and live action directly by the camera. For his interior scenes, "Zeman often uses small drawn scenes which are placed near the camera so as to appear large. A small area of a corner of the scene will be cut away, and through this the actual scene and the live actors will be photographed."[46]

The results of this attention to detail create the sort of delightful storybook quality that can be such an attractive aspect of steampunk. Howard Waldrop's delight is infectious, like a child savoring his first magic theater experience:

> There's a scene of a train coming down a track—the *train* is drawn; the *wheels* and the *tracks* are animated; the (real) engineer stands on an open platform in the engine's cab and (real) people lean out of the (drawn) passenger car. (It's so simple and powerful it takes your breath away.)[47]

Elsewhere, Waldrop notes:

> Actors walk through back-projected sets; at the same time they're walking *behind* animated full-sized paper cutouts of spinning flywheels and meshing gears, all this in front of a painted set in the middle-background. For maybe five seconds of screen time.[48]

A variety of other whimsical touches abound. When Count Artigas reaches for a pistol to shoot down Hart's departing balloon, it doesn't fire. He hands it to his assistant, who shrugs and, in close-up, *winds up* the pistol, which now rapidly spits out bullets. In another scene two fish, mirror images of each other, collide, melt into each other, and are transformed into a beautiful white butterfly that flutters easily away into the depths. As for the actors portraying the villains—at least the live-action ones as opposed to the paper cutouts and puppets—they behave on screen *like* puppets in a sort of Victorian slapstick manner, as if slightly pixilated (which they doubtless are, in one way or another). And yes, there's a trusty frock-coated gentleman appearing atop a steam coach and occasionally tooting his little trumpet for no apparent reason, other than it's the thing to do. All the while the music score rattles and bangs away, sometimes as a deranged harpsichord accompanying and imitating the actions of the bizarre machines, and sometimes as more velvety sounds in the strings cushioning the romantic moments.

Karel Zeman brings the imagination of Jules Verne and the vision of Georges Méliès into the world of today's steampunk culture. As first mate on the decks of Captain Nemo's *Nautilus*, he brings on board with him a most improbable machine. Cranked by hand, it is a clatter of intermittent movements and an engagement of wheels and gears. The beam of light it emits penetrates the darker reaches of our imagination. Through its agency, still images move, reality dreams, and a "never-was" converges with a "might-be." This fabulous apparatus is called the motion picture, and it magically traverses time and space, reality and fantasy. It provokes and disorients us, as all steampunk fantasies should do. Ursula Le Guin once best described the effect: "When fantasy is the real thing, nothing, after all, is realer."[49]

Notes

1. Jeff VanderMeer, *The Steampunk Bible*, coauthored with S. J. Chambers (New York: Abrams, 2011), 9. Writing in *Locus*, issue 315, April 1987, Jeter stated, "Personally, I think Victorian fantasies are going to be the next big thing, as long as we can come up with a fitting collective term . . . something based on the appropriate technology of the era; like 'steampunks,' perhaps."

2. Howard Waldrop and Lawrence Person, "The Fabulous World of Jules Verne," *Locus online* (13 October 2004), n.p., http://voyagesextraordinaires.blogspot.com/2007/12 Fabulous-world-of-julesvere1958.html (4 February 2012).

3. See Thomas C. Renzi, *Jules Verne on Film* (Jefferson, N.C.: McFarland, 1998), 52–58.

4. Verne's fifty-four-volume series, *Voyages extraordinaires*, was inaugurated in 1866 with *The Adventures of Captain Hatteras* and over the next half century would comprise sixty-four works.

5. Pauline Kael, "The Deadly Invention," quoted in *5001 Nights at the Movies* (New York: Henry Holt, 1982), 179.

6. For details about Czech animation in the 1940s through the early 1960s, see Harriet R. Polt, "The Czechoslovak Animated Film," *Film Quarterly* 17, no. 3 (Spring, 1964): 31–40. These quotations are from pages 32–34.

7. *Na kometě* (*Off on a Comet*) can be seen in its entirety on www.youtube.com/watch?v=LQe5_zKeNzA, and *Ukradena vzducholod* (*The Stolen Airship*) on www.you tube.com/watch?v=1dobJ1PJcDk.

8. Quoted in Jan Velinger, "Karel Zeman—Author of Czech Animated Films Including the Mixed-Animation Classic, 'Journey to the Beginning of Time,'" www.radio.cy/en/section/czechs/karel-zeman.

9. See www.london.czechcentres.cz/programme/travel-events/karel-zeman.

10. Mike Ashley, "When Steampunk Was Real," in *Steampunk Prime: A Vintage Steampunk Reader*, ed. Mike Ashley (New York: Nonstop Press, 2012), 8.

11. Herbert R. Lottman, *Jules Verne: An Exploratory Biography* (New York: St. Martin's Press, 1996), 44.

12. Novalis, *Henry von Ofterdingen*, trans. Palmer Hilty (New York: Frederick Ungar, 1982), 77.

13. Quoted in John C. Tibbetts, *The Gothic Imagination* (New York: Palgrave Macmillan, 2011), 354.

14. Lottman, *Jules Verne: An Exploratory Biography*, 335–336.

15. Lottman, *Jules Verne: An Exploratory Biography*, 101–103.

16. Peter Costello, *Jules Verne: Inventor of Science Fiction* (New York: Scribner, 1978), 186.

17. Isaac Asimov, *Asimov on Science Fiction* (New York: Doubleday, 1981), 185.

18. Kingsley Amis, *New Maps of Hell* (New York: Harcourt, Brace, 1960), 34.

19. Arthur C. Clarke, Introduction to Jules Verne, *From the Earth to the Moon* (New York: Dodd, Mead, 1962), viii.

20. Lottman, *Jules Verne: An Exploratory Biography*, 303.

21. Lottman, *Jules Verne: An Exploratory Biography*, 295.

22. Costello, *Jules Verne: Inventor of Science Fiction*, 165.

23. Brian Aldiss, *Billion Year Spree* (New York: Doubleday, 1973), 96.

24. In *The Begum's Fortune*, the evil Professor Schultz builds a secret arms factory intended to produce weapons of mass destruction against its targets. "It will be a whole battery hurled through space," explains Schultz, describing the operation of the cannon and its shells, "to carry flame and death into a town by covering it with a shower of inextinguishable fire!" "The Begum's Fortune," in *Strange Signposts: An Anthology of the Fantastic*, ed. Sam Moskowitz (New York: Holt, Rinehart and Winston, 1966), 109.

25. This remarkable but little-known story, which contains a clockwork man of demonic aspect, reveals the influence of the German master of the Gothic tale, E. T. A. Hoffmann, particularly in tales like "The Sandman," which features clockwork automatons. See "Master Zacharias," in *Science Fiction: Stories and Contexts*, ed. Heather Masri (New York: Bedford/St. Martin's, 2008), 478–503. All quotations are taken from this edition.

26. Masri, *Science Fiction: Stories and Contexts*, 486.

27. Masri, *Science Fiction: Stories and Contexts*, 494.

28. In its description and operation, it prefigures modern rocketry, particularly the Nazi V-2 rockets and the ICBMs of today. All quotations from *For the Flag* are taken from an anonymous translation first published in America in 1897 and later republished by Hurst and F. M. Lupton in 1903.

29. Verne's trip to America in 1867 on *The Great Eastern* steamship had a profound impact on his books. Upon returning to France after six days of tours of New York, Brooklyn, Albany, and Niagara Falls, he set portions of *20,000 Leagues Under the Sea* and twenty-nine other novels in the areas he had observed. "It is hard to think of any other major nineteenth-century writer," claims biographer William Butcher, "who rejected his roots to the extent of attempting to think in another culture." See William Butcher, *Jules Verne* (New York: Thunder's Mouth Press, 2006). See 209, 75–182. Even before this, Verne's reading of two American writers, James Fennimore Cooper and Edgar Allan Poe, had had a decisive impact on his own work.

30. Jules Verne, *For the Flag*, 4.

31. Jules Verne, *For the Flag*, 38.

32. Jules Verne, *For the Flag*, 115.

33. In Wells's later story, also published in Verne's lifetime, "The New Accelerator" (1903), two men take a drug that speeds up their bodies' systems and observe the retarded movements of people, animals, and vehicles, a mimicking of film's slow-motion effect. And foreshadowing the camera's high-angle shot, the narrator of *The War of the Worlds* describes the evacuation of London as if "seen from a balloonist's perspective." See Thomas C. Renzi, *H. G. Wells: Six Scientific Romances Adapted for Film* (Metuchen, N.J.: Scarecrow Press, 1992), 6.

34. Terry Ramsaye, "Robert Paul and *The Time Machine*," in Harry M. Geduld, *The Definitive Time Machine* (Bloomington: Indiana University Press, 1987), 196.

35. Quoted in Ramsaye, "Robert Paul and *The Time Machine*," 196.

36. In "Master Zacharias" the mad clockmaker, Zacharias, declares, "I cannot die, I, the first watchmaker in the world; I, who, by means of these pieces and diverse wheels, have been able to regulate the movement with absolute precision! Have I not subjected time to exact laws, and can I not dispose of it like a despot? Before a sublime genius had arranged these wandering hours regularly, in what vast uncertainty was human destiny plunged? . . . I have regulated time, time would end with me! It would return to the infinite, whence my genius has rescued it." See Masri, *Science Fiction: Stories and Contexts*, 491.

37. Quoted in Costello, *Jules Verne: Inventor of Science Fiction*, 188. In *The Carpathian Castle* (1889) Verne imagines an apparatus that only tangentially could be considered a progenitor to the talking picture. He made use of Edison's improved phonograph with its wax cylinders, used in conjunction with mirrored reflections, to convince a superstitious crowd of people that the ghost of a dead opera singer can be seen and heard. But even here, avers biographer Peter Costello, "no hint of the possibilities of the film camera seems to have reached him. [*The Carpathian Castle*] in no way presages film or television," 181.

38. Perhaps more than just a footnote is the fact that when Wells's *First Men on the Moon* was published in 1901, a year before the appearance of Méliès's *Trip to the*

Moon, the narrator refers to a story by Jules Verne called *Trip to the Moon*. Why did he not cite Verne's original title *From the Earth to the Moon*? Did this perhaps influence Méliès's subsequent choice of title?

39. Quoted in John Frazer, *Artificially Arranged Scenes: The Films of Georges Méliès* (Boston: Hall, 1979), 99.

40. Costello, *Jules Verne: Inventor of Science Fiction*, 147.

41. Lynda Nead, *The Haunted Gallery: Painting, Photography, Film*, c. 1900 (New Haven and London: Yale University Press, 2007), 222–230.

42. Frazer, *Artificially Arranged Scenes: The Films of Georges Méliès*, 99.

43. Frazer, *Artificially Arranged Scenes: The Films of Georges Méliès*, 149.

44. Pauline Kael, "The Deadly Invention," in *5001 Nights at the Movies*, 179.

45. Harriet R. Polt, "The Czechoslovak Animated Film," *Film Quarterly*, Vol. 17 (Spring 1964), 37–38.

46. Polt, "The Czechoslovak Animated Film," 37–38.

47. Waldrop and Person, "The Fabulous World of Jules Verne," *Locus online*, n.p.

48. Waldrop and Person, "The Fabulous World of Jules Verne," *Locus online*, n.p.

49. Ursula Le Guin, "From Elfland to Poughkeepsie," in *The Language of the Night: Essays on Fantasy and Science Fiction, Ursula K. Le Guin*, ed. Susan Wood (New York: Perigree Books, 1979), 95.

Bibliography

Aldiss, Brian. *Billion Year Spree*. New York: Doubleday, 1973.

Amis, Kingsley. *New Maps of Hell*. New York: Harcourt, Brace, 1960.

Ashley, Mike. "When Steampunk Was Real." 8–10 in *Steampunk Prime: A Vintage Steampunk Reader*, ed. Mike Ashley. New York: Nonstop Press, 2012.

Asimov, Isaac. *Asimov on Science Fiction*. New York: Doubleday, 1981.

Butcher, William. *Jules Verne*. New York: Thunder's Mouth Press, 2006.

Clarke, Arthur C. Introduction to Jules Verne, *From the Earth to the Moon*. New York: Dodd, Mead, 1962.

Costello, Peter. *Jules Verne: Inventor of Science Fiction*. New York: Scribner, 1978.

Frazer, John. *Artificially Arranged Scenes: The Films of Georges Méliès*. Boston: Hall, 1979.

Jeter, K. W. "Steampunks." *Locus* 315 (April 1987), quoted in Rick Klaw, "The Steam-Driven Time Machine." 349–356 in *Steampunk*, ed. Ann and Jeff Vander-Meer. San Francisco: Tachyon Publications, 2008.

Kael, Pauline. "The Deadly Invention." 179 in *5001 Nights at the Movies*. New York: Holt, 1982.

Le Guin, Ursula, "From Elfland to Poughkeepsie." 83–95 in *The Language of the Night: Essays on Fantasy and Science Fiction, Ursula K. Le Guin*, ed. Susan Wood. New York: Perigree Books, 1979.

Lottman, Herbert R. *Jules Verne: An Exploratory Biography*. New York: St. Martin's Press, 1996.

Miller, Cynthia. "Steampunk." 351–356 in John C. Tibbetts, *The Gothic Imagination*. New York: Palgrave Macmillan, 2011.

Nead, Lynda. *The Haunted Gallery: Painting, Photography, Film, c. 1900*. New Haven and London: Yale University Press, 2007.

Novalis. *Henry von Ofterdingen*. Trans. Palmer Hilty. New York: Frederick Ungar, 1982.

Polt, Harriet R. "The Czechoslovak Animated Film." *Film Quarterly* 17, no. 3 (Spring 1964): 31–40.

Ramsaye, Terry. "Robert Paul and *The Time Machine*." 196–203 in *The Definitive Time Machine*, ed. Harry M. Geduld. Bloomington: Indiana University Press, 1987.

Renzi, Thomas C. *H. G. Wells: Six Scientific Romances Adapted for Film*. Metuchen, N.J.: Scarecrow Press, 1992.

———. *Jules Verne on Film*. Jefferson, N.C.: McFarland, 1998.

VanderMeer, Jeff, and S. J. Chambers. *The Steampunk Bible: An Illustrated Guide to the World of Imaginary Airships, Corsets and Goggles, Mad Scientists, and Strange Literature*. New York: Abrams Image, 2011.

Velinger, Jan. "Karel Zeman—Author of Czech Animated Films Including the Mixed-Animation Classic, 'Journey to the Beginning of Time.'" www.radio.cy/en/section/Czechs/karel-zeman (10 February 2012).

Verne, Jules. *For the Flag*, anonymous translation. London: Hurst and F. M. Lupton, 1903.

———. "Master Zacharias." 478–503 in *Science Fiction: Stories and Contexts*, ed. Heather Masri. New York: Bedford/St. Martin's, 2008.

———. "The Begum's Fortune." 105–117 in *Strange Signposts: An Anthology of the Fantastic*, ed. Sam Moskowitz. New York: Holt, Rinehart and Winston, 1966.

Waldrop, Howard, and Lawrence Person. "The Fabulous World of Jules Verne," *Locus online*, 13 October 2004. http://voyagesextraordinaires.blogspot.com/2007/12/fabulous-world-of-jules-verne-1958.html (February 2012).

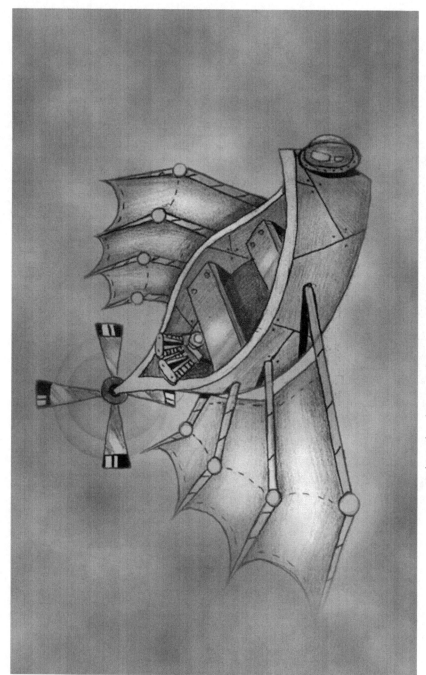

Airships: the ultimate in luxury travel. Copyright Jody Steel

CHAPTER EIGHT

Airships East, Zeppelins West: Steampunk's Fantastic Frontiers

Cynthia J. Miller

Steampunk is a generative force that brings motion and vitality to the worlds in which it appears. It mobilizes and transforms—animates, reconstructs, and renews—bringing fantastic machines to life, and with them, the dreams and ambitions of their creators. Gears whir, propellers gyrate, and mechanical marvels surge, flip, roll, and hum. Just as its anachronistic blending of technologies bends time, steampunk also folds space, collapsing near and far, bringing imaginative creations to geographic frontiers at the far corners of the world and providing a geographic playground for the frontiers of the imagination.

Reaching those frontiers has often called for wondrous forms of transportation to carry people and ideas across land, sea, and air: intricate flying machines and brightly colored balloons; trains and automobiles powered by steam; imposing undersea vessels; and even rocket-powered high-wheeled bicycles. Rescued from the dustbin of impossibility, inventions such as Leonardo da Vinci's fifteenth-century ornithopter and Samuel Pierpont Langley's much later Aerodrome have found life, and flight, in the steampunk universe as the genre's call to motion urges artists, writers, and filmmakers onward.

While fantastic transportation of all sorts, from rockets to motorcars, is a hallmark of steampunk's mingling of the strange and the familiar, it is the airship that truly serves as an icon of the genre's assault on the frontiers of time and space. Sleek, silver-skinned vessels that crawl through the skies, casting shadows over nineteenth-century worlds below, airships, in their many forms and guises, embody steampunk's imaginative power, even as they reference present-day nostalgia for the early years of flight. These slow-moving giants of the sky impart a sense of wonder to travel, blurring the lines between past and present, as they carry intrepid voyagers east and west, as far as their imaginations will go.

This chapter, then, examines the role of the airship in steampunk's engagement with frontiers, old and new, in film and literature—serving as spectacle, symbol of progress, and vessel of exploration and independence—and argues that the presence of airships, wherever they are found, embodies the promise that frontiers still exist. Airship captains and pirates are, in much the same ways as their historical predecessors, intrepid adventurers who defy the boundaries of convention and chart courses that few others follow—and in the same way, their anachronistic adventures signal the onset of a new era made possible by technology. Whether serving as an icon of "progress" in an alternate history or a gleaming, lighter-than-air testimony to the magic of the machine; gliding across the Wild West, in televised series such as *The Adventures of Brisco County, Jr.* (1993–1994), or the Exotic East, in literary works such as Joe Lansdale's novel *Zeppelins West* (2001), steampunk airships conquer both time and space and proclaim the air the frontier of the speculative future.

Steampunk's Fantastic Transportation

Steampunk's wondrous conveyances have served gentlemen explorers and lower-class dreamers, alike. In early "scientific romance" and other proto-steampunk novels and stories, such as Jules Verne's *20,000 Leagues Under the Sea* (1869), intellectuals, scientists, and well-bred adventurers journeyed to the far reaches of the known world in imaginative inventions such as the famous underwater vessel the *Nautilus*, while in a slightly later work, *The Steam House, Part I: The Demon of Cawnpore* (1880), four Englishmen journey across exotic India in a huge steam-powered mechanical elephant. These well-heeled adventurers are joined, however, by figures of another sort—rough-and-tumble, dissatisfied, working-class characters who also seek to leave their mark on the world. They are the innovators of the New World, using fantastic technology in relentless pursuit of the American Dream—the heroes of what has come to be known as the "Edisonade." As Jeff Vander-Meer explains in *The Steampunk Bible*:

> The Edisonade was the science fiction form of the dime novel and typically featured a young boy inventor escaping his stagnating environment and . . . heading West using a steam vehicle built from scratch.[1]

The earliest of these, Edward S. Ellis's oft-imitated "The Huge Hunter, or the Steam Man of the Prairies" (1868), featured the titular Steam Man as a rickshaw-pulling figure that conveys the tale's protagonist westward to fortune and glory.[2] Ellis's tale would inspire many, but among those, it was Luis Senarens whose dime novel stories expanded the domain of proto-steampunk, as he chronicled the inventions and adventures of Frank Reade, and the two generations of descendants that would follow him: "distinguished inventors of marvelous machines in the line of steam and electricity."[3] Senarens's tales of the Age of Invention featured the globe-trotting Reades and their spectacular array of futuristic creations: all-terrain vehicles like the *Thunderer*, an eight-wheeled tank-ship hybrid heralded as the "New Electric Terror"; the Steam Horse, "a new method of rapid travel without need of rails"; submarines; flying boats; and so much more.[4]

As steampunk scholars such as VanderMeer and Jess Nevins note of these early proto-steampunk works, the ties that exist between their anachronistic inventions and the wider systems of power in their narrative worlds are complex.[5] Imperialism, social class, repression, and ethnocentric notions of progress run rampant through their tales of expansion and conquest.[6] Products of their era, these adventures cast for the working class are shot through with what VanderMeer terms "unapologetic racism and jingoism."[7] Fantastic science and technology, in these tales, facilitates the exploitation and domination of far-off lands and their inhabitants, in ways that mirror the real-life exploits of adventurer-explorers of their day, such as Martin and Osa Johnson, Albert Blinkhorn, and Campbell Beasley, all of whom yielded to the tendency to cast exotic Others and their locales as supporting players in their own bids for fame and fortune.[8]

In the Edisonades' gentlemanly counterparts, these political-philosophical issues come under a bit more scrutiny—openly interrogated in some, while, in others, simply laid bare, offering readers the opportunity to consider the implications of technological advancement in the service of political and social power. In sometimes highly divergent ways, both Verne and his British contemporary H. G. Wells overtly commented on prevailing notions of progress through their narratives of gentlemen adventurers. Both displayed an awareness of the potential for misuse of the great power wielded by scientists and inventors, interweaving their science fiction narratives with cautionary warnings. Verne, however, confined his observations to issues of science and technology, while Wells, recognizing that such misuse seldom happened without the blessing of government and industry—and often, the support of the public at large—was inclined to craft broader cautionary tales about the relationship between science and power.

Later in the twentieth century, as steampunk moved toward an identity as a distinct and self-conscious genre, themes of extraordinary transportation that held the power to obliterate frontiers became more highly elaborate, and flying machines, underwater vessels, fantastic vehicles, and even subterranean conveyances conquered air, sea, and land. Drawing on inspiration provided by the "iron mole" featured in Edgar Rice Burroughs's novel *At the Earth's Core* (1914), steampunk pioneer James Blaylock created the "subterranean prospector" of *The Digging Leviathan* (1984)—a digging machine designed to travel to the center of the Earth. Gurney steam carriages traversed the roadways of William Gibson and Bruce Sterling's *The Difference Engine* (1991), while dirigibles and dreadnoughts advanced the interests of the British Empire. Imaginative visions such as these were carried forward in publications like the 1999 illustrated series *The League of Extraordinary Gentlemen*. Written by renowned graphic novelist Alan Moore and illustrated by Kevin O'Neill, the series merged several science fictional worlds that featured warring airships and an updated version of Verne's fantastic vessel *Nautilus*.

That same year, steampunk's time-defying inventions filled the silver screen, as a former Civil War hero and his inventor sidekick—headquartered in a Victorian steam train brimming over with gleaming brass gadgetry and marvels of scientific advancement—rescued President Ulysses S. Grant from captivity, in Barry Sonnenfeld's *Wild Wild West* (1999). The pair battled the evil Dr. Arliss Loveless and his giant mechanical spider as it strode across the barren Western landscape, in order to save the president and the country. The glistening gears and long, lingering close-ups of larger-than-life mechanisms gave testimony to the film's fascination with anachronistic technology.

While its affection for and appropriation of Victorian aesthetics and technology carried forward in the genre's late-twentieth-century texts, there was a critical difference in steampunk's contemporary sociopolitical outlook. As Nevins discusses, steampunk writers are all too aware of the realities that the Edisonade

> writers were ignorant of or chose to dismiss. . . . Accompanying this lack of innocence is an anger and a rebellion against much of what the Edisonade's [sic] stood for.[9]

That "anger and rebellion" at proto-steampunk's seemingly unconsidered approach to social and political issues resulted in twentieth-century steampunk writers' tendency to deconstruct or parody their predecessors; later generations critiqued, from a contemporary sociopolitical stance, those who came before, frequently demonstrating more affinity for the sentiments of Wells than Senarens, or even Verne, and seeing in steampunk a vehicle for social change. This stance, in turn, influenced the ways in which steampunk's fantastic creations have approached the frontiers of time and space.

As the genre entered the twenty-first century, its literary and cinematic presence expanded by leaps and bounds, with novels by authors such as Cherie Priest, Scott Westerfeld, and China Miéville, and films such as *The League of Extraordinary Gentlemen* (2003), *Van Helsing* (2004), and *The Golden Compass* (2007). Its library of tales, however, has embraced notions of egalitarianism and espoused the expansion of knowledge and experience over conquest and exploitation, frequently offering active critique of the latter. As adventurers of all classes and castes—captains and pirates alike—have ventured forth, they have done so in amazing vehicles and vessels that carried them to the far corners of the globe. Among these, airships—balloons, flying ships, zeppelins—have served as one of the genre's most versatile icons. As these fantastic flying machines have taken flight in steampunk, they have given expression to the organic impulses of alternative history—blending steam, propellers, balloons, and all manner of vehicular form—while at the same time, remaining lightly tethered to the "real world" conception of the airship, prior to its passing into the annals of history.

The Spectacle of Flight

The history of flight has always been one of imaginative spectacle. From the paper and cloth contraptions of the Montgolfiers in 1783, to eighteenth- and nineteenth-century gliders, aerodromes, and autogyros, to the Wright brothers' first heavier-than-air flight at the dawn of the twentieth century, flight has beckoned humans to create—to innovate—and to dream. Nineteenth-century aeronautical pioneer Sir George Cayley spoke of the air as "an uninterrupted navigable ocean that comes to the threshold of everyman's door," but even as Cayley's era came and went, no practical vessel existed for controlled flight.[10] The motorized, steerable balloon—the dirigible—was seen as aviation's best hope, and as Botting relates, "The quest for the right combination of design, power and material enlivened the skies over several nations."[11] Scientists and showmen, engineers and aristocrats all rose to the challenge of making dirigible flight a reality. Some had wings, others sails, still others, paddle wheels. England, France, and Germany all engaged their most creative scientific and military minds in order to bring into being the mammoths of the skies now known collectively as "airships."

Journalists and cartoonists envisioned flights of fancy: balloon taxis cruising for fares in the airspace above city streets, intercity balloon coaches, and a worldwide network of lighter-than-air passenger transports. Drawings and designs ranged from the impractical to the outlandish. An early dolphin-shaped dirigible lowered its tail to ascend and raised its tail for descent.[12] A French clockmaker created and built his own model powered by clockworks. Designers envisioned airborne horses, birds under harness, and even a screw-shaped airship that was meant to literally bore through the air as a drill bit pierces wood. Some even laid claim to success: in 1834, the European Aeronautical Society opened the world's first airline office in London, promoting ticket sales for passenger airship service between London and Paris on an oar-powered dirigible named the *Eagle*—a vessel that burst during inflation and was torn to pieces by a mob of angry investors.[13] For some, these were machines that dreams were made of; for others, who lost fortunes or sustained injuries, they were the stuff of nightmares.

After years of failure—fabric ripped midair, disastrous fires, uncontrollable navigation—Count Ferdinand von Zeppelin launched the rigid airship that would become synonymous with his name in July 1900. Over ten thousand Germans, Austrians, and Swiss gathered in Friedrichshafen to witness the launch that captured the imaginations of royalty and commoners alike. Rumored to be "as high as a church and as long as an oceangoing steamer," the dirigible was, in fact, 407 feet long, contained seventeen separate balloon compartments filled with hydrogen gas, and carried two aluminum gondolas. It was towed on a raft into the open water of Lake Constance, and the now-historic words "Airship ready for takeoff" were uttered, signaling the beginning of a new era in manned flight.[14] The dirigible rose, but its voyage came to a halt only eighteen minutes later. The initial flight of the *Zeppelin* was, at best, a marginal success, but, as journalist-explorer Eugene Wolf declared, "One thing it did show—dirigible flight is a reality."[15]

Indeed, dirigible flight *was* a reality, and once refined, it became integrated into elegant travel, commercialism, and warfare. "Zeppelin Fever"—fascination for what Flaherty called "those domesticated dinosaurs of the sky"—spread throughout the Western world.[16] Spectacular travel posters were commissioned by the Zeppelin-Hamburg line to advertise its flights within Germany, as well as to Brazil and the United States. Post offices issued special airmail stamps, and commemorative medals were struck in honor of inaugural flights. Postcards, picture books, sheet music, and even towels were emblazoned with the airships' likenesses, a number of which still exist, along with thousands of glass negatives, only hinting at the impact of the *Zeppelin* on its era and those that followed. Each summer, since 1975, the Städtisches Bodensee-Museum in Friedrichshafen has mounted special exhibits celebrating the zeppelin's golden age, such as "The *Hindenburg* as

AIRSHIP
ANDY

FRANK V. WEBSTER

Popular literature reflected the public's love affair with airships.

a Flying Hotel," "The World Flight of the *Graf Zeppelin*," and "The South American Voyages," which are viewed by some three hundred thousand visitors.[17] As fantastic vessels that brought about the conquest of Cayley's "ocean" of the air—the frontier of the sky—dirigibles captured and held imaginations around the world for generations.

The age of the colossus of the air came to a close, however, beginning in 1937, when the *Hindenburg* was destroyed by a disastrous fire as onlookers watched in horror. After the *Hindenburg* disaster, passenger flights using hydrogen-inflated airships were no longer permitted. The following year, Germany announced the annexation of Austria, rekindling fears of a European war, and helium sales to the country—the major manufacturer of airships—were halted for fear that the vessels would be used for military purposes. But while smaller nonrigid blimps served as convoy escorts, large rigid airships had no part in the war. In early 1940, the two remaining zeppelins were destroyed and their metal harvested for military aircraft, and their hangars were leveled to facilitate takeoffs of Luftwaffe bombers. By 1944, Allied bombers had destroyed all the zeppelin construction facilities, and all remnants of the grandeur that was the airship were gone. The mystique of the airship, however, remained, with vessels such as the zeppelin becoming symbols of a lost Golden Age.

Airships as Magical Technology

All across science fiction, anachronistic or not, lighter-than-air conveyances were also playing major roles. Edgar Allan Poe's "The Balloon Hoax" (1844), Verne's *Five Weeks in a Balloon* (1863), and Mark Twain's *Tom Sawyer Abroad* (1894) all feature spectacular balloons, as did numerous other tales. But in 1887, a new airship was written into being: Verne's heavier-than-air ship-turned-flying machine, the *Albatross*. A hybrid wonder of imagination, it sailed through the skies under the power of thirty-seven propellers reaching up from its deck, with its brash inventor Robur at the helm, in *The Clipper of the Clouds*:

> Some strange phenomenon had occurred in the higher zones of the atmosphere, a phenomenon of which neither nature nor the cause could be explained. To-day [sic] it appeared over America; forty-eight hours afterwards it was over Europe; a week later, it was in Asia over the Celestial Empire.[18]

It was not long before other sky-faring vessels took on a proto-steampunk character. In Rudyard Kipling's story "With the Night Mail" (1905), a journalist's account of a night on a nuclear-powered airship is set in the year 2000, when airships are as ubiquitous as the steamships of Kipling's day. With names like *Zephyr*, *Helios*, and *Thunderbolt*, these early images of flying machines reflected many of the fantastic imaginings of their day and—unfettered by compliance with the laws of physics or the dictates of practicality—adapted, parodied, and amplified them in ways that exceeded the wildest dreams of even their most ingenious real-world counterparts. Kipling wrote of the captivating technology—the Fleury Ray—that made steel-hulled dirigibles possible:

> Fleury's Ray dances in violet-green bands and whirled turbillions of flame. The jointed U-tubes of the vacuum-chamber are pressure-tempered colloid (no glass would endure the strain for an instant) and a junior engineer with tinted spectacles watches the Ray intently. It is the very heart of the machine—a mystery to this day.[19]

This speculative practice of combining meticulous technological detail with expansive imagination has come to characterize the anachronistic creations of contemporary steampunk: the ability to envision painstakingly accurate, yet fantastic, technologies. As Lavie Tidhar contends: "The underlying theme of all fiction within the Steampunk sphere resorts to that moment whereby technology transcends and becomes, for all intents and purposes, magical."[20]

In her essay "Reclaiming the Machine," Rebecca Onion argues that the interest of steampunk authors and creators lies less in the transcendent qualities of nineteenth-century technology than in its "spectacular failures"—as exemplars of the era's sense of "daring"—citing the airship as prime among these.[21] She suggests that it is the association with large-scale disaster, such as the tragedy of the *Hindenburg*, and all the lesser-known calamities and misfortunes that preceded it, that has given the airship its prominent place in steampunk's multitextual universe. The airship's symbolic value is, however, far more complex, as is suggested by its persistence in popular culture in the face of its inability to persist in the history of flight. These colossal ships represent humans' attempts to control the forces of nature. Their failures, great and small, are intimately bound up with their successes—two sides of the same coin, if you will—comprising the magic of possibility and the possibility of magic.

Magic, as Marcel Mauss observed, is inextricably linked to the wish—the desire for fantasy to be fulfilled, and for longings, dreams, and visions to become a reality—it represents the attempt to move beyond the realm of

Airships render distances irrelevant and barriers negligible. *Copyright Jody Steel*

known possibilities, into the desired unknown.[22] For much of human history, flight had been one such fantasy, linked to utopian visions of travel, conquest, and advancement of the human condition.[23] The ability to fly, itself a marvel, would lead to untold wonders of its own—not merely breaking barriers of time (turning weeks of travel into days) and space (collapsing the distance between locations) but altering the face of communication, warfare, and scientific discovery. The rise of technologies of flight, then, was both a response to a collective yearning for magic and magical in its own right, casting scientists and engineers as modern-day magicians. Dostoyevsky alluded to this interconnection of man, magic, and technology when he declared, "Since man cannot live without miracles, he will provide himself with miracles of his own making."[24]

In their time, and for generations to come, vessels of lighter-than-air travel were certainly just that—miraculous—if not for their beauty, for their sheer size:

> The *Diana* was the newly launched pride of British Imperial Airways, an orca shape eight hundred fifty feet long sheathed in silver-gray doped cotton, more than two hundred feet around at the broadest point, a third of the way between blunt nose and cruciform tailfins.[25]

While the rise of technology in society is typically associated with the death of magic, destroying, as Richard Stivers notes, "the sense of mystery that seems essential to human existence," airships, in fact, create, maintain, and retrieve that essential sense of mystery, carrying it forward for generations.[26] Perhaps more than any other means of fantastic transport, these mammoths of the air are artifacts of modern magic, and the inventors and designers who brought them into being, conjurers who bent lightning to their will and harnessed the wind. Their captains and crew—the brave hero, the dogged intellectual, and the inquisitive "everyman"—manned airships to the east and zeppelins to the west, in search of adventure, glory, and knowledge. From Senarens's young Frank Reade Jr., to Joe Lansdale's disembodied head of Buffalo Bill Cody, to Cherie Priest's Andan Cly, all embodied a spirit of adventure so far-reaching that it could not help but stretch beyond the bounds of the nineteenth century.[27]

The airships that plied the skies of the real world in the early twentieth century evoked, for both their passengers and those who watched them glide overhead, an overwhelming sense of awe. Their seemingly effortless progress among the clouds, and their stately arrivals and departures, matched the gentility of the environment they provided for those on board. Steampunk's imaginative airships represent a similar constellation of magical sky-faring technologies, daring pilots, and genteel passengers, and evoke a similar sense of wonder—one deepened by the fact that their imaginary voyages are more fantastic than any undertaken in the real world. Steampunk thus creates, through its airships, what Margaret Rose cites as "an imaginative engagement between the present and the past" through overlapping forms of meaning making, or what Steffen Hantke terms a "unique historical ability to reflect the present moment."[28] Airships arose, in their real-world incarnations, in an era marked by innovation and the consumption of spectacle—a time when grand theatrical performances, World's Fairs, and motion pictures thrilled their audiences; city skylines glowed with the power of alternating current while neon lit their streets; and ocean liners taller than an eight-story building carried thousands across the Atlantic in a single passage. Even in such an era, these grand vessels of the sky seemed dazzling and anachronistic, long before they were appropriated and rearticulated in late-twentieth-century literature, art, and film.

Fantastic Frontiers

Magical . . . spectacular . . . evocative . . . the airship transcends its assemblage of beams, propellers, gears, and valves to become something laden with meaning, wonder, and nostalgia. This transcendence into magic also offers a means for understanding the vessel's ability to create and re-create fantastic frontiers. On majestic vessels that "bore them onward high above the reams of mortals," airship voyagers were "awed and silent while all the wondrous panorama of our world was spread out before them like some grand landscape under the wand of a mighty magician."[29] The powerful airships rendered irrelevant geographic obstacles that had hitherto excluded all but the heartiest adventurers: mountains, seas, glaciers, and jungles all melted away, no longer able to impede either adventure or progress across the frontiers of civilization. Truly, for airship voyagers, the sky was not the "limit," but rather the promise of limitlessness. Writing in 1905, Brazilian airship pioneer Alberto Santos-Dumont—already famous for his jaunts in Parisian skies—imagined the God's-eye view of the world that an "aerial yacht" of the near future might give its owner and his guests:

> We shall watch the stars rise. We shall hang between the constellations and the earth. We shall awake to the glory of the morning. So day shall succeed to day. We shall pass frontiers. Now we are over Russia—it would be a pity to stop—let us make a loop and return by way of Hungary and Austria. Here is Warsaw! Let us set the propeller working full speed to change our course. Perhaps we shall fall in with a current that will take us to Belgrade?[30]

This notion of seemingly endless possibility is a hallmark of the age of the airship, and part of its ongoing appeal. Paul Di Filippo, author of *The Steampunk Trilogy* (1995), celebrates the perception of unfettered growth that existed in this era of invention and discovery: "There were still frontiers. There were fewer laws and governing bodies. Who wouldn't want all of those things back?"[31] Frontiers signaled opportunity, but this was often tied to class and caste, with travel-as-experience often limited to those of wealth or status. Technological advancement altered that relationship, loosening, or at least shifting, the links between social class and the means of experiencing the world. Just as the Grand Tour had valorized experiencing the known world for European elites of the seventeenth and eighteenth centuries, and the "Cook's Tour" via rail transit had opened cultural and geographic frontiers for the middle class in the mid-nineteenth century, airships continued the tradition of grand travel, by promising to make the enterprise of long-distance voyages fast, effortless, and spectacular—with journeys as wondrous as their destinations.

In steampunk literature and film, airship travelers—from the genteel elite, to globe-trotting inventors, to rough-and-ready working-class adventurers—continue to reach out to explore and redefine the frontier. To the east, west, north, south, and points in between, the footprints of bold airship adventurers may be found, as they experience people and places few Victorian travelers ever saw. A dozen zeppelins, floating like "brightly colored cigars" that "God had clumsily dropped from his humidor," deliver Buffalo Bill Cody—or his head, at least, in a Mason jar mounted atop a steam-driven robot—and his Wild West performers to the Exotic East for a performance before the emperor of Japan, in Joe R. Lansdale's *Zeppelins West*.[32] From the promenade deck of *Old Paint*, the traveling show's main airship, Cody looks out over the exotic land below:

> Japan swelled up to meet them, showed them fishing villages of stick and thatch and little running figures. Farther inland the sticks gave way to thousands of colorful soldier tents tipped with wind-snapped flags as far as the eye could see. Samurai, in bright leather, carrying long spears with banners attached and swords at their sides, lifted their helmet-covered heads to watch the zeppelins drop.[33]

Similarly, scientist and explorer Langdon St. Ives voyages by zeppelin to South America in James Blaylock's short story "Lord Kelvin's Machine." Standing at the rocky rim of a volcanic cone, he surveys a landscape so unfamiliar, it could as easily be lunar as Peruvian, the mountainside falling "two thousand feet toward steamy, open fissures, the entire crater glowing like the bowl of an enormous pipe."[34] Northern frontiers are portrayed as equally breathtaking—and treacherous. The daring young inventor Frank Reade and his sister Kate (a *female* airship pilot) are featured in numerous dime novel illustrations of their proto-steampunk polar adventures, breaking through icebergs and enacting near-impossible rescues in desolate northern seas with their helicopter airships, after other seasoned (real world) Arctic explorers, such as Roald Amundsen and dirigible captain Umberto Nobile, were lost or stranded.[35]

Zeppelins and balloons alike are buffeted by the strong winds of other northern skies in Philip Pullman's novel *The Golden Compass* (as well as in its film adaptation). Svalbard, home of ice bears and magical Northern Lights, is portrayed in tales of

> slow crawling glaciers, of the rocks and ice floes where the bright-tusked walruses lay in groups of a hundred or more, of the seas teeming with seals . . . of the great grim iron-bound coast, the cliffs a thousand feet or more high . . . the coalpits and the fire mines where the bearsmiths hammered out mighty sheets of iron and riveted them into armor.[36]

It is not difficult to envision anachronistic airships in frontiers such as these. They seem of a piece, set apart from everyday life—like St. Ives's "tiny airship" at the foot of the Peruvian mountains, "moored like an alien vessel amid the bunch grasses and tola bush," or Frank Reade's "gallant craft" at the Pole, as it "soared on higher and higher," narrowly avoiding an enormous iceberg.[37] These exotic, otherworldly frontiers outside the world generally known to Victorians provide the perfect setting for all manner of retrofuturism, and the appearance of zeppelins, flying ice ships, and helicopter dirigibles does not particularly trouble the reader's or viewer's received sense of place.

Airships' most remarkable quality, however, is their ability to endow the most ordinary of settings with an air of spectacle. As Onion illustrates, the airship, in its many forms, has been adapted, appropriated, and reenvisioned in a range of cultural texts that extend far beyond literature and film, from the transformation of a child's bedroom into an airship interior, to the crafting of zeppelin-themed jewelry.[38] Each of these adaptations is, in fact, a narrative form that demonstrates the power of the airship as an icon of anachronistic creativity, illustrating their ability to intrude into more "known" settings and transport the essence of the frontier—and the magic of possibility—with them. As they do so, they do, in fact, trouble our sense of place; they clearly do not belong. But the disjuncture their presence creates serves to highlight their symbolic loading, calling forth the complex aspirations of power and glory, futuristic visions of travel and conquest, and daring innovations in science and technology that brought them into being in their own Golden Age. Thus, images of these sky-faring vessels, hovering over London or moored above the Empire State Building in New York, serve an evocative function similar to the sight of Lansdale's anachronistic airborne Wild West convoy or Kipling's fleet of "air mail" dirigibles. Whether crawling unremarked over a sleepy Western town, or filling the air like "a shoal of monstrous flying sharks,"[39] these fantastic vessels do not simply draw attention to retrofuturism's disjuncture of time, place, and technology. In their creative engagement between past and present, they serve as a spectacular reminder of that two-sided coin—the magic of possibility and the possibility of magic—and embody a promise that, somewhere, frontiers still exist.

> What shall we tell you?
> Tales, marvelous tales
> Of ships and stars and isles where good men rest
> Where nevermore the rose of sunset pales
> And winds and shadows fall towards the West[40]

Notes

1. Jeff VanderMeer and S. J. Chambers, *The Steampunk Bible* (New York: Abrams Image, 2011), 41.

2. Edward Ellis, "The Huge Hunter, or the Steam Man of the Prairies," originally published in *Beadle's American Novel*, no. 45 (August, 1868).

3. Paul Guinan and Anina Bennett, *Frank Reade: Adventures in the Age of Invention* (New York: Abrams Image, 2012), 17.

4. Many of these were published under the pseudonym "Noname."

5. VanderMeer and Chambers, *The Steampunk Bible*, 30, 41.

6. See Michael Adas, *Machines as the Measure of Men: Technology and Ideologies of Western Dominance* (New York: Cornell University Press, 1990).

7. VanderMeer and Chambers, *The Steampunk Bible*, 42.

8. The Johnsons were known for their adventure explorations of Kenya, the Congo, British North Borneo, and the Solomon Islands from 1913 to 1936, which resulted in numerous books as well as films such as *Simba* (1928) and *Congorilla* (1931). Safari adventurer Albert Blinkhorn filmed *The Capture of a Sea Elephant and Hunting Wild Game in the South Pacific* in 1914. Campbell Beasley produced

The Captain Beasley Expedition that same year and *In the Amazon Jungle with Captain Beasley* the next.

9. VanderMeer and Chambers, *The Steampunk Bible*, 42.

10. Douglas Botting, *The Giant Airships* (Alexandria, Va.: Time-Life Books, 1980), 6.

11. Botting, *The Giant Airships*, 6.

12. Known humorously as "Egg's Folly," the airship was designed by Swiss engineers John Pauly and Durs Egg, in 1816.

13. Botting, *The Giant Airships*, 21.

14. Botting, *The Giant Airships*, 17.

15. "A Monster Airship: Successful Ascent Made by Scientists in Switzerland," *New York Times*, 28 July 1900, n.p., http://query.nytimes.com/gst/abstract.html?res= F60B13F63A5F1B738DDDA00A94DF405B808CF1D3 (2 February 2012).

16. Thomas Flaherty, unpublished letter, n.d., courtesy of Time-Life Books. See also Guillaume de Syon, *Zeppelin! Germany and the Airship, 1900–1939* (Baltimore, Md.: Johns Hopkins University Press, 2001).

17. Flaherty, unpublished letter.

18. Jules Verne, *The Clipper of the Clouds* (London: Sampson Low, Marston, Searle, & Rivington, 1887), 3.

19. Rudyard Kipling, *With the Night Mail: A Story of 2000 A.D. (Together with Extracts from the Contemporary Magazine in Which It Appeared)* (Toronto: University of Toronto Libraries Press, 2011).

20. Lavie Tidhar, "Steampunk," *Internet Re-View of Science Fiction*, March 2005, 26 October 2010, www.irosf.com/q/37 zine/article/10114 (8 October 2011).

21. Rebecca Onion, "Reclaiming the Machine: An Introductory Look at Steampunk in Everyday Practice," *Neo-Victorian Studies* 1, no. 1 (Autumn 2008): 138–163, www.neovictorianstudies.com/past.../NVS%201–1%201–Onion.pdf (10 October 2011).

22. Marcel Mauss, *A General Theory of Magic* (London: Routledge, 2001).

23. Bayla Singer, *Like Sex with Gods: An Unorthodox History of Flying* (College Station: Texas A&M University Press, 2003).

24. Fyodor Dostoyevsky, *The Brothers Karamazov: A Novel in Four Parts and an Epilogue* (New York: Penguin Classics, 2003), 333.

25. S. M. Stirling, *The Peshawar Lancers* (New York: Roc, 2003), 15.

26. Richard Stivers, *Technology as Magic: The Triumph of the Irrational* (New York and London: Continuum, 2001).

27. For readers who are unfamiliar, the disembodied head of Buffalo Bill Cody captained the zeppelin *Old Paint* in Joe Lansdale's *Zeppelins West* (2001), while Andan Cly served as airship captain and pirate in Cherie Priest's novels *Boneshaker* (2009) and *Ganymede* (2011).

28. Margaret Rose, "Extraordinary Pasts: Steampunk as a Mode of Historical Representation," *Journal of the Fantastic in the Arts* 20, no. 3 (2009): 319; Steffen Hantke,

"Difference Engines and Other Infernal Devices: History According to Steampunk," *Extrapolation* 40, no. 3 (Fall 1999): 244–254.

29. Guinan and Bennett, *Frank Reade*, 58.

30. Alberto Santos-Dumont, "The Future of Air-Ships," *Fortnightly Review* 83 (1905): 447.

31. Cited in Peter Berbigal, "The Age of Steampunk: Nostalgia Meets the Future, Joined Carefully with Brass Screws," Boston.com, 26 August 2007, www.boston.com/news/globe/ideas/articles/2007/08/26/the_age_of_steampunk (12 September 2011).

32. In a notable bit of steampunk intertextuality, the robot was made by none other than Frank Reade, who hoped that the great impresario's mechanical body would help promote his corporation.

33. Joe R. Lansdale, *Zeppelins West* (Burton, Mich.: Subterranean Press, 2001), 14.

34. James P. Blaylock, "Lord Kelvin's Machine," in *Steampunk*, ed. Ann VanderMeer and Jeff VanderMeer (San Francisco: Tachyon Publications, 2008), 17.

35. Nobile was an Italian aeronautical engineer and promoter of semirigid airships who was, in fact, involved in a polar airship crash that gave rise to an international rescue mission. Amundsen, a Norwegian explorer who was the first to reach the South Pole (1912), and first to undisputedly reach the North Pole (1925), disappeared during the rescue attempt.

36. Philip Pullman, *The Golden Compass* (New York: Yearling, 2001), 224.

37. Blaylock, "Lord Kelvin's Machine," 17; Guinan and Bennett, *Frank Reade*, 152.

38. Onion, "Reclaiming the Machine," 150.

39. Michael Moorcock, "Benediction: Excerpt from the Warlord of the Air," in *Steampunk*, ed. Ann VanderMeer and Jeff VanderMeer, 13.

40. James Elroy Flecker, "Prologue," in *The Golden Journey to Samarkand* (Ann Arbor: University of Michigan Library, 1913), 2.

Bibliography

Adas, Michael. *Machines as the Measure of Men: Technology and Ideologies of Western Dominance*. New York: Cornell University Press, 1990.

Anonymous. "A Monster Airship: Successful Ascent Made by Scientists in Switzerland." *New York Times*, 28 July 1900. http://query.nytimes.com/gst/abstract.html?res=F60B13F63A5F1B738DDDA00A94DF405B808CF1D3 (2 February 2012).

Berbigal, Peter. "The Age of Steampunk: Nostalgia Meets the Future, Joined Carefully with Brass Screws." Boston.com, 26 August 2007. www.boston.com/news/globe/ideas/articles/2007/08/26/the_age_of_steampunk (12 September 2011).

Blaylock, James P. "Lord Kelvin's Machine." 17–52 in *Steampunk*, ed. Ann VanderMeer and Jeff VanderMeer. San Francisco: Tachyon Publications, 2008.

Botting, Douglas. *The Giant Airships*. Alexandria, Va.: Time-Life Books, 1980.

Dostoyevsky, Fyodor. *The Brothers Karamazov: A Novel in Four Parts and an Epilogue.* New York: Penguin Classics, 2003.

Ellis, Edward. "The Huge Hunter, or the Steam Man of the Prairies." Originally published in *Beadle's American Novel,* no. 45. August, 1868.

Flaherty, Thomas. Unpublished letter, n.d. Courtesy of Time-Life Books.

Flecker, James Elroy. "Prologue." In *The Golden Journey to Samarkand.* Ann Arbor: University of Michigan Library Press, 1913.

Guinan, Paul, and Anina Bennett. *Frank Reade: Adventures in the Age of Invention.* New York: Abrams Image, 2012.

Hantke, Steffen. "Difference Engines and Other Infernal Devices: History According to Steampunk." *Extrapolation* 40, no. 3 (Fall 1999): 244–254.

Kipling, Rudyard. *With the Night Mail: A Story of 2000 A.D. (Together with Extracts from the Contemporary Magazine in Which It Appeared).* Toronto: University of Toronto Libraries Press, 2011.

Lansdale, Joe R. *Zeppelins West.* Burton, Mich.: Subterranean Press, 2001.

Mauss, Marcel. *A General Theory of Magic.* London: Routledge, 2001.

Moorcock, Michael. "Benediction: Excerpt from the Warlord of the Air." 13–16 in *Steampunk,* ed. Ann VanderMeer and Jeff VanderMeer. San Francisco: Tachyon Publications, 2008.

Onion, Rebecca. "Reclaiming the Machine: An Introductory Look at Steampunk in Everyday Practice." *Neo-Victorian Studies,* no. 1 (Autumn 2008): 138–163. www.neovictorianstudies.com/past.../NVS%201–1%201–Onion.pdf (10 October 2011).

Priest, Cherie. *Boneshaker.* New York: Tor Books, 2009.

——. *Ganymede.* New York: Tor Books, 2011.

Pullman, Philip. *The Golden Compass.* New York: Yearling, 2001.

Rose, Margaret. "Extraordinary Pasts: Steampunk as a Mode of Historical Representation." *Journal of the Fantastic in the Arts* 20, no. 3 (2009): 319–333.

Santos-Dumont, Alberto. "The Future of Air-Ships." *Fortnightly Review* 83 (1905): 443–454.

Singer, Bayla. *Like Sex with Gods: An Unorthodox History of Flying.* College Station: Texas A&M University Press, 2003.

Stirling, S. M. *The Peshawar Lancers.* New York: Roc, 2003.

Stivers, Richard. *Technology as Magic: The Triumph of the Irrational.* New York and London: Continuum Publishing, 2001.

de Syon, Guillaume. *Zeppelin! Germany and the Airship, 1900–1939.* Baltimore, Md.: Johns Hopkins University Press, 2001.

Tidhar, Lavie. "Steampunk." *Internet Re-View of Science Fiction.* March 2005. 26 October 2010. www.irosf.com/q/37 zine/article/10114 (8 October 2011).

VanderMeer, Ann, and Jeff VanderMeer, eds. *Steampunk.* San Francisco: Tachyon Publications, 2008.

VanderMeer, Jeff, and S. J. Chambers. *The Steampunk Bible: An Illustrated Guide to the World of Imaginary Airships, Corsets and Goggles, Mad Scientists, and Strange Literature*. New York: Abrams Image, 2011.

Verne, Jules. *The Clipper of the Clouds*. London: Sampson Low, Marston, Searle, & Rivington, 1887.

A history that never was. *Copyright Jody Steel*

CHAPTER NINE

Enacting the Never-Was: Upcycling the Past, Present, and Future in Steampunk

Suzanne Barber and Matt Hale

Scrounging through the "junkyard" of history,[1] steampunk authors and artisans employ the nineteenth century, and more generally the documented past, as a reservoir of conceptual and material fragments of previous cultures and ways of being. It is from these temporally rendered units of human creation that steampunks craft counterfactual histories. While a number of recent studies have examined the literary, graphic, and artistic qualities of steampunk within popular media, few have directly observed the expressive forms and creativity of those individuals who self-identify *as* steampunks. As such, this chapter will explore the artistic behaviors of steampunks by directly attending to their communicative practices and the ways that they re-create both time and material into new and atemporal forms.

This chapter is rooted in folkloristic methodology and combines narrative and performative analysis of vernacular practice. The data from this text derive from ethnographic fieldwork conducted among members of the Alternate History Track (henceforth AHT) at Dragon*Con in Atlanta, Georgia, in 2010. Dragon*Con is a North American popular culture convention, or "con" as convention goers call it, that focuses on "science fiction and fantasy, gaming, comics, literature, art, music, and film."[2] Since its inception in 1987 with just over a thousand attendees, Dragon*Con has grown exponentially. Today, it attracts over forty thousand congoers who inundate downtown Atlanta with costumes and commerce. Over the four-day Labor Day weekend, fans participate in hours of programming and entertainment including themed discussion panels, concerts, costume contests, and workshops.

The AHT is one of thirty-six individual themed fan tracks that host such activities. We will focus on one AHT event, a theatric panel titled History Interactive, wherein audience members were given a variety of historic scenarios to reconstruct and perform for one another with the aid of props (video footage from the panel is available online).[3] By analyzing History Interactive, we will illustrate that steampunk performative enclaves where history, counterfactuality, and play merge are generated through both narratological and material means. For the sake of simplicity, we will call this figurative position the never-was. Secondly, building from the theories of author and futurist Bruce Sterling, we will discuss steampunk as an atemporal phenomenon. Finally, we will suggest that steampunk is not only an artistic form through which steampunk cosplayers[4] and enthusiasts express their aesthetic sensibilities but that it can also act as a site of critical discourse about the past, present, and projections of the future.

Tinkering with Time and Matter

Like the Victorians themselves, steampunks are complicated. They are retrospective futurists continually building their present from the remnants of the past. Steampunks look to the "wonderful, glorious remains of . . . previous cultures [and] . . . previous mindsets and . . . use elements from that treasure trove to actually craft things that are appropriate to [their] future."[5] Whether refashioning outdated ideologies or "mental antiques,"[6] or repurposing pieces of discarded objects, steampunks employ that which was prior to construct their fantastic costumes, contraptions, and stories from whatever scraps of the past that they feel are worth salvaging. Steampunks do not replicate the past. They instead reshape and refine elements of prior temporalities into refurbished forms in a process known as upcycling.[7] Upcycling is the creation of forms from waste materials that attempt to be of a higher quality and more sustainable nature than the compositional elements from which they were derived. With their propensity to piece together alternate worlds from conceptual/material structures and discourses of the past, it is safe to say that steampunks are, if nothing else, tinkerers.

A steampunk's costume is an "atemporal" object, a thing that is not so much "matter out of place"[8] as it is matter out of time. Steampunk costumers transform their bodies into ensembles of referential discourse that blend multiple temporalities into a single form. It is deeply dialogic and purposefully intertextual and gains much of its aesthetic effect through the juxtaposition of elements from wildly different sociotemporal contexts. In this sense, steampunk costumes behave as wearable chronotopes,[9] objects that open up communicative possibilities into other spaces and other times, including fictionalized events that historically never existed. These material forms are animated by and embedded within narratives of alternative realities, counterfactual pasts filled with retrofuturistic fashion and steam-powered technologies.

Steampunks manage multiple temporalities through their costumes and the stories that they enact through them. These temporalities include, but are not limited to, (1) the historic past as it is recounted within the historical record; (2) an imagined alternate past that never was; (3) the "actual" present, that is to say, the temporal context in which a costume was created or worn or when a narrative was performed; (4) a counterfactual or "virtual" present precipitated by divergences from the historical record in an alternate past; and finally (5) a speculative future, the horizon of potentialities built upon the precedent of that which came before it.

The simultaneous temporality of alternate history is anchored by the concept of the Jonbar hinge, an occurrence within a timeline with two or more possible outcomes, one that sets in motion a chain of events leading to the present reality and another that initiates a divergence from the grand narrative of history. This point of divergence within the historical record creates in its wake an alternate history. Taking its name from a Jack Williamson short story,[10] the Jonbar hinge, what Karen Hellekson has alternatively called the "nexus event,"[11] provides a critical pivot point between history, a story that chronicles the events that took place prior to the present, and counterfactual history, a story based upon but dissimilar to history. That is to say, an alternate history might parallel, converge with, or diverge from what the historical record tells us happened within the past, but it does not replicate it. While steampunk literature explores the "what ifs" of history through textual means, steampunk cosplayers embody and enact this speculative space through costume, adornment, and performance.

History Interactive

A crowd of fifty or so congoers wearing top hats, corsets, and goggles filed into the beige and gold meeting space inside the ground floor of the Westin hotel on Peachtree Street Northwest. They found seating, struck up conversations, posed for photos, and thumbed through their Dragon*Con programming guidebooks while they waited for the panel to commence. At the front of the room sat a lengthy but narrow table with a tablecloth draped across it. On top of the tablecloth was a variety of props: rope, feather boas, fake weaponry, an assortment of novelty hats, to name but a few. Ace Talkingwolf and Jamie Haeuser cohosted and moderated the event. Talkingwolf wore a medium-height top hat with a brass monocle atop its brim, black trousers, a white loose-fitting Victorian shirt, and a black vest. He had a black holster slung over his shoulder that held in place a pistol made of recycled materials. Talkingwolf made his way to the prop table and conferred with Haeuser before grabbing a wireless microphone, turning it on, and asking for a volunteer. As requested, a member of the audience rose to the occasion and took his place beside Talkingwolf and Haeuser.

Facing the prop table alongside his volunteer, Talkingwolf said, "Do me a favor. Pick a single item here that's not an article of clothing. Pick that one," he suggested. The volunteer did as he was told and selected the object. "Not that one. You don't want that one." He pointed to a different item; again Talkingwolf's assistant followed his directions to the letter. "Not that one. Pick the one with the handle," Talkingwolf whispered into the microphone.

"This one?" the volunteer asked.

"Yeah," Talkingwolf replied softly. "Now turn around and hold it up." The volunteer faced the audience and raised the six-inch-long gray plastic chain-saw blade into the air by its handle. Speaking in an upbeat radio show personality's voice, Talkingwolf read a fictional message from the panel's sponsor. "Doctor Benamin's famous rectal thermometer, known for its comfort design. Now, with a new turbo auto-enema attachment. That's Doctor Benamin's comfort design rectal thermometer and its new turbo auto-enema attachment from the makers of Electro-Cath. Catheters for gentlemen." With those few words, Talkingwolf's performance had marked the beginning of the panel, one mode of communication bracketed off from another. The audience shifted from the realm of quotidian conversation, a social space filled with disconnected discourses. Discussion subsided and the audience tuned into their hosts. The spectators cheered as Talkingwolf finished his monologue and turned the floor over to Haeuser.

Haeuser was dressed in a black top and corset accented with distressed brass buttons, a long black skirt, and a burgundy collar around her neck.

Ace Talkingwolf presides. *Copyright Jody Steel*

She wore a teardrop-shaped black hat embellished with a plume of black feathers and a stream of amber silk that descended down her back. Haeuser explained the rules to the audience. The audience was to be broken down into six small groups of individuals. Each team would then receive a Jonbar hinge scenario that posed a particular question of what circumstances might have come to fruition had certain historical events happened differently. The scenarios were varied and included historical events that extended well beyond the Victorian era. What would have happened if Saint Patrick had drowned on his way to Ireland, or if James Cook had never discovered Australia? What if Queen Victoria had had no children, or if John Wilkes Booth hadn't assassinated Abraham Lincoln? Though each of the preceding vignettes would certainly be a productive entryway into the exploration of the steampunk vernacular, we will instead limit our focus to two scenes in particular. With that, we shall turn our attention to William Tecumseh Sherman, general of the Union Army during the American Civil War, and the outcome of his speculative death at the Battle of Chickamauga in 1863.

According to historical records, General Sherman didn't die in the Battle of Chickamauga, nor did he do so for another twenty-eight years. In fact,

General Sherman led his destructive "march to the sea" into Savannah, Georgia, and eventually confederate surrender in 1865. This is what history tells us happened during the American Civil War, but for the participants of History Interactive, this master narrative, its motifs, *dramatis personae*, and plot points, became the figurative brick and mortar with which to build a history that never was, to imagine what might have been. The group of six audience members who were assigned to this particular Jonbar hinge met briefly before their performance to create a loose script after selecting a few props, chiefly a large plastic sword. With plot and materials in hand, Sherman's speculative death at Chickamauga was set in motion. One member of the group, a tall woman sporting brass goggles and a retrofuturistic wireless headset, narrated the tale for the audience as the other five members enacted the scene:

> So Sherman was at Chickamauga and he died, but not in battle. What really happened was [she pauses] he was promptly eaten by a zombie. [The member of the group playing Sherman is overcome by three zombies. He falls to the floor. The audience laughs and applauds.] After this, zombie Sherman led his army of darkness into Atlanta and desiccated the city. [Zombie Sherman stands and lumbers forward with his arms extending forward with his zombie cohort.] . . . On his way to Ford's Theatre, President Lincoln, zombie hunter [wielding his plastic sword], got the urgent call on the wireless telegraph that there was a disaster in Atlanta and decided to go and fight the zombie horde singlehandedly, where he was [she pauses] promptly eaten by a zombie. The zombie horde continued to take over Atlanta, and since there was no one left in the country to save the world from the zombies, it turned into sort of a zombie theme park [the zombies hop up and down, waving their arms in excitement, mimicking a theme park ride], and Six Zombies over Atlanta became very popular for the mundanes to come and visit and hopefully not be eaten. Eventually, it evolved . . . into Dragon*Con, which is why you see all of the zombies walking around Atlanta around Labor Day.

While General Sherman was a historical figure reanimated from the nineteenth century, the time frame that most steampunks anchor their creative acts in, another group of performers at the panel was given a Jonbar hinge that surpassed that vintage by nearly a millennium. Their scenario centered on what might have happened if the first Viking settlement had survived. Although Sherman's story had been brought to life with a minimal use of props, this group utilized multiple props, fake plush muscles, novelty Viking and plastic World War I Prussian helmets, soft rubber weaponry, and an articulating skunk hand puppet. While Sherman's narrative was told from the vantage of the present conditions of 2010, this performance focused on a group of Viking settlers in the year 1900 celebrating their own past through narrative and performance. The narrator opened the scene:

> Narrator: Welcome class of 1900 to Leif Erikson University. As you know, nine hundred years ago today is the anniversary of our first successful colony here on North American soil. So, in celebration of that we're going to . . . [have the] very [first] celebration of the Thanksgiving.
>
> Anders: Argh! [Anders yells as he waves his prop war hammer into the air.]
>
> Professor: We here at Leif Erikson University are very excited about this first celebration and to commemorate it, we have had our first annual canoe burning and we had a great turnout for that, and we are now looking forward to our first ever Thanksgiving play written by our first creative arts writing major, Anders Erikson.
>
> Anders: Argh! [Again, Anders yells and raises his hammer.]
>
> Professor: And also, by our first dramatic arts major, Bournfork. [Bournfork holds his arms into the air, displaying a sword in one hand and a tightly closed fist.] A round of applause please.
>
> Narrator: [The narrator shifts lower in pitch.] Nine hundred years ago, at the shores of North America, our first Viking settlers came ashore.
>
> Bournfork: Argh! [He raises his weapon.]
>
> Narrator: After burning their boats behind them to show their dedication to this new world colony [the two Vikings pantomime the destruction of their own ships], they came in contact with the natives. A beautiful Native American princess came forth bearing gifts of food for the settlers. [The "native" slowly walks up to the two Vikings holding a plush skunk puppet.] Of course, being the brutally awesome Vikings that we are, we immediately killed her and stole all of the food. [The Vikings pummel the "native" with their foam weapons until she falls to the floor, and then they take the stuffed skunk from her and pretend to eat it.]
>
> Bournfork: Argh!
>
> Anders: Argh!
>
> Narrator: Now in honor of said celebration, we will commence with our annual game of beserker ball. [The two Vikings exchange blows with their weapons.]

Anders: Argh! Die! [Anders hits Bournfork in the head with his hammer.]

Bournfork: [Falls dramatically to his death as he says] If only my mother were here.

Narrator: Congratulations, sir. As the Beowulfs, you go on to win berserker ball, and you get the honor of slaying the princess again.

Anders: Arghh! [Just as before, though this time without his comrade, Anders ceremonially attacks the "native" princess.]

Professor: Congratulations.

Anders: Arrghh, arrghh, arghh! [Anders waves his weapon into the air as he yells, followed by applause from the audience.]

Steampunks do not relegate their tinkering to material objects alone. As the previous two scenes illustrate, steampunks are equally temporal as well as material bricoleurs. Borrowing from the work of Lévi-Strauss in an expanded sense, the bricoleur collects and retains elements, whether material, ideological, discursive, etc., "on the principle that 'they may always come in handy.'" Deriving from the French verb *bricoler* meaning to tinker, the bricoleur artfully cobbles together these rudiments into a cohesive assemblage, or *bricolage*.[12] As temporal bricoleurs, steampunks return to those abandoned aspects of the past and "put them together in a new way."[13] Through narrative, steampunks are able to create stylistic coherence between material objects that are from contradictory temporal contexts, enabling Vikings, zombies, Civil War generals, plastic props, re-creations of Victorian costumes, and futuristic objects to cohabit atemporal space.

Plausibility, Atemporality, and the Endless Grand Narrative

Weaving together intertextual citations to the historical record and to popular and local culture, the actors within these two scenes engendered the never-was into a performative reality, a space set off from ordinary communication opening up into a realm of upkeyed performance and of play and fantasy.[14] By reenacting a history that never was, this troupe of congoers not only explored an unknowable hypothetical past through intertextual signification but also created solidarity between multiple temporalities. Divergent timelines, both actual and virtual, coexist, as do technologies, fashion, and ideologies of vastly different sociotemporal contexts, linked together for an aesthetic effect. Through narrative, the past is recalled, decontextualized, and recontextualized within new communicative space, taking on new meaning relative to the referents it has been reset in proximity to; this is true of the narrativization of Sherman's untimely death.[15] Within what folklorist Richard Bauman calls the "narrative event"—that is, the moment in which a narrative is performed—the narrator and her coperformers replayed a chain of events that took place within the past (both actual and imagined), recounted through storytelling within the present, what Bauman distinguishes as the "narrated event."[16] Although the content of the narrative indicates that the events within the story had taken place sometime between the Battle of Chickamauga in 1863 and the conclusion of the American Civil War in 1865, there are multiple points of anachronism and divergence from the historical record that exist simultaneously and equally alongside historical fact. First, let's look to those points of asynchronicity, where history and alternate history diverge.

The wireless radio telegraph by which President Lincoln received word of the devastating zombie attacks in Atlanta is untimely in the sense that it was first patented by Guglielmo Marconi in 1896. Secondly, Lincoln's assassination at Ford's Theatre in 1865 could have never taken place as he was instead killed by General Sherman and his zombie minions within this alternate timeline. These divergences are aberrations from the "parent narrative"[17] of the historical record that resulted in the formation of the Six Zombies over Atlanta theme park and finally the establishment of Dragon*Con. Again, these plot-forwarding and world-building discursive structures dovetail with the narratively constituted never-was reality of both the local (Dragon*Con and Atlanta) and the "larger-than-local" context[18] (North American history and the developments of nineteenth-century technologies/industrialization). Within the narrative event, we have further complications of cohabiting temporalities. The narrator who guided us through the unfolding events of this alternate past wore a wireless headset that looked as if it belonged to a future that had never happened; likewise she also referenced a common Internet meme where Abraham Lincoln is made, among many other anachronistic things, a zombie hunter. Furthermore, several members of the performing group wore twentieth-century clothing alongside their new-antique steampunk attire, while the entire performance space was filled with twenty-first-century technologies—iPods, cell phones, wireless microphones, a PA system—all of this framed by the contemporary architectural design of the Westin hotel itself.

Within the nineteenth-century Viking Thanksgiving celebration scene, we can see that although the narrative in question diverges from the historical record, this alternate history is modeled on historical grand narrative, popular conceptions of Vikings throughout human history, as well as local realities. Steampunks balance between complete ahistorical content and historical reproduction. Situated between these two points is historical plausibility. One must diverge from history in order to imagine alternate pasts, but at the same time, one must also create new histories that are plausible. As such, the speculative arts share borders with both science fiction and fantasy. On one hand, alternate history is not future oriented, at least not in the same way that science fiction is. It is not usually set within a near or distant future that is yet to come, unless, however, this future was precipitated by a Jonbar hinge within the past. Likewise, alternate history narratives, either as vernacular practice or literature, typically do not take place in an imaginary world of complete magic and fantasy. Steampunk is neither pure science fiction nor pure fantasy, but a hybrid of history, science fiction, and fantasy.

Steampunks reconstruct pieces of the past into new and often more sustainable forms, into fashions, inventions, and new ongoing discourses while simultaneously diverging from the metanarrative of the historical record. Despite the muddying of fact and fiction within History Interactive, steampunk communities are not exclusively engaged in the deconstruction of history. Steampunks do dismantle history, but they put it back together again, even if it looks remarkably different from how it started or if there are a few spare parts that somehow don't quite make it into the final product. For steampunks, deconstruction permits fabrication. It creates elements, both discursive and material, that can be repurposed rather than discarded. This quality of repurposing, craftsmanship, and care of the former material and ideologies in steampunk represents a reaction to the unsustainable projects of modernism, the infinite quest for speed and the rejection of yesterday's knowledge of hypermodernity, and the nihilism and "superficiality"[19] of postmodernism.

Anyone attending an alternate history convention will soon realize that steampunks feel no incredulity toward historical master narratives as postmodernism is typically characterized.[20] In fact, knowledge of historical narrative is a resource that can be harnessed to create more complicated and historically accurate costuming. It is a reserve of information that one might use to flesh out a persona or backstory by interweaving his character's actions with those of historical figures or events. As General Sherman's zombie-induced demise illustrates, one must first learn, value, and understand history before one can successfully diverge from it. Though Sherman was eaten by a zombie, he still pressed forward, marching toward the sea, synchronous with the events (albeit as a zombie) that history tells us he took part in.

Steampunk narrative systems could then be understood as a hyponarrative structure—that is, as petits récits, or little narratives—embedded within an endlessly revisable and dynamic master narrative matrix.[21] That is to say that both levels, the local and the grand or global, are dialogically linked sets of discourses. They are dependent upon one another and are thus mutually constitutive. The local and the global, the little narrative and the master narrative, are reconceptualized as endlessly expandable accordion-like narrative constructs, a discursively rendered fabric of space/ time ripe for perpetual recycling, refashioning, and revision. Steampunks approach historical narrative as a virtual "midden yard . . . [cluttered] with artifacts and ideas that are relevant to [their] lives today [that also]. . . provide some connection to [their] past."[22] In this sense, history becomes, like the infinitely consumable digital textual environment in which many steampunks augment their local communities beyond their local reality, an "endless [grand] narrative"[23] of source material from which to construct reimaginings of the past within the present. This field of narrative discourse, therefore, blends together locality and popular media, individuality and collectivity, the past and the present, constituted through "the volitional, temporal action[s]"[24] of human actors.

This system of intertextual and dialogic embeddedness was most apparent in one scene at History Interactive that focused on the premature demise of Saint Patrick. The sketch's narrator informed the audience that Saint Patrick had drowned before returning to the shores of Ireland. Had Saint Patrick made it ashore (as he did in historical reality), she explained, he and his crew would have trampled a collection of magical shamrocks. Because Saint Patrick perished, however, these rare shamrocks were left to be consumed by the local inhabitants, the leprechauns. After eating the shamrocks, the leprechauns grew tremendously, which the narrator jokingly put forward as an explanation as to "why there are some tall Irish people." The now-enlarged leprechauns' leader, "King Conan O'Brien . . . drove the snakes out of Ireland and into the NBC Executive Suites." [A young man portraying O'Brien entered the scene accessorized with a shiny plastic crown and a bejeweled walking cane. He then attacked a fellow cast member who was wearing a lengthy snakelike hat with his cane.] The narrator spoke up once more, saying the leprechauns "steamed the shamrocks and [she paused] they were punks." The scene ended and the audience applauded. As we can see here, this particular example illustrates how steampunks create a cohesive whole from wildly divergent elements, from the historical record, popular culture, folklore, and mythology, even connecting steampunk subculture to the hypothetical evolution of leprechaun anatomy.

Although atemporality has acted as a verbal stand-in for anachronism or temporal pastiche, which in some ways it is, it is also more than that. Bruce Sterling suggests that atemporality is a kind of "agnosticism, . . . a calm, pragmatic, serene skepticism about the historical narratives."[25] Though we can see ironic play, virtuality, and deconstruction in History Interactive, all hallmarks of postmodernism, historical plausibility allows steampunks to simultaneously diverge from historical narratives while still ascribing to and asserting their importance. In fact, these convergences and divergences help steampunks to endlessly revise, update, and gain new perspective on existing master narratives as well as to create new ones, because, as Sterling points out, the old ones "just don't map onto what is going on."[26] By bricoleuring elements from the past into forms within the present, steampunks create proximity between temporal artifacts that would have never cohabited a single moment in time. This temporal juxtaposition generates the genre's dual illuminative capability.[27] As an aesthetic system, steampunk invites the reassessment and critique of abandoned forms from the past from the vantage of the present while transforming the past into a vista from which to assess the present.

Upcycling the Past, Sustaining the Present, Building the Future

In "The User's Guide to Steampunk," Sterling tells us that while "the 19th-century world was crude, limited and clanky, . . . the 20th-century world is calamitously unsustainable."[28] At its most basic state, steampunk is an aesthetic genre and a diffused but coherent form of sartorial, literary, and artful entertainment. At the same time, alternate history also provides a field of discursive and critical possibilities. As within any tradition that persists through time and space, stasis is impossible. Elements are discarded as they fall out of fashion. Over time, old ways of doing, thinking, and behaving are seen from a new temporal perspective and, as a result, are placed into a relational framework with that of the new. Each performance, every costume, embellishment, gadget, or narrative constructed within the present, is pregnant with dialogic and indexical connections that link these communicative actions to the discourses of the past.[29] It is within the dialogic constitution of alternate histories that steampunks are able to not only recycle the words and material culture of others but also, in essence, upcycle them into new, more culturally and environmentally sustainable forms.

The past, however, is not without its problems. As Sterling reminds us, "When you raise the dead, they bring their baggage."[30] Steampunks revise and selectively re-create the past much in the same fashion as they upcycle the discarded waste materials of times prior into new forms within their present. Rather than whitewashing history and creating a sepia-toned utopian dream of the past (which is itself a trope within steampunk fiction and cosplay practices), many steampunks confront the complex issues that were part and parcel of the historical time frame from which they construct their alternate worlds (the maltreatment and murder of the native princess motif, for instance). Within these counterfactual play frames, such concerns become centers of gravity for critical discourse. By recentering the nineteenth century within a twenty-first-century context, steampunks are able to confront issues relating to gender inequality, colonization and imperialism, environmental conquest, late consumer capitalist notions of human/object relations, and so on. On one hand, they minimize the distance between the never-was and historical narrative by creating incredibly detailed costumes, gadgets, and accessories, many of which are historically accurate in terms of materials, construction techniques, style, and form (excluding those atemporal elements like ray guns or steam-powered computers),[31] as well as character backstories and personas that are plausibly interwoven into the fabric of the past so as to re-create it but not to divorce it from historical narrative. On the other hand, steampunks highlight and maximize the intertextual gaps that underscore their creative modulation and re-creation of history.[32]

While steampunks might choose to borrow feminine fashion from the nineteenth century, for example, they do so while questioning the gender assumptions of the Victorian era. To return to History Interactive as a case in point, nearly all of the skits generated and performed by the panelists parodied or commented upon these issues. In one scene, Queen Victoria, who was played by a young man in a Utilikilt, died childless and heirless because she, as a proper Victorian lady, would not engage in the "improper acts" of sexual behavior. She told each of her suitors that "it is improper for a lady to be seen without clothes by a gentleman," despite their pleas that she consider the future of her realm. After falling to the floor and dying, a battle for the former queen's royal throne ensues. In this case, Victorian attitudes about gender and sexuality have been exaggerated and transformed into a parodic/ allegorical narrative and performative construct.

Another participant in History Interactive named Katie McAlister played a Martian prison officer charged with the task of transporting British criminals to a Martian penal colony (which had been established as a result of James Cook's failure to discover Australia). Shortly after landing on Mars, the prisoners revolted, capturing McAlister's character and successfully claiming the Martian colony as their own. After her group's skit was over, she returned to her chair and draped a large sash over her shoulder that read "Votes for women and sentient automata." She told us that she had become interested in steampunk philosophy from exposure to the aesthetic in films, literature, and cons. She explained:

> I got more and more interested in the concept of imagining this alternate history and the potential for creativity and the things that people can create. From a costuming perspective, you can create some very cool stuff and . . . it's a way to imagine the past and all of the things we really like about the past [while] also . . . questioning the role of women in a way that a lot of the literature from the period really does not. You can imagine women as explorers and heroes in a way that very few books from the actual Victorian era really did.

McAlister's comments, her costume, and her role as a Martian prison officer reflect layers of maximizing the intertextual gap created by the dialogic nature of the History Interactive panel specifically but also of alternate history subculture in general. While her costume and performance

McAlister transposing the Victorian era. *Copyright Jody Steel*

indexically refer back to the past, they simultaneously challenge Victorian gender relations and empire building, while still asserting the importance of past ways of life as a model from which to create the present. Though McAlister was wearing a corset and other Victorian clothing, she was detaching these material forms from their sociotemporal context within the past, transposing them to the present, and using them as a means to critique the past from which they came while also reclaiming them as aesthetic forms.

Though we have concentrated on the particularities of History Interactive as an expressive act that reflects the larger cultural network from which it originated, we can see that the creative and artistic processes that come into focus within this local reality are present within the larger mediated steampunk and alternate history discourses. If we look at this locality and turn our attention to publications like SteamPunk Magazine,[33] blogs like Jeni Hellum's Multiculturalism for Steampunk,[34] vernacular video and multimedia productions like the 2010 short film The Candy Shop: A Fairy Tale About the Sexual Exploitation of Children,[35] online forum discussions, or countless alternate history conventions like AnachroCon in Atlanta, Georgia, or the Steampunk World's Fair in Piscataway, New Jersey, we can see that steampunks engage with the past as both a reservoir of ready-made referential forms and also as a productive vantage from which to make sense of and transform the present. In each of these mediated forms, steampunks approach the past as a field of former possibilities. The past, then, is a narratively constituted field of discarded objects and temporal pieces, some of which are worth reclaiming and reusing; others are left behind as they are no longer useful, and still others are created into new forms that exceed the prior potentialities that they once had. Steampunks are tinkerers who refashion the past anew into the never-was in order to imagine, prepare for, and build a future that is yet to come.

Notes

1. Alan Moore, "An Interview with Alan Moore," SteamPunk Magazine 3 (September 2007): 23.

2. Dragon*Con, "Welcome to Dragon*Con!," DragonCon.org 2011, www.Dragoncon.org (5 December 2011).

3. History Interactive Panel video footage is available at the following address: http://youtu.be/4GqoYyuUwpc. The Dragon*Con Steampunk Fashion Show 2010 is accessible at http://youtu.be/9tdxBYtdHos, as is the parade, at the following URL: http://youtu.be/1fwRVfn28aE. To see a small sampling of some of the informal interviews

that we conducted at Dragon*Con 2010, see our youtube.com channel at www.youtube
.com/user/AeneasPictures/featured.

4. Cosplay is a portmanteau of the words costume and play, used to describe
the act of donning a costume and/or accessories as well as the corporeal and verbal
stylings of a particular character/generic idea as a means to represent that figure in
performance.

5. Moore, "An Interview with Alan Moore," 23.

6. Bruce Sterling, *Tomorrow Now: Envisioning the Next Fifty Years* (New York:
Random House, 2002), 14.

7. It should be understood that steampunks engage in recycling as well as upcycling; however, we have chosen to focus primarily on the latter of these two forms
of creative reuse.

8. Mary Douglas, *Purity and Danger: An Analysis of Concepts of Pollution and Taboo* (1966; reprint, New York: Routledge, 2003).

9. Mikhail Bakhtin, *The Dialogic Imagination*, ed. Michael Holquist (Austin:
University of Texas Press, 1981).

10. Jack Williamson, *The Legion of Time* (New York: Bluejay Books, 1952).

11. Karen Hellekson, *The Alternate History: Refiguring Historical Time* (Kent,
Ohio: Kent State University Press, 2001), 5.

12. Claude Lévi-Strauss, *The Savage Mind* (Chicago: University of Chicago Press,
1966), 16–36.

13. Moore, "An Interview with Alan Moore," 23.

14. Gregory Bateson, "A Theory of Play and Fantasy," *Psychiatric Research Reports*
2 (1955): 39–51, and Erving Goffman, *Frame Analysis: An Essay of the Organization
of Experience* (Cambridge: Harvard University Press, 1974).

15. Richard Bauman and Charles Briggs, "Poetics and Performances as Critical
Perspectives on Language and Social Life," *Annual Review of Anthropology* 19 (1990):
59–88.

16. Richard Bauman, *Story, Performance, and Event: Contextual Studies of Oral
Narrative* (Cambridge: Cambridge University Press, 1986).

17. P. J. Falzone, "The Final Frontier Is Queer: Aberrancy, Archetype and Audience Generated Folklore in K/S Slashfiction," *Western Folklore* 64, no. 3/4 (2005):
252–256.

18. Amy Shuman, "Dismantling Local Culture," *Western Folklore* 52, no. 2/4
(1993): 345–364.

19. Fredric Jameson, *Postmodernism, or, the Cultural Logic of Late Capitalism* (Durham, N.C.: Duke University Press, 1992), 9.

20. Jean François Lyotard, *The Postmodern Condition: A Report on Knowledge*
(Minneapolis: University of Minnesota Press, 1979).

21. Manfred Jahn, *Narratology: A Guide to the Theory of Narrative*, Version 1.8
(Cologne, Germany: English Department, University of Cologne, 2005).

22. Jake von Slatt, "Introduction," in *SteamPunk Magazine: The First Seven Years: Issues #1–7* (Charleston: Combustion Books, 2011), 3.

23. Alan Kirby, *Digimodernism: How New Technologies Dismantle the Postmodern and Reconfigure Our Culture* (New York: Continuum, 2009), 161.

24. Henry Glassie, "Tradition," in *Eight Words for the Study of Expressive Culture*, ed. Burt Feintuch (Urbana: University of Illinois, 2003), 178.

25. Bruce Sterling, "Atemporality for the Creative Artist," paper presented at the Transmediale 10, Berlin, Germany (2010).

26. Sterling, "Atemporality for the Creative Artist."

27. Rachel A. Bowser and Brian Croxall, "Introduction: Industrial Evolution," *Neo-Victorian Studies* 3, no. 1 (2010): 5, www.neovictorianstudies.com (July 2011).

28. Bruce Sterling, "The User's Guide to Steampunk," *SteamPunk Magazine* 5 (April 2009): 30–32.

29. Richard Bauman and Charles Briggs, "Genre, Intertextuality, and Social Power," *Journal of Linguistic Anthropology* 2, no. 2 (1992): 147–148, in regard to the temporalizing and indexical possibilities of genre invocation.

30. Sterling, "The User's Guide to Steampunk," 33.

31. Many steampunk objects are, however, often built with a level of craftsmanship and detail that they appear as if they could have plausibly existed in the nineteenth century. It is not a form of material verisimilitude (these objects are not constructed in such a way as to hide the fact that they never actually existed, but are instead created in such a way as to both synchronize with and diverge from the material forms particular to the nineteenth century). Artifacts of this sort often are mechanical and articulable and are constructed of materials that do not merely veneer an antique or Victorian aesthetic on top of contemporary objects. Instead, steampunk cosplayers and inventors create material products that are frequently heavy, are bulky, and actually do things. They emphasize depth, meaning historical plausibility, craftsmanship, and care, and they are made of materials that balance between function and form. In short, these types of materials are diametrically opposed, for one example, to mass-produced cellular phone or laptop covers with gears and cogs that are sold as steampunk accessories, objects that lack an element of depth, craftsmanship, and individuality that is so vital to steampunk material culture.

32. Bauman and Briggs, "Genre, Intertextuality, and Social Power," 147–148.

33. "Home Page," *SteamPunk Magazine* (2012), www.steampunkmagazine.com (21 January 2012).

34. Jeni Hellum, "Home Page," *Multiculturalism for Steampunk* (2012), www .thesteamerstrunk.blogspot.com (18 May 2011).

35. *The Candy Shop: A Fairytale about the Sexual Exploitation of Children*, Stop the Candy Shop (2012), www.stopthecandyshop.com/the-film (14 August 2011).

Bibliography

Bakhtin, Mikhail. *The Dialogic Imagination*. Ed. Michael Holquist. Austin: University of Texas Press, 1981.

Bateson, Gregory. "A Theory of Play and Fantasy." *Psychiatric Research Reports* 2 (1955): 39–51.

Bauman, Richard. *Story, Performance, and Event: Contextual Studies of Oral Narrative*. Cambridge: Cambridge University Press, 1986.

Bauman, Richard, and Charles Briggs. "Genre, Intertextuality, and Social Power." *Journal of Linguistic Anthropology* 2, no. 2 (1992): 131–172.

———. "Poetics and Performances as Critical Perspectives on Language and Social Life." *Annual Review of Anthropology* 19 (1990): 59–88.

Bowser, Rachel A., and Brian Croxall. "Introduction: Industrial Evolution." *Neo-Victorian Studies* 3, no. 1 (2010): 1–45. www.neovictorianstudies.com (12 July 2011).

The Candy Shop: A Fairytale about the Sexual Exploitation of Children. Stop the Candy Shop (2012). www.stopthecandyshop.com/the-film (14 August 2011).

Douglas, Mary. *Purity and Danger: An Analysis of Concepts of Pollution and Taboo*. 1966; reprint, New York: Routledge, 2003.

Dragon*Con. "Welcome to Dragon*Con!" Dragoncon.org. 2011. www.DragonCon.org (5 December 2011).

Falzone, P. J. "The Final Frontier Is Queer: Aberrancy, Archetype and Audience Generated Folklore in K/S Slashfiction." *Western Folklore* 64, no. 3/4 (2005): 243–261.

Glassie, Henry. "Tradition." 176–197 in *Eight Words for the Study of Expressive Culture*, ed. Burt Feintuch. Urbana: University of Illinois, 2003.

Goffman, Erving. *Frame Analysis: An Essay of the Organization of Experience*. Cambridge: Harvard University Press, 1974.

Hellekson, Karen. *The Alternate History: Refiguring Historical Time*. Kent, Ohio: Kent State University Press, 2001.

Hellum, Jeni. "Home Page." Multiculturalism for Steampunk. 2012. www.thesteamerstrunk.blogspot.com (18 May 2011).

"Home Page." *SteamPunk Magazine*. 2012. www.steampunkmagazine.com (21 March 2011).

Jahn, Manfred. *Narratology: A Guide to the Theory of Narrative*. Version 1.8. Cologne, Germany: English Department, University of Cologne, 2005. www.Uni-koeln.de/~ame02/pppn.htm (7 December 2011).

Jameson, Fredric. *Postmodernism, or, the Cultural Logic of Late Capitalism*. Durham, N.C.: Duke University Press, 1992.

Kirby, Alan. 2009. *Digimodernism: How New Technologies Dismantle the Postmodern and Reconfigure Our Culture*. New York: Continuum, 2009.

Lévi-Strauss, Claude. *The Savage Mind*. Chicago: University of Chicago Press, 1966.

Lyotard, Jean François. *The Postmodern Condition: A Report on Knowledge*. Minneapolis: University of Minnesota Press, 1979.

Moore, Alan. "An Interview with Alan Moore." *SteamPunk Magazine* 3 (September 2007): 22–23.

Sterling, Bruce. *Tomorrow Now: Envisioning the Next Fifty Years*. New York: Random House, 2002.

———. "Atemporality & the Passage of Time." Paper presented at the European Graduate School, Saas-Fee, Switzerland, 2009.

———. "Atemporality for the Creative Artist." Paper presented at the Transmediale 10, Berlin, Germany, 2010.

———. "The User's Guide to Steampunk." *SteamPunk Magazine* 5 (April 2009): 30–33.

Vermeulen, Timotheus, and Robin van den Akker. "Notes on Metamodernism." *Journal of Aesthetics and Culture* 2 (2010): 1–14.

Von Slatt, Jake. "Introduction." 2–3 in *SteamPunk Magazine: The First Seven Years: Issues #1–7*. Charleston: Combustion Books, 2011.

Williamson, Jack. *The Legion of Time*. New York: Bluejay Books, 1952.

Newsie strike picket signs at the pro-union rally at Steampunk World's Fair. *Art by Jody Steel; original photography by Michael Salerno*

CHAPTER TEN

Objectified and Politicized: The Dynamics of Ideology and Consumerism in Steampunk Subculture

Diana M. Pho

Steampunk's fascination with the effects of retrofuturistic, neo-Victorian technology upon society elevates the importance of the steampunk object. Steampunk fan identity, then, becomes connected to a currently developing ideology concerning steampunk things: a reactive stance against the omnipresent, slightly menacing, and mostly incomprehensible role of technology in the average person's life today. As an aesthetic, steampunk appeals to those who express discontent with the lack of tactile-focused beauty and the sense of disembodiment contained within today's technological design.[1] It is not surprising, then, that in discussions about the purpose and meaning of technology in human lives, questions concerning steampunk subculture's political possibilities emerge. Furthermore since the style is widely described as "neo-Victorian," subcultural participants and observers have questioned whether the appropriation of the Victorian aesthetic is progressively subversive, conservatively nostalgic, or something in between. Thus, in order to examine the political dimensions of this community, I will focus on how one hotly debated issue is addressed among steampunks: the commodification of steampunk objects.

Steampunk objects are wildly enjoyable subcultural markers that have gained popularity in the mainstream.[2] Indeed, the role of steampunk objects as signifiers has often been conflated with the community's definition of steampunk itself, and in previous scholarship, academics and writers also debated its terminology.[3] A current consensus, however, is explained aptly by Stefania Forlini: steampunk is "about things—especially technological things—and our relationship to them."[4] Moreover, a steampunk object cannot be limited to one medium. Because of the impact of new media and social media in disseminating steampunk images and performances, the definition of a steampunk object ranges from art objects to mediatized images to webzines and blogs to archived performances and rallies. All of these I view as viable "steampunk objects" for critique; including this diverse assortment under the umbrella of the steampunk object stresses the importance of how current media technologies proliferate the creation of objects in today's postmodern cultural discourse. As Philip Auslander notes: "Media and information technologies have created not only a storehouse of images that has led to aesthetic practices based on pastiche and appropriation but also the environment in which cultural discourses are disseminated."[5]

Steampunk objects, both textual and visual, have been assessed critically before.[6] With its increasing application to other art forms, however, I propose that the aesthetic should also be assessed in terms of performance: specifically as a performative promise in keeping with anthropologist Deborah Kapchan's concept of "lived aesthetics"—artistic practices that are performed such as music and theater that contain creative potential that "enacts rather than infers and by its very action accomplishes its goal."[7] Hence, through new media cultural production, steampunk objects become more than clever exercises in anachronism but may promise the progressive mobilization of ideas, or what cultural theorist Stephen Duncombe refers to as the "ethical spectacle."[8] There is evidence, however, of the deferment of this political interpretation in favor of apolitical commercialization, or even ideologically ambiguous messages. This chapter, then, will address how various ideologies concerning the treatment of steampunk objects are embraced, rejected, and proliferated in a postindustrial information economy and how steampunk's postmodern, mediatized identity serves both in conjunction with and in reaction against anticonsumerist stances.

On Methodology: Interrogating "Neo-Victorian" and "Steampunk" Using Web 2.0

Firstly, I must note the debates concerning the meaning of neo-Victorianism and of steampunk, two words whose definitions have remained unstable. The suffix "neo-" has been debated extensively in Victorian scholarship over whether "neo-" refers to a subversion of the Victorian era or a repetition of it; this, in turn, complicates its inclusion as part of the steampunk aesthetic.

Victorian literature scholars Ann Heilmann and Mark Llewellyn both argue that the term "neo-Victorian" does not necessarily suggest a certain political stance:

> To suggest that all neo-Victorian texts—literary, filmic, (audio)visual—are progressive (politically, culturally, aesthetically, literarily), and always represent the "new, modified, or more modern style" just because they appear "in conjunction with a genre," is problematic. . . . There are plenty of texts that might fit these broader terms of neo-Victorianism by genre alone but which are also inherently conservative because they lack imaginative re-engagement with the period, and instead recycle and deliver a stereotypical and unnuanced reading of the Victorians and their literature and culture; as Christian Gulteben notes, there is a danger in the balance between correcting "historical injustice" and what "can be construed cynically as the compliance with the hegemony of the politically correct'."[9]

I agree that it is intellectually hazardous to automatically assign a political slant to the neo-Victorian aesthetic, and furthermore, to apply the same warning to steampunk. Thus, I propose "neo-Victorian" does not mean a reenactment or a repetition of a historical aesthetic trend, but an *interpretation* of the Victorian; and through various interpretations, biases anywhere on the political map unfold. By logical extension to steampunk, I refer to Mike Perschon's argument for steampunk as an "empty" aesthetic that functions as "neo-Victorian, retrofuturistic, technofantasy": "[an] array of visual markers which, when combined, constitute the look popularly understood as steampunk."[10] This definition does not disregard the political or nonpolitical perspectives but instead broadens *steampunk* to account for dynamic viewpoints: "the steampunk glass isn't half-full or half-empty: it's empty, awaiting the artist to fill it with something."[11] Hence, steampunk style cannot be easily ideologically categorized.

New media offer a space where the debates over "what is steampunk" and "how political is steampunk" are enacted through textual arguments and performative examples. Given how dispersed the steampunk community is, the Internet provides the network in which participants locally and globally interact. Individual and localized opinions, which may become lost in mass media and larger pop culture, become magnified and resonate throughout this virtual community. One blog post, tweet, meme, or image, then, repeatedly incites the ideological debate, resulting in new permutations of opinion that continue to mold the community's sociopolitical leanings. As porous a venue as cyberspace can be in formulating ideology, however, virtual spaces also provide niches within the subculture, creating virtual barriers that different politically inclined steampunk participants do not cross. Social media and new media can simultaneously galvanize individual opinions while also dividing an international fandom; thus, the tools of Web 2.0 serves as both a platform and as a micromedia by which current ideological fluctuations within the steampunk community can be gauged. With the exponential growth of steampunk websites, blogs, and online fan communities, it is impossible to give a complete assessment of the steampunk ideological debate in cyberspace. Nevertheless, the increasing visibility of the topic across this virtual space reveals the development of steampunk away from a community who uncritically enjoys an applied aesthetic into a substantially self-reflexive social group.

Person/Machine: Elaborating on the Steampunk as Cyborg

A steampunk's subcultural identity (and any possible political ideology) is intimately connected to an ethical stance concerning the steampunk object. This mind-set is rooted in a positive integration, both imaginatively and literally, of retrofuturistic technology into the human body: steampunks are performing cyborgs, according to Hans-Thies Lehmann's "technically-infiltrated body"[12] and Donna Haraway's "A Cyborg Manifesto."[13] Not only is the human mechanized in steampunk, but the machine also becomes humanized. The New York City–based steampunk anarchist group Catastrophone Orchestra and Arts Collective declares that:

> Steampunk machines are real, breathing, coughing, struggling and rumbling parts of the world. They are not the airy intellectual fairies of algorithmic mathematics but the hulking manifestations of muscle and mind, the progeny of sweat, blood, tears, and delusions. The technology of steampunk is natural; it moves, lives, ages, and even dies.[14]

Instead of the circuitry and microchips of 1980s cyberpunk or the minimalist design of today's Apple products, steampunk mechanics are based on imperfections and mortality, two extremely human qualities. The anthropomorphism of the machine and the self-identification with the cyborg self is further embodied by persona creation. The "steamsona" is a widely recognized subculture phenomenon, though not all steampunk participants have one. On one hand, the steamsona is recognized as a role-playing identity; a steamsona may use false prosthetic limbs, wheelchairs, and monogoggles as extensions of a cyborg self. Furthermore, the cyborg identity extends not only to physical applications but virtual ones as well, with steamsonas emerging on Facebook, Tumblr, and Second Life.[15]

On the other hand, the cyborg steampunk is also a literal reality as people with disabilities actively participate in the subculture. For example, Elsa Sjunneson, who is partially blind, has written about her relationship between steampunk and disability. She understands the steampunk community as a space where she can acknowledge her impairment and even styled her blind cane to fit with the aesthetic. At the same time, however, she is openly critical of able-bodied others who are not reflective of their decision to incorporate disabilities into their steamsona: "I sometimes find it insulting when a fully able person decides to take their abilities (such as being able to see out of both eyes) and chooses to sacrifice it for the game of character. Ableism isn't just about using words like 'cripple'; it isn't just about how the bulk of able-bodied society assumes that we are all helpless; it's also about taking disability and acting like it is a cool thing that we can just take off at the end of the day."[16] Unchecked bouts of ableism is something that steampunk blogger Jaymee Goh also warns of when she advocates for creating welcoming spaces for differently abled people: "Steampunks with disabilities are part of that everyone, and while it may seem, at first glance, to be a huge use of resources accommodating their immediate needs, remember that what's good for one subsection of the community can be extended to all other subsections of the community."[17] On her blog in an article titled "With This Steam-Powered Prosthetic Arm, I Could Be as Strong as . . . a Normal Person," Goh also highlights other steampunks with disabilities and how they have adapted themselves to participate in the scene.

Certainly, as the steampunk community has expanded, the associations between fantastical technology and practical applications are being bridged; for example, the University of Massachusetts, Lowell, is designing a Steampunk and Art Therapy course for people with autism in cooperation with ModVic, a company specializing in steampunk and neo-Victorian home restoration; additionally, they plan to develop a program on steampunk design for living assistance devices such as canes, wheelchairs, and listening devices.[18] Therefore, the person/machine in the steampunk community is slowly being recognized on dual social levels as play and as lived experience.

What all three examples emphasize are the ethical implications between a steampunk's imaginative cyborg identity versus a participant's actual one. Despite criticisms about the current state of the subculture, the discussion about human and nonhuman technological ethics can be interpreted as part of a larger agenda toward egalitarian treatment of all body types where the technically infiltrated body is seen in an optimistic light. Again, to compare steampunk attitudes toward this hybridity against its manifestations in cyberpunk, the augmented human body in cyberpunk often results in the subject's loss of humanity or its subjugation by the government or multinational corporations. On the other hand, steampunk takes a more positive view: the steampunk aesthetic—and in turn, members of its community—recognizes that the cyborg does not necessarily result in the creation of a more advanced form of humanity, and more significantly, steampunks prioritize the intimate and social experiences that exist between the individual and the machine. Hence, the cyborg in the steampunk subculture can exist as being real and imagined, physical as well as virtual; thus, a complex understanding of interpersonal relations between steampunks and their various expressions of performed technologically integrated identities becomes manifested in ideological debates as steampunks attempt to interpret their stylistic choices alongside political standpoints.

DIY Expressions: Artisans as the "Punks" of Steampunk

The extent to which a performative identity engages with technology contributes to the various ethical responses made between people and the steampunk object, mediated in part by the Internet and social media. Well-known steampunk websites and blogs highlight various objects and facilitate a community of admirers and self-involved producers. One of the most well known is the Steampunk Workshop, run by maker Jake von Slatt. Coauthor of *The Steampunk Bible* Jeff VanderMeer cites von Slatt's website as one of the first that recognizes the importance of the community in steampunk engagement.[19] In fact, von Slatt believes that the most important aspect of the Steampunk Workshop is not its function as an archive for his DIY creations but its use in spreading information about steampunk's DIY philosophy and its roots in maker culture: "I actually consider my true work to be the web pages that describe the construction of each piece, the piece itself merely the byproduct of the workshop experience," von Slatt acknowledges.[20] Websites, blogs, and virtual spaces, then, can serve as vehicles for the dissemination of steampunk objects, while also becoming steampunk objects in their own right.

Along with the philosophy that anyone can create and maintain steampunk objects, the ethical relationship between creators and their work has been described using politically charged terminology. For example, Art Donovan, steampunk artist and the curator for the Oxford Museum's 2010 steampunk exhibit, explains that "the 'punk' is an important reference to an outsider attitude. In Steampunk this attitude manifests itself in the form of the lone wolf artist, the DIY (Do-It-Yourself) craftsman, and the amateur engineer, who are not beholden to any contemporary style of ideology."[21]

Such political statements have not been ignored by others. Communications scholar Dru Pagliassotti contemplates steampunk's ideological potential to suggest these are only nascent ideas at present:

> Such sociopolitical commentary hasn't been as prevalent in steampunk. Although the do-it-yourself ethic of punk has been retained by steampunk, which cherishes a literary history of mad scientists and crackpot inventors and attracts its share of engineers, designers, and costumers, there is less of a sense that the steampunk movement is innately oppositional. True, in the broadest sense, DIY opposes mass marketing and consumerism, but thus far anticonsumerism hasn't emerged as a unifying theme for the movement. [22]

VanderMeer, in contrast, argues that the "punk" of steampunk highlights a reactionary response that is distinctly progressive: "The parallel couldn't be more obvious: Steampunks seek to reject the conformity of the modern, soulless, featureless design of technology—and all that it implies—while embracing the inventiveness and tech origins of Victorian machines. They also seek to repair the damage caused by industrialization, . . . a progressive impulse to reclaim the dead past in a positive and affirmative way."[23] Indeed, progressive steampunks have taken on the performative trappings of the aesthetic. Steamsona elements such as scene names are used by many anticonsumerist progressives such as von Slatt and more radical anachro-punks (punks who also identify as anarchists) such as *SteamPunk Magazine* founder Magpie Killjoy, its former editor C. Allegra Hawksmoor, and the Catastrophone Orchestra and Arts Collective of Queens, New York.

Steamsona pseudonyms do not imply that their identity as political actors is false, but instead, their steamsonas reflect authentic beliefs. This authenticity of self in persona creation has been noticed in other studies concerning subcultural communities, such as anthropologist Tom Boellstorff's work on Second Life.[24] In fact, these steampunks promote progressive stances against consumerism as part of their steampunk identity: von Slatt comments, "Steampunks eschew the consumerism of popular culture. . . . Steampunks want to buy something once and then pass it on to our children. Even better, we want to make something once, something that we will use every day for the rest of our lives."[25] Advocates for the DIY/maker aspect of steampunk are also more likely "lifestylists," such as the bloggers behind the Greyshade Manor, who write about renovating an old Victorian homestead using modern methods that are environmentally friendly and historically accurate to Victorian times: "Like the literature, the lifestyle

Steampunk "demotivational poster" of Abraham Lincoln.

begins with speculation: What would reality be like if all the best parts of the past had continued on but the best parts of the present had also developed?"[26] These acts of DIY creation and green living fall in line with Forlini's proposal that the steampunk aesthetic fosters a newfound sense of ethics toward things:

> In reading things, we learn to see our fundamentally posthuman condition, our profound embeddedness in what the science and technology studies tradition refers to as socio-technical network of humans and nonhumans.[27]

In keeping with my previous observations on the steampunk as cyborg, the range of media outlets that advocates for a progressive treatment of steampunked objects implies that technology is more than an addition to the human body/self-identity, but part of Forlini's "socio-technical network of humans and nonhumans" that above all prioritizes the social effects of steampunked objects.

Satirical Subversions:
Political Humor in Steampunk

The political efficacy of the ethical relationship between steampunks and their objects, however, is complicated by the subcultural humor that pushes the boundaries of ideological sincerity. Humor is prevalent in the style's application: most popularly as pastiche, or "steampunk versions" of modern-day objects that emphasize idiosyncratic juxtapositions or allude to pop culture. Pastiche has long been recognized as an attraction, Pagliassotti notes:

> Steampunk bloggers often, at least in the introductions to their blogs, adopt an (ironic) imitation of Victorian writing style, and steampunk costumers and roleplayers often emulate the archetypical literary characters found in Victorian and pulp adventure stories. At times, works of steampunk fiction and art have also offered pastiches of well-known writers or artists of the Victorian period.[28]

For example, the popular performance group the League of S.T.E.A.M. is inspired by the Ghostsbusters; created in 2007, the League's popularity has resulted in a Web series, a touring staple on the convention circuit, and a feature role in Panic! at the Disco's music video "The Ballad of Mona Lisa."[29] Thus, the commodification of steampunk through new media initiatives leads to gains in "subcultural capital," to reference Sarah Thornton's work.[30] Additionally, pastiche results in steampunked historical figures, with their images circulating the Internet as memes. The most common is Abraham Lincoln with a Gatling-gun arm titled "Steampunk: Yeah, it's kind of like that."[31]

Mockingly critical political commentary appears in steampunk visual media and performances as well, usually centered upon a participant's steamsona. One example is Lord Featherstone (the steamsona of Brute Force artist/owner Thomas Willeford), who is a member of BORG: Britannic Officers Reconnaissance Group. In the group's poster created by Willeford, a military officer with a monogoggle stares sternly ahead; the acronym is a tongue-in-cheek reference to the assimilating enemy from Star Trek, and BORG's motto is a commentary about British imperialism: "Resistance is Bloody Futile . . . you will be colonized." Such images acknowledge the problems of the historical past with ironic self-reflexivity, reminding us of colonial-era violence from a smug, contemporary distance. Whether this satirical piece proves that the community at large encourages postcolonial perspectives is yet to be seen, though examples do crop up online, usually the results of steamsona play at conventions. Wampanoag tribe member Monique Poirier, for instance, plays a Native American scientist; in the image titled "Postcolonialism at Work," she is poisoning Professor Elemental, a British "chap-hop" rapper dressed in safari gear.[32]

Steamsona performances like these can take lighthearted jabs against historical oppression but also blend satire with more blatant expressions of progressive engagement relevant to today's political climate. The pro-union flash mob that I participated in during the Steampunk World's Fair in Somerset, New Jersey, in May 2011 is a prime example of this expression of steampunked political engagement. Organized by Miriam Roçek performing as "Steampunk Emma Goldman"—an homage to the famous nineteenth-century Jewish anarchist—this pro-union rally supported both real and

BORG Poster from Brute Force Leather. *Courtesy of Thomas Willeford*

"Postcolonialism at Work." *Courtesy of Monique Poirier and Paul Alborough*

fictional union causes, according to their promotional copy on the event's Facebook page:

> Let us remember the labor organizers, the struggles, and the world-changing activism of the past! If you appreciate the 8 hour day, weekends, or safety standards, you have a 19th century union to thank. This flashmob [sic] will be a combination 19th century strike and modern day pro-labor demonstration. Come in working-class period garb, your regular steampunk garb, or even modern union t-shirts, and support the cause of your choice, and by doing so, support them all.

We will stand, simultaneously, by the Newsboy's Strike of 1899, the Cripple Creek Miner's Strike of 1894, the Interplanetary Aetheric Pilot's Strike of 2204, and the Wisconsin State Employees of Right the Hell Now.[33]

Over sixty people attended, many of them wielding signs that were character appropriate; a pair of young newsies, for instance, held protest signs that said "Newsies Need Fair Pay!" and "Pulitzer and Hearst Unfair to Labor!"[34] while aristocratic steampunks demonstrated a "counterprotest" by waving signs that said slogans like "Why Work When You Can Inherit?" and "Get Back to Work Peasants!"[35] Roçek enacted another rally at the Great New England Steampunk Convention in September 2011 to support the gay rights activist group FCK H8 under the banner "Fornicate Hate"[36] and has protested at Occupy Wall Street as well, which drew attention from the *New York Times*.[37]

The creation of alternate identities to foster political action in the form of satire and parody corresponds with the activist strategy that Stephen Duncombe calls a progressive "ethical spectacle": political action that is "directly democratic, breaks down hierarchies, fosters community, allows for diversity, and engages with reality while asking what new realities might be possible."[38] To Duncombe, the obvious illusion presented in an ethical spectacle is part of its attraction, whether in the form of dance parties in the streets, people dressing up as "Monopoly-inspired" Billionaires for Bush, or Reverend Billy's "No shopping" sermons.

Likewise, steampunk's performative revisionism, rooted in the idea of re-appropriating the past to create a better future, is a common theme in much of steampunk's developing ideology. The Catastrophone Orchestra writes in their artist's manifesto that "we are rebuilding yesterday to ensure our tomorrow. . . . We are archeologists of the present, reanimating a hallucinatory history."[39] Magpie Killjoy believes that the DIY steampunk tinkerer can advocate for sustainable living and "help people realize that progress is not necessarily linear: we might have to go back in order to go forward."[40] Furthermore, neo-Victorian scholars Bowser and Croxall note how steampunk's hybrid temporality is key to understanding the style's usage:

> Indeed, steampunk looks to the present to illuminate the past, the past to illuminate the present, the future to illuminate the past, and the past to illuminate the future: its most defining feature may therefore be the jumbling of markers from different time periods in order to illuminate compatibility.[41]

Steampunk's "illuminating compatibility" compares historical problems to contemporary ones yet also considers their theatrical quality as further assurances of political authenticity; these actions gesture toward a fantastical utopia through their creative excess. Performance theorist Jill Dolan suggests that utopian performance can enact affective change upon the audience, which reveals the possibility of enacting an optimistic ideal through civil engagement.[42] Thus, political actions that become "steampunked" open up an imaginative space where ideological messages are framed not only as historical pastiche but as relevant and engaging postmodern commentary that gestures toward a utopic horizon.

The Commercial and the Colonial: Steampunk Palin and the Gatehouse Gazette

Yet the steampunk aesthetic does not easily align itself with a progressive or leftist perspective, despite the previous examples: the comic book *Steampunk Palin* is a case in point. Published in January 2011 and created by Ben Dunn, the comic provoked controversy in the steampunk and sci-fi communities; word about it spread like wildfire through a hilarious online review from the website *Comics Alliance*. Moreover, a self-titled website dedicated to *Steampunk Palin* helped spread its recognition online. This website suggests a feminist stance criticizing Palin's fetishization by the public: "Sarah Palin is a magnet for sexism from both the right and left. It is hard to imagine a male politician being sexualized, but a good looking middle aged female politician becomes the Alaskan Snow MILF."[43] The actual comic, however, does not seem to be a feminist critique as much as it seeks to pander toward pop culture's fetishization of Palin and of steampunk: the comic hypersexualizes her steampunked image and includes eight pin-up spreads of Palin in steampunk gear. Additionally, the story connects her frequent intellectual gaffes to steampunk tropes. In the comic, the world has run out of oil, and so Palin suggests using steam power; when her proposed power source is tested, though, an explosion results, and Palin is rebuilt into a steam-powered body. Other major political figures are also steampunked after the explosion; Barack Obama becomes the cyborg "Robama," and John McCain sports a cybernetic arm. The bipartisan group goes on to defeat Al Gore, who oddly enough, is the head of the remaining oil/nuke conglomerate. *Comics Alliance* reviewer Chris Murphy mentions that the comic achieves its humorous effect, but it's unclear whether the humor was a result of the author's success or failed execution of political commentary: "I was laughing pretty hysterically at the events of the 15–page story for reasons I'm going to go ahead and assume are *not intended by the authors*. Thus, I'm not afraid to declare *Steampunk Palin* to be so bad it's good."[44]

Steampunk Palin comic cover. *Courtesy of Ben Dunn*

Steampunk in this case, then, is a framework that compliments Palin's attractiveness and her ineptitude while also making fun of the greater political sphere. The comic highlights the irrational functionality of steampunk mechanics despite its popularity as a visual aesthetic, which is compared to the public's focus on Palin's sex appeal and its ridicule of her many political blunders. Palin is not the only figure lampooned through the application of this style; the entire American political system is satirized as being overwrought and ineffective when it becomes steampunked. Only in a ridiculous retrofuturist world, according to Ben Dunn, can Democrats and Republicans unite to fight against a common enemy, and that political enemy is a complete ideological mash-up that is not reflective of the real-life politician's platform in any way. No wonder this comic inflamed steampunk fans who believe in steampunk's utopic potential. Many steampunks expressed their rage over the comic as mocking the subculture,[45] though many more outside commentators in the science fiction community expressed their disgust over any further type of media featuring Palin.[46]

The comic's overarching message is not a criticism against conservative or progressive values, however, but it *questions the very politicization of the aesthetic.* This analysis of *Steampunk Palin* has been overlooked by many, unfortunately, primarily because subculture participants and outside observers alike chose to focus upon the comic's timeliness in capitalizing upon steampunk's growing appeal and the then-popular attraction of ridiculing Palin; thus, the comic worked in compliance with consumerism rather than jockeying against it. Indeed, the negative reaction from many who accused the comic as being a "bad" example of steampunk is not because the comic was necessarily poorly produced or badly written, but because it was obviously commercial. In this case, political humor in steampunk is not truly subversive against commodification but vulnerable to any form of commercial hijacking. Duncombe's "ethical spectacle" is not the only ideological avenue for steampunk objects, and in fact, as *Steampunk Palin* demonstrates, they can also fall in accordance with Fredric Jameson's observation of pastiche as being a politically empty gesture "without any of parody's ulterior motives, amputated of the satiric impulse, devoid of laughter or of any conviction that alongside the abnormal tongue that you have momentarily borrowed, some healthy linguistic normality still exists."[47] In this manner, *Steampunk Palin* speaks to a progressive audience, but not necessarily to an anticonsumerist one, and certainly exposes the fallibility of establishing ideological associations in visual culture.

Steampunk objects have also taken a decidedly nonradical and even conservatively nostalgic position, such as the steampunk webzine *The Gatehouse*

Gazette. Founded in 2008 specifically as an alternative to the anarchist-run *SteamPunk Magazine*, the *Gatehouse Gazette* was created by steampunks "who felt that there had never been much 'punk' in steampunk to begin with and they wondered whether they couldn't produce a magazine of their own."[48] The *Gatehouse Gazette*, though it initially claimed to be "apolitical" and in later issues refers to its content as being "activist,"[49] continuously uses terminology that harkens back to language used by the West to objectify the non-Western other. In their November 2009 issue, for example, *Gatehouse* describes steampunk's self-sufficiency as a "return to primitivism," and their March 2010 issue sparked controversy for using the term "Victorientalism" to describe Asian steampunk.[50] In the *Gatehouse Gazette*'s final issue, titled "Empire Revisited: Astounding Tales from the Colonies," the zine editor Nick Ottens unabashedly expressed a nostalgic view toward pro-imperialist sentiments:

> Neo-Victorianism isn't imperialist revival but does recreate the style and storytelling of an era in which England ruled a quarter of the world's population. The romance of the empire has been part of the steampunk ethos for more than a decade. Whether it's imperialist adventure in the colonies or megalomania in old Blighty, the empire is always there, prominently or lurking in the shadows, when you're entering the nineteenth century. Rather than trying to hide it because we're anti-colonialists now, let's be honest and upfront about the fact that we admire the pomp and spirit of the globetrotting Victorians. Once we identify what we like, we can confidently either discuss or ignore what we don't. The Victorians perpetrated a lot of wrongs after all but it's ridiculous to pretend that steampunk wants nothing to do with empire because of it.[51]

The occupation of an anticonsumerist stance is not necessarily a politically progressive position, either. Left-wing makers, anarchists, and nostalgically imperialist steampunks alike all claim the DIY, anticommercial ethos as part of their political philosophy; thus, steampunk's relation to materialism can be transformed into an ideologically flexible concept that can be commandeered by anyone on the ideological spectrum.

Another contradictory twist upon steampunk's claimed ideology versus its practiced one is the subculture's rampant materialism, which poses an ethical dilemma that pits the community's anticonsumerist manifesto with the reification of the financially successful independent artist. While steampunks pride themselves on creativity, many also seek to profit from it, resulting in an overflow of handcrafted work, much of it being fashion accessories and outfits. Engagement with steampunked objects often correlates with the Victorian fascination with the accumulation of things, and new media perpetuate this mind-set too. In fact, the emphasis on "owning stuff" complies with Thornton's observation about accumulating subcultural capital through consumerism.[52] On self-vending websites such as Etsy and eBay, thousands of steampunk items are sold, and major steampunk online boutiques exist such as Steampunk Couture, Clockwork Couture, Brute Force Studios, and the Steampunk Emporium. As a result, the steampunk maker's message about DIY and self-sustainability is countered with the anxiety for the financial viability of steampunk objects in an oversaturated artists' marketplace.

This blatant push for commercial artistic success is emphasized by Evelyn Kriete, co-moderator of the popular LiveJournal community *steamfashion*: "And I would definitely like to see steampunk prove to be a viable market to support the numerous artists in the trend. . . . On the other hand, if mainstream products and fans who have just gotten into steampunk end up stealing the spotlight from long-established steampunk artists who need to make a living off of their work, then it's a terrible thing."[53] To Kriete, the purpose of steampunk is clear; it is a "trend" that should be utilized for its marketing potential as opposed to its political potential. Kriete's fear that "long-established" artists will be obscured by "fans who have just gotten into steampunk" speaks to Thornton's subcultural hierarchy.[54] Indeed, in the steampunk community, the rising popularity of individual artists has been equated by some with the need for their commercial success. In fact, because of successful makers and designers such as Brute Force Studios and ModVic, many amateur artist groups are seeking to replicate them, usually by forming troupes or art collectives called "crews" (in reference to airship pirate crews) and soliciting their skills in prop-making, costuming, and panel-speaking as services to conventions. In competition with these groups, however, are popular media and corporations that develop steampunk-themed products to appeal to the mainstream, and many of the indie steampunk antics that pop up on YouTube have now been picked up by pop artists such as Panic! at the Disco, Lady Gaga, Bush, and Justin Bieber.[55]

Conclusion: Steampunk as Historicity's Palimpsest

In conclusion, people's divergent attitudes toward the political uses of their subcultural objects have been sites of tension within the steampunk community. Yet these tensions are not unique to this community alone but are also reflected in dominant culture's attitudes toward consumerism, environmental living, and technological advances. Much like how neo-Victorian reimagines the Victorian for our age, steampunk style's gestures toward historical moments speak to Jameson's historicity: "a relationship to the present which somehow defamiliarizes it and allows us that distance from immediacy which is at length characterized as historical perspective."[56] Steampunk's historicity also coincides with conclusions made about current adaptations of Victorian novels into film and television, situating steampunk's current handling of ideological questions inside a larger scope around the public's fascination with the Victorian.[57]

Unlike Jameson's lament that historicity leads only to a nonpolitical void in the text, however, I offer Linda Hutcheon's assurance that, instead of hollowness, "what postmodernism does, as its very name suggests, is confront and contest any modernist discarding or recuperating of the past in the name of the future. It suggests no search for the transcendent, timeless meaning but rather a re-evaluation of, and a dialogue with the past in light of the present."[58] Thus, the political anxiety about steampunk's commodification speaks to today's concerns over materialism and politics. In that sense, steampunk's political promise insofar has been an incomplete one: not overthrowing dominant paradigms but working alongside them and easily applicable across a wide variety of political preferences. Within its incompleteness, though, lies its greatest potential, as expressed by Duncombe: "when it is impossible to think of an alternative, then maybe the solution is to think about the impossible."[59] The results of steampunk's cultural production using remixed histories and overlapping cultural references can be described, perhaps, as a palimpsest of historical moments, where the final result—our imagined pasts pasted over historical realities—privileges neither the past nor the present but gestures toward an as yet unrealized utopian blending of both. The conversation of ideology is not yet fully realized, and tracking its evolution would be of great interest to scholars: not only for those interested in neo-Victorianism but across other interdisciplinary fields. As Christine Ferguson recently argued in her article about steampunk ideology, scholars looking at steampunk or other taste cultures cannot make easy assumptions about "how ideological critique and historiographic reflection is or might be incorporated into subcultural aesthetics."[60] Indeed, as the ideological designs behind steampunk become reevaluated and reinvented, its aesthetic form and function will nevertheless continue to provide a social gauge upon which to assess today's sociopolitical attitudes.

Notes

1. For instance, as science fiction author Gail Carriger writes about steampunk in her essay, "Which Is Mightier, the Pen or the Parasol?": "Functionality has become

something shameful, a tiny thing to be hidden away behind plastic and metal. . . . We steampunk DIYers force cogs and gears back out into the open." *Steampunk II: Steampunk Reloaded*, ed. Jeff and Ann VanderMeer (San Francisco: Tachyon Press, 2010), 402.

2. Virtually accessible mediatized images also serve as easy inspiration for creators of steampunk objects. Scott Westerfeld, author of the best-selling steampunk *Leviathan* trilogy, once quipped that whenever he needs to find inspiration, he does a Google search on "steampunk." Panel at Book Expo America 2010, "Steampunkery: Why Are Today's Teens Embracing 19th-Century Technologies?," http://vimeo.com/12054016 (20 July 2012).

3. Various definitions of steampunk exist, a symptom of the postmodern nature of the community. Rachel Bowser and Brian Croxall, in their introduction to *Journal of Neo-Victorian Studies* special issue on steampunk (www.neovictorianstudies.com/past_issues/3–1%202010/NVS%203–1–1%20R-Bowser%20&%20B-Croxall.pdf (20 July 2011), define it as "a kind of cultural memory work, wherein our projections and fantasies about the Victorian era meet the tropes and techniques of science fiction, to produce a genre that revels in anachronism while exposing history's overlapping layers," which is an efficient explanation of the steampunk style, though I favor Mike Perschon's definition of steampunk, which is elaborated upon further in my essay "Advocating for the Aesthetic," 14 July 2011, *STEAMED!*, http://ageofsteam.wordpress.com/2011/07/14/advocating-for-aesthetic (29 July 2011).

4. Stefania Forlini, "Technology and Morality: The Stuff of Steampunk," *Journal of Neo-Victorian Studies* 3, no. 1 (2010): 72, www.neovictorianstudies.com/past_issues/3–1%202010/NVS%203–1–3%20S-Forlini.pdf (20 July 2011).

5. Philip Auslander, *Presence and Resistance: Postmodernism and Cultural Politics in Contemporary American Performance* (Ann Arbor: University of Michigan Press, 1992), 17.

6. This special issue, titled "Steampunk, Science, and (Neo)Victorian Technologies," came out in 2010 and was guest edited by Rachel A. Bowser and Brian Croxall.

7. Deborah Kapchan, "The Promise of Sonic Translation: Performing the Festive Sacred in Morocco," *American Anthropologist* 110, no. 4 (December 2008): 470.

8. Stephen Duncombe, *Dream: Re-Imagining Progressive Politics in an Age of Fantasy* (New York: New Press, 2007), 134.

9. Ann Heilmann and Mark Llewellyn, *Neo-Victorianism: The Victorians of the Twenty-First Century, 1999–2009* (New York: Palgrave MacMillan, 2010), 6.

10. Mike Perschon, "Steam Wars," *Journal of Neo-Victorian Studies* 3, no. 1 (2010): 128, www.neovictorianstudies.com/past_issues/3–1%202010/NVS%203–1–5%20M-Perschon.pdf (20 July 2011). This definition does not disregard the political or non-political positions that steampunk participants hold, but instead broadens the usage of the term *steampunk* to account for a wide range of viewpoints.

11. Perschon, "Advocating for the Aesthetic."

12. Hans-Thies Lehmann, *Postdramatic Theater*, trans. Karen Jürs-Munby (New York: Routledge, 2006), 162.

13. Donna Haraway, "A Cyborg Manifesto: Science, Technology, and Socialist-Feminism in the Late Twentieth Century," in *Simians, Cyborgs and Women: The Reinvention of Nature* (New York: Routledge, 1991), 149.

14. Catastrophone Orchestra and Arts Collective, "What, Then, Is Steampunk?," *SteamPunk Magazine* 1 (2004): 4, www.steampunkmagazine.com/pdfs/SPM1–web.pdf (20 July 2011).

15. Examples of online steampunk spaces such as the Ning social networks Steampunk Empire and Dieselpunks, the forum Brass Goggles, and the expansive worlds of New Babbage, NeoVictoria, Caldeon, and others on Second Life.

16. Elsa Sjunneson, "A Word About Eyepatches: A Personal Essay," 12 June 2011, *Beyond Victoriana*, http://beyondvictoriana.com/2011/06/12/a-word-about-eyepatches-a-personal-essay-guest-blog-by-elsa-sjunneson (20 July 2011).

17. Jaymee Goh, "With This Steam-Powered Prosthetic Arm, I Could Be as Strong as . . . a Normal Person," 1 May 2010, *Silver Goggles*, http://silver-goggles.blogspot.com/2010/05/repost-for-blogging-against-disablism.html (20 July 2011).

18. Bruce Rosenbaum, interview with the author, November 2011.

19. Jeff VanderMeer and S. J. Chambers, *The Steampunk Bible* (New York: Abrams Image, 2011), 104.

20. Jake von Slatt, as quoted in Forlini, "Technology and Morality: The Stuff of Steampunk," *Journal of Neo-Victorian Studies* 3, no. 1 (2010): 77, www.neovictorianstudies.com/past_issues/3–1%202010/NVS%203–1–3%20S-Forlini.pdf (20 July 2011).

21. Art Donovan, *The Art of Steampunk* (East Petersburg, Pa.: Fox Chapel Publishing, 2011), 24.

22. Dru Pagliassotti, "Does Steampunk Have Politics?," in *The Mark of Ashen Wings*, 19 February 2009, http://drupagliassotti.com/2009/02/11/does-steampunk-have-politics (30 July 2011).

23. VanderMeer and Chambers, *The Steampunk Bible*, 99.

24. Tom Boellstorff, *Coming of Age in Second Life* (Princeton, N.J.: Princeton University Press, 2008), 121.

25. Jake von Slatt, "A Steampunk Manifesto," in *The Steampunk Bible*, 219.

26. Greyshade Estate, "Towards a Steampunk Lifestyle," *The Greyshade Estate*, 28 September 2010, http://greyshadeestate.blogspot.com/2010/09/towards-steampunk-lifestyle.html (29 July 2011).

27. Forlini, "Technology and Morality," 91.

28. Dru Pagliassotti, "Does Steampunk Have an Ideology?," *The Mark of Ashen Wings*, 19 February 2009, http://drupagliassotti.com/2009/02/13/does-steampunk-have-an-ideology (30 July 2011).

29. The official music video can be viewed on YouTube at www.youtube.com/watch?v=gOgpdp3lP8M (20 July 2011).

30. Specifically, I reference Thornton's ethnographic research into the UK dance social scene in *Club Cultures: Music, Media and Subcultural Capital*, where she conceptualized "subcultural capital" as a combination of aestheticized resistance marked

by consumerism and social connections within the subcultural community. Sarah Thornton, *Club Cultures: Music, Media and Subcultural Capital* (Middletown, Conn.: Wesleyan University Press, 1996).

31. Steampunk Lincoln is a frequent costume choice at steampunk conventions and has also resulted in two series starring the president, titled *Steampunk Lincoln* (http://steampunklincoln.webstarts.com/index.html) and *Time Lincoln* (www.antarctic-press.com/html/version_01/viewitem.php?id=5521&bk=search .php?search=time%20lincoln).

32. Monique Poirier, "Postcolonialism at Work," *Moniquilliloquies*, http://moniquill.tumblr.com/post/5757645850/bookishbeth-post-colonialism-at-work-native (31 July 2011).

33. Miriam Roçek, quoted from Facebook, May 2011.

34. Ay-leen the Peacemaker, "Steampunk World's Fair Part II: The Fairening," 9 June 2011, *Tor.com*, www.tor.com/blogs/2011/06/steampunk-worlds-fair-ii-ayleen -the-peacemaker (30 July 2011).

35. Magpie Killjoy, "Steampunk World's Fair 2011," *Birds Before the Storm*, 23 May 2011, www.birdsbeforethestorm.net/2011/05/2011–steampunk-worlds-fair (30 July 2011).

36. Miriam Roçek, interview with the author, July 2011.

37. Christopher Matthews, "A Radical's Legacy: Emma Goldman Lives On at Occupy Wall Street, and on the Rental Market," *The Local East Village on the New York Times*, 22 December 2011, http://eastvillage.thelocal.nytimes.com/2011/12/22/ emma-goldman-lives-radicals-former-address-up-for-rent-and (15 January 2012).

38. Duncombe, *Dream: Re-Imagining Progressive Politics in an Age of Fantasy*, 126.

39. Catastrophone Orchestra, "What, Then, Is Steampunk?," 4–5.

40. Killjoy, interview, "The Future of Steampunk: A Roundtable Interview," 410.

41. Bowser and Croxall, *Journal of Neo-Victorian Studies*, 5.

42. Jill Dolan, *Utopia in Performance: Finding Hope at the Theater* (Ann Arbor: University of Michigan Press, 2005), 21.

43. "Steampunk Palin," *Steampunk Palin*, http://steampunkpalin.com (28 July 2011).

44. Chris Murphy, "'Steampunk Palin' Comic More Insane Than You Imagined," *Comics Alliance*, 20 January 2011, www.comicsalliance.com/2011/01/20/steampunk -palin-comic (20 January 2011).

45. Murphy, "'Steampunk Palin' Comic More Insane Than You Imagined."

46. Mark Frauenfelde, *Steampunk Palin* comic book, *BoingBoing*, 21 January 2011, http://boingboing.net/2011/01/21/steampunk-palin-comi.html (29 July 2011). When BoingBoing profiled this on their website, a slew of criticisms arose expressing disgust and fatigue over pop culture's obsession with Palin, who they thought didn't deserve so much media focus. This, of course, reflects the site's progressive readership. Very few of the comments mentioned how this comic was a satire about Palin and the American political system.

47. Fredric Jameson, *Postmodernism, or, the Cultural Logic of Late Capitalism* (Durham, N.C.: Duke University Press, 1992), 17.

48. Nick Ottens, "History of the *Gatehouse Gazette*," *The Gatehouse Gazette*, November 2011, www.ottens.co.uk/gatehouse/History%20of%20the%20Gatehouse%20Gazette.pdf (15 February 2011).

49. Ottens, "History of the *Gatehouse Gazette*."

50. The debate over the term "Victorientalism" provoked contention among European steampunks who saw no issue with the term and steampunks of color who were greatly offended by it. See Jaymee Goh's article "Countering Victorientalism," 7 March 2010, http://silver-goggles.blogspot.com/2010/03/countering-victorientalism.html; *Beyond Victoriana*'s "The Semantics of Words & the Antics of Fashion: Addressing 'Victorientalism,'" 7 March 2010, http://beyondvictoriana.com/2010/03/07/beyond-victoriana-17the-semantics-of-words-the-antics-of-fashion-addressing-victorientalism; the Anti-Oppression Linkspam community on *Dreamwidth*, http://linkspam.dreamwidth.org/tag/victorientalism; and the *Gatehouse Gazette*'s response "In Defense of Victorientalism," 11 March 2010, www.ottens.co.uk/gatehouse/2010/03/in-defense-of-victorientalism for reference.

51. Nick Ottens, "Farewell to Empire," *The Gatehouse Gazette*, November 2011, www.ottens.co.uk/gatehouse/gazette-21 (15 February 2012).

52. Sarah Thornton, "The Social Logic of Subcultural Capital," in *The Subcultures Reader*, ed. Ken Gelder and Sarah Thornton (New York: Routledge, 1997), 202.

53. Evelyn Kriete, interview, "The Future of Steampunk: A Roundtable Interview," in *Steampunk II: Steampunk Reloaded*, 412.

54. Thornton, "The Social Logic of Subcultural Capital," 209.

55. In addition to Panic! at the Disco's "The Ballad of Mona Lisa" music video, Lady Gaga's video "Alejandro," Bush's album *The Incredible Machine*, and Justin Bieber's video rendition of "Santa Claus Is Coming to Town" in Santa's steampunk workshop in the North Pole are examples of popular artists engaging with the style.

56. Jameson, *Postmodernism*, 284.

57. Heilmann and Llewellyn, *Neo-Victorianism: The Victorians in the Twenty-First Century, 1999–2009*, 215.

58. Linda Hutcheon, "Representing the Postmodern," in *A Postmodern Reader*, ed. Joseph Natoli and Linda Hutcheon (New York: State University of New York Press, 1993), 261.

59. Duncombe, *Dream: Re-Imagining Progressive Politics in an Age of Fantasy*, 167.

60. Christine Ferguson, "Surface Tensions: Steampunk, Subculture, and the Ideology of Style," *Journal of Neo-Victorian Studies* 4, no. 2 (2011): 84, www.neovictorianstudies.com/issues/NVS%204-2-4%20C-Ferguson.pdf (1 March 2012). Ferguson's article was published right before this article's revisions were turned in for this anthology. Admittedly, I confess some excitement about her discussion of the topic, particularly because of my involvement in her research. While she brings up relevant points that coincide with my own, we differentiate on how we construct our arguments around the development of ideology in steampunk.

Bibliography

Anti-Oppression Linkspam community. http://linkspam.dreamwidth.org/tag/victor ientalism (15 February 2012).

Auslander, Philip. *Presence and Resistance: Postmodernism and Cultural Politics in Contemporary American Performance*. Ann Arbor: University of Michigan Press, 1992.

Ay-leen the Peacemaker (Diana M. Pho). "Steampunk World's Fair Part II: The Fairening" 9 June 2011. *Tor.com*. www.tor.com/blogs/2011/06/steampunk-worlds -fair-ii-ayleen-the-peacemaker (30 July 2011).

———. "The Semantics of Words & the Antics of Fashion: Addressing 'Victoriental-ism.'" *Beyond Victoriana*. 7 March 2010. http://beyondvictoriana.com/2010/03/07/ beyond-victoriana-17the-semantics-of-words-the-antics-of-fashion-addressing -victorientalism (15 February 2012).

Bieber, Justin. "Santa Claus Is Coming to Town" (*Arthur Christmas* version). Music video. www.youtube.com/watch?v=nAI_xI9wQnE (15 February 2012).

Boellstorff, Tom. *Coming of Age in Second Life: An Anthropologist Explores the Virtually Human*. Princeton, N.J.: Princeton University Press, 2008.

Book Expo America 2010. "Steampunkery: Why Are Today's Teens Embracing 19th-Century Technologies?" Video. http://vimeo.com/12054016 (20 July 2011).

Bowser, Rachel A., and Brian Croxall. "Introduction: Industrial Evolution." *Journal of Neo-Victorian Studies* 3, no. 1 (2010): 1–45. www.neovictorianstudies.com/ past_issues/3–1%202010/NVS%203–1–1%20R-Bowser%20&%20B-Croxall.pdf (20 July 2011).

Brass Goggles. "The Steampunk Forum at Brass Goggles." http://brassgoggles.co.uk/ forum (28 July 2011).

Bush. *The Incredible Machine*. CD. 2010.

Carlson, Marvin. *Performance: A Critical Introduction*, 2nd ed. New York: Routledge, 1996.

Carriger, Gail. "Which Is Mightier, the Pen or the Parasol?" 399–403 in *Steampunk II: Steampunk Reloaded*, ed. Ann VanderMeer and Jeff VanderMeer. San Francisco: Tachyon Press, 2010.

Catastrophone Orchestra and Arts Collective. "What, Then, Is Steampunk?" *Steam-Punk Magazine* 1 (2004): 4–5. www.steampunkmagazine.com/pdfs/SPM1–web.pdf (20 July 2011).

Dolan, Jill. *Utopia in Performance: Finding Hope at the Theater*. Ann Arbor: University of Michigan Press, 2005.

Donovan, Art. *The Art of Steampunk*. East Petersburg, Pa.: Fox Chapel Publishing, 2011.

Duncombe, Stephen. *Dream: Re-Imagining Progressive Politics in an Age of Fantasy*. New York: New Press, 2007.

Dunn, Ben. *Steampunk Palin*. San Antonio, Tx.: Antarctic Press, 2010.

Ferguson, Christine. "Surface Tensions: Steampunk, Subculture, and the Ideology of Style." *Journal of Neo-Victorian Studies* 4, no. 2 (2011): 66–90. www.neovictor ianstudies.com/issues/NVS%204–2–4%20C-Ferguson.pdf (1 March 2012).

Forlini, Stefania. "Technology and Morality: The Stuff of Steampunk." *Journal of Neo-Victorian Studies* 3, no. 1 (2010): 1–45. www.neovictorianstudies.com/past _issues/3-1%202010/NVS%203-1-3%20S-Forlini.pdf (20 July 2011).

Frauenfelde, Mark. *Steampunk Palin* comic book. *BoingBoing*. 21 January 2011. http:// boingboing.net/2011/01/21/steampunk-palin-comi.html (29 July 2011).

Gatehouse Gazette 21: Empire Revisited: Astounding Tales from the Colonies. Ed. Nick Ottens. www.ottens.co.uk/gatehouse/gazette-21 (15 February 2012).

Gelder, Ken, and Sarah Thornton, eds. *The Subcultures Reader*. New York: Routledge, 1997.

Goh, Jaymee. "Countering Victorientalism." *Silver Goggles*. 7 March 2010. http:// silver-goggles.blogspot.com/2010/03/countering-victorientalism.html (15 February 2012).

———. "With This Steam-Powered Prosthetic Arm, I Could Be as Strong as . . . a Normal Person." *Silver Goggles*. 1 May 2010. http://silver-goggles.blogspot.com/2010/05/ repost-for-blogging-against-disablism.html (20 July 2011).

Gray, Jonathan, Cornel Sandvoss, and C. Lee Harrington. *Fandom: Identities and Communities in a Mediated World*. New York: New York University Press, 2007.

Greyshade Estate. "Towards a Steampunk Lifestyle." *The Greyshade Estate*. 28 September 2010. http://greyshadeestate.blogspot.com/2010/09/towards-steampunk -lifestyle.html (29 July 2011).

Haraway, Donna. "A Cyborg Manifesto: Science, Technology, and Socialist-Feminism in the Late Twentieth Century." 149–181 in *Simians, Cyborgs and Women: The Reinvention of Nature*. New York: Routledge, 1991.

Hebdige, Dick. *Subculture: The Meaning of Style*. New York: Routledge, 1979.

Heilmann, Ann, and Mark Llewellyn. *Neo-Victorianism: The Victorians in the Twenty-First Century, 1999–2009*. New York: Palgrave Macmillan, 2010.

Jameson, Fredric. *Postmodernism, or the Cultural Logic of Late Capitalism*. Durham, N.C.: Duke University Press, 1992.

Kapchan, Deborah. "The Promise of Sonic Translation: Performing the Festive Sacred in Morocco." *American Anthropologist* 110, no. 4 (December 2008): 467–483.

Killjoy, Magpie. "Steampunk World's Fair 2011." *Birds Before the Storm*. 23 May 2011. www.birdsbeforethestorm.net/2011/05/2011–steampunk-worlds-fair (30 July 2011).

Lady Gaga. "Alejandro." Music video. www.youtube.com/watch?v=niqrrmev4mA (15 February 2012).

League of S.T.E.A.M. http://leagueofsteam.com (20 July 2011).

Lehmann, Hans-Thies. *Postdramatic Theater*. Trans. Karen Jürs-Munby. New York: Routledge, 2006.

Matthews, Christopher. "A Radical's Legacy: Emma Goldman Lives On at Occupy Wall Street, and on the Rental Market." *The Local East Village on the New York Times*. 22 December 2011. http://eastvillage.thelocal.nytimes.com/2011/12/22/ emma-goldman-lives-radicals-former-address-up-for-rent-and (15 January 2012).

Muggleton, David, and Rupert Weinzierl, eds. *The Post-Subcultures Reader*. New York: Berg, 2003.

Murphy, Chris. "'Steampunk Palin' Comic More Insane Than You Imagined." *Comics Alliance*. 20 January 2011. www.comicsalliance.com/2011/01/20/steampunk -palin-comic (29 July 2011).

Natoli, Joseph, and Linda Hutcheon, eds. *A Postmodern Reader*. New York: State University of New York Press, 1993.

Ottens, Nick. "History of the *Gatehouse Gazette*." *The Gatehouse Gazette*. November 2011. www.ottens.co.uk/gatehouse/History%20of%20the%20Gatehouse%20Gazette.pdf (15 February 2012).

———. "In Defense of Victorientialism." *The Gatehouse Gazette*. 10 March 2010. www.ottens.co.uk/gatehouse/2010/03/in-defense-of-victorientalism (15 February 2012).

Pagliassotti, Dru. "Does Steampunk Have an Ideology?" *The Mark of Ashen Wings*. 19 February 2009. http://drupagliassotti.com/2009/02/13/does-steampunk-have -an-ideology (30 July 2011).

———. "Does Steampunk Have Politics?" *The Mark of Ashen Wings*. 19 February 2009. http://drupagliassotti.com/2009/02/11/does-steampunk-have-politics (30 July 2011).

Panic! at the Disco. "The Ballad of Mona Lisa." Music video. www.youtube.com/watch?v=gOgpdp3lP8M (20 July 2011).

Perschon, Mike. "Advocating for the Aesthetic." *STEAMED!* 14 July 2011. http://ageofsteam.wordpress.com/2011/07/14/advocating-for-aesthetic (29 July 2011).

———. "Steam Wars." *Journal of Neo-Victorian Studies* 3, no. 1 (2010): 127–166. www.neovictorianstudies.com/past_issues/3-1%202010/NVS%203-1-5%20M -Perschon.pdf (20 July 2011).

Poirier, Monique. "Postcolonialism at Work." *Moniquilliloquies*. 23 May 2011. http://moniquill.tumblr.com/post/5757645850/bookishbeth-post-colonialism-at-work -native (31 July 2011).

Roçek, Miriam. Interview with the author. July 2011.

Rosenbaum, Bruce. Interview with the author. November 2011.

Second Life. *Steampunk on Second Life*. http://secondlife.com/destinations/roleplay/steampunk (29 February 2011).

steampunk fashion. http://steamfashion.livejournal.com (20 July 2010).

Steampunk Empire. www.steampunkempire.com (20 July 2011).

"Steampunk Palin." *Steampunk Palin*. http://steampunkpalin.com (28 July 2011).

Sjunneson, Elsa. "A Word About Eyepatches: A Personal Essay." *Beyond Victoriana*. 12 June 2011. http://beyondvictoriana.com/2011/06/12/a-word-about-eyepatches -a-personal-essay-guest-blog-by-elsa-sjunneson (20 July 2011).

Sutton-Smith, Brian. *The Ambiguity of Play*. Cambridge: Harvard University Press, 1997.

Thornton, Sarah. *Club Cultures: Music, Media and Subcultural Capital*. Middletown, Conn.: Wesleyan University Press, 1996.

————. "The Social Logic of Subcultural Capital." 198–215 in *The Subcultures Reader*, ed. Ken Gelder and Sarah Thornton. New York: Routledge, 1997.

VanderMeer, Ann, and Jeff VanderMeer, eds. *Steampunk II: Steampunk Reloaded*. San Francisco: Tachyon Press, 2010.

VanderMeer, Jeff, and S. J. Chambers. *The Steampunk Bible: An Illustrated Guide to the World of Imaginary Airships, Corsets and Goggles, Mad Scientists, and Strange Literature*. New York: Abrams Image, 2011.

PART III

RETROFITTING THINGS

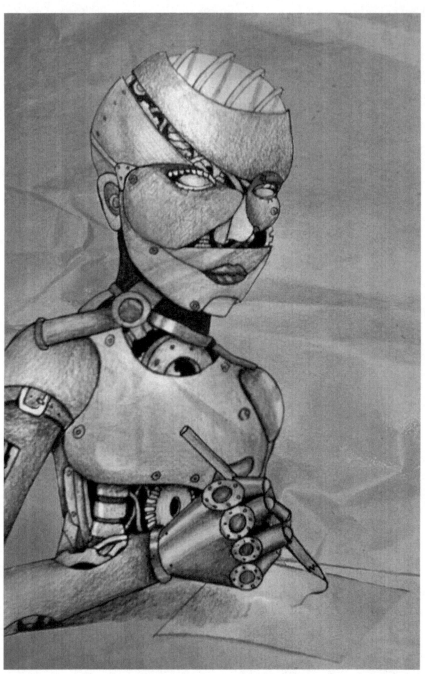

Machines making machines. *Copyright Jody Steel*

CHAPTER ELEVEN

"Love the Machine, Hate the Factory": Steampunk Design and the Vision of a Victorian Future

Sally-Anne Huxtable

The term "steampunk" was coined to refer to a branch of "cyberpunk" fiction that concerned itself with Victorian-era technology. However, steampunk is more than that. Steampunk is a burgeoning subculture that pays respect to the visceral nature of antiquated technology. It's about "steam," as in steam engines, and it's about "punk," as in counterculture.

—Margaret Killjoy, "From the Editor" (2012)

Since the coining of the term *steampunk* by the writer K. W. Jeter in 1987, this (originally somewhat tongue-in-cheek) term has taken on a life of its own, transforming from a speculative-fiction subgenre into a set of ideas, beliefs, and practices that include literature, graphic novels, music, politics, art, design, cultural theory, material culture, and virtual reality. Steampunk thus encompasses a complex network of cultural and political ideas as well as personal and artistic practices and modes of consumption that are, most usually, developed, discussed, and disseminated via online communities. Indeed, the emergence of steampunk as a subculture during the era of the Internet means that steampunk most definitely exists in the "real" or "material" world—and it is very much about negotiating materiality and the relationship between the individual, the body, and society as a whole. However, the crucial debates about the function and nature of steampunk are based in cyberspace, as are the means of sharing, disseminating, producing, and consuming many forms of the visual and material literary culture of steampunk.

The focus of this chapter is design, particularly the relationship between objects, clothing, and art (be they designs in the real world and/or in virtual reality) and the diverse sets of ideas and practices that are posited (and posted) as steampunk. Although it will acknowledge the notion of steampunk as part of what Kahn and Kellner have called a "Post-Modern adventure" of fluid Internet "post-subcultures"[1] with a number of diverse ideas as to what steampunk does or does not mean, this chapter will primarily focus upon the ways in which a number of examples and readings of steampunk art and design have been influenced and informed by highly activist, antiestablishment, intellectual, and sometimes esoteric modes of discourse. The ideas and discussions that are particularly relevant to this notion of steampunk are those championed in SteamPunk Magazine, which actively celebrates steampunk as a radically political, egalitarian, culturally diverse, and inclusive cultural alternative to mainstream culture. In my exploration of this activist form of steampunk approach to design, I wish to draw comparison between the concerns and ideas of these advocates of radical steampunk and many of the beliefs espoused by design reformers such as William Morris, Oscar Wilde, and Walter Crane in the second half of the nineteenth century. It is my contention that both "movements"—if one can describe them as such—offer a set of ideas that seek to rethink the relationships between humans and objects as well as the aesthetics and role of design in society both in the present and for the future.

Steampunk as Social Critique

In the first edition of SteamPunk Magazine, the New York City–based activists the Catastrophone Orchestra and Arts Collective explain their radical definition of steampunk:

> Steampunk is a re-envisioning of the past with the hypertechnological perceptions of the present. Unfortunately, most so-called "steampunk" is simply dressed-up, recreationary nostalgia: the stifling tearooms of Victorian imperialists and faded maps of colonial hubris. This kind of sepia-toned yesteryear is more appropriate for Disney and suburban grandparents than it is for a vibrant and viable philosophy or culture.[2]

It is this particular strand of steampunk that informs my exploration of the ways in which both writers and designers have articulated the idea that steampunk should function as something far more profound than a form of neo-Victorian escapist role-play. Indeed, many proponents of radical or

STEAMPUNK MAGAZINE
PUTTING THE PUNK BACK INTO STEAMPUNK
[LIFESTYLE, MAD SCIENCE,
THEORY & FICTION]

#1

MICHAEL MOORCOCK * ABNEY PARK *
DARCY JAMES ARGUE * THOMAS TRUAX *
G. D. FALKSEN * J. T. HAND * MARGARET
P. KILLJOY * CORY GROSS

Nicholas Kole, front cover, *SteamPunk Magazine* 1 (2007). *Courtesy of Nicholas Kole*

anarchic steampunk maintain that it not only should serve as a critique of both Victorian and contemporary society but also must act as a catalyst for a wholesale transformation of Western capitalist society. This attitude is exemplified by Kate Franklin and James Schafer, who are the administrators of the Steampunk Facebook community page and the founders of Parliament and Wake, a website that offers an alternative approach to history, including "Good Wars That Never Were," a critique of the unthinking militarism that has infiltrated many areas of steampunk culture, as well as ideas for future social change such as "More Than Nostalgia: Steampunk as Blueprint for an Imagined Future."[3] Franklin and Schafer's article "Why Steampunk (Still) Matters" in issue eight of SteamPunk Magazine outlines their belief in steampunk as a politically radical set of ideas that might offer future pathways for society. They are highly scathing of members of the community who indulge in the subculture as a form of escapist fantasy, particularly author G. D. Falksen's assertion that "steampunk is Victorian science fiction,"[4] claiming that they "undermine the beliefs and actions of those who do want to use steampunk as a platform for social change."[5] Steampunk, according to Franklin and Schafer, should offer a vision that balances both utopian and dystopian concepts:

> While the application of the steampunk aesthetic to history is an inspiring means to understand and critique our present, we believe applying that dissatisfied, innovative aesthetic to Brave New Worlds is a better way to visualize and thus achieve alternate futures.[6]

It is in this spirit that the contributors to SteamPunk Magazine and a number of designers seek to appropriate and reimagine certain aspects of Victorian visual and material culture as an expression of resistance against the perceived uniformity and insipidness of contemporary consumer culture. The core of this critique is the rejection of capitalist modes of manufacture and consumption and the increasingly blandly functional nature of design. As the Catastrophone Orchestra explain in the first issue of SteamPunk Magazine:

> Authentic Steampunk is not an artistic movement but an aesthetic technological movement. The machine must be liberated from efficiency and designed by desire and dreams. The sleekness of optimal engineering is to be replaced with the necessary ornamentation of true function. Imperfection, chaos, chance and obsolescence are not to be seen as faults, but as ways of allowing spontaneous liberation from the predictability of perfection.[7]

Inspired by a set of ideas and beliefs that question the supremacy of the "perfection" and homogeneity of most twenty-first-century design—such as, for example, the near-idolatry afforded in some quarters toward Apple products such as the iPhone and MacBook Air—this statement positions steampunk as a movement that will produce objects with the potential to cause us to rethink the aesthetics of design. Indeed it was Professor Calamity, a member of the same collective, who, on the now defunct *SteamPunk Magazine* forum The Gaslamp Bazaar, coined the phrase "Love the machine, hate the factory," which forms the title of this chapter. The science fiction and fantasy author Richard Harland encapsulates this attitude in his online discussion of steampunk:

> Contemporary machines lack steampunk appeal because the inner parts are all boxed away, and the outer casings are bland and homogenized. Harking back to past technology is a harking back to machines that *look* like machines, with the real feel and mystery of all their working parts.[8]

However, there is also the implication here that steampunk should question not only the aesthetic and social function of design but also the physical and emotional relationship between humans and designed objects, particularly machines. The notion of the mystery and excitement of machines relates directly to Victorian science fiction, which originally inspired steampunk, a fictive genre rich with flying and time machines as in the work of H. G. Wells and Jules Verne. Indeed, Rebecca Onion has explored the profound emotional and intellectual importance of the machine to steampunk, as well as the rejection of this contemporary culture of dull technologies. She comments that:

> Steampunks fetishise cogs, springs, sprockets, wheels, and hydraulic motion. They love the sight of the clouds of steam that arise during the operation of steam-powered technology. Many of the people who participate in this subculture see reading, constructing, and writing about steam technology as a highly libratory counterculture practice (hence, the addition of the word "punk").[9]

As Onion makes clear, rethinking the connection between humans and the machine is vital to radical steampunk, but the reconsideration of the fundamental relationship between humans and design and the rejection of the faddishness of capitalist design culture is also essential to these ideas.

Loving the Machine

The idea that good design should not be subject to fashion was essential to design reform of the second half of the nineteenth and the early twentieth century, particularly the Arts and Crafts movement. Indeed, the similarities between steampunk concepts about the relationship between the individual, society, and the machine and the ideas of many Victorian advocates of Arts and Crafts ideologies are markedly similar in many ways. Both reject what they see as the mindlessness of the mass production of objects and clothing. However, there is a frequent misunderstanding that the protagonists of the Victorian Arts and Crafts movement were wholeheartedly opposed to machinery. As has been well recorded, handcrafted objects and a belief in the pleasures of labor were central to the movement, but what is less discussed is that even ardent believers in handcrafting, such as the Arts and Crafts designer and socialist William Morris, could see a new reformed role for the machine, and even for the factory, in lightening the workload of laborers. Professor Calamity's motto "Love the machine, hate the factory" also refuses that traditional notion of the factory as a symbol of mass production and wage slavery, in much the same way as William Morris does in his 1884 essay "A Factory as It Might Be." In this essay originally published in *Justice*, the journal of the Social Democratic Federation, Morris accepts machines insofar as they might alleviate human toil, and also factories if they can be redesigned as (green) sites of pleasure, tranquility, and happy labor. He declares:

> Furthermore machines of the most ingenious and best approved kinds will be used when necessary, but will be used simply to save human labour; nor indeed could they be used for anything else, in such well-ordered work as we are thinking about; since, profit being dead, there would be no temptation to pile up wares whose apparent value as articles of use, their conventional value as such, does not rest on the necessities or reasonable desires of men for such things, but on artificial habits forced on the public by the craving of the capitalists for fresh and ever fresh profit.[10]

However, radical steampunk takes this anticapitalist rhetoric of the machine further than Morris as it reclaims the very machine that enslaved the mass of workers and consumers in the nineteenth and twentieth centuries. It reimagines technology as something that no longer functions as a yoke but that facilitates freedom and equality. As steampunk activists Ben Sargent and Mary Lin write in their manifesto "Why Steampunk?":

> In modern times, we realize that science and technology industries have perpetuated great wrongs, particularly against nature, with in some cases dire, unintended consequences. Steampunk takes us back to a time of greater innocence and idealism, to those moments when decisions could have been made to move the fate of the earth and humanity in a different direction. Steampunk allows the psyche to get it right; to blend art and science towards a more harmonious result. . . . women had very few opportunities in Victorian society; steampunk offers an opportunity to right that wrong by giving women a level

playing field on which they can wow their male co-explorers and conspirators with their inventive genius without losing their gender identity.[11]

Sargent and Lin envision and advocate both the collective and individual practice of steampunk in the arts and sciences as a means of creating inclusive and sustainable forms of living while refusing the negative aspects of Victorian culture and morality including gender inequality, colonialism, and other forms of discrimination. This radical form of steampunk speaks of the importance of handcrafting but also the beauty of machines—albeit, generally, steam and clockwork machines (if they are electric they become steampunked to look as if they are driven by cogs and gears and steam)—and their interconnectivity with humans both as makers and users. In the editorial to issue six of *SteamPunk Magazine*, C. Allegra Hawksmoor notes:

> We adore the machines that come from an age before endless replication reduced everything into soulless copies of itself—lacking any sort of individuality, and plastered with labels warning us not to interfere with machines whose workings we cannot possibly understand.[12]

Steampunk takes the machine and reworks and aestheticizes it so that it is appreciated for its beauty as well as its functionality. The machine is also celebrated for its very "machineness," for the ways in which machine and human can live in future concord—a world in which working machines become the epitome of Morris's famous dictum: "Have nothing in your houses that you do not know to be useful or believe to be beautiful."[13] The sentiment of loving the machine effectively revises for the twenty-first century the Arts and Crafts philosophy of C. R. Ashbee, who wrote in 1901: "We do not reject the machine, we welcome it. But we desire to see it mastered."[14] In steampunk the machine no longer needs to be mastered; humans and technologies can live in joyous harmony, something that becomes increasingly apparent when one explores the fascination of many steampunks wearing prostheses.

The melding of human and machine has been explored by a number of designers such as Ian Finch-Field (also known as Skinz-N-Hydez), who features his work on the alternative art showcase deviantART.com. Commissioned steampunk objects such as Finch-Field's handcrafted brass, copper, and leather Steampunk Leg and his Glove-O-Love blur the lines between decorative art, body modification, garment, and machine.[15] Although currently fantasy, the future possibility of cyborgs, or of beautifully fashioned mechanical limbs, is tantalizing to steampunks. This captivation with the

Skinz-N-Hydez (Ian Finch-Field), Steampunk Leg, brass, copper, and leather, 2009, http://skinz-n-hydez.deviantart.com. *Courtesy of Ian Finch-Field*

idea of melding the body with steam or clockwork technology has even reached the mainstream with actor Kenneth Branagh's portrayal of the villainous steam-powered cyborg Dr. Arliss Loveless in the 1999 film *Wild Wild West*.[16] Certainly in terms of serious steampunk design, although the wearing of such prostheses is undoubtedly playful, the dream implicit in such works seems to be that one day soon human and machine will be in total accord, just as human and horse were until the twentieth century. As these fantastical limbs and devices indicate, not all steampunk machines are useful or even work. Indeed, many still do inhabit the imaginative world of Victorian science fiction. However, they are also serious explorations of the potentially beneficial ways in which lovingly crafted machines might supplant the ugly technologies of the present.

DIY and the World (Wide Web) of Home Crafting

The key to this critique of contemporary design is, I believe, the encouragement of a culture of do-it-yourself amateur art and design and "tinkering" within the steampunk community. It is pertinent to note here that it is no coincidence that the development of steampunk as a form of design practice has coincided with the craft revival of the last decade, and that the development of online marketplaces such as eBay, Etsy.com, and Folksy .co.uk have facilitated the emergence of this do-it-yourself culture of art, craft, fashion, and design. As the creators of *SteamPunk Magazine* outline in their submission guidelines at the back of issue number one, "We are interested in nearly every form of DIY, although engineering, crafts and fashion are particularly dear to us."[17] Libby Bulloff expands this idea in her article "The Future of Steampunk Fashion in Two Parts" in issue number seven of *SteamPunk Magazine*:

> Many of us are suffering from the effects of the economic recession in the United States and elsewhere in the world, or else renouncing materialism and capitalist money systems. Therefore, steampunk's rise as a fashion aesthetic is timely, as the very best of it is handmade, upcycled, collected, and one-of-a-kind. Fighting the mainstream by DIY is both cunning and affordable. One does not have to be rich or thin to look great in casual steampunk garb, and the most fantastic items for padding your steampunk wardrobe usually don't have a little label discerning them as steampunk, either. . . . Don't limit yourself to wearing only clothes with a Victorian flair. Other antique, vintage, and ethnic influences definitely bring new interest to your wardrobe, and keep the mainstream from copying your look.[18]

Issue two of the magazine includes instructions by Rachel E. Pollock for a "Sew Yourself a Lady Artisan's Apron," a DIY project that pays homage to the work wear of the Victorian artisan but, in the context of radical steampunk, subverts Victorian stereotypes, ideas, and imagery, such as the gendered notion of the male craftsman or engineer, and creates suitable period protective clothing to allow women to create machines and/or objects. The emphasis on steampunk

FRONT VIEW

— straps adjustable w/snaps or bachelor buttons
— two D-rings for clips & caribiners
— pocket watch patch pocket on Ⓛ pocket (R?)
— leather pen strap @ top Ⓛ bodice
— rivets reinforce patch pockets

CRAFT & DYE APRON DESIGN

R.E. POLLOCK 2007

1¼"-1½" width

1½"-2" width

BACK VIEW

Rachel E. Pollock, "Sew Yourself a Lady Artisan's Apron," *SteamPunk Magazine* 2, (2007): 33. *Courtesy of Rachel E. Pollock*

fashion as both a mode of individual expression and a form of sustainable design and consumption set against a mainstream "fashion industry" based on novelty and constant innovation bears much comparison with the ideas of design reformers of the second half of the nineteenth century. As Oscar Wilde—who along with his wife Constance was a formidable advocate of dress reform—noted in 1887 on the exigencies of fashion at that time:

> Women's dress can easily be modified and adapted to any exigencies of the kind; but most women refuse to modify or adapt it. They must follow the fashion, whether it be convenient or the reverse. And, after all, what is a fashion?

From the artistic point of view, it is usually a form of ugliness so intolerable that we have to alter it every six months.[19]

Just as Wilde advocated what would today be called the "upcycling" of clothing, radical steampunk positions itself as a culture of recycling, sustainability, and hands-on crafting and do-it-yourself. The evidence of this growing trend can be seen on sites like Etsy.com where a search of handmade items using the term "steampunk" throws up a plethora of objects, albeit with varying degrees of relationship to what is generally regarded as the steampunk aesthetic of cogs, gears, Kraken, dirigibles, corsets, goggles, and top hats. One popular aspect of this trend in handcrafting is the phenomenon of "steampunking," where designers and crafters take "found objects" and transform and redesign them into recognizable "steampunk" objects. Perhaps the best-known and most celebrated examples of these are the beautiful and functional "steampunked" laptops and PCs of Richard "Doc" Nagy, also known as Datamancer. However, if one cannot afford Nagy's extraordinary creations, a number of websites offer their readers the cheaper option of following instructions for "steampunking" their own laptops.[20]

In the late nineteenth century, suggestions for home crafts also abounded. In addition to the "taste" or advice manuals by authors such as Mary Eliza Haweis, Charles Eastlake, and Margaret Oliphant that advised on interior decoration and dress in the Aesthetic style,[21] the 1870s and 1880s saw an onslaught of essays, lectures, and pamphlets offering detailed instructions on making one's own "Art" or "Aesthetic" objects or transforming existing objects into this style. These offerings on the production of amateur home arts such as *Bazaar*'s book *Artistic Amusements* (1882)[22] and *Sylvia's Home Journal*'s book *Sylvia's Book of Artistic Knickknacks* (1882),[23] instructed the reader in all manner of artistic employments in which she (and they were firmly aimed at a female readership) might indulge. Suggestions included "Decalcomonie," which is "the art of transferring pictures to china, wood, leather, silk or to the walls of a room";[24] painting on china, ivory, and terracotta; "Imitations of the quaint lacquer work articles from Japan" (a suggestion that utilized lampblack to gain the desired effect; one can only wonder at the horrors that would have been produced if anyone ever followed these instructions);[25] "Rustic work"; and "Imitation of Japanese Inlaid Work."[26] Thus for those who could not afford the work of designers or retailers such as Morris & Co. or Liberty & Co. or who preferred to make their own crafts, such DIY texts were immeasurably helpful. Likewise, when considered from the viewpoint of polemicists such as Morris, the very fact of encouraging people to make handicrafts functioned as a form of resistance to the

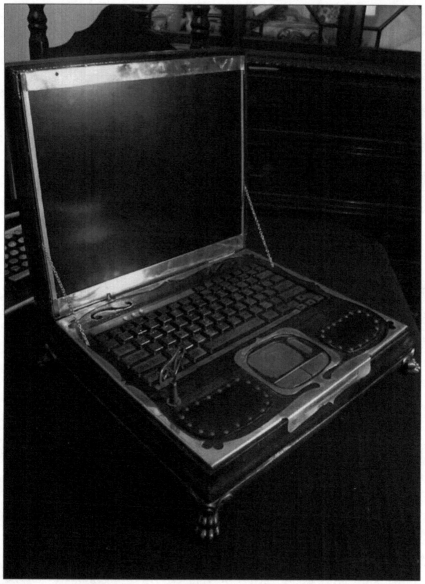

Richard Nagy (Datamancer), steampunked laptop, 2007, www.datamancer.net. *Courtesy of Richard Nagy*

slavery and toil required to make mass-produced goods. These texts effectively democratized the idea of craft and facilitated the physical, emotional, and spiritual experience of making objects. Oscar Wilde expounded these ideas on his lecture tour of America in 1882:

> It must always be remembered that what is well and carefully made by an honest workman, after a rational design, increases in beauty and value as the years go on. . . . Now, what you must do is to bring artists and handicraftsmen together. Handicraftsmen cannot live, certainly cannot thrive, without such companionship. Separate these two and you rob art of all spiritual motive.[27]

In addition to the generally genteel art of dressmaking, *SteamPunk Magazine* also offers a more eclectic approach to DIY. Each issue offers several projects for its readers to try, including Johnny Payphone's set of instructions to replicate his remarkable invention, "the Penny Fakething," which is a normal bicycle dismantled and reassembled in a style reminiscent of the iconic Edwardian penny-farthing, in issue number two. Other DIY schemes outlined may, perhaps, be more risky than is, perhaps, suitable (or safe) for the gentler readers of the magazine. Projects include casting metal and an "Emergency Welding Machine" in issue five, both practical and spiritual alchemy in issue seven, and creating your own artificial island from "the deathless oceans" in issue seven.[28] This emphasis on self-sufficiency is most paramount in *The Steampunk's Guide to the Apocalypse*, a publication penned by Margaret Killjoy, Colin Foran, and Professor Calamity that combines practical survivalism, political rhetoric, and a hearty dose of humor—chapter four is titled "Scoundrels and the Defense Therefrom."[29] Professor Calamity writes:

> Today's post-apocalyptic stories are a bit darker and more nihilistic perhaps, but they remain projects of the Victorians. The heroes are not the strongest or most "savage," but the ones who use their intelligence and ethics as their compass in the wastelands. In many ways, like steampunk itself, the post-apocalypse is both a critique of the world of technology and a celebration of our own innate ingenuity.[30]

This dystopian outlook is, perhaps, the polar opposite of William Morris's vision of a postrevolutionary pastoral London where handcrafting and joy in labor reign supreme in his 1890 utopian work *News from Nowhere (Or an Epoch of Rest)*.[31] However, the centrality of the idea of people making objects themselves remains a constant in these visions of the future, be they

[the author and subject of the
article pose together here in a
drawing by one "Rachel"]

Johnny Payphone with Penny Fakething: "All of the Danger of the Original with None
of the Authenticity," reproduction of charcoal drawing based on an original photograph,
SteamPunk Magazine 2 (2007): 34. *Courtesy of Rachel Olson*

utopian or dystopian. William Morris discusses the uses and abuses of the machine but never its potential beauty, whereas Steampunk reconfigures nineteenth- and early-twentieth-century Arts and Crafts ideas by extolling both the utility and the aesthetic possibilities of machines. Just as Morris appreciated the technologies and beauties of other eras, particularly those of the Middle Ages, maybe the lapse and free flow of time allows us to aestheticize machines that seemed new and threatening to an inhabitant of the nineteenth century. Now it is the newer forms of machines—the internal combustion engine and machines driven by electricity such as mp3s, smartphones, laptops, tablets, and computers—that threaten. Conversely, such machines are utterly essential to steampunk's Internet presence despite the threat they might pose, particularly through the homogeneity and utilitarian nature of their design. Thus, even the computer and all of its accessories can be rendered safe and beautiful by being "steampunked" and encased in the tactile sensualities of wood, leather, and brass.

Steampunk as a subculture with a focus on do-it-yourself design and dress has coincided with the rapid rise of websites such as Etsy.com and Folksy .co.uk, which sell all manner of handcrafted goods and provide a worldwide community as well as local communities for crafters. Over the last decade these sites have become instrumental in the rebirth of the visibility of craft and as both shopping sites and sources of ideas and inspiration for crafters. The vast majority of "steampunk" pieces are accessories or objects of jewelry that take inspiration from and are frequently made from timepieces and small mechanical gears. The other most popular "symbol" is the Kraken, or giant squid or octopus from Jules Verne's science fiction novel *20,000 Leagues Under the Sea* (1869). This visual vocabulary of cogs, clocks, and Kraken provides steampunk with a symbolic language not dissimilar from the sunflowers, lilies, and peacock feathers of Victorian Arts and Crafts and Aestheticism, and it has spawned many amused Internet discussions about crafters who attempt to sell all manner of objects as "steampunk," including the category "Not Remotely Steampunk" on Regretsy, a website that highlights the weird, wonderful, and downright awful on Etsy.[32]

Nevertheless, what might be deemed "quality" steampunk objects for sale are usually, but not always, rendered in materials and colors thought to be suitable for a Victorian adventurer or explorer, frequently rejecting the bright aniline dyes and colors that Victorian Aestheticism and Arts and Crafts also rejected. Thus, we see a lot of use of brown materials, particularly leather, as well as the frequent use of brass. Just as Victorian design reformers with varied ideological stances, for instance, William Morris and

Christopher Dresser, were generally as concerned with the quality of materials used in the manufacture of objects as they were with visual appearance of their design, the focus in much steampunk art, design, and dress is upon materiality, particularly the "feel" of objects and clothing. In this instance the ideas of touch and tactility, such as those put forward by Eve Sedgwick, become highly pertinent to the experience of these multisensual aspects of design rather than simply following visual keys.[33] Rebecca Onion outlines the luxurious nature of the materials favored by steampunk designers: "The steampunk ideology prizes brass, copper, wood, leather, and papier-mâché—the construction materials of this bygone time."[34] As opposed to the perceived artificiality and banality of contemporary materials, the smoothness, coldness, softness, stiffness, pliability, roughness, hardness, warmth, shininess, dullness, scent, and sound of these materials are, I believe, central to their appeal. Steampunk design is, indeed, often notable for the use of constituents such as brass, glass, and leather. Such materials evoke and rework a form of "authenticity" (as opposed to the perceived "artificiality" of twentieth- and twenty-first-century plastics and synthetic textiles) that suggests a very specific kind of nineteenth-century aesthetic—that of the designer or inventor who melds these materials together in an alchemy of creation.

Conclusion: Rebuilding the Machine

Tinkering with history is not a new thing. For centuries people have imagined or reimagined the past in order to re-form the present and shape the future. To dismiss this as a form of nostalgia vastly oversimplifies the issues and discourses of the relationship between past and present in dissident forms of design. The great Aesthetic critic Walter Pater dreamed that a study of the worlds of Hellenic, medieval, and Renaissance culture would revolutionize the experience of being human in the nineteenth century, writing in 1868 that "we cannot conceive the age; we can conceive the element it has contributed to our culture; we can treat the subjects of the age bringing that into relief."[35] The fluid and constantly variable nature of steampunk and steampunk art and design culture means that it necessarily contains a mass of, seemingly, irreconcilable paradoxes: utopian/dystopian; craft/industry; surface/whole; immediate communication/gradual handicraft. Indeed, just as various forms of idealism, utopianism, community, and political activism were vital to the practice of Arts and Crafts art and design in the second half of the nineteenth century, so they are central to that of steampunk in the beginning of the twenty-first. Professor Calamity's radical phrase—"Love the machine, hate the factory"—embraces the power and beauty of designed objects, particularly machines, but rejects cultural conformity, drudgery, and banal aesthetics, which is at the core of this work.

In nineteenth- and early-twentieth-century Britain, advocates of cultural reform such as Carlyle, Ruskin, Haweis, Pater, Morris, and Ashbee, among others, took what they believed to be the beauties and positive qualities of the past and used them to critique contemporary society. Activists like Morris and Ashbee also extolled the virtues of communality, something that Ashbee lived out with his short-lived Guild of Handicraft community in the first years of the twentieth century. Likewise, this brand of radical and anarchic steampunk has endeavored to offer a vision of an alternative future in which factory-made, mass-produced, and homogenous design is abandoned. Instead they conceptualize an aesthetic that celebrates the beauty of machines, the materiality of objects and dress, the significance of collectivity, the importance of the quality of individuality, and the act of artistic creation itself.

It may be that many advocates of radical steampunk do not necessarily realize the ways in which their own critique of contemporary culture, and their sense of communality found through the Internet, chimes with the ideals of those who sought to reform society in the nineteenth and the early twentieth centuries. As Margaret P. Ratt writes in the first edition of *SteamPunk Magazine*, "For the most part, we look at the modern world about us, bored to tears, and say, "no, thank you. I'd rather have trees, birds, and monstrous mechanical contraptions than an endless sprawl that is devoid of diversity."[36] While some steampunks have built virtual utopias such as New Babbage in Second Life and seem as happy with virtual objects and design as they would be with the "real," the dissident DIY designers of radical steampunk seem determined to use the Internet to disseminate the ideas, plans, and diagrams that they hope will transform culture and society as we know it. It just remains to be seen if they manage to turn their uchronian dreams into utopian or dystopian reality.

Notes

1. Richard Kahn and Douglas Kellner, "Internet Subcultures and Oppositional Politics," in *The Post-Subcultures Reader*, ed. David Muggleton (London: Berg, 2003), 299–314.

2. Catastrophone Orchestra and Arts Collective, "What, Then, Is Steampunk?," *SteamPunk Magazine* 1 (2007): 6, www.combustionbooks.org/downloads/SPM1–web .pdf (20 January 2012).

3. James Schafer and Kate Franklin, "Parliament and Wake," www.parliament andwake.com (30 January 2012).

4. G. D. Falksen, "Steampunk 101," 2009, www.tor.com/blogs/2009/10/steam punk-101 (10 January 2012).

5. James Schafer and Kate Franklin, "Why Steampunk (Still) Matters," *Steam-Punk Magazine* 8 (2012): 5, www.combustionbooks.org/downloads/spm8–web.pdf (9 February 2012).

6. Schafer and Franklin, "Why Steampunk (Still) Matters," 13.

7. Catastrophone Orchestra and Collective, "What, Then, Is Steampunk?"

8. Richard Harland, "Worldshaker and Liberator: Steampunk," 2009, www.richardharland.net/worldshaker/WS.steampunk/WS.steampunk.index.htm (30 January 2012).

9. Rebecca Onion, "Reclaiming the Machine: An Introductory Look at Steampunk in Everyday Practice," *Neo-Victorian Studies* 1, no. 1 (Autumn 2008): 39, www.neovictorianstudies.com/past_issues/Autumn2008/NVS%201–1%20R-Onion .pdf (10 January 2012).

10. William Morris, "A Factory as It Might Be, Part III," *Justice* (31 April 1884): 2.

11. Ben Sargent and Mary Lin, "Why Steampunk? Manifesto," *Inventing Earth* http://inventingearth.org/page/why-steampunk-manifesto (20 January 2012).

12. C. Allegra Hawksmoor, "Editorial," *SteamPunk Magazine* 6 (2009): 2, www.steampunkmagazine.com/pdfs/spm6–web.pdf (12 January 2012).

13. William Morris, "The Beauty of Life," *Hopes and Fears for Art* (London: Longmans, Green, 1919), 110.

14. Charles Robert Ashbee, *An Endeavour Towards the Teachings of J. Ruskin and W. Morris, Being a Brief Account of the Work, the Aims and the Principles of the Guild of Handicraft* (London: Edward Arnold, 1901), 47.

15. Ian Finch-Field, "Skinz-N-Hydez," deviantART, http://skinz-n-hydez.de viantart.com (25 January 2012).

16. Barry Sonnenfeld, *Wild Wild West* (Warner Bros, 1999).

17. "Submit to No Master! But Submit to Us!" *SteamPunk Magazine* 1 (2007): 72, www.combustionbooks.org/downloads/SPM1–web.pdf (20 January 2012).

18. Libby Bulloff, "The Future of Steampunk Fashion in Two Parts," *SteamPunk Magazine* 7 (2010): 31–36, www.combustionbooks.org/downloads/spm7–web.pdf (15 January 2012).

19. Oscar Wilde, "Literary and Other Notes," in *The Woman's World*, November 1887, reprinted in *The Works of Oscar Wilde*, Vol. 4 (New York: Nottingham Society, 1909), 205–206.

20. Melissa Smith, "How to Make a Steampunk Laptop," www.ehow.com/ how_7185801_make-steampunk-laptop.html (29 February 2012).

21. Charles Lock Eastlake, *Hints on Household Taste* (London: Longmans, Green, 1872); Mrs. (Margaret) Oliphant, *Dress*, Macmillan Art at Home Series, ed. William J. Loftie (London: Macmillan, 1878); Mrs. (Mary Eliza) Haweis, *The Art of Decoration* (London: Chatto and Windus, 1881).

22. *Artistic Amusements, Being Instructions for a Variety of Artwork for Home Employment, and Suggestions for a Number of Novel and Saleable Articles for Fancy Bazaars* (London: The Bazaar Office, 1882).

23. *Sylvia's Book of Artistic Knickknacks Containing Illustrations of Many Fancy Articles Suitable for Bazaars with Instructions as to Their Production, Directions for Painting on Various Materials and for Tapestry Painting Are Included* (London: Ward, Lock, 1882).

24. *Artistic Amusements*, 14.

25. *Artistic Amusements*, 31.

26. *Sylvia's Book of Artistic Knickknacks*, 332.

27. Oscar Wilde, "Interior and Exterior House Decoration," 1882, *The Works of Oscar Wilde*, Vol. 6 (New York: Nottingham Society, 1909), 283.

28. David Dowling, "An Introduction to Casting," *SteamPunk Magazine* 5 (2009): 48–56, www.combustionbooks.org/downloads/spm5–web.pdf (25 January 2012); Zac Zinin, "Emergency Welding Machine," *SteamPunk Magazine* 5 (2009): 62–63, www.combustionbooks.org/downloads/spm5–web.pdf (25 January 2012); Benjamin Bajenski and C. Allegra Hawksmoor, "On Alchemy," *SteamPunk Magazine* 7 (2010): 44–53, www.combustionbooks.org/downloads/spm7–web.pdf (25 January 2012).

29. Margaret Killjoy, Colin Foran, and Professor Calamity, *The Steampunk's Guide to the Apocalypse*, 2nd ed. (New York: Combustion Books, 2011), 35.

30. Professor Calamity, "Appendix B: The End Is Nigh: Victorians and the First Post-Apocalypse," in *The Steampunk's Guide to the Apocalypse*, 58.

31. William Morris, *News from Nowhere (or an Epoch of Rest)* (Kelmscott: Kelmscott Press, 1892). The work was originally serialized in the Socialist journal *Commonweal* in 1890 and published in a revised form as a novel in 1892.

32. www.regretsy.com/category/not-remotely-steampunk (20 January 2012). The phenomenon has even inspired a "chap-rap" on YouTube titled "Just Glue Some Gears on It (and Call It Steampunk)" by a gentleman identifying himself as Sir Reginald Pikedevant, http://youtu.be/TFCuE5rHbPA (15 January 2012).

33. Eve Kosofsky Sedgwick, *Touching Feeling: Affect, Performativity, Pedagogy* (Duke, N.C.: Duke University Press, 2003).

34. Onion, "Reclaiming the Machine," 139.

35. Walter Pater, "Poems by William Morris," *The Westminster Review* 34 (October 1868): 310.

36. Margaret P. Ratt, "Issue One: Putting the Punk Back into SteamPunk," *SteamPunk Magazine* 1 (2007): 2, www.combustionbooks.org/downloads/SPM1–web.pdf (20 January 2012).

Bibliography

Artistic Amusements, Being Instructions for a Variety of Artwork for Home Employment, and Suggestions for a Number of Novel and Saleable Articles for Fancy Bazaars. London: The Bazaar Office, 1882.

Ashbee, C. R. *An Endeavour Towards the Teachings of J. Ruskin and W. Morris, Being a Brief Account of the Work, the Aims and the Principles of the Guild of Handicraft.* London: Edward Arnold, 1901.

Craftster. www.craftster.org (20 January 2012).

Eastlake, Charles Lock. *Hints on Household Taste.* London: Longmans, Green, 1872.

eBay. www.ebay.com (20 January 2012).

Etsy. www.Etsy.com (20 January 2012).

Falksen, G. D. "Steampunk 101." 2009. www.tor.com/blogs/2009/10/steampunk-101 (15 January 2012).

Finch-Field, Ian. "Skinz-N-Hydez." deviantART. http://skinz-n-hydez.deviantart.com (25 January 2012).

Folksy. www.folksy.co.uk (20 January 2012).

Harland, Richard. "Worldshaker and Liberator: Steampunk." 2009. www.richard harland.net/worldshaker/WS.steampunk/WS.steampunk.index.htm (30 January 2012).

Haweis, Mrs. (Mary Eliza). *The Art of Decoration.* London: Chatto and Windus, 1881.

Kahn, Richard, and Douglas Kellner. "Internet Subcultures and Oppositional Politics." 299–314 in *The Post-Subcultures Reader*, ed. David Muggleton. London: Berg, 2003.

Killjoy, Margaret, Colin Foran, and Professor Calamity. *The Steampunk's Guide to the Apocalypse*, 2nd ed. New York: Combustion Books, 2011.

Morris, William. "A Factory as It Might Be, Part III." *Justice* (31 April 1884): 2.

———. *News from Nowhere (or an Epoch of Rest).* London: Kelmscott Press, 1892.

———. "The Beauty of Life." In *Hopes and Fears for Art.* London: Longmans, Green, 1919.

"Not Remotely Steampunk." Regretsy. www.regretsy.com/category/not-remotely -steampunk (20 January 2012).

Oliphant, Mrs. (Margaret). *Dress.* Macmillan Art at Home Series, ed. William J. Loftie. London: Macmillan, 1878.

Onion, Rebecca. "Reclaiming the Machine: An Introductory Look at Steampunk in Everyday Practice." *Neo-Victorian Studies* 1, no. 1 (Autumn 2008): 138–163. www .neovictorianstudies.com/past_issues/Autumn2008/NVS%201–1%20R-Onion. pdf (10 January 2012).

Pater, Walter. "Poems by William Morris." *The Westminster Review*, n.s., 34 (October 1868): 300–312.

Pikedevant, Sir Reginald. "Just Glue on Some Gears (and Call It Steampunk)." YouTube. http://youtu.be/TFCuE5rHbPA (15 January 2012).

Sargent, Ben, and Mary Lin. "Why Steampunk? Manifesto." *Inventing Earth.* http:// inventingearth.org/page/why-steampunk-manifesto (20 January 2012).

Schafer, James, and Kate Franklin. "Parliament and Wake." www.parliamentand wake.com (30 January 2012).

Sedgwick, Eve Kosofsky. *Touching Feeling: Affect, Performativity, Pedagogy.* Duke, N.C.: Duke University Press, 2003.

Smith, Melissa. "How to Make a Steampunk Laptop." *ehow.* www.ehow.com/how_7185801_make-steampunk-laptop.html (29 February 2012).

Sonnenfeld, Barry. *Wild Wild West.* Warner Bros, 1999.

"The Steampunk Forum at Brassgoggles." http://brassgoggles.co.uk/forum (15 January 2012).

SteamPunk Magazine 1–8 (2007–2012). www.steampunkmagazine.com (15 January 2012).

Sylvia's Book of Artistic Knickknacks Containing Illustrations of Many Fancy Articles Suitable for Bazaars with Instructions as to Their Production, Directions for Painting on Various Materials and for Tapestry Painting Are Included. London: Ward, Lock, 1882.

Wilde, Oscar. *The Works of Oscar Wilde.* 10 vols. New York: Nottingham Society, 1909.

The Difference Engine grows up. *Copyright Jody Steel*

CHAPTER TWELVE

Steve Jobs versus the Victorians: Steampunk, Design, and the History of Technology in Society

Amy Sue Bix

Steampunk aficionados often appreciate fantastically designed submarines, robot dirigibles, and even modified Victorian-style laptops for their own sake, as expressions of technological fun and creative energy. But on closer analysis, steampunk literature, film, and art also supply excellent commentary on important issues regarding the past, present, and future of technologies. How should objects be designed? Should they follow established historically inspired lines, or try to establish an innovative language of modernity? Who shapes our machines, and what establishes our context of technological choice? What values does technology reflect and/or impose? Who decides and who benefits; as historian David Noble has asked, "Progress for whom? Progress for what?"[1]

The book accompanying the 2009–2010 steampunk exhibit at Oxford University's Museum of the History of Science explained, "Steampunk is a unique fantasy version of nineteenth century Victorian England, now imbued with high-tech digital devices, fantastic steam-powered machines, and all manner of surreal electro-mechanical contraptions. . . ."[2] Those familiar with the genre will know of a multitude of other reference points, from jewelry and costumes available through online craft outlets, to Hollywood's version of *The League of Extraordinary Gentlemen* (2003), television shows such as *The Wild, Wild West* (1965–1969), and a wealth of books, graphic novels, and fan-fiction versions of *Star Wars* robots and weaponry.[3]

Engineers, artists, and designers themselves frequently represent the ultimate visual thinkers, both by nature and educated professional preference.

Accordingly, this chapter focuses on the artifacts of steampunk, primarily (but never apart from) its literature, films, or do-it-yourself costuming and role-playing subculture. To open with an instant-classic example, the 2007 "Datamancer steampunk laptop," created by Richard Nagy, embeds a modern computer within a gleaming copper and brass case, lifted on small claw-foot legs. Instead of pressing an unobtrusive "on" button, a gesture so automatic today as to become meaningless, users activate the laptop through the more hands-on, conscious effort of turning a scrolled key.[4]

This chapter poses two major questions: first, what were the real-life Victorians' ideas about what machines should look like, and how does that historical depth connect to steampunk? Second, what does the emergence of steampunk reveal about the history of how our technological aesthetics have evolved? What was the mind-set that brought design from ornately detailed brass and glass to today's "blobjects," as Scott Westerfeld has called them, or "jellybeans," to use Jake von Slatt's disparaging term?[5] Steampunk can serve as an excellent subject of reflection for historians of technology, precisely because steampunk writing, art, and design all place material technologies at the center of their conceptions. Stefania Forlini has written:

> As a sub-genre of science fiction, [steampunk] explores the difference an object can make. . . . As a craft and lifestyle movement, it produces material things . . . to challenge contemporary technological design and help us reconsider the value of things. In both its literary and material manifestations, steampunk is about learning to read all that is folded into any particular created thing—that is, learning to connect the source materials to particular cultural, technical, and environmental practices, skills, histories, and economies of meaning and value."[6]

Victorians' Machine Vocabulary

At its best, steampunk captures and re-creates Victorians' love of what historian David Nye calls the "technological sublime."[7] Iron and glass combined as fundamental materials to form England's then-radical Iron Bridge (first completely made of cast iron, 1779) and the Crystal Palace of London's Great Exhibition of 1851, both entrancing crowds. Symbolizing the wonders of new machinery, President Ulysses Grant personally started the giant Corliss engine that powered Philadelphia's 1876 Centennial Exposition.[8] Steampunk imagery draws on essential sources in Victorian and Edwardian machinery, both actual historical developments (steam locomotives, airships) and classic science fiction (notably, H. G. Wells and Jules Verne).[9]

Steampunk's pseudo-celebration of nineteenth-century material technology engages basic questions about design aesthetics. To borrow a phrase made popular in the title of Owen Jones's influential 1856 design sourcebook, what was the Victorians' "grammar of ornament"?[10] How have our default assumptions about technological appearance evolved over the decades? Who decides what is visually attractive, socially relevant, and/or functionally appropriate, and how can we prioritize or balance those sometimes compatible, perhaps contradictory goals?

In hearkening back to the Victorian era, steampunk pays tribute to nineteenth-century leaders' enthusiasm for technology and their efforts to champion and accelerate invention. New patent legislation passed in Britain, France, and elsewhere aimed to clarify procedures and make registration more accessible. By the 1880s, the British patent office received more than twenty thousand applications each year, and by 1911, the United States had issued more than one million patents. Many real-life Victorian inventions, of course, relied on the gears, flywheels, pistons, levers, and gauges that have become the visual identifiers of steampunk. To take a few examples, in the 1870s, after watching a device in a steamship's engine room count the turns of a propeller, Ohio bar owner James Ritty invented the cash register that used internal wheels to track transactions and stop dishonest clerks from pocketing profits. Victorians loved toy automatons, dancing figures powered by clockwork and balances, or mechanical savings banks in the form of elephants or dogs that mechanically grabbed and deposited coins. Some inventions predated Rube Goldberg in the extended intricacy of their steps; in 1893, two British men patented a device to brew tea automatically; the ringing of a preset alarm clock triggered rods, levers, and bars that turned on the gas, poured water down a pipe into the teapot, and finally turned off the burner.[11] In creating and manufacturing new machines, Victorians had to decide on a vocabulary of appearance. Their technological design did not start from scratch. It was no coincidence that early railway passenger coaches and automobiles often imitated the shape and decorations of horse-drawn carriages, often manufactured by the same firms; the same workmen alternated between painting stripes and curlicues on carriages and cars.[12]

While today's steampunk speaks a visual language symbolizing possible future paths of older technology, it is vital to realize that Victorians themselves wrestled with the same challenge of inventing an iconography of machine design, without converging on consensus. Far from reveling in the metal of steam-engine boilers, many Victorian designers sought to disguise it behind Egyptian, Napoleonic, or other fanciful excess. Boulton and Watt

The iconic Victorian machine: every lever, wheel, and cylinder in view. *Copyright Jody Steel*

themselves encased steam engines inside an architectural frame of Tuscan or Doric columns. Other nineteenth-century manufacturers transformed steam engines into "miniature Greek temples," using elaborately curved Corinthian capitals to support the working beam, or even adding laurel wreaths. The circa 1855 "Gothic steam engine" (displayed now at Dearborn's Henry Ford Museum) features soaring pointed arches and pierced geometric ornamentation, all coated in pure white.[13] Design historian Julie Wosk suggests that in the days when newspapers headlined gory accounts of steam-boiler explosions and train derailments, manufacturers embraced such visually familiar ornamentation as a way to reassure a terrified public. By linking intimidating machinery to classical Greece and Rome, Victorians sought to present steam engines as "enduring, stately, and, most important, safe additions to the social milieu."[14] As art historians Charlotte Gere and Michael Whiteway explain, "Nineteenth-century designers assumed a culturally sophisticated and well-informed audience . . . and expected subtle references to earlier civilizations to be understood and appreciated." For a twenty-first-century Western audience, trained to expect flimsy plastic and particle board in Walmart-ized forgettable consumer form, it is now Victorian iron itself that represents dignity and impressiveness, even (or perhaps, especially) when lacking the incongruous ornamentation.[15]

Victorian buildings that housed the new technologies, from water-pumping stations to railroad stations, similarly embraced romanticized foreign camouflage, presenting "factory chimneys as Italian campaniles and warehouses as Egyptian palaces."[16] Robert Stephenson's 1850 Britannia railway bridge crossing the Menai Strait echoed the colossal lines of Egyptian design, while Isambard Kingdom Brunel wanted to decorate some of his bridges with sphinxes. Train stations incorporated medieval castle towers, Moorish-style arches, or secularized Gothic pinnacles. Brunel's 1841 Great Western Railway train shed in Bristol featured a Tudor-style roof complete with fake hammer beams, but later urban terminals dramatically covered platforms with arching metal girders and impressive spans of glass, reflecting the aesthetic and technical influence of Crystal Palace architecture.[17]

Numerous commentators, including Bruce Sterling and Jake von Slatt, have suggested that modern steampunk's appeal lies partly in its celebration of vintage workmanship.[18] Steampunk designer Art Donovan has written, "No longer satisfied with the injection-molded plastic design of today's mass-produced products, steampunk artists are crafting a romantic new standard for modern goods by taking traditional nineteenth century materials and applying them to twenty-first century technology. . . . These artists prefer the 'transparent' honesty of the handcrafted object. . . ."[19] Ironically, the Victorians themselves were caught up in parallel debates over art versus factory, individual creativity versus mass production. An aesthetic and philosophical backlash against both the process and products of mechanized industry spawned John Ruskin's Arts and Crafts movement. Ruskin, Augustus Pugin, William Morris, and others proclaimed a new artistic taste that fetishized a preindustrial dignity of labor and attempted to recapture the seemingly superior tradition, soul, harmony, and high quality of handmade goods.[20]

Steampunkers often portray the Victorian era as the last refuge of fine craftsmanship, an image brought to life in the clocks with hand-cut gears and chains made by Eric Freitas.[21] But in reality, mass production was already well under way by the early Victorian era. To take just one example, by the 1820s, clockmaker Eli Terry had improved and patented water-powered machinery for cutting wooden clockwork parts. By dramatically reducing the cost and increasing the volume of production, Terry and other early-nineteenth-century manufacturers transformed clocks from a handcrafted luxury item into a smaller, affordable purchase brought to even rural families by a network of peddlers.[22] United States firms especially came to specialize in what historians have called "armory practice," embracing the shop use of jigs, fixtures, and "go/no-go" gauges, plus pattern pieces and machines such as the Blanchard copying lathe. Though in practice manufacturers still could not always meet the goal of producing perfectly interchangeable parts, the system allowed factory owners to replace experienced craftsmen with cheaper, unskilled machine tenders. Indeed, it was this "American system of manufactures" that intrigued observers at the 1851 Crystal Palace exhibition, not just the items on display but the process of production with special-purpose machines.[23]

The aesthetics of Victorian design actually grew quite chaotic, borrowing and mixing elements of Queen Anne style, Gothic Revival, medievalized, Renaissance, and Baroque principles. Owen Jones modeled the interior decoration of the 1851 Great Exhibition on the bold color combinations of Spain's Alhambra, making it a garish parade of multicolored stripes rather than a more sober wood and metal monotone. Oscar Wilde's Aesthetic movement added an exoticist obsession with India, Japan, China, Persia, and other non-Western civilizations.[24]

As a self-consciously individualized aesthetic, steampunked machine creations, movie imagery, and book illustrations accommodate substantial scope for variation and brightness, especially in the realm of fashion and accessories. But in practice, generalizations of shadowy colors, dark woods, and metallic tones often dominate. Steampunk sculptors, writers, and designers, of course, are not historic reenactors; artistic license permits them a certain fluidity in interpreting Victorian machine style. Yet in its way, the common steampunk definition of nineteenth-century technology as brass and glass, gears and levers, is as narrowly blinded as the popular cultural stereotype of the Victorian era as scared of sexuality. Just as modern scholarship has shown the wide existence and variation in Victorian sex lives, Victorian technological life proves more complex and often contradictory than commonly recognized. Long term, the rich potential of steampunk lies in recapturing and building on the Victorians' true diversity of design, meant to convey varying ideas of beauty and cultural gravitas. Steampunk designs, such as Ian Crichton's 2009 spaceship model "Celestial Sphere 'Britannia'" or Jesse Newhouse's 2008 steampunked iPod dock "Gramophonobox MKII" might well, if built by actual Victorians, have incorporated classical columns in their structures. Some steampunk artists have created objects that reflect the Victorians' eclecticism; for instance, the 2008 "Victrola Eye-Pod" built by Joey Marsocci ("Dr. Grymm") incorporates classically scrolled legs, while Richard Nagy's 2008 "Archbishop" PC suite beautifully reflects the nineteenth century's infatuation with Gothic influences.[25]

The Evolution of Machine Aesthetics

It was the real-life Victorians' wealth of aesthetic influences and the intellectual vigor of the design debate that fostered the continued evolution of design ideals into the twentieth century. Breaking with Ruskin's hatred of mechanization, many Americans in the Arts and Crafts movement, such as Frank Lloyd Wright, sought to reconcile industrial modernization with quality.[26] An emerging horror of ornamental overabundance led to a fascination with simplicity, the inherent grace of technology itself. By the post–World War I period, Americans especially saw themselves as shaping a new Machine Age. As a 1980s Brooklyn Museum of Art exhibit demonstrated, in "this new consciousness . . . history seemed irrelevant, traditional styles and pieties outmoded. The machine in all its manifestations—as an object, a process, and ultimately a symbol—became the fundamental fact of modernism."[27] From the record-setting flights of Charles Lindbergh, to the reverential machine photographs of Margaret Bourke-White, from experimental television sets to Buckminster Fuller's Dymaxion automobile, the interwar era headlined the glories of modernized technology. Even the Great Crash of 1929 failed to fatally dent excitement over the opening of the Golden Gate Bridge, Hoover Dam, the Empire State Building, the Tennessee Valley Authority, and the 1939–1940 New York World's Fair, with its Depression-proof theme, "Building the World of Tomorrow."

European and American Machine Age aesthetics embraced mass production, clean lines, and new materials such as Bakelite and aluminum. Reflecting the Bauhaus maxim, "Art and Technology: A New Unity," designers such as Ludwig Mies van der Rohe, Le Corbusier, and Marcel Breuer incorporated the chrome and tubular steel of bicycles into minimalized chairs and cantilevered tables.[28] Futurist artists, such as Giacomo Balla, painted lines of the automobile to signify the transformation of the world by speed itself, a value later reaffirmed by the airplane, radio, and Space Age modernism. The later American art movement, Precisionism, celebrated an industrialized world as peaceful and powerful. In the 1920s and 1930s, the Ford Motor Company paid Charles Sheeler to document its vast River Rouge factory. His resulting photographs and paintings showed a world dominated by crossed conveyor belts and other industrial machinery, with human presence minimized or altogether absent. The 1930 image tellingly titled "American Landscape" showed impressive smokestacks replacing trees, an industrial canal rather than a meandering river, but as a polished construction that did not mourn the absence of either individual humanity or untouched nature. Other Precisionists, such as Ralston Crawford, went even further in showing water towers, grain elevators, factories, and endless roadways as clean and bright geometric abstractions, glorious for their very starkness.[29]

Steampunk in many ways represents a rejection of this modernist sensibility, relishing roughness and often a patched-together appearance as more honest than prefabricated pseudo-perfection. Art Donovan declared, "Due to the modern methods of mass production and the need to cheaply produce billions of units, modern design now suffers from an androgynous 'digital silhouette' whereby one cannot visually tell the difference between a cell phone and a remote, or even a flat screen TV and a computer."[30] Yet steampunk's very popularity underscores the value of a historical understanding of how our pared-down iPod design mentality evolved. Steampunk represents commentary not just on nineteenth-century versus twenty-first-century technologies, but on what came in between. For instance, the transition is readily apparent in electric kettles and other new appliances made by Berlin's Allgemeine Elektricitäts-Gesellschaft around 1910, which stripped away all decorative links to traditional domestic possessions of the elite, embracing a standardized geometric form that implied accessibility to all owners.

Early-twentieth-century industrial designers, such as Raymond Loewy, Henry Dreyfuss, Norman Bel Geddes, and Walter Dorwin Teague, defined "the modern" specifically by its contrast to older aesthetics. They feverishly applied fluid streamlining (and its domestic equivalent, cleanlining) to create new icons: aerodynamic locomotives, tapered-front automobiles, even teardrop-shaped pencil sharpeners.[31] It was no coincidence that American manufacturers passionately pursued industrial design, especially during the Depression. At a time when many ordinary people worried that rapid mechanization had displaced workers and helped spawn mass unemployment, innovative appearances reassured doubters that mechanization truly represented progress. Planned obsolescence suggested that mass production was ultimately necessary to restore mass consumption and a supposedly universal path to prosperity, defined by an abundance of possessions.[32]

Plastic especially seemed to create its own aesthetic, from the smooth curves of stackable chairs, to the striking shapes of Bakelite jewelry, to glossy art deco radio cases. Corporate boosters touted the wonders of plastic, nylon, and other synthetic materials, presenting those novel substances as naturally superseding the Victorians' metals, silk, and wood, while offering better-than-natural characteristics of strength and versatility. Chicago's 1933 Century of Progress Exposition blazoned the promise/warning, "Science finds, industry applies, man conforms." DuPont adopted the slogan, "Better Things for Better Living Through Chemistry." Of course, today's environmentalists have made it impossible to ignore the global toll of pollution and oil dependence. Designers created many products to be beyond repair; rather than fixing a broken Swatch watch, consumers were intended simply to purchase replacements. Steampunk underlines the immoral cast of such a disposable society, contrasting floods of cheap plastic to the romance of solid metal.[33]

Similarly, when electricity was relatively new, ordinary people marveled at the silent, invisible force that lit rooms at the flick of a switch, safe (unlike candle or gaslight) for even children to operate. In the late nineteenth and early twentieth centuries, both physicians and patients placed faith in the miraculous magic of electricity to cure everything from headaches to impotence.[34] Today, electricity's mystery has been evaporated by its ubiquity, restoring retro allure to its dramatic opposite, the sheer physicality, noise, and novelty of steam.

Even the dangers of steam, remote in practice and, indeed, completely outside the awareness of most people today, have acquired a certain strange fascination, even retro glamor. Alarmed by reports of engineers who held down the safety valves to steamboats or locomotives to attain reckless velocity, nineteenth-century legislators passed pioneering safety regulations and inspection provisions. For the Victorians, *Frankenstein* (1818) underlined the simultaneous fear and admiration of change, with the danger that machinery might overpower man. To a modern audience jaded and cauterized by the potential for nuclear holocaust, chemical poisoning, global warming, and environmental degradation, nineteenth-century technologies have lost their horrors. We know now that Victorian industrialization did not destroy humanity; in fact, once steampunkers reenvision it to work around child labor, pollution, and poverty, the machinery itself, stripped of such realities, becomes benign, even charming.

Today's design aesthetic is machines without noise, machines without visible risk, machines without machinery. Automobile functioning has become opaque, forcing backyard mechanics to submit vehicles to dealer-controlled computer diagnostics. Steampunk ideals, therefore, restore machinery to a place of visible consciousness. Ideally, steampunk can invigorate delight in machinery and a brave fascination with both its potential and (mostly fictional) dangers. Steampunk reveals a sense of awe combined with a sense of humor and a sense of complex ambiguity about the relationship between technology and society. In portraying a Victorian-style technology often infused with twenty-first-century sensibilities, steampunk can also capture a consciousness of modern sustainability imperatives. Not coincidentally, it also links to the 1960s/1970s "appropriate technology" and computer-liberation movements, the ethic of technology by and for the people, freed from monopoly by corporate marketing.[35]

244 ~ Amy Sue Bix

Art Donovan maintains that steampunk "celebrates a time when new technology was produced not by large corporations, but by talented and independent artisans and inventors."[36] Bricoleurs relish that user-created ideal both as a guarantee of intellectual freedom and as a statement against the dominance of commercialized mass production. But from a historical perspective, the image of the independent inventor proves more complex. In fact, the Victorian-era machine shop proved the catalyst for cooperative investigation and innovation. More than that, the nineteenth century fostered the birth of modern corporate organization, especially in the United States, where railroads and rapidly expanding firms such as DuPont embraced the "visible hand" of professional management hierarchies, horizontal mergers, and vertical integration. Victorian managers originated the idea of standardizing and governing the process of invention itself. German chemical companies created research laboratories to create synthetic dyes and pharmaceuticals. Thomas Edison, whose mythologized public image still defines what many people envision as the embodiment of a lone genius, created what some historians have considered the world's first industrial research laboratory at Menlo Park, New Jersey, in 1876. In what Edison reportedly termed his "invention factory," he explicitly aimed to turn out "a minor invention every ten days and a big thing every six months or so." To compensate for his own lack of formal scientific education, Edison hired key staff such as theoretical physicist Francis Upton, who could ground Edison's empirical brainstorming in formal mathematical reality. Providing his team with top-quality laboratory equipment, machine tools, and a technical library, Edison collaborated his way to the grand total of 1,093 patents filed under his name.[37] By the beginning of the twentieth century, the Bell Telephone Company, General Electric, DuPont, and Westinghouse had all established research laboratories that recruited engineers and scientists such as Charles Steinmetz and brilliant inventors such as Nikola Tesla to labor within the capital-intensive mega-organization.[38]

Nevertheless, steampunk raises a deeper question: have modern trends of standardized test-centered education and cultural shifts in childhood squashed old-fashioned curiosity and the joy of technical exploration? The philosopher/motorcycle mechanic Matthew Crawford has written about the artificial separation of mental and manual skills, about the lost rewards of completing tangible tasks.[39] During the early twentieth century and through the Cold War, numerous radio operators, rocket scientists, and future mechanics honed their technical skills in attics, sheds, or basements by building radio sets from Heathkits or simply taking apart old clocks.[40] Gever Tulley, a cofounder of the Tinkering School, has advocated for letting youngsters do "dangerous things," such as playing with fire and zapping objects in microwave ovens, as learning exercises.[41] Many engineering educators bemoan that current students lack the hands-on awareness of previous generations, and San Francisco's Exploratorium, Stanford University, and numerous other institutions are attempting to reopen license for children to do manual experiments.[42]

Steve Jobs, Steampunk, and Technological Desire

As many (though by no means all) fans of popular culture know, Steve Jobs was part of that cohort of self-taught tinkerers and hackers. The company he birthed, Apple, may appear the absolute antithesis of steampunk ideals, as the world's most valuable company, measured by market capitalization, in summer 2011. But strikingly, Jobs was in many ways just as obsessed with the grammar of object design and technological art as are adherents of steampunk culture. It reveals a wealth of perspective on the history of technology to recognize that Jobs's design ideals were situated 180 degrees apart from those of steampunk. One key mantra for Apple was "Simplicity is the ultimate sophistication." Jobs commanded his staff to absorb design history, to take aesthetic cues from the streamlined "pure" forms of a classic Cuisinart or Porsche, mass-produced Tiffany glass, Bauhaus modernism, Braun electronics, and Eames chairs. He reverenced the Zen-inspired architecture of I. M Pei and fashion sense of Issey Miyake, who personally created Jobs's iconic black mock turtleneck. Along with designer Jonathan Ive, Jobs defined Apple through a philosophy of simplicity, connecting the entire conception of all products from manufacture, through packaging, to end-stage user experience.[43]

Like steampunk artists, Jobs positioned his design as a conscious reaction against the (different) trends he detested among other technology creators. In contrast to the metallic high-tech hulks of other manufacturers, Apple housed its machines first in low-key beige cases, then in playfully shaped shells of eye-popping multicolor translucent plastic. Jobs designed his computers to appear "friendly"; not only did the start-up icon feature a smiling "Happy Mac" face, but the original Mac case itself echoed the contours of the user's own head. Obsessive design vision led Jobs to focus attention on minute details of his products, refining them over successive iterations, even down to the precise lines of a chamfer. He took the quest for minimalism to extremes, even seeking to abolish an on/off switch and computer function keys as unnecessary clutter. Jobs insisted on eliminating noisy internal fans, creating a straightforward single-button mouse, and developing a white-background screen to simulate the appearance of paper, all against the resistance of engineers who vowed those specifications were impossible. With a perfectionist personality, he even mandated ideal proportions for internal circuit boards, invisible to ordinary users.[44]

Jobs and Steve Wozniak founded Apple as a deliberate democratization of technology, part of the great transformation of computers from behemoth mainframes into accessible, affordable home devices liberated for user-friendly writing, games, art, and music. Their 1975 Homebrew Computer Club hackers' unconventional subculture emerged from the West Coast hippie era, *Whole Earth* strain of revolutionary experimentation, reclaiming computers from banks, corporate monopoly, and the military-industrial complex.[45] That spirit of rebellion was condensed into the famous/infamous "1984" Super Bowl ad, with Apple representing the renegades smashing the Big Brother fascism of IBM. Such corporate history makes it all the more ironic that Jobs wound up merely redirecting the source of control, attempting to ensure that users could not violate his interpretations of the appropriate computer experience. Apple corporate culture became notably hostile to hackers, with machines that limited opportunities to add customized peripherals, with cases literally built to discourage nonspecialists from opening them.[46]

Yet in the end, the mottos dear to Apple's self-definition, "insanely great" and "think different," also represent part of the imaginative ideal behind steampunk. Jobs believed that good technology must carry an emotional appeal to users, a design vision that nurtured the "cult" of Macintosh. Visually, there is a striking opposition between the pure-white, oversimplified cord marking advertising that introduced the iPod and the florid intricacies of steampunk creations. But though applied in radically different aesthetic and historical directions, that same sheer passion for design and an unembarrassed love of technology give steampunk its richness and resonance. Rebecca Onion has commented, "Steampunks express the sense that, when one is in the act of communing with a machine, one can access the pure pleasure of understanding."[47] Many early adopters and aficionados of Apple products also prize that sense of connecting to and through what they consider well-designed technology. To many design professionals and ordinary users, Apple devices exuded soul. Paola Antonelli, design curator at New York's Museum of Modern Art, remembered that upon first acquiring a Macintosh, she felt, "It was like a little pug dog looking at me. It wasn't just something I worked with; it kept me company. It had such personality and such life."[48]

For hard-core steampunk artists, such notions represent anathema; to them, the iPod manifests the worst of dull or even dehumanizing design, the isolation and isolating tendencies of contemporary techno-driven desire. The postmortem praise and even mythologizing of Steve Jobs reinforced the equally passionate feeling of those who love iPads, iPods, and iPhones that such devices, used with awareness and sensitivity, can reinforce self-expression and empower users. Clearly, such deeply held convictions resist reconciliation, yet in the end, both sides come back to the primacy of design choices and what they signify about technology's creators and users, and the cultures in which they are embedded. Not coincidentally, Jobs himself devoted careful attention to what he called the "magical" meeting points for dialogue between engineering/science and the humanities; his deep interest in liberal arts subjects, such as calligraphy and the history of font design, directly shaped his computer-age vision.

Intellectually, though the analogies are not perfect, it can be useful to think of steampunk as a history of technology running parallel to the "what if" strand of military history.[49] Robert Cowley writes, "Counterfactual history may be the history of what didn't happen, a shadow universe, but it casts a reflective light on what did. Why did certain events (and the trends and trajectories that grew out of them) dominate, and not others? At what point did possibilities become impossibilities?"[50] What if Charles Babbage had succeeded in producing functioning computers generations ago?[51] In its exploration of alternate-reality technological possibilities, steampunk serves as a useful corrective to technological determinism, errors in assuming that technological "progress" autonomously develops along certain paths and people merely follow.[52]

Steampunk provides excellent perspective on important ideas in the history of technology, including scholar Melvin Kranzberg's famous first "law of technology": "Technology is neither good nor bad; nor is it neutral."[53] Fundamentally, technology never develops in a vacuum. The steampunk genre provides useful insight into ways that technological development expresses the essential influence of human choice and social context. Like design in the Victorian era and ever since, steampunk still offers the heart of a creative dialogue between technological change and the contested mentality of modernity.

Notes

1. David Noble, *Forces of Production* (Oxford: Oxford University Press, 1986).

2. Art Donovan, *The Art of Steampunk* (East Petersburg, Pa.: Fox Chapel Publishing, 2011), 24.

3. Mike Perschon, "Steam Wars," *Neo-Victorian Studies* 3, no. 1 (2010): 127–166, www.neovictorianstudies.com (29 February 2012). On the rapidly evolving definitions

of steampunk, see Jess Nevins, "Prescriptivists vs. Descriptivists: Defining Steampunk," *Science Fiction Studies* 38, no. 3 (November 2011): 513–518.

4. Donovan, *The Art of Steampunk*, 26.

5. "Scott Westerfeld on *Leviathan*," in *The Steampunk Bible*, ed. Jeff VanderMeer and S. J. Chambers (New York: Abrams, 2011), 66–68; Rebecca Onion, "Reclaiming the Machine: An Introductory Look at Steampunk in Everyday Practice," *Neo-Victorian Studies* 3, no. 1 (2010): 138–163, www.neovictorianstudies.com (29 February 2012).

6. Stefania Forlini, "Technology and Morality: The Stuff of Steampunk," *Neo-Victorian Studies* 3, no. 1 (2010): 72–98, www.neovictorianstudies.com (28 February 2012).

7. David Nye, *American Technological Sublime* (Cambridge: MIT Press, 1996).

8. For more on the history of actual Victorian technology, see William Rosen, *The Most Powerful Idea in the World: A Story of Steam, Industry, and Invention* (New York: Random House, 2010); Thomas J. Misa, *A Nation of Steel: The Making of Modern America, 1865–1925* (Baltimore: Johns Hopkins University Press, 1999); Maury Klein, *The Power Makers: Steam, Electricity, and the Men Who Invented Modern America* (New York: Bloomsbury Press, 2008); Alan Marcus and Howard Segal, *Technology in America: A Brief History* (New York: Wadsworth Publishing, 1998).

9. VanderMeer and Chambers, *The Steampunk Bible*. For further analysis of steampunk and history, see Jason Jones, "Betrayed by Time: Steampunk and the Neo-Victorian in Alan Moore's *Lost Girls* and *The League of Extraordinary Gentlemen*," *Neo-Victorian Studies* 3, no. 1 (2010): 99–126, www.neovictorianstudies.com (28 February 2012).

10. Owen Jones, *The Grammar of Ornament* (London, 1856); reprint (New York: Van Nostrand Reinhold, 1972).

11. Stephen van Dulken, *Inventing the 19th Century: 100 Inventions that Shaped the Victorian Age* (New York: New York University Press, 2001).

12. On American attitudes toward industrialization, see Leo Marx, *The Machine in the Garden: Technology and the Pastoral Ideal in America* (New York: Oxford University Press, 1964) and John Kasson, *Civilizing the Machine: Technology and Republican Values in America, 1776–1900* (New York: Grossman, 1976).

13. www.thehenryford.org/exhibits/pic/1997/97.aug.html (28 February 2012).

14. Julie Wosk, *Breaking Frame: Technology and the Visual Arts in the Nineteenth Century* (New Brunswick: Rutgers, 1994), xii.

15. Charlotte Gere and Michael Whiteway, *Nineteenth Century Design: From Pugin to Mackintosh* (New York: Abrams, 1993), 10, 13.

16. Gere and Whiteway, *Nineteenth Century Design*, 10–11.

17. Michael Freeman, *Railways and the Victorian Imagination* (New Haven: Yale University Press, 1999).

18. Bruce Sterling, "The User's Guide to Steampunk," and Jake von Slatt, "A Steampunk Manifesto," in VanderMeer and Chambers, *The Steampunk Bible*.

19. Donovan, *The Art of Steampunk*, 25–26.

20. Pamela Todd, *The Arts & Crafts Companion* (New York: Bulfinch Press, 2004).

21. Donovan, *The Art of Steampunk*, 59–61.

22. David Jaffee, "Peddlers of Progress and the Transformation of the Rural North, 1760–1860," *The Journal of American History* 78, no. 2 (September 1991): 511–535; John Joseph Murphy, "Entrepreneurship in the Establishment of the American Clock Industry," *The Journal of Economic History* 26, no. 2 (June 1966): 169–186.

23. Merritt Roe Smith, *Harpers Ferry Armory and the New Technology* (Ithaca, N.Y.: Cornell University Press, 1980); David Hounshell, *From the American System to Mass Production, 1800–1932: The Development of Manufacturing Technology in the United States* (Baltimore: Johns Hopkins University Press, 1985).

24. Wendy Kaplan, *The Arts and Crafts Movement in Europe and America* (London: Thames and Hudson, 2004).

25. Donovan, *The Art of Steampunk*, 77, 83, 88, 106.

26. Todd, *The Arts & Crafts Companion*.

27. Richard Guy Wilson, Dianne H. Pilgrim, and Dickran Tashjian, *The Machine Age in America, 1918–1941* (New York: Abrams, 1986, 2001), 23.

28. Eric Knowles, *100 Years of the Decorative Arts* (New York: MITCH, 2006).

29. Terry Smith, *Making the Modern: Industry, Art, and Design in America* (Chicago: University of Chicago Press, 1993).

30. Donovan, *The Art of Steampunk*, 26.

31. Jeffrey L. Meikle, *Twentieth-Century Limited* (Philadelphia: Temple, 2001).

32. Amy Sue Bix, *Inventing Ourselves Out of Jobs: America's Debate over Technological Unemployment, 1929–1981* (Baltimore: Johns Hopkins University Press, 2001).

33. Jeffrey L. Meikle, *American Plastic* (New Brunswick: Rutgers, 1997); Stephen Fenichell, *Plastic: The Making of a Synthetic Century* (New York: HarperBusiness, 1996); Penny Sparke, ed., *The Plastics Age: From Bakelite to Beanbags and Beyond* (Woodstock, N.Y.: Overlook Press, 1992).

34. Carolyn de la Pena, *The Body Electric* (New York: New York University Press, 2005). See also David Nye, *Electrifying America: Social Meanings of a New Technology, 1880–1940* (Cambridge: MIT Press, 1992).

35. E. F. Schumacher, *Small Is Beautiful: A Study of Economics as if People Mattered* (London: Blond and Briggs, 1973).

36. Donovan, *The Art of Steampunk*, 4.

37. William Pretzer, *Working at Inventing: Thomas A. Edison and the Menlo Park Experience* (Baltimore: Johns Hopkins University Press, 2002); Matthew Josephson, *Edison: A Biography* (New York: McGraw-Hill, 1959); Paul Israel, "Inventing Industrial Research: Thomas Edison and the Menlo Park Laboratory," *Endeavour* 26, no. 2 (2002): 48–54.

38. Ernst Homburg, "The Emergence of Research Laboratories in the Dyestuffs Industry, 1870–1900," *British Journal for the History of Science* 25, no. 1 (March 1992): 91–111; Leonard Reich, *The Making of American Industrial Research: Science and Business at GE and Bell, 1876–1926* (Cambridge, Mass.: Cambridge University Press, 2002); Steven Usselman, "From Novelty to Utility: George Westinghouse and

the Business of Innovation During the Age of Edison," *Business History Review* 66 (Summer 1992): 251–304.

39. Matthew Crawford, *Shop Class as Soulcraft: An Inquiry into the Value of Work* (New York: Penguin, 2009).

40. Kristen Haring, *Ham Radio's Technical Culture* (Cambridge: MIT Press, 2008).

41. Gever Tulley, *50 Dangerous Things You Should Let Your Children Do* (New York: NAL Trade, 2011).

42. "The Tinkering Studio," The Exploratorium; http://tinkering.exploratorium .edu (28 February 2012). "Teaching Kids to Tinker so They Can Design Tomorrow's Machines," Stanford University News Service, http://news.stanford.edu/pr/92/920630Arc2145.html (28 February 2012).

43. Walter Isaacson, *Steve Jobs* (New York: Simon and Schuster, 2011).

44. Isaacson, *Steve Jobs.*

45. John Markoff, *What the Dormouse Said: How the Sixties Counter-Culture Shaped the Personal Computer Industry* (New York: Penguin, 2006); Fred Turner, *From Counterculture to Cyberculture: Stewart Brand, the Whole Earth Network, and the Rise of Digital Utopianism* (Chicago: University of Chicago Press, 2008).

46. Isaacson, *Steve Jobs.*

47. Rebecca Onion, "Reclaiming the Machine."

48. James B. Stewart, "How Jobs Put Passion into Products," *New York Times*, 7 October 2011, www.nytimes.com/2011/10/08/business/how-steve-jobs-infused -passion-into-a-commodity.html?_r=1&scp=1&sq=How%20Jobs%20Put%20 Passion%20Into%20Products&st=cse (28 February 2012).

49. For more on steampunk as a counterfactual exercise, see Patrick Jagoda, "Clacking Control Societies: Steampunk, History, and the Difference Engine of Escape," *Neo-Victorian Studies* 3, no. 1 (2010): 46–71, www.neovictorianstudies.com (28 February 2012).

50. Robert Cowley, ed., *What Ifs? Of American History* (New York: Berkeley, 2004), xiii–xiv.

51. William Gibson and Bruce Sterling, *The Difference Engine* (New York: Bantam, 1991).

52. Merritt Roe Smith and Leo Marx, *Does Technology Drive History?* (Cambridge: MIT Press, 1994).

53. Melvin Kranzberg, "Technology and History: 'Kranzberg's Laws,'" *Technology and Culture* 27, no. 6 (July 1986): 544–560. See also Langdon Winner, "Do Artifacts Have Politics?," in *The Whale and the Reactor: A Search for Limits in an Age of High Technology* (Chicago: University of Chicago Press, 1986), 19–39.

Bibliography

Bix, Amy Sue. *Inventing Ourselves Out of Jobs: America's Debate over Technological Unemployment, 1929–1981.* Baltimore: Johns Hopkins University Press, 2001.
Cowley, Robert, ed. *What Ifs? Of American History.* New York: Berkeley, 2004.

Crawford, Matthew. *Shop Class as Soulcraft: An Inquiry into the Value of Work*. New York: Penguin, 2009.

de la Pena, Carolyn. *The Body Electric*. New York: New York University Press, 2005.

Donovan, Art. *The Art of Steampunk*. East Petersburg, Pa.: Fox Chapel Publishing, 2011.

Fenichell, Stephen. *Plastic: The Making of a Synthetic Century*. New York: Harper Business, 1996.

Forlini, Stefania. "Technology and Morality: The Stuff of Steampunk." *Neo-Victorian Studies* 3, no.1 (2010): 72–98. www.neovictorianstudies.com (28 February 2012).

Freeman, Michael. *Railways and the Victorian Imagination*. New Haven: Yale University Press, 1999.

Gere, Charlotte, and Michael Whiteway. *Nineteenth Century Design: From Pugin to Mackintosh*. New York: Abrams, 1993.

Gibson, William, and Bruce Sterling. *The Difference Engine*. New York: Bantam, 1991.

Haring, Kristen. *Ham Radio's Technical Culture*. Cambridge: MIT Press, 2008.

Homburg, Ernst. "The Emergence of Research Laboratories in the Dyestuffs Industry, 1870–1900." *British Journal for the History of Science* 25, no. 1 (March, 1992): 91–111.

Hounshell, David. *From the American System to Mass Production, 1800–1932: The Development of Manufacturing Technology in the United States*. Baltimore: Johns Hopkins University Press, 1985.

Isaacson, Walter. *Steve Jobs*. New York: Simon and Schuster, 2011.

Israel, Paul. "Inventing Industrial Research: Thomas Edison and the Menlo Park Laboratory." *Endeavour* 26, no. 2 (2002): 48–54.

Jaffee, David. "Peddlers of Progress and the Transformation of the Rural North, 1760–1860." *Journal of American History* 78, no. 2 (September 1991): 511–535.

Jagoda, Patrick, "Clacking Control Societies: Steampunk, History, and the Difference Engine of Escape." *Neo-Victorian Studies* 3, no. 1 (2010): 46–71. www.neovictorianstudies.com (28 February 2012).

Jones, Jason. "Betrayed by Time: Steampunk and the Neo-Victorian in Alan Moore's *Lost Girls* and *The League of Extraordinary Gentlemen*." *Neo-Victorian Studies* 3, no. 1 (2010): 99–126. www.neovictorianstudies.com (28 February 2012).

Jones, Owen. *The Grammar of Ornament*. London, 1856. Reprint: New York: Van Nostrand Reinhold, 1972.

Josephson, Matthew. *Edison: A Biography*. New York: McGraw-Hill, 1959.

Kaplan, Wendy. *The Arts and Crafts Movement in Europe and America*. London: Thames and Hudson, 2004.

Kasson, John. *Civilizing the Machine: Technology and Republican Values in America, 1776–1900*. New York: Grossman, 1976.

Klein, Maury. *The Power Makers: Steam, Electricity, and the Men Who Invented Modern America*. New York: Bloomsbury Press, 2008.

Knowles, Eric. *100 Years of the Decorative Arts*. New York: MITCH, 2006.

252 〜 Amy Sue Bix

Kranzberg, Melvin. "Technology and History: 'Kranzberg's Laws.'" *Technology and Culture* 27, no. 3 (July 1986): 544–560.
Marcus, Alan, and Howard Segal. *Technology in America: A Brief History*. New York: Wadsworth Publishing, 1998.
Markoff, John. *What the Dormouse Said: How the Sixties Counter-Culture Shaped the Personal Computer Industry*. New York: Penguin, 2006.
Marx, Leo. *The Machine in the Garden: Technology and the Pastoral Ideal in America*. New York: Oxford University Press, 1964.
Meikle, Jeffrey L. *American Plastic*. New Brunswick: Rutgers, 1997.
———. *Twentieth-Century Limited*. Philadelphia: Temple, 2001.
Misa, Thomas J. *A Nation of Steel: The Making of Modern America, 1865–1925*. Baltimore: Johns Hopkins University Press, 1999.
Murphy, John Joseph. "Entrepreneurship in the Establishment of the American Clock Industry." *Journal of Economic History* 26, no. 2 (June 1966): 169–186.
Nevins, Jess. "Prescriptivists vs. Descriptivists: Defining Steampunk." *Science Fiction Studies* 38, no. 3 (November 2011): 513–518.
Noble, David. *Forces of Production*. Oxford: Oxford University Press, 1986.
Nye, David. *American Technological Sublime*. Cambridge: MIT Press, 1996.
———. *Electrifying America: Social Meanings of a New Technology, 1880–1940*. Cambridge: MIT Press, 1992.
Onion, Rebecca. "Reclaiming the Machine: An Introductory Look at Steampunk in Everyday Practice." *Neo-Victorian Studies* 3, no. 1 (2010): 138–163. www.neovictorianstudies.com (28 February 2012).
Perschon, Mike. "Steam Wars." *Neo-Victorian Studies* 3, no. 1 (2010): 127–166. www.neovictorianstudies.com (28 February 2012).
Pretzer, William. *Working at Inventing: Thomas A. Edison and the Menlo Park Experience*. Baltimore: Johns Hopkins University Press, 2002.
Reich, Leonard. *The Making of American Industrial Research: Science and Business at GE and Bell, 1876–1926*. Cambridge: Cambridge University Press, 2002.
Rosen, William. *The Most Powerful Idea in the World: A Story of Steam, Industry, and Invention*. New York: Random House, 2010.
Schumacher, E. F. *Small Is Beautiful: A Study of Economics as if People Mattered*. London: Blond and Briggs, 1973.
Smith, Merritt Roe. *Harpers Ferry Armory and the New Technology*. Ithaca, N.Y.: Cornell University Press, 1980.
Smith, Merritt Roe, and Leo Marx. *Does Technology Drive History?* Cambridge: MIT Press, 1994.
Smith, Terry. *Making the Modern: Industry, Art, and Design in America*. Chicago: University of Chicago Press, 1993.
Sparke, Penny, ed. *The Plastics Age: From Bakelite to Beanbags and Beyond*. Woodstock, N.Y.: Overlook Press, 1992.
Sterling, Bruce, "The User's Guide to Steampunk." 12–13 in VanderMeer and Chambers, *The Steampunk Bible*. New York: Abrams, 2011.

Stewart, James B. "How Jobs Put Passion Into Products." *New York Times*, 7 October 2011. www.nytimes.com/2011/10/08/business/how-steve-jobs-infused-passion -into-a-commodity.html?_r=1&scp=1&sq=How%20Jobs%20Put%20Passion%20 Into%20Products&st=cse (28 February 2012).

Streitfeld, David. "Erasing the Boundaries." *New York Times*, 12 February 2012. www.nytimes.com/2012/02/13/technology/keeping-consumers-on-the-digital -plantation.html?scp=1&sq=%22erasing%20the%20boundaries%22&st=Search (28 February 2012).

Todd, Pamela. *The Arts & Crafts Companion*. New York: Bulfinch Press, 2004.

Tulley, Gever. *50 Dangerous Things You Should Let Your Children Do*. New York: NAL Trade, 2011.

Turner, Fred. *From Counterculture to Cyberculture: Stewart Brand, the Whole Earth Network, and the Rise of Digital Utopianism*. Chicago: University of Chicago Press, 2008.

Usselman, Steven, "From Novelty to Utility: George Westinghouse and the Business of Innovation During the Age of Edison." *Business History Review* 66 (Summer 1992): 251–304.

van Dulken, Stephen. *Inventing the 19th Century: 100 Inventions that Shaped the Victorian Age*. New York: New York University Press, 2001.

VanderMeer, Jeff, and S. J. Chambers. *The Steampunk Bible: An Illustrated Guide to the World of Imaginary Airships, Corsets and Goggles, Mad Scientists, and Strange Literature*. New York: Abrams, 2011.

Von Slatt, Jake. "A Steampunk Manifesto." 216–218 in VanderMeer and Chambers, *The Steampunk Bible*. New York: Abrams, 2011.

Wilson, Richard Guy, Dianne H. Pilgrim, and Dickran Tashjian. *The Machine Age in America, 1918–1941*. New York: Abrams, 1986, 2001.

Winner, Langdon. "Do Artifacts Have Politics?" 19–39 in *The Whale and the Reactor: A Search for Limits in an Age of High Technology*. Chicago: University of Chicago Press, 1986.

Wosk, Julie. *Breaking Frame: Technology and the Visual Arts in the Nineteenth Century*. New Brunswick, N.J.: Rutgers, 1994.

Part mechanic, part magician, steampunk inventors shape the machines that shape the world. *Copyright Jody Steel*

CHAPTER THIRTEEN

Remaking the World:
The Steampunk Inventor
on Page and Screen

A. Bowdoin Van Riper

Engineers and inventors lurk at the margins of the steampunk universe: in but not quite of it.[1] They are set apart by their clothes—boots more robust, or goggles more elaborate than fashion dictates—by the tools protruding from their waistcoat pockets, or simply by their conviction that the world can and should be remade to suit human needs. They project the practicality and directness of an explorer, an airship captain, or an officer in a frontier regiment, but the unknown into which they venture is technological, not geographical. Engineers are only occasionally the heroes of steampunk tales, but they are seldom absent, and with good reason. Marginal as they may first appear, engineers are pivotal figures within the steampunk universe: makers of the world that they, and all those who swirl around them, inhabit.

Steampunk is defined by the unexpected intrusion of the modern into the historical, and technology is the nexus of that intrusion. The technological fantastic—nineteenth-century machines with twentieth-century capabilities—lies at the conceptual core of steampunk fiction, film, and visual art, and the fusion of Victorian technological aesthetics and contemporary attitudes is emblematic of the steampunk subculture. Steampunk's stories of fantastic technologies also, however, involve a second intrusion of the modern into the historical. They take place in the nineteenth century, but the stories' creators and audiences come to them fully aware of—and the stories thus reflect—technology's complex twentieth- and twenty-first-century legacy.

The portrayal of engineers in steampunk reflects this dual historical consciousness. It balances nineteenth-century admiration of engineers with twentieth-century wariness of them, and reflects both delight in the wonders they can produce and anxiety over the havoc those wonders can wreak. Steampunk engineers are agents of progress—reinforcing and perfecting the status quo—but they are also transgressive, disruptive figures whose actions have (intentionally or not) the capability to shake it to the core. Steampunk engineers carry, on their collective shoulders, the legacy of Thomas Edison, whose relentless experiments with incandescent bulbs enabled him to light the world, but also that of J. Robert Oppenheimer, whose determination to solve the "technically sweet" problem of building an atomic bomb brought civilization to the brink of self-destruction. What follows is an examination of the dual historical consciousness—the *second* intrusion of the modern into the historical—as it is played out in steampunk's portrayals of three archetypal engineer-inventor characters: the technocrat, the lone inventor-hero, and the inventor-sidekick. Fantastic machines make steampunk what it is; this chapter, therefore, considers the people who make the machines.

The Engineer as Icon

The recognition of engineers as heroes was a product of "the long nineteenth century": the years between the French Revolution and the First World War. The epic technological changes collectively known as the Industrial Revolution—new methods of manufacturing, new transportation systems, new building materials, and new kinds of public works—provided a steady stream of projects where engineers could make their reputations. The emergence of a mass literary culture—a product of rising literacy rates, the falling cost of printing, and the emergence of new institutions like lending libraries and illustrated newspapers—created new opportunities to chronicle the latest technological achievements and the men behind them.[2] Engineering's gradual coalescence into a profession brought engineers, as a group, a new degree of middle-class respectability—permanently separating them, in the public mind, from the craftsmen and laborers who gave form to their ideas.[3] Finally, less tangible but no less important, the cultural mood of the long nineteenth century aligned with that of the nascent engineering profession. Belief that the remaking of nature for human benefit was an absolute, unambiguous good united the two, making it easy to celebrate those whose work made that dream into reality.

The industrializing nations of the era embraced real-world engineers with a fervor once reserved for statesmen and religious leaders. Individual engineers—Archimedes, Vitruvius, da Vinci—had achieved fame before, but never in such numbers. The masterminds behind major civil engineering projects—Robert Stevenson of the Bell Rock Lighthouse, Marc Brunel of the Thames Tunnel, Ferdinand de Lesseps of the Suez Canal, and John Roebling of the Brooklyn Bridge—were hailed like victorious generals, conquerors of nature rather than nations. The creators of new electrical technologies— Michael Faraday, Charles Steinmetz, Nikola Tesla, and Thomas Edison among them—were routinely painted as latter-day wizards. The popular press chronicled their exploits, and writers like Samuel Smiles penned adoring biographies, bestowing sobriquets that became as well known as their real names. Diminutive Isambard Kingdom Brunel, creator of the Great Western Railway and designer of the biggest steamships in the world, was "the Little Giant"; highway engineer Thomas Telford was "the Colossus of Roads"; and Edison, named for the location of his New Jersey workshop, became "the Wizard of Menlo Park."[4]

Real engineers became icons of physical vigor, practical knowledge, and ingenuity for an age that valued all three. Their fictional counterparts were, if anything, even more impressive. They invented their way to fame, fortune, and adventure in tales such as Jules Verne's *From the Earth to the Moon* (1865), Edward Everett Hale's "The Brick Moon" (1869), and Harry Enton's *Frank Reade and His Steam Man of the Plains* (1876). They helped to defeat the "Yellow Peril" in Jack London's genocidal fantasy "The Unparalleled Invasion" (1910), and to save the entire planet in Garrett P. Serviss's *Edison's Conquest of Mars* (1898), creating spaceships and superweapons for a counterattack against the Martian invaders from H. G. Wells's *The War of the Worlds* (1898).

Engineers remained hero figures well into the twentieth century. General George W. Goethals, superintendent of the Panama Canal project; Frank Crowe, who oversaw the building of Boulder (later Hoover) Dam; and Joseph Strauss, designer of the Golden Gate Bridge, were lauded—like their nineteenth-century predecessors Telford, Roebling, and Brunel—for their skill in subduing and reshaping nature. New fields of technological endeavor, born with the century, yielded their own hero figures: Donald Douglas in aviation, Philo T. Farnsworth in electronics, and Robert Goddard in rocketry.[5] Heroic fictional engineers proliferated as well, in boys' adventure stories like the "Tom Swift" series, mainstream novels like John Buchan's *The Thirty-Nine Steps* (1915), and science fiction tales like E. E. Smith's *The Skylark of Space* (1928) and George O. Smith's *Venus Equilateral* (1947). At the movies, Randolph Scott oversaw the building of the *Union Pacific* (1939), and John Wayne drove a tunnel through the Andes in *Tycoon* (1947). Other films, freed from the real-world limitations imposed by available materials and the laws of physics, depicted more ambitious projects: a transatlantic tunnel in *The Tunnel* (1935), for example, or a nuclear-powered rocket in *Destination Moon* (1950).

The decline of the heroic engineer as an archetypal figure, which began gradually in the aftermath of the Second World War and steepened over the second half of the century, was partly a reflection of engineers' growing anonymity. The great civil engineering projects of the postwar era—the Interstate Highway System or the World Trade Center, for example—were less likely to be associated with a particular individual than those of the pre-war period or the nineteenth century. Postwar leaps in technology were also likely to emerge from corporate research and development laboratories and thus lack a single, identifiable engineer-parent. This decline was reinforced by the growing subtlety—the *un*-obviousness—of even world-altering break-throughs. The transistor, developed at Bell Labs in 1947, made possible the microelectronics revolution, but few outside the electronics industry could readily explain what it did.[6]

The cultural reputation of engineers was also eroded by a series of highly publicized technological failures in the 1940s and 1950s: the collapse of the Tacoma Narrows Bridge, the U. S. Navy's wartime struggle with "dud" torpedoes, and the midair disintegration of de Havilland Comet and Lock-heed Electra airliners. Engineers were also tainted by association with tech-nologies that, to many, seemed as much a curse as a blessing. They were the public face of the automation of production lines, of the computerization of record keeping and payroll systems, and of superhighway projects that destroyed once-vibrant urban neighborhoods. They were also implicated in the military-industrial complex that President Eisenhower warned against in his farewell address to the nation. They stood, slide rules in hand, behind the ever-expanding stockpiles of bombs and missiles that put Armageddon a single political miscalculation away.

The erosion continued for the remainder of the century, fed by revelations about napalm and Agent Orange, Chernobyl and *Challenger*, and reinforced by the growing uneasiness of many in the West with the narrow, reductive worldview engineers were presumed to hold. The heroic engineer who trans-formed the world gave way, as an archetypal character, to the self-absorbed engineer who endangered it. Over the last four decades of the twentieth cen-tury, fictional engineers unleashed a steady stream of malevolent computers, genetically engineered monsters, homicidal robots, and planet-destroying weapons. Only those relegated to sidekick status (like Q in the James Bond films, or Scotty in *Star Trek*), or explicitly defined as rebels *against* their profession (like the conscience-stricken computer expert in *Wargames*) were exempt.[7] The rest—like the overambitious genetic engineers of Michael Crichton's novel *Jurassic Park* (1990)—came labeled: "potentially useful, but dangerous if left unattended."[8]

Technocrats

The idea that individual scientists and engineers could actively shape the fate of nations runs through much of nineteenth-century science fiction. Captain Nemo, of Jules Verne's *20,000 Leagues Under the Sea* (1869), harbors such ambitions, as does Robur, the hero of Verne's *Clipper of the Clouds* (1885) and *Master of the World* (1904). Jacobus Lanningdale conceives the biological weapons that enable the West to defeat an expansion-minded China in Jack London's short story "The Unparalleled Invasion" (1907), and Thomas Edison redraws the balance of power in the solar system in Garrett P. Serviss's *Edison's Conquest of Mars* (1898). In *Edison's Conquest of Mars*, it is Edison himself who parleys with the king of the defeated Martians, assuring him that Earth's intentions were defensive rather than imperialistic. The skills necessary to solve complex technical problems are, in such tales, readily transferred to the realm of politics. The realities of twentieth-century politics, however, suggest otherwise.[9]

William Gibson and Bruce Sterling's *The Difference Engine* (1991) revives the nineteenth-century fantasy of the engineer-statesman with gusto.[10] Set in an alternate nineteenth century where the British government funded construction of Charles Babbage's "analytical engine"—an immense, brass-geared, steam-driven mechanical computer—it imagines Charles Darwin, Isambard Kingdom Brunel, and Babbage himself as members of the Radical Industrial Lords, the dominant political party of the age. The "Rads," as they are known, are the ultimate technocrats: prizing rationalism and efficiency over even the most hallowed traditions. Under their rule, aristocratic privileges have been curtailed, religion dethroned, and a radical meritocracy introduced. Britain's computer monopoly (France's attempt to build a similar device, the Great Napoleon, ends in failure) makes it the world's lone superpower—able to dominate the globe both economically and politically. Brunel, in Gibson and Sterling's 1855, is not only Britain's most eminent engineer but also—after the unexpected death of Byron—the country's prime minister.[11]

The technocrats' success is tempered, however, by notable failures. All their scientific and technological knowledge and problem-solving ability cannot dispel the polluted air, thick with coal and wood smoke, that covers

London like a blanket. Nor can they alleviate the noxious smell rising from the Thames (still used as an open sewer), which culminates—in the alternate 1855 of *The Difference Engine* as in our 1855—in an eruption of stench that Londoners dubbed the Great Stink. Brunel, for all his mastery of the material world, is as vulnerable as any politician to fractiousness within his own party and verbal assaults from the opposition. Calling his ministers to account for their lack of support in a two-day debate over a vote of no confidence, he is left with no choice but to issue an ultimatum. "I must be master in this House," he declares, "or else resign my office—abandoning this nation to the purported leadership of men whose intentions are increasingly stark in their clarity. Gentlemen, the choice is yours."[12] His government is equally embattled outside of Parliament, harried by violent revolutionaries whose mysterious leader uses the *nom de guerre* Captain Swing.[13] The technocrats are, ultimately, no more successful than any other politicians in remaking society in their image. The barriers they face—like waste heat and friction in a machine—can only be minimized, not eliminated.

Stephen Baxter's *Anti-Ice* (1993) is a more fanciful tale, and its hero's success in remaking the world around him is more complete. Sir Josiah Traveller is already famous when the story begins in the mid-1850s: a millionaire industrialist and engineering genius, described by one character as the "inheritor of the mantle of Brunel" and "the Leonardo of our age."[14] Anti-ice is a mysterious substance that, when heated, releases unimaginable quantities of energy. Traveller is not only the world's foremost expert on its use—his scarred face and prosthetic nose testimony to its terrible power—but also the holder of a virtual monopoly on the Earth's only known supply, which was deposited in Antarctica when a comet struck the Moon centuries earlier. *Anti-Ice* begins at the height of the Crimean War, and Traveller enters the story and the war literally holding the fate of nations (in the form of an anti-ice artillery shell) in his hands.

Traveller's shell, like Nemo's submarine and Edison's disintegrator ray, sweeps away all opposition before it. It demolishes the besieged, seemingly impregnable fortress of Sevastopol, kills thousands of its Russian defenders, and ends the war at a stroke. A nineteenth-century version of the tale might have ended with Traveller's accepting the Russian surrender, or attempting (Nemo-like) to enforce global peace and disarmament through intimidation. *Anti-Ice*, however, is a product of the late twentieth century, and Traveller exists within the long cultural shadows cast by its history. Like Leo Szilard, Enrico Fermi, and other veterans of the Manhattan Project, he is appalled by the devastation wrought by his handiwork and renounces all further work on munitions. Like Wernher von Braun, he pours his heart and soul into

peaceful applications, including space travel. Britain becomes the most pros-
perous nation on Earth and, thanks to its monopoly on anti-ice weapons, the
most powerful. Yet, when Traveller tries to prevent a second use of anti-ice
weapons to end the Franco-Prussian War in 1871, he finds himself—like J.
Robert Oppenheimer in the early 1950s—brushed aside by a government
whose interests no longer align with his. Orleans is destroyed by an anti-
ice rocket, the war ends, and Britain becomes, for better or worse, master
of Europe. History thus moves on, and Traveller—once the most powerful
man in Europe—is pushed to the sidelines, left to observe events rather than
shape them. An epilogue delivers a final ironic underscoring of his ultimate
impotence: Traveller's pioneering space voyage, by revealing a new source of
anti-ice, breaks Britain's monopoly and opens the door to a world in which
his terrible weapons will become ubiquitous.

Independents

The independent inventor-hero is a defining figure in the nineteenth-century
and turn-of-the-century tales to which steampunk is, in part, an homage. With
a video-telegraph on his workbench, a time machine in his closet, and an airship in his backyard, he embodies the uncomplicated fascination with new
machines and the unswerving belief in progress that pervaded Western culture
before the First World War. Endlessly creative, boundlessly energetic, and
wildly ambitious, he and his fellow fictional inventors relentlessly expanded
the boundaries of the possible, confident—as were their readers—that no machine they created could prove to be more curse than blessing. When Frank
Reade Jr. and his partner use Reade's robot "steam man" and "steam horse" to
casually run down and kill a gang of Wild West outlaws, pausing only to drive
iron spikes from the horse's hoof through the skull of the last dazed survivor, it
is presented as thrilling high adventure.[15] As the twentieth century unfolded,
however, reading (and viewing) audiences grew less willing to treat all technological innovation as benign progress. The heroic independent inventor gradually faded from popular culture, replaced by the eccentric-genius inventor, the
bumbling inventor, and the misguided (or actively malevolent) inventor. The
new independent inventors reflected new popular attitudes toward technology: they were agents of mayhem (albeit sometimes comic) and chaos (albeit
sometimes productive) rather than seamless, orderly progress—pivotal figures
in what Brian Attebery dubs the "exploding gadget plot."[16]

Steampunk retains the independent inventor-hero as a character—
both for fidelity to the *kind* of story being told and for his ability to drive
the plot—but paints his actions in the darker, more complicated shad-

From small experiments come revolutionary advances . . . or catastrophic failures. *Copyright Jody Steel*

ings common to twentieth-century tales of invention. Nowhere is this transition more striking than in the evolution of Captain Nemo, the hero of Jules Verne's *20,000 Leagues Under the Sea* and *The Mysterious Island* (1874). Nemo, as written by Verne, is a dark, brooding, mysterious figure haunted by demons from his past: the independent inventor as Byronic hero. The darkness in Nemo's soul manifests itself in his actions—sinking naval vessels without warning, threatening to drown the narrator and his companions—but not in his inventions, which remain unproblematic monuments to his genius and skill.

Depictions of Nemo in post-1945 films, however, render the inventions (as well as the man) dark and morally ambiguous. The 1954 adaption of *20,000 Leagues* ends with a mushroom-shaped cloud rising over Nemo's secret island base, and a voiceover that makes clear he had harnessed the power of the atom.[17] The 1961 film *The Mysterious Island* features giant creatures (bees, a crab, a flightless prehistoric bird): the products of experiments by the not-actually-dead Nemo. The 2003 film *The League of Extraordinary Gentlemen* arms the *Nautilus* with a guided missile capable of destroying an entire building at a stroke. All three technologies are morally tainted at best and signs of outright irresponsibility at worst. Atomic energy and submarine-launched missiles evoke the real-world role of nuclear-armed submarines as guarantors of "Mutual Assured Destruction." The bioengineered beasts of *The Mysterious Island* resonate with H. G. Wells's novel *The Island of Doctor Moreau* (1896), as well as 1950s films—such as *Them!* (1954), *Tarantula* (1955), and *The Beginning of the End* (1957)—in which creatures of unnatural size symbolize science run amok.[18]

Langdon St. Ives, the hero of four novellas and two novels by steampunk pioneer James P. Blaylock, is (by design) an inventor-hero in the classic nineteenth-century style. An explorer and adventurer as well as an inventor, he travels the world battling wild beasts, the elements, and evildoers alike: including Dr. Ignacio Narbondo—an equally classic nineteenth-century mad scientist. The novel *Lord Kelvin's Machine* (1992) describes three of St. Ives's encounters with the fantastic device of the title, created by Britain's greatest nineteenth-century physicist: William Thomson, Lord Kelvin.[19] In the first, a comet is on a collision course with the Earth, and St. Ives (while busy with Narbondo's latest evil plot) must also subvert Kelvin's misguided, potentially catastrophic plan to avert the collision by using the machine to temporarily switch off Earth's magnetic field. In the second, Narbondo steals the machine and threatens to use it to pull steel-hulled ships to the bottom of the ocean if he is not paid an appropriate ransom. In the third, St. Ives himself acquires the machine and uses it to travel through time (rewriting history as he goes) to save his beloved, Alice, from death at Narbondo's hands. St. Ives, of course, succeeds in each case—the comet misses, the ships remain afloat, and Alice lives—but in every case Lord Kelvin's machine is a dangerous wild card: not a tool to be casually used but an agent of disruption to be carefully managed.

The catastrophe that opens, and sets the stage for, Cherie Priest's *Bone-shaker* (2009) highlights—with a distinctly twenty-first-century sensibility—the dangers that can ensue when such devices run out of control. Leviticus Blue, a classic independent inventor, is hired to design and build a giant self-propelled drill that miners can use to penetrate the frozen ground of the Yukon Territory, where gold has been discovered. Laboring in the basement workshop of his Seattle home, he completes "Dr. Blue's Incredible Bone-Shaking Drill Engine," but its first, unannounced test goes horribly wrong. The "Boneshaker" runs out of control beneath the city, undermining and collapsing much of downtown, and releasing a noxious gas from within the Earth that reanimates the corpses of those killed in the disaster.[20]

The image of the dead city hangs like a cloud over the exuberant frontier world of *Boneshaker*. Its crumbled buildings and poisoned dead call forth memories of other engineering missteps—Bhopal, Chernobyl, the Twin Towers—for twenty-first-century readers, much as the mushroom cloud in Disney's *20,000 Leagues* evoked memories of Hiroshima and the burgeoning nuclear arms race for Cold War audiences. The lone inventors of steampunk display the boldness, the exuberance, and the creativity of their nineteenth-century forebears, but they cannot—because we, the readers and viewers, cannot—reclaim the innocence with which they brought gleaming new machines into the world.

Sidekicks

Technocrats serve the state, and independent inventor-heroes serve themselves, but sidekicks—the third class of steampunk inventors—serve the hero. Eccentric even by the standards of a subgenre defined by its eccentricity, sidekicks have two qualities in common: limitless creativity and their absolute loyalty. Their mastery of machines gives them the power to remake the world at will, but rather than exercise that power on their own they cede it to the hero. Their inventions invariably prove to be beneficial—and, more often than not, essential—to the hero's success, or even his survival.

In the steampunk-Western television series *The Adventures of Brisco County, Jr.* (1993–1994), for example, the title character twice borrows Professor Albert Wickwire's homemade rocket—once to pursue a speeding train, and once to destroy a marauding tank—and both times would have been helpless without it. In the final episode of the series' only season, Wickwire comes to the rescue in person. Arriving in the nick of time aboard a dirigible of his own design, he plucks Brisco and two companions from the roof of a burning building surrounded by outlaws, saving the hero when he cannot save himself. Federal agent James West, shot at point-blank range in the film *Wild Wild West* (1999), rises to fight again, saving the president and the nation, because his partner Artemus Gordon supplied him with an experimental bulletproof vest. Likewise, in the film *Jonah Hex* (2010), Hex is able to complete a seemingly impossible mission—infiltrating a heavily guarded warehouse and destroying its contents—only because his friend Smith has equipped him with crossbow-like pistols that light and launch rocket-propelled dynamite projectiles. An army of ruthless killers is no match for a single reckless hero if he is backed by a gunsmith capable of inventing the rocket-propelled grenade eighty years early.

Exotic technology enables the inventor-sidekick to save the day, but it also poses the near-constant risk of making him look like a fool or a lunatic. Inventor-sidekicks, as a group, have limitless creativity and extraordinary ingenuity but a badly underdeveloped sense of practicality. The fact that a particular machine *can* be built is, for them, more than reason enough to build it, and they indiscriminately embrace every technological possibility that flashes into their heads. Early in the horror-adventure film *Van Helsing* (2004), Carl—the friar who accompanies monster-hunter Gabriel Van Helsing on his adventures—concocts a large flask of an evil-looking yellow liquid in his laboratory, freely admitting that he has no idea what it might be used for. Artemus Gordon of *Wild Wild West* takes the mania for invention to even greater extremes, devising—among other gadgets—a miniature compressed-air power saw, a woman's dress with flame throwers in its capacious false bosom, and a rocket-powered flying bicycle.

The dramatic conventions of adventure stories ensure, of course, that all these strange devices—no matter how absurd they seem at first glance—will prove to be not only useful but also essential. By the end of *Wild Wild West*, Gordon's miniature saw has enabled him to free a kidnapped woman from a cage in the villain's lair, and the lethally loaded dress has enabled Gordon and West to escape from captivity themselves. The flying bicycle, though it can achieve takeoff speed only by plunging over the edge of a canyon and diving hundreds of feet toward the ground below, proves to be an ideal platform for dropping nitroglycerin bombs on the villain's ultimate weapon: a giant robotic spider. Even Carl's mysterious yellow liquid proves its worth in *Van Helsing*. Fleeing, alongside Van Helsing, from a horde of a hundred or more enraged vampires, he flings the flask at them in desperation. It strikes the stone floor of the castle through which they are running, shatters, and releases the liquid, which blossoms instantly into artificial sunlight that fills every crevice of the room and obliterates the vampires *en masse*. Carl, relieved and delighted, cries out exultantly: "I know what it does! I know what it does!"

The relationship between Carl and Van Helsing, like that between Gordon and West, is defined by mutual exasperation underlain with grudging admiration—a reflection, perhaps, of that between Agent 007 and Q in the James Bond films. In steampunk, however, such tensions are the exception rather than the norm. Brisco County's interactions with Wickwire, and Jonah Hex's with Smith, reflect genuine warmth. In the short-lived 1995 steampunk-Western television series *Legend*, dime novelist Ernest Pratt enjoys both a fruitful partnership and a deep friendship with master inventor Janos Bartok (a thinly disguised version of Nikola Tesla). Bartok's inventions enable Pratt to live out the daring exploits of the supposedly real hero of his books, Nicodemus Legend, and Pratt's willingness to use them to fight evildoers and defend the innocent serves Bartok's desire to see justice done in the often-lawless West. Alexia Maccon enjoys an even closer partnership with one Madame Lefoux, who supplies her with cunningly designed weapons, in Gail Carriger's *Changeless* (2010). The two women feel, from their first meeting in Lefoux's millinery shop (the laboratory and workshop are hidden beneath, behind a secret door), an immediate and intense bond.[21] They are, instantly, not just partners but soul mates. Maccon, who acts as a covert agent for Queen Victoria, appreciates why Lefoux so enjoys her own double life; Lefoux in turn understands Maccon's need for—and relishes the challenge of creating—an "ordinary" parasol with hidden pockets in its canopy, a powerful electromagnet in its handle, and a concealed dart gun in its shaft.

Madame Lefoux wears her hair cut "scandalously" short, dresses in the latest male fashions—tailored breeches, waistcoat, top hat, and a cravat like a "silken waterfall"—but presents, and thinks of, herself as unambiguously female.[22] Her bond with Maccon belongs to the Victorian tradition of emotionally intense "romantic" friendships, and Carriger, from the first meeting between the two, allows it to tease at the blurred line between the homosocial and the homosexual. Both in that and in the fact that it involves two women, however, the partnership in *Changeless* is an exception to genre convention. Virtually all other inventor-hero alliances in steampunk are bonds between men, and even the most intense—Pratt and Bartok in *Legend*, or Jim West and Artemus Gordon in the television series *The Wild, Wild West* (1965–1969)—are, literally and figuratively, played straight. The professional quietly overshadows the personal, and the partnership is defined by the meshing of the partners' complementary skills rather than the intertwining of their mental landscapes or their emotional lives.

The relationship between steampunk heroes and their inventor-sidekicks thus models, in miniature, an idealized relationship between technology and society. The inventor is autonomous within his laboratory and workshop but clearly understood (by both) to be subordinate to the hero in the context of the wider world. The inventor produces a steady stream of wonders, to the hero's great and undeniable benefit, but the hero is free to choose among them and use them as he sees fit. The hero, in turn, helps to keep the inventor grounded in reality, his skepticism acting as a brake on useless, impractical, or potentially dangerous projects. There are, as a result, no terrifying surprises.

Conclusion

Nineteenth- and early-twentieth-century tales of exotic machines were defined by their exuberant celebration of technology's promise, and their valorization of those who unleashed it. Similar tales from the late twentieth and twenty-first centuries are defined by their anxiety over technology's potential for destruction and their suspicion that its makers—through carelessness, shortsightedness, or indifference—will wreak havoc on society. Steampunk, rooted in one era but created in the other, reflects both attitudes. It acknowledges both the promise and the peril that new technology brings, and its engineer-inventor characters reflect that complexity. They share their nineteenth-century counterparts' ability, and desire, to remake the world, but their awareness of the constraints on their efforts (and the consequences of a misstep) would be alien to their fictional and historical forebears. That awareness—like steampunk's vision of technology as an inherently double-edged sword—is imported from the twentieth and twenty-first centuries, and its presence keeps the techno-optimism of the engineer-inventor characters from seeming as naïve as it often does in nineteenth-century tales. Steampunk's inventors, like the machines they create, engage us by being simultaneously alien and familiar.

All of steampunk's inventor characters live in a world with fewer *structural* restraints than ours on technological innovation. "The entirety of knowledge could almost be comprehended by a single individual," notes author Paul Di Filippo. "There were still frontiers. There were fewer laws and governing bodies.

Who wouldn't want all those things back?"[23] Untroubled by government regulations, environmental impact statements, and zoning laws, steampunk inventors are thus free to keep airships in their barns and build drill engines in their basements. They are free to create whatever machine seizes their imaginations at the moment, to pursue ideas as far as their engineering skills will allow, and to dream the biggest dreams their imagination can conceive. The same lack of restriction, however, means that there may not be anyone close at hand to point out the fatal flaw in their latest mechanical brainchild, or ask them whether there is a good reason to invent it at all.

The other characters that surround steampunk's inventor characters thus face a complex dilemma. They cannot afford to shut off the flow of wondrous machines that abound from the inventors' workshops; their prosperity, their security, and their ability to build a better world depend on embracing them. Entering into that embrace unaware of the risks that the machines may pose, however, is as great a danger as ignoring them entirely. The tales told about the three types of inventors discussed here—technocrats, free agents, and sidekicks—reflect different solutions to that challenge, some conscious, others accidental. The challenge, however, is the same in each case, and the same as the one that humankind faces as it contemplates technological change at the dawn of the twenty-first century: how to reliably tell a blessing from a curse.

Notes

1. There are substantial differences, in the real world, between engineers and inventors. Engineers are credentialed and licensed, while inventors are not; engineers' work is grounded in theory and mathematics, while inventors' work is (often, but not always) craft based; and engineers typically work as members of large teams, while inventors are often solitary. These distinctions have existed since the mid-nineteenth century, though they were less sharply drawn—and the boundary between them more fluid—than is the case today, and steampunk tends to use both terms indiscriminately. In the context of this chapter, I have tried to use the terms precisely when discussing real-world historical context and loosely—following the lead of the specific work under discussion—when discussing fictional characters.

2. Useful overviews include David P. Billington, *The Innovators: The Engineering Pioneers Who Transformed America* (New York: Wiley, 1996) and Tom F. Peters, *Building the Nineteenth Century* (Cambridge: MIT Press, 1996). On the intertwining of the industrial revolution and the communications revolution, see Asa Briggs and Peter Burke, *A Social History of the Media: From Gutenberg to the Internet*, 3rd ed. (Cambridge, UK: Polity Press, 2010), 105–120.

3. R. A. Buchanan, *A History of the Engineering Profession in Britain, 1750–1914* (London: Kingsley, 1989); Edwin T. Layton Jr., *The Revolt of the Engineers: Social*

Responsibility and the American Engineering Profession (Baltimore: Johns Hopkins University Press, 1986).

4. For a case study of the valorization process, see Wyn Wachhorst, *Thomas Alva Edison: An American Myth* (Cambridge: MIT Press, 1983) and Randall E. Stross, *The Wizard of Menlo Park: How Thomas Alva Edison Invented the Modern World* (New York: Broadway Books, 2008).

5. See Thomas P. Hughes, *American Genesis: A Century of Invention and Technological Enthusiasm, 1870–1970* (New York: Viking, 1989) and David P. Billington and David P. Billington Jr., *Power, Speed, and Form: Engineers and the Making of the Twentieth Century* (Princeton, N.J.: Princeton University Press, 2006).

6. Case studies of this phenomenon in the microelectronics industry—arguably the most significant of the post-1945 era—include Michael Riordan and Lillian Hoddeson, *Crystal Fire: The Invention of the Transistor and the Birth of the Information Age* (New York: Norton, 1998); Michael Hiltzik, *Dealers of Lightning: Xerox PARC and the Dawn of the Computer Age* (New York: HarperBusiness, 2000); and Katie Hafner, *Where Wizards Stay Up Late: The Origins of the Internet* (New York: Simon & Schuster, 1996).

7. The definitive history of the engineer's changing image in popular culture remains to be written. David J. Skal, *Screams of Reason: Mad Science and Modern Culture* (New York: Norton, 1998) and Christopher Frayling, *Mad, Bad, and Dangerous?: The Scientist and the Cinema* (London: Reaktion Books, 2005) provide useful context, however.

8. Stephen Jay Gould, "Jurassic Park," in *Past Imperfect: History According to the Movies*, ed. Mark C. Carnes (New York: Henry Holt, 1995), 30–35.

9. Jack London, "The Unparalleled Invasion," www.jacklondons.net/writings/StrengthStrong/invasion.html (12 February 2012); Garrett P. Serviss, *Edison's Conquest of Mars*, www.gutenberg.org/ebooks/19141 (12 February 2012).

10. William Gibson and Bruce Sterling, *The Difference Engine* (New York: Spectra, 1992).

11. Herbert L. Sussman, "Cyberpunk Meets Charles Babbage: *The Difference Engine* as Alternative Victorian History," *Victorian Studies* 38, no. 1 (Autumn 1994): 1–23.

12. Gibson and Sterling, *The Difference Engine*, 409.

13. Nicholas Spencer, "Rethinking Technological Ambivalence: Technopolitics and the Luddites in William Gibson and Bruce Sterling's *The Difference Engine*," *Contemporary Literature* 40, no. 3 (Autumn 1999): 403–429.

14. Stephen Baxter, *Anti-Ice* (New York: Harper Voyager, 1993), 23.

15. Paul Guinan and Anina Bennett, *Frank Reade: Adventures in the Age of Invention* (New York: Abrams Image, 2012), 36–37.

16. Brian Attebery, "Beyond Captain Nemo: Disney's Science Fiction Films," in *From Mouse to Mermaid: The Politics of Film, Gender, and Culture*, ed. Elizabeth Bell et al. (Bloomington: Indiana University Press, 1995), 151–152.

17. J. P. Telotte, "Science Fiction as True-Life Adventure: Disney and the Case of *20,000 Leagues Under the Sea*," *Film & History* 40, no. 2 (Fall 2010): 66–79.

18. William J. Schoell, *Creature Features: Nature Turned Nasty in the Movies* (Jefferson, N.C.: McFarland, 2008), 43–68.

19. James P. Blaylock, *Lord Kelvin's Machine* (New York: Ace, 1992). Lord Kelvin, a real historical figure, also plays a small role in S. M. Stirling's steampunk alternate-history novel *The Peshawar Lancers* (2003), and a caricatured version of him is the villain in the steampunk-influenced 2009 film version of Verne's *Around the World in Eighty Days*.

20. Cherie Priest, *Boneshaker* (New York: Tor Books, 2009), 15–20.

21. Gail Carriger, *Changeless* (New York: Orbit, 2010), 85–94.

22. Carriger, *Changeless*, 80.

23. Quoted in Peter Bebergal, "The Age of Steampunk," *Boston Globe*, 26 August 2007, Ideas section, 10, http://bardhaven.wordpress.com/2007/08/27/steampunk -boston (15 February 2012).

Bibliography

Attebery, Brian. "Beyond Captain Nemo: Disney's Science Fiction Films." 148–60 in *From Mouse to Mermaid: The Politics of Film, Gender, and Culture*, ed. Elizabeth Bell, Lynda Haas, and Laura Sells. Bloomington: Indiana University Press, 1995.

Baxter, Stephen. *Anti-Ice*. New York: Harper Voyager, 1993.

Bebergal, Peter. "The Age of Steampunk." *Boston Globe*. 26 August 2007, Ideas section, 10. http://bardhaven.wordpress.com/2007/08/27/steampunk-boston (15 February 2012).

Billington, David P. *The Innovators: The Engineering Pioneers Who Transformed America*. New York: Wiley, 1996.

Billington, David P., and David P. Billington Jr. *Power, Speed, and Form: Engineers and the Making of the Twentieth Century*. Princeton, N.J.: Princeton University Press, 2006.

Briggs, Asa, and Peter Burke. *A Social History of the Media: From Gutenberg to the Internet*, 3rd ed. Cambridge, UK: Polity Press, 2010.

Buchanan, R. A. *A History of the Engineering Profession in Britain, 1750–1914*. London: Kingsley, 1989.

Carriger, Gail. *Changeless*. New York: Orbit, 2010.

Frayling, Christopher. *Mad, Bad, and Dangerous? The Scientist and the Cinema*. London: Reaktion Books, 2005.

Gibson, William, and Bruce Sterling. *The Difference Engine*. New York: Spectra, 1992.

Gould, Stephen Jay. "Jurassic Park." 30–35 in *Past Imperfect: History According to the Movies*, ed. Mark C. Carnes. New York: Holt, 1995.

Guinan, Paul, and Anina Bennett. *Frank Reade: Adventures in the Age of Invention*. New York: Abrams Image, 2012.

Hafner, Katie. *Where Wizards Stay Up Late: The Origins of the Internet*. New York: Simon & Schuster, 1996.

Hiltzik, Michael. *Dealers of Lightning: Xerox PARC and the Dawn of the Computer Age.* New York: HarperBusiness, 2000.

Hughes, Thomas P. *American Genesis: A Century of Invention and Technological Enthusiasm, 1870–1970.* New York: Viking, 1989.

Layton, Edwin T., Jr. *The Revolt of the Engineers: Social Responsibility and the American Engineering Profession.* Baltimore: Johns Hopkins University Press, 1986.

London, Jack. "The Unparalleled Invasion." www.jacklondons.net/writings/Strength Strong/invasion.html (12 February 2012).

Peters, Tom F. *Building the Nineteenth Century.* Cambridge: MIT Press, 1996.

Priest, Cherie. *Boneshaker.* New York: Tor, 2009.

Riordan, Michael, and Lillian Hoddeson. *Crystal Fire: The Invention of the Transistor and the Birth of the Information Age.* New York: Norton, 1998.

Schoell, William J. *Creature Features: Nature Turned Nasty in the Movies.* Jefferson, N.C.: McFarland, 2008.

Serviss, Garrett P. *Edison's Conquest of Mars.* www.gutenberg.org/ebooks/19141 (12 February 2012).

Skal, David J. *Screams of Reason: Mad Science and Modern Culture.* New York: Norton, 1998.

Spencer, Nicholas. "Rethinking Technological Ambivalence: Technopolitics and the Luddites in William Gibson and Bruce Sterling's *The Difference Engine.*" *Contemporary Literature* 40, no. 3 (Autumn 1999): 403–429.

Stross, Randall E. *The Wizard of Menlo Park: How Thomas Alva Edison Invented the Modern World.* New York: Broadway Books, 2008.

Sussman, Herbert L. "Cyberpunk Meets Charles Babbage: *The Difference Engine* as Alternative Victorian History." *Victorian Studies* 38, no. 1 (Autumn 1994): 1–23.

Telotte, J. P. "Science Fiction as True-Life Adventure: Disney and the Case of *20,000 Leagues Under the Sea.*" *Film & History* 40, no. 2 (Fall 2010): 66–79.

Wachhorst, Wyn. *Thomas Alva Edison: An American Myth.* Cambridge: MIT Press, 1983.

Clockwork woman of mystery. *Art by Jody Steel; mask by Maurice Herzing*

CHAPTER FOURTEEN

Steampunk's Legacy: Collecting and Exhibiting the Future of Yesterday

Jeanette Atkinson

In creating a striking visual and material culture, set within an alternative historical timeline, steampunks are challenging traditional representations of history and what constitutes "authentic" heritage. This, potentially, contests the curatorial voice within Western museums. This chapter engages with these challenges through examining recent exhibitions of steampunk art and material culture and encounters between curators and steampunks, with the aim of furthering the understanding of the power relations between museums and countercommunities such as steampunks.

Although I became aware of steampunk several years ago through books and social media, I began researching the culture after visiting the *Steampunk* exhibition at the Museum of the History of Science in Oxford, United Kingdom (UK), in late 2009. This exhibition led me to question the relationship between communities such as steampunks and museums, consider the potential challenges to the concept of authenticity in heritage, and explore whether steampunk material culture is being collected as well as exhibited by museums.

A definition of heritage in this context is pertinent here. While "heritage" literally means something that is inherited,[1] in this chapter I am more concerned with how it embodies identity and sociocultural practices. Of particular relevance is the definition by Graham, Ashworth, and Tunbridge, who state, "Heritage is that part of the past which we select in the present of contemporary purposes, be they economic, cultural, political or social."[2] In choosing specific aspects of the past in order to construct "meaning and identity making,"[3] steampunks are potentially in conflict with museums' notions of heritage. This authorized heritage discourse,[4] or official heritage, is "a type of canon formation, where heritage objects and places become selected for their adherence to canonical criteria, such as aesthetic excellence, relevance to national identity or scientific significance."[5] In contrast, steampunk material culture, with its nostalgia for Victorian styles and technology, is unofficial heritage that lacks "formal protection by legislation, [is] under-represented in public collections, [and is] under-valued according to canonical criteria." Despite this, "unofficial heritage, curated within communities, is a majority practice"[6] that challenges, and potentially subverts, official heritage both in what constitutes heritage and what is considered an authentic representation of history. The aim of this chapter, therefore, is to discuss examples of collaboration between museums and steampunk communities in the UK context, whether the relationship might lead to steampunk material culture being collected as well as exhibited, and to examine perspectives on authenticity in relation to heritage.

The findings in this chapter draw on research interviews with a small cohort of museum professionals and steampunk artists who were either involved in the design and installation of steampunk exhibitions or have been part of collaboration between steampunks and museums. Three case studies in the UK were chosen: Leicestershire County Council Heritage and Art Service (LCCH&AS); the Museum of the History of Science (MHS), Oxford; and Kew Bridge Steam Museum (KBSM), London. MHS and KBSM have hosted steampunk exhibitions, and LCCH&AS has provided steampunk communities with access to relevant collections, as inspiration for their material culture.[7]

Research Context

Leicestershire County Council Heritage and Art Service holds the Symington Collection of Corsetry, Foundation and Swimwear. R. & W. H. Symington & Co. Ltd., based in Market Harborough in Leicestershire, produced garments from the 1830s through to the late twentieth century. The Symington factory building now houses Harborough Museum, which is part of LCCH&AS, in addition to Harborough District Council and Harborough Library. Built up from small beginnings in the 1830s, the Symington business moved into the factory building in 1861. By 1881, they were exporting their corsets to Australasia, and then to North and South America and to Africa, and they became a public company in 1898.[8] After World War I, with less demand for corsets, the business started to produce a wider range of foundation garments, including the well-known "liberty bodice." The introduction of new fabrics revolutionized foundation wear after World War II, and Symington extended their range again to supply the teenage market and provide swimwear.

The 1960s saw the takeover of the company by Courtaulds. Although they worked with large retail companies to produce garments, demand reduced to the point where part of the building was sold to Harborough District Council in 1980, and the business finally closed in May 1990.[9] Ten years previously, the Symington Collection—a wide range of corsets, foundation wear, and swimwear—had been presented to LCCH&AS. The section of the collection most relevant to the steampunk community, and therefore this chapter, is corsets and specifically those from 1860 to the early twentieth century.

From 13 October 2009 to 21 February 2010, the Museum of the History of Science, part of the University of Oxford, presented the exhibition *Steampunk*. Working closely with the MHS, it was guest curated by the American artist and designer Art Donovan and described as "the first museum exhibition of Steampunk art."[10] Donovan provided the impetus for the exhibition but also drew on the permanent collections at the museum for inspiration in the creation of some of his artworks. The early scientific instruments at MHS "include the collections of astrolabes, sundials, quadrants, early mathematical instruments generally (including those used for surveying, drawing, calculating, astronomy, and navigation) and optical instruments (including microscopes, telescopes and cameras), together with apparatus associated with chemistry, natural philosophy and medicine,"[11] all perfect inspiration for steampunk artists. Eighteen international artists took part in the exhibition, and events supporting it included live mannequins in steampunk clothes. The objects ranged from lights and goggles to jewelry, brass spiders, laptops and keyboards, clockwork attachments, and steampunk figures and masks.[12] While the exhibition was housed in its own gallery, this led through to a complementary display of museum objects, so locating the steampunk artworks within the context of the scientific instruments. Work produced by students from secondary school art, design, and technology departments, as part of *The Great Steampunk Art and Design Competition*, also accompanied the main exhibition,[13] so engaging further with the local community.

Kew Bridge Steam Museum, on the site of the original Kew Bridge Pumping Station, is run by the Kew Bridge Engines Trust and Water Supply Museum Limited. The museum opened in 1975 and houses five historic beam engines and various water-pumping engines.[14] From 4 June to 29 August 2011 the museum held an extensive exhibition titled *The Greatest Steampunk Exhibition*. Following on from the MHS exhibition, but with a greater range of objects, the exhibition included artwork, posters, costumes, wigs, hats,

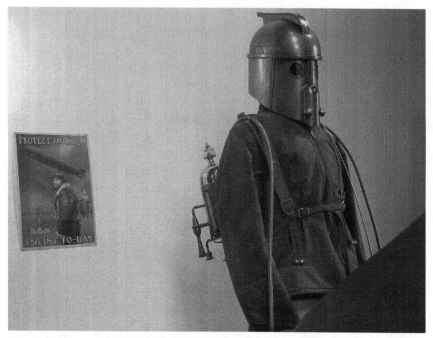

Protect the Skies, steampunk exhibition at Kew Bridge Steam Museum, London, UK. *Photo: Annie Mole, London Underground Tube Diary (http://london-underground.blogspot .co.uk), CC BY 2.0*

jewelry, machines, and a steampunk bed, which was made in the museum's forge, in addition to science and sci-fi inspired creations. Organized jointly between the Victorian Steampunk Society (VSS)[15] and the Kew Bridge Engines Trust, the exhibition interwove steampunk objects within galleries of steam-pumping engines throughout the museum. Extensive events supported the displays, including workshops, a steampunk music weekend, and a fashion show titled *Fashion Punk*.[16]

MHS and KBSM were chosen as case studies for this chapter to demonstrate how museums and steampunk communities work together to produce exhibitions. MHS, being the first exhibition of steampunk art, at least in the UK,[17] revealed how productive this initial contact could be, and KBSM built on this, taking the collaboration further. Research examined the motivations for both MHS and KBSM in holding their exhibitions, assessed whether any of the objects might ultimately form part of their permanent collections, and determined whether further engagement with steampunk communities is an ongoing priority. To establish this, semistructured interviews were undertaken with Professor Jim Bennett, director of MHS, and John Naylor, steampunk artist, chair of the VSS, and organizer of the Asylum (a three-day steampunk event held in Lincoln, UK), who was closely involved in the design and implementation of the KBSM exhibition.

LCCH&AS is intended as a counterpoint to these more formal engagements with steampunk communities. While there is a range of museums that form part of LCCH&AS, their Collections Centre does not, itself, hold exhibitions. Instead they offer access to the collections there, or at their museums, for interested groups. As part of my research, I interviewed Philip Warren, principal curator at the LCCH&AS to discuss collaboration with steampunk communities. Having provided access for steampunks to their collections, they demonstrate not only engagement with but also influence on the production of steampunk material culture.[18]

Steampunk Communities and Museums: From Temporary Exhibitions to Permanent Collections?

Steampunk at MHS was the first major collaboration between a museum and steampunks to produce a formal exhibition. However, as John Naylor informed me, steampunks have been collaborating with heritage organizations and museums for some time now, particularly as part of the steampunk event, the Asylum, which has taken place annually in Lincoln, UK, since 2008. Steampunks embrace historic venues, and Lincoln provides the perfect backdrop for the Asylum. Lincoln Castle, around which the events take place, also hosts exhibitions of steampunk art and material culture, in part due to the enthusiasm of the manager, who "loves steampunk,"[19] and some of the objects that were on display at KBSM are expected to be shown at the castle during the Asylum in September 2012.

Based on conversations with research participants, the objects displayed in the MHS and KBSM exhibitions have not gone on to form part of either their permanent collections or those of other museums (however, steampunk objects are being collected by private collectors and possibly some private galleries in the United States[20]). Although steampunk material culture has been predominantly displayed by science and industrial museums,[21] and venues such as Snibston Discovery Museum, Coalville, Leicestershire (part of the LCCH&AS),[22] have engaged actively with steampunk communities, apparently it is not yet being collected. This may be due to the type of museum currently showing temporary exhibitions of steampunk objects. Although the objects, inspired as they are by Victorian technology and science fiction/fantasy literature, especially the work of Jules Verne and H. G. Wells, find a place among the steam, clockwork, or science exhibits, they are perhaps too "otherworldly" and not indicative of a branch of science to find a permanent place there. A decorative arts museum such as the Victoria and Albert Museum (V&A), London (which Philip Warren suggested), or the Hunt Museum, Limerick, Ireland (an exhibition titled *The Art of Steampunk* with objects based on The Hunt Collection ran from October 2011 to January 2012), may be more appropriate places. Indeed, images of a steampunk wedding have already been uploaded to the V&A website,[23] indicating a potential home for steampunk objects.

The Design Museum, London, has also been suggested.[24] This indicates that although steampunk is associated with science—through its links to science fiction and steam-technology-inspired material culture—it is perceived by museums seeking to add to their collections to be a form of design or decorative art. In this sense, steampunk material culture can be likened to the Arts and Crafts movement. Rebecca Onion suggests "in their disaffection for the technology of their own time, steampunks echo the anger of the antimoderns of the late nineteenth and early twentieth century, who, through the Arts and Crafts movement, advocated a return to a premodern "middle" landscape."[25] With aims of producing handmade objects, rather than machine made, the Arts and Crafts movement may not appear an obvious influence for steampunks with their love of steam-powered machines. The ethos of do-it-yourself is strong in the culture, though, and it is this, together with knowing the various craft methods, the techniques, and how machines work, that resonates with the Arts and Crafts movement.

With its links to Victorian culture and technology and a strong manufacturing ethos, steampunk is, as John Naylor asserts, "embedded in the western psyche. . . . We're brought up with it, we have a literacy based on steampunk, a visual and a technological literacy, that we've grown up with as children and all generations have got that."[26] This implies that, in Western societies at least,[27] its material culture will be collectable for museums as well as private collectors. Museums collect material culture for many reasons, including identity, values, connoisseurship, and knowledge, as well as the location, society, and culture in which they are based.[28] They also need to collect contemporary culture in order to remain relevant.[29] Based on John Naylor's assessment of steampunk, therefore, it is likely that museums will collect a material culture that is embedded in our psyche, as well as temporarily exhibit it.[30]

So, museums may well collect steampunk art and material culture in the future, but do steampunks want their objects to be collected? Steampunks were closely involved in the UK exhibitions under discussion in this chapter, but that does not equate to their wanting to be part of permanent collections. The history of museums may be a factor here. From the mid-to late nineteenth century—during Queen Victoria's reign—museums as the "forms and institutions of high culture" became part of "the purpose of civilizing the population as a whole."[31] Steampunks embrace certain aspects of Victorian society but critique others, including racism, sexism, and the colonial agenda. This suggests that steampunks would not want to be part of a "civilizing" museum mission. Being part of a museum collection also risks mainstreaming steampunk, and reactions to their culture being appropriated as part of the background design for pop star Justin Bieber's Christmas 2011 music video, for example, demonstrate how little they appreciate this.[32]

This does not take into account, however, how engaged some steampunks are with museums. The opportunity to "travel to other places in time,"[33] to experience "living" Victorian technology, can be achieved through museums. In addition to the events strongly supported by steampunks at the MHS and KBSM exhibitions, steampunks organize their own museum-related visits and events, often through social media. For example, the League of Bournemouth Steampunks (in the UK) arranged an off-hours visit to the Museum of Electricity (an Edwardian power station) in Dorset in December 2010.[34] More recently, the Steampunk Opium Wars took place at the National Maritime Museum, Greenwich, London, on 16 February 2012.[35] On the same day in Canada, Steampunk Ottawa were returning to the Canadian Museum of Nature, Ottawa, Ontario, "to complete our safari through the wild halls of this most esteemed establishment."[36] In the United States, the Charles River Museum of Industry and Innovation in Waltham, Massachusetts, holds monthly steampunk meet-ups[37] and an annual steampunk festival,[38] and in Alameda, California, the Crystal Palace Steampunk Oktoberfest Ball in October 2012 hosts "a special exhibition of Steampunk-inspired inventions and devices to be displayed at the ball and will present awards to the most adventurous, most creative, and most original inventions."[39]

New Zealand is not to be outdone in the arranging of steampunk events and exhibitions. The third exhibition organized by the League of Victorian Imagineers, titled *Steampunk: Tomorrow as It Used to Be*, was held at the Forester Gallery in Oamaru (in New Zealand's South Island) in 2011. Launched by a street party, the town, which holds regular Victorian festivals, has embraced steampunk, with the mayor stating that "Oamaru had become a centre for Steampunk and the movement had taken on a 'literal head of steam.'"[40] These examples demonstrate that engagement, accessibility, and power relations are important, as I discuss later in this chapter. So long as there is full collaboration between museums and steampunks as regards what is collected and how it is exhibited, then steampunks might indeed be willing to be part of a permanent relationship that showcases and gives a voice to their culture.

It is perhaps a little soon for museums to be accessioning objects yet, though. Certainly Philip Warren suggested that we are not yet at that stage:

> I think lots of museum curators would probably just go "well, that seems a bit weird" and that might just be a trend, so I'll wait for twenty years and see if it actually manifests itself as being culturally important and then I'll try to do something about it and put on an event.[41]

Coupled with concerns that steampunk might "just be a trend" is the fact that, as a culture, it is very much in flux, having already had two distinct phases. The first dated from the late 1970s and early 1980s through to 1991, when Gibson and Sterling's book *The Difference Engine* was published; the second phase began in the early 1990s and continues today.[42] So, collecting the material culture now may give only a snapshot of this particular time and phase. Museums may be waiting until the culture is more established, more of "a fixture" in our society, before it warrants being accessioned into museum collections. As Jim Bennett explains:

> I don't think we are ready for such a thing. I think the movement is too active in a way to be museum-ized. I know I put on an exhibition, but the exhibition was part of the movement; it left nothing to our collection whatsoever. We didn't acquire any of those objects. We never intended to. It was always meant to be a phenomenon, not something that would become part of our permanent collections.[43]

Funding issues may also be a factor in whether steampunk material culture is collected by museums. In the current financial situation, museums have to justify more than ever the reasons why they would choose to acquire specific objects, and priorities for collecting are not the same as those for exhibiting. Money is not the only factor, however. Museums can "lack curators with adequate knowledge of their subject area, and the know-how to purchase in the market place."[44] As most steampunk art and material culture is produced commercially and is being bought by private collectors, this lack of knowledge is inhibiting the collecting of contemporary art and culture in the UK. While some funding measures were put in place in the UK in 2007, through grants from the Art Fund and the Heritage Lottery Fund, more work is needed to address a perceived lack of knowledge transfer and to establish closer links between museums and the higher education sector.[45]

Museum Collections and the Production of Steampunk Material Culture

Steampunks embrace steam and clockwork technology and Victorian aesthetics and clothing, using them as inspiration for their clothes and material culture. While steampunks adapt them to suit their own aesthetics and desire for a nonconformist approach to contemporary technology, museum collections are definitely one of the many influences. In our interview, Philip Warren described how groups of steampunks have used the collections at the LCCH&AS. During viewing sessions of the collections in 2011, he found that:

> What they were interested in, principally, were our nineteenth-century corsets and understanding how they were made and constructed, and they were very interested in the fact that they were very different from the corsets that the female steampunks were wearing.[46]

So, steampunks, while they were clearly influenced by images of Victorian corsets, adapted them to their own purposes. Typically, the corsets are worn over, rather than under, clothes, and unlike traditional corsets,[47] may have straps over the shoulders, so demonstrating that it is the look, rather than the function, that is important.

As with many subcultures, steampunks choose to wear the clothes they do for a variety of reasons, including performing for their fellow steampunks and any audiences. They are engaging in "active participation in their own self-display via heritage."[48] This is their own perception of heritage, demonstrating their identity and meaning making, rather than the authorized discourse espoused by museums. Nevertheless, there is an authenticity in steampunk clothes (not "costumes," as John Naylor was keen to point out). For steampunks, "authenticity" is a rendition as close as possible to their vision of an alternative present. It is a negotiated authenticity, mediated through the cultural or subcultural norms that define the boundaries of their community. The Symington corset collections, therefore, provide key influences in design and construction, so adding both to the knowledge and techniques that are an essential part of the steampunk ethos and to the negotiated authenticity of their constructed identities and reenvisioned history.

At the MHS, while the collections were inspirational to artists, particularly Art Donovan, the guest curator, they were just that—an inspiration, not a means of dictating what should or should not be included in an object. Various scientific instruments from differing eras might be called on, therefore, as inspiration, providing a "mash-up" of styles, time periods, and scientific purpose. Brian Catling criticized this mash-up in the MHS Broadsheet No. 9, describing the steampunk art as being "highly detailed and intensely wrought sculptural objects that nest like swollen and outrageous cuckoos alongside the museum's permanent collection of scientific and optical instruments."[49] He did, though, modify this somewhat later in his article, admitting that "the crafted metaphor when set in contrast to the factual inventions that inspired them, could expose something of the drive that stirs them both into life."⁵⁰ This proved to be the case, because, as Jim Bennett explained in *The Art of Steampunk: Extraordinary Devices and Ingenious Contraptions from the Leading Artists of the Steampunk Movement*:

> A room through which the visitors exited contained original Victorian and Edwardian instruments and machines that exemplified the roots of Steampunk art. The reactions of our visitors supported the museum's policy of the varieties of appreciation. Objects that would scarcely have been noticed elsewhere in the museum were examined with care and pleasure. Instruments that would have been dismissed as beyond understanding were embraced for their sculptural and decorative qualities; they were enjoyed as relics of a past visual culture. In the gallery devoted to Steampunk art, the visitors had engaged easily with the display, had savoured and valued the pleasure of seeing work that was thoughtful, original, finely made, and amusing, and they carried that sensibility into the gallery of historic instruments. No amount of exhortations from us about varieties of appreciation could have achieved this, but here we could see the policy working. Steampunk gave us that opportunity.⁵¹

This suggests that the steampunk objects had indeed "expose[d] something of the drive that stirs them both into life."⁵²

The MHS collections were a more obvious influence on the construction of some of the objects than KBSM. While the Victorian steam technology and beam engines of Kew Bridge were a sympathetic setting for many of the objects, it was less clear where the link to the inspiration came from with this exhibition. Many of the exhibits drew on the same type of metals and demonstrated a complex machinelike construction, but science fiction influences were also in evidence. Goggles featured large, be they brass, leather and fur, or a combination of the two. Highlights included *Darth Vapour* and a steampunked Borg, both heads created by Thadeus Tinker.⁵³ The label stated that these objects "hint at how classic sci-fi could have been." Across from the borg was the *Universum Steampunk Hot-Air Engine*, created by Jos de Vink⁵⁴ and the *Cathedral Steampunk Hot-Air Engine*, both amazing constructions in brass powered by candles.

Clockwork insects and jewelry incorporating eyes demonstrated the complexity of steampunk visual and material culture, and these intricate objects contrasted with the scale of the *Thunderbuss Sonic Hunting Rifle*, which hinted at both the past and future. Links to H. G. Wells could be seen in the *Time Machine Steampunk Hot Air Engine*, which was almost astronomical in its appearance (perhaps influenced by the collections at the MHS?). An exhibition label introduced a group of steampunk objects as "faux taxidermy and curios," linking them back to the "cabinets of curiosity and displays of the weird and wonderful [that] were very popular in the Victorian period and

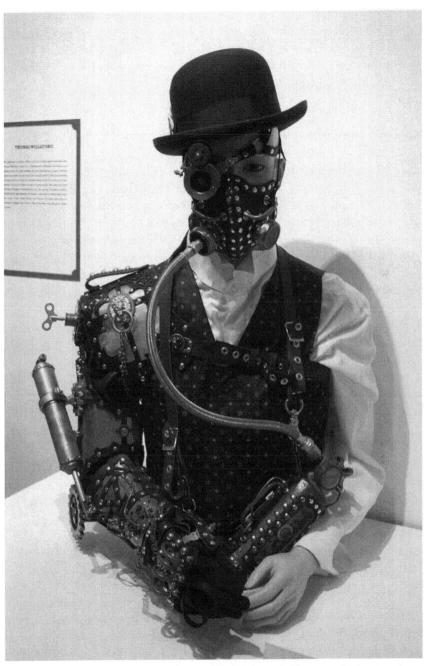

Steampunk exhibition at the Museum of the History of Science, Oxford, UK. *Photo: openingscene @Flickr CC BY-ND 2.0*

are still so with Steampunks." This confirms that steampunks draw on Victorian influences and aesthetics, and yet they also parody and rebel against them; while the movement has an underlying core of Victoriana, it is also highly individualized, with each steampunk creating his or her own identity and so a unique interpretation of the culture.

Visitors were invited to create their own steampunk material culture in a section set aside for this purpose, so engaging the audience with one of the main steampunk tenets—do it yourself. This philosophy sets steampunk firmly within the subculture genre. As de la Haye explains, "Within the stylistic boundaries of sub-cultures, there is much emphasis upon personal expression and clothes are often home-made or customized to individualize off-the-peg garments."[55] This individualization was also demonstrated in the clothes on display, which linked both the Victorian and contemporary eras. Next to the hundred-inch and ninety-inch engines stood the *Bomb Disposal Specialist, Her Majesty's Engineers*. In another piece created by Thadeus Tinker, a former soldier, the text accompanying the outfit connected a neo-Victorian ensemble to the very real dangers soldiers and bomb disposal experts face in military conflicts. Next to the Boulton and Watt engine, a lady's steampunk day dress in blue tartan and lace combined "steam" from Victorian times and "punk" from the 1970s. Designed by Lady Elsie and with homage to Vivian Westwood, the accompanying text explained that the aim was to make a piece of "wearable steampunk art."[56]

Power Relations in Museums and Communities

Both the MHS and KBSM are science museums, and neither attracts the same numbers of visitors that large museums, such as the Ashmolean Museum of Art and Archaeology and the Pitt Rivers Museum, both in Oxford, or the British Museum and the Victoria and Albert Museum, both in London, can command. It is interesting that these are the museums engaging with steampunk. What does that say about them? Jim Bennett explained the rationale for engaging with steampunks in Gary Moskowitz's online article:

> When we see a movement that is using this cultural capital in original and attractive ways, we want to be part of that. From our point of view, it is a creative movement in the arts that has a currency and popularity.[57]

In our interview, Bennett also agreed that the MHS was pleased with the increased visitor numbers, not least because "the steampunk communities engaged strongly with the exhibition, and were very keen to adopt the events that we put on."[58] Increased visitor numbers was also a factor for KBSM, who approached the VSS with the idea of an exhibition.[59] However, I believe that it goes deeper than that. Both museums are innovators in engaging with steampunks. They are inventive museums that are reaching out to a wider community, and perhaps, they can afford to take risks in their exhibitions that some larger museums cannot.

This raises the question of power relations between the steampunk communities involved in these particular exhibitions and the museums themselves. On asking Jim Bennett and John Naylor, it became apparent that "the collaboration required significant negotiation, in order to ensure that, at MHS, science was paramount, but also the best steampunk objects possible were on display."[60] This meant that both the museum's "voice" and the communities' were evident.

> The arrangement with Art [Donovan] was that he would be the curator. . . . he selected the artists. He knew the range of people, internationally, who might contribute; he selected them and he invited them to be part of the show. . . . After that, I took over and did the rest of what a curator would normally do, that's to say, I arranged the thing, tried to make sense of it all in our space. If there's a guest curator and a local curator, we would always divide things that way. . . . We did the design, in terms of the panels and the labels and all of that.[61]

At Lincoln, it is most definitely a joint collaboration: "they try to accommodate us, we try to accommodate them; it's almost symbiotic."[62] This suggests in both cases that it is possible for museums to give up power, to grant equal status to communities, and by doing so become stronger institutions.[63] The ability to share power and status may be due to the types of museums under discussion here. Both Hilda Hein[64] and Steven Conn[65] advocate there is a hierarchy of museums, in which art and the museums in which it is displayed are privileged, particularly over craft or functional objects. Hein also suggests "there is a comparable hierarchy within and between museums of science, natural history, and technology, where 'pure' science is at the top of the scale, followed by applied and utilitarian discovery."[66] This has implications not only for where steampunk material culture might be displayed or collected but also for how it is classified—art, design, scientific invention, or example of a sociocultural phenomenon. In some ways it is all of these, indicating that museums need to be flexible and inclusive when embracing a subculture such as steampunk and its associated material culture.

In terms of the exhibitions under discussion in this chapter, both the steampunk communities and the museums demonstrated that they formed mutually beneficial relationships and were examples of inclusive communities. Museums are in the business of access and welcoming visitors, but they have not always been that accessible, or reached out to communities.[67] This is now changing, with museums engaging strongly with a wide variety of communities.[68] The ethos of the VSS is also to engage, so demonstrating that these particular steampunk communities aim to be inclusive rather than exclusive. The VSS website states:

> The VSS both facilitate and support a range of events and activities for the UK Steampunk community and are always happy to respond to enquiries from organizations looking to learn more about the genre. We also organize and run the Premier UK Steampunk festival "Weekend at the Asylum."[69]

Steampunks appear, from the literature and my research, to be both communities of interest, in that they share common interests, irrespective of location, particularly through social media, and communities of practice, where they again share interests but also "engage in joint activities and discussions, help each other, and share information."[70] In our interview, Philip Warren noted that many of the steampunks that he had worked with had arrived separately or in small groups: "The only thing that defined them as a group was in terms of their dress and their appearance," so indicating that this particular group was very much a community of interest. Members of steampunk communities join together in having common interests in the type of clothes they choose to wear, the material culture they carry and make, the materials they prefer to use, and the desire for a knowledge of how objects work—knowledge that is not easily available with today's technology.[71]

These interests in terms of the production of their material culture cross over into a community of practice. Committed steampunks definitely practice what they preach—they make or customize their clothes, material culture, and technology. For them, do-it-yourself is part of being a steampunk. Although someone who had bought all of their clothes and accessories (even from vintage retailers), rather than making or customizing them, would be welcomed, I suspect, from what John Naylor and Philip Warren said, that they would be encouraged to start customizing their look. This would help to avoid mainstreaming of the culture. As Libby Bulloff explains:

> As long as steampunks encourage each other to make their own clothing, or at the very least buy garments from small, independently owned design houses . . . the mainstream won't usurp the spirit behind Steampunk. If we give up on constantly homing and reenvisioning our aesthetic, then we lose.[72]

A steampunk aesthetic is highly individualized, but remaining authentic to the values of the subculture is an important part of belonging to a community of practice. By learning and refining one's practice, a stronger engagement in, and contribution to, the community is possible.[73]

Exhibiting the "Essence" of a Community

While museums do not educate their audiences on how to be steampunks, their collections do provide important influences and inspirations for the production of steampunk material culture, and in exhibiting those products it is possible to gain some insight into the "essence" of the community. This insight is achievable, John Naylor argues, only

> provided the exhibition is fully rounded. You can't just put objects in place, in isolation, and get the very essence of steampunk. You've got to include everything, from the signage and labeling; these are important. The placement, the way people are introduced to objects, is important, whether you are going for a deliberate placement of these objects or a single steampunk experience.[74]

The interpretation of the exhibition is everything, though; otherwise it would be viewing abstract objects with no context. As the exhibitions under discussion demonstrate, placing steampunk objects within a science museum gives a very particular context to those objects. An art museum would provide a very different feel to the exhibition, one that perhaps is not so approachable, nor would it demonstrate the obvious scientific and industrial influences on steampunk.

What of a design museum, though? Jim Bennett suggested that this, or possibly a fashion museum, might be the place for a permanent collection. There is a design, and certainly a craft, element to steampunk material culture, as Jim Bennett explained about the objects in the MHS exhibition: "they didn't represent technological developments; they were developments in design, I guess."[75] Steampunk is about finding out how machines work; "by ripping open, reconstructing, and inhabiting machines, steampunks hope to access the unknowable terrain of postmodern material culture."[76] They then redesign them, refashioning them to a steampunk aesthetic. As Jay Strongmans explains in his stunningly visual book *Steampunk: The Art of Victorian Futurism*:

> Steampunk . . . tries to imagine the innovations of our present and our future as if the Victorians themselves were designing and manufacturing them. In essence then, this movement is fuelled by a love of Neo-Victorianism mixed with a healthy dose of 21st Century post-punk attitude and an embracing of the aesthetics of do-it-yourself technology.[77]

The artist that steampunks look to as embodying the art and science of steampunk lies further back in history, though: Leonardo da Vinci,[78] who took both objects and people apart to find out how they worked and designed and constructed amazing machines. When da Vinci's work was exhibited as part of *Universal Leonardo*, a Europe-wide exhibition program from 2006–2007, museum venues ranged from the Galleria degli Uffizi in Florence, to the Museum of the History of Science, Oxford, and the University of Oxford Botanic Garden.[79] This demonstrates the breadth of the artist that steampunks identify with and gives a sense of where and how steampunk art and material culture could be exhibited and collected.

Conclusion

Currently, steampunk art and material culture are being exhibited in a variety of museums but are not being collected. Steampunk, with its revisioning of technology, does not easily fit into traditional science collections; instead it is in collections of art galleries that steampunk may find a place. Yet, this risks stultifying a vibrant living culture, a "rich and flexible world,"[80] and can offer only the perspective of that specific moment in time. It also risks making a history of steampunk as a subculture,[81] so losing the essential social aspect of steampunk, which could be the result if objects are seen out of context as works of art. As John Naylor explained, "One of the key aspects to steampunk is social interaction, so you have to offer social events at the same time [as the exhibition]. You've got to engage with people."[82] In addition, as Knell points out, "Object collections often fail historians looking for evidence of the history of social practices. Unlike archival materials, objects are not good at retaining information, particularly if collection management has been poor."[83] By placing objects within a decorative arts or a design museum, or even a social history museum, the objects can be seen within the context that they both aspire to and rebel against. Both the social aspect and the machine aesthetic can come through. As Jeter declares in his introduction to *Infernal Devices*:

> A fascination with Victorian tech is at its heart a salutary acceptance of the machine-ness of machines—and correspondingly an acceptance of the humanity of human beings. . . . Thus we perceive flesh-and-blood Victorians—even the fictional ones—as being more genuine than ourselves. They had lives; we have marketing. . . . Steampunk enthusiasts are engaged, however unknowingly, in nobler fun than mere mental cosplay. May God bless and increase their tribe; human beings might yearn for lost things, but never for unreal things.[84]

To some extent, the social aspect and the machine aesthetic were achieved with steampunk novels through the exhibition *Out of This World: Science Fiction but Not as You Know It* at the British Library, London, from 25 May to 25 September 2011. Showcasing works by writers such as K. W. Jeter, James P. Blaylock, Bryan Talbot, Michael Moorcock, William Gibson, and Bruce Sterling, the genre was set within a broad scope, demonstrating that science fiction—and by inclusion, steampunk—can "raise people's awareness of the potential of science whilst also entertaining them. . . . [But] it can do so much more, by way of social commentary and studying the human condition in unusual circumstances."[85] In order to promote the essence and values of steampunk and communicate them to nonsteampunk audiences, the context of the culture, not just its objects, needs to be collected, and it is this, as much as the newness of the genre, that may be inhibiting museums in their acquisition of steampunk objects.

Notes

1. Richard Prentice, "Heritage: A Key Sector in the 'New' Tourism," in *Heritage, Museums and Galleries: An Introductory Reader*, ed. Gerard Corsane (London and New York: Routledge, 2005), 244.

2. Brian Graham, Gregory John Ashworth, and John E. Tunbridge, "The Uses and Abuses of Heritage," in *Heritage, Museums and Galleries: An Introductory Reader*, ed. Gerard Corsane (London and New York: Routledge, 2005), 30.

3. Laurajane Smith, *Uses of Heritage* (London and New York: Routledge, 2006), 13.

4. Smith, *Uses of Heritage*.

5. Susie West, "Introduction," in *Understanding Heritage in Practice*, ed. Susie West, Understanding Global Heritage (Manchester and Milton Keynes: Manchester University Press in association with the Open University, 2010), 1.

6. West, "Introduction," 1.

7. I was influenced, in part, in my methodology of researching steampunk communities by Amy C. Wilkins, *Wannabes, Goths and Christians: The Boundaries of Sex, Style, and Status* (Chicago: University of Chicago Press, 2008).

8. Philip Warren, *Foundations of Fashion: The Symington Corsetry Collection, 1860–1990* (Leicester, UK: Leicestershire County Council, Museums, Arts and Records Service, 2001); LCC, "Collections Online: Symington Collection of Corsetry, Foundation & Swimwear: Symington History, Part 1," *Leicestershire County Council Heritage Services*, n.d., http://museums.leics.gov.uk/collections-on-line/GetSingle Collection.do?collectionKey=68 (24 January 2012).

9. Warren, *Foundations of Fashion*; LCC, "Collections Online: Symington Collection of Corsetry, Foundation & Swimwear: Symington History, Part 2," *Leicestershire County Council Heritage Services*, n.d., http://museums.leics.gov.uk/collections -on-line/GetSingleCollection.do?collectionKey=68 (24 January 2012).

10. MHS, "Exhibition Programme for 'Steampunk'" (Museum of the History of Science, 2009).

11. MHS, "MHS—Museum of the History of Science, Oxford: History," *Museum of the History of Science*, 2011, www.mhs.ox.ac.uk/about/history (25 January 2012).

12. MHS, "Broadsheet No. 9: Steampunk" (Museum of the History of Science, 2009); Art Donovan, *The Art of Steampunk: Extraordinary Devices and Ingenious Contraptions from the Leading Artists of the Steampunk Movement* (East Petersburg, Pa.: Fox Chapel Publishing, 2011).

13. MHS, "MHS—Museum of the History of Science, Oxford: Steampunk."

14. KBSM, "The Greatest Steampunk Exhibition June 4th–August 29th—Kew Bridge Steam Museum, London," *Kew Bridge Steam Museum*, 26 May 2011, www .kbsm.org/news/2011–archive/224-the-greatest-steampunk-exhibition-june-4th-august-29th (25 January 2012).

15. See VSS, "The Victorian Steampunk Society," n.d., http://thevss.yolasite.com (25 January 2012).

16. KBSM, "The Greatest Steampunk Exhibition: Publicity Leaflet" (Kew Bridge Steam Museum, 2011).

17. For information on steampunk art exhibitions in the United States, see "Steampunk Art Exhibition 2008—YouTube," YouTube, 2008, www.youtube .comwatch?v=Piw9X-O5jsw&feature=related, and video sculptures by Tim Tate at Lenny Campello, "Tim Tate Steampunk Opening at Pentimenti Gallery, Philadelphia—YouTube," YouTube, 2008, www.youtube.comwatch?v=Qx1JjzqExnI (12 February 2012).

18. Three other interviews were requested, in order to provide a more balanced viewpoint on these exhibitions and collections. Although two of the three potential participants responded and agreed to take part, time constraints meant that it was not possible to conduct the interviews.

19. John Naylor, interview with the author.

20. John Naylor, interview with the author.

21. Bradford Industrial Museum has an exhibition running from December 2011 to May 2012; see Bradford Council, "Steampunk—What's on—Bradford Museums & Galleries," n.d., www.bradfordmuseums.org/whatson/event_detail.php?ID=368 (11 February 2012).

22. For Snibston's most recent steampunk event, see LCC, "New Age of Discovery—Events—Snibston—Leicestershire County Council," 2012, www.leics.gov.uk/discovery (11 February 2012).

23. V&A, "Wedding Fashion: Wedding of Mary Corey March and Christopher Paul Saari," 2010, www.vam.ac.uk/things-to-do/wedding-fashion/546 (11 February 2012).

24. Jim Bennett, interview with the author.

25. Rebecca Onion, "Reclaiming the Machine: An Introductory Look at Steampunk in Everyday Practice," *Neo-Victorian Studies* 1, no. 1 (2008): 138–163, www .neovictorianstudies.com; Jeff VanderMeer and S. J. Chambers, *The Steampunk Bible* (New York: Abrams Image, 2011).

26. John Naylor, interview with the author.

27. Although see Diana M. Pho, "Beyond Victoriana | A Multicultural Perspective on Steampunk," n.d., http://beyondvictoriana.com (12 February 2012).

28. Susan M. Pearce, "Collecting Reconsidered," in *Interpreting Objects and Collections*, ed. Susan M. Pearce, Leicester Readers in Museum Studies (London and New York: Routledge, 1994), 193–204; Simon J. Knell, "Altered Values: Searching for a New Collecting," in *Museums and the Future of Collecting* (Aldershot, UK: Ashgate Publishing, 2004), 1–46.

29. Anna Steen, "Samdok: Tools to Make the World Visible," in *Museums and the Future of Collecting*, ed. Simon J. Knell (Aldershot, UK: Ashgate Publishing, 2004), 196–203.

30. Although libraries are collecting steampunk books, see Mike Ashley, *Out of This World: Science Fiction But Not as You Know It* (London: The British Library, 2011).

31. Tony Bennett, *The Birth of the Museum: History, Theory, Politics* (London and New York: Routledge, 1995), 19.

32. "Santa Claus Is Coming to Town" (*Arthur Christmas* version)," YouTube, 6 December 2011, www.youtube.comwatch?gl=GB&v=nAI_xI9wQnE (5 March 2012); tridecalogism, "The Negative Side of Steampunk Going Mainstream," *Manbehindthecurtain*, 7 February 2012, http://manbehindthecurtain.ie/2012/02/07/the-negative-side-of-steampunk-going-mainstream (5 March 2012).

33. Cornelius Holtorf, "Heritage Values in Contemporary Popular Culture," in *Heritage Values in Contemporary Society*, ed. George S. Smith, Phyllis Mauch Messenger, and Hilary A. Soderland (Walnut Creek, Calif.: Left Coast Press, 2010), 47.

34. Engineer, "BourneSteamPunk.com » Visit to the Museum of Electricity, Christchurch on Sunday 5th December," *BourneSteamPunk.com*, 24 November 2010, http://bournesteampunk.com?p=244 (5 March 2012).

35. "The Steampunk Opium Wars—Untold London," *Untold London*, 2012, http://untoldlondon.org.uk/events/entry/the_steampunk_opium_wars (5 March 2012).

36. Ay-leen the Peacemaker, "Steampunk Events for February 2012 | Tor.com," *Tor.com*, n.d., www.tor.comblogs/2012/01/steampunk-events-february-2012 (5 March 2012).

37. CRMI, "Steampunk | Charles River Museum of Industry & Innovation," *Charles River Museum of Industry & Innovation*, n.d., www.crmi.org/events-2/steam punk (5 March 2012).

38. "Steampunk Festival—Non-Profit Organization—Waltham, MA | Facebook," *Facebook.com*, n.d., www.facebook.comCRMISteampunkFestival (5 March 2012).

39. "The Steampunktoberfest Ball," *The Period Events and Entertainments Re-Creation Society, Inc.*, n.d., www.peers.org/steampunk.html (5 March 2012).

40. Ben Guild, "Street Party Marks Opening of Steampunk Exhibition | Otago Daily Times Online News : Otago, South Island, New Zealand & International News," *Otago Daily Times*, 17 October 2011, www.odt.co.nz/regions/north-otago/182556/street-party-marks-opening-steampunk-exhibition (5 March 2012).

41. Philip Warren, interview with the author.

42. Jess Nevins, "Introduction: The 19th-Century Roots of Steampunk," in *Steampunk*, ed. Ann VanderMeer and Jeff VanderMeer (San Francisco: Tachyon Publications, 2008), 3.

43. Jim Bennett, interview with the author.

44. Jane Glaister and Helen Wilkinson, *Collections for the Future* (London: Museums Association, 2005), 17.

45. Sally Cross and Helen Wilkinson, *Making Collections Effective* (London: Museums Association, 2007), 24–25.

46. Philip Warren, interview with the author.

47. See Warren, *Foundations of Fashion*, for examples.

48. Bella Dicks, *Culture on Display: The Production of Contemporary Visitability* (Maidenhead, UK: Open University Press, 2003), 119; see also Terry Wallace, "Went the Day Well: Scripts, Glamour and Performance in War-Weekends," *International Journal of Heritage Studies* 13, no. 3 (2007): 200–223; Rachel A. Bowser and Brian Croxall, "Introduction: Industrial Evolution," *Neo-Victorian Studies* 3, no. 1 (2010): 1–45, www.neovictorianstudies.com; Jeanette Atkinson, "Engagement and Performance: Created Identities in Steampunk, Cosplay and Re-enactment," in *The Cultural Moment in Heritage Tourism: New Perspectives on Performance and Engagement*, ed. Laurajane Smith, Emma Waterton, and Steve Watson (London: Routledge, 2012), 113–130.

49. Brian Catling, "Steampunk: A Calibration of Longing," in *MHS Broadsheet No. 9: Steampunk* (Oxford: Museum of the History of Science, 2009).

50. Catling, "Steampunk: A Calibration of Longing."

51. Jim Bennett and Art Donovan, "Foreword," in *The Art of Steampunk: Extraordinary Devices and Ingenious Contraptions from the Leading Artists of the Steampunk Movement* (East Petersburg, Pa.: Fox Chapel Publishing, 2011), 19.

52. Catling, "Steampunk: A Calibration of Longing."

53. Thadeus Tinker, "Major Tinker's Emporium—Steampunk in Great Britain," n.d., http://tinkers-emporium.synthasite.com (10 February 2012).

54. Jos de Vink, "Heteluchtmachines (Introduction to Jos De Vink's Work)," n.d., http://home.kpn.nl/gvink01/index.html (10 February 2012).

55. Amy de la Haye, "Travellers' Boots, Body-Moulding, Rubber Fetish Clothes: Making Histories of Sub-Cultures," in *Making Histories in Museums*, ed. Gaynor Kavanagh (London and New York: Leicester University Press, 1996), 144.

56. Tinker, "Major Tinker's Emporium—Steampunk in Great Britain."

57. Gary Moskowitz, "What's with Steampunk?," 2010, www.moreintelligentlife.co.uk/content/lifestyle/gary-moskowitz/steampunk (11 February 2012).

58. Jim Bennett, interview with the author.

59. John Naylor, interview with the author.

60. John Naylor, interview with the author.

61. Jim Bennett, interview with the author.

62. John Naylor, interview with the author.

63. For a discussion of this in relation to non-Western communities, see Christina F. Kreps, "Non-Western Models of Museums and Curation in Cross-Cultural Perspective," in *A Companion to Museum Studies*, ed. Sharon Macdonald (Oxford and Malden, Mass.: Blackwell Publishing, 2006), 457–472; see also Eilean Hooper-Greenhill, *Museums and the Interpretation of Visual Culture* (London and New York: Routledge, 2000).

64. Hilda Hein, "Looking at Museums from a Feminist Perspective," in *Gender, Sexuality and Museums: A Routledge Reader*, 1st ed., ed. Amy K. Levin (London: Routledge, 2010), 53–64.

65. Steven Conn, *Museums and American Intellectual Life, 1876–1926*, illustrated ed. (Chicago: University of Chicago Press, 2000).

66. Hein, "Looking at Museums from a Feminist Perspective," 56.

67. Stephen Weil, "The Museum and the Public," in *Museums and Their Communities*, ed. Sheila Watson, Leicester Readers in Museum Studies (London: Routledge, 2007), 32–46.

68. Sheila Watson, "Museums and Their Communities," in *Museums and Their Communities*, 1–23.

69. VSS, "The Victorian Steampunk Society."

70. Etienne Wenger, "Communities of Practice: A Brief Introduction," *Communities of Practice*, 2006, www.ewenger.comtheory/index.htm (12 February 2012).

71. See Onion, "Reclaiming the Machine: An Introductory Look at Steampunk in Everyday Practice," for a discussion of how the iPod is anathema to steampunks.

72. VanderMeer and Chambers, *The Steampunk Bible*, 150.

73. Etienne Wenger, *Communities of Practice: Learning, Meaning, and Identity* (Cambridge: Cambridge University Press, 1998), 7.

74. John Naylor, interview with the author.

75. Jim Bennett, interview with the author.

76. Onion, "Reclaiming the Machine: An Introductory Look at Steampunk in Everyday Practice," 144–145.

77. Jay Strongman, *Steampunk: The Art of Victorian Futurism* (London: Korero Books, 2011), 12.

78. Catastrophone Orchestra and Arts Collective, "What, Then, Is Steampunk? Colonizing the Past so We Can Dream the Future," *SteamPunk Magazine* 1 (Fall 2006): 4–5, www.steampunkmagazine.com (12 January 2012).

79. University of the Arts, London, "Universal Leonardo: Leonardo Da Vinci Online › Exhibitions List," 2012, www.universalleonardo.org/exhibitions.php (12 February 2012).

80. VanderMeer and Chambers, *The Steampunk Bible*, 206.

81. de la Haye, "Travellers' Boots, Body-Moulding, Rubber Fetish Clothes: Making Histories of Sub-Cultures."

82. John Naylor, interview with the author.

83. Knell, "Altered Values: Searching for a New Collecting," 29–30.

84. K. W. Jeter, "Introduction: On Steampunk and 'Steampunk,'" in *Infernal Devices*, Kindle (Nottingham: Angry Robot, 2011), location 36–48.

85. Ashley, *Out of This World: Science Fiction But Not as You Know It*, 6.

Bibliography

Ashley, Mike. *Out of This World: Science Fiction But Not as You Know It*. London: The British Library, 2011.

Atkinson, Jeanette. "Engagement and Performance: Created Identities in Steampunk, Cosplay and Re-enactment." 113–130 in *The Cultural Moment in Heritage Tourism: New Perspectives on Performance and Engagement*, ed. Laurajane Smith, Emma Waterton, and Steve Watson. London: Routledge, 2012.

Ay-leen the Peacemaker. "Steampunk Events for February 2012 | Tor.com." *Tor.com*, n.d. www.tor.comblogs/2012/01/steampunk-events-february-2012 (5 March 2012).

Bennett, Jim, and Art Donovan. "Foreword." 18–19 in *The Art of Steampunk: Extraordinary Devices and Ingenious Contraptions from the Leading Artists of the Steampunk Movement*. East Petersburg, Pa.: Fox Chapel Publishing, 2011.

Bennett, Tony. *The Birth of the Museum: History, Theory, Politics*. London and New York: Routledge, 1995.

Bowser, Rachel A., and Brian Croxall. "Introduction: Industrial Evolution." *Neo-Victorian Studies* 3, no. 1 (2010): 1–45. http://neovictorianstudies.com (5 March 2012).

Bradford Council. "Steampunk—What's on—Bradford Museums & Galleries," n.d. www.bradfordmuseums.org/whatson/event_detail.php?ID=368 (11 February 2012).

Campello, Lenny. "Tim Tate Steampunk Opening at Pentimenti Gallery, Philadelphia—YouTube." YouTube. 2008. www.youtube.comwatch?v=Qx1JjzqExnI (12 February 2012).

Catastrophone Orchestra and Arts Collective. "What, Then, Is Steampunk? Colonizing the Past so We Can Dream the Future." *SteamPunk Magazine* 1 (Fall 2006): 4–5. www.steampunkmagazine.com (5 March 2012).

Catling, Brian. "Steampunk: A Calibration of Longing." In *MHS Broadsheet No. 9: Steampunk*. Oxford: Museum of the History of Science, 2009.

Conn, Steven. *Museums and American Intellectual Life, 1876–1926*. Illustrated ed. Chicago: University of Chicago Press, 2000.

CRMI. "Steampunk | Charles River Museum of Industry & Innovation." *Charles River Museum of Industry & Innovation*, n.d. www.crmi.org/events-2/steampunk (5 March 2012).

Cross, Sally, and Helen Wilkinson. *Making Collections Effective*. London: Museums Association, 2007.

Dicks, Bella. *Culture on Display: The Production of Contemporary Visitability*. Maidenhead, UK: Open University Press, 2003.

Donovan, Art. *The Art of Steampunk: Extraordinary Devices and Ingenious Contraptions from the Leading Artists of the Steampunk Movement*. East Petersburg, Pa.: Fox Chapel Publishing, 2011.

Engineer. "BourneSteamPunk.com » Visit to the Museum of Electricity, Christchurch on Sunday 5th December." *BourneSteamPunk.com*, 24 November 2010. http://bournesteampunk.com?p=244 (5 March 2012).

Glaister, Jane, and Helen Wilkinson. *Collections for the Future*. London: Museums Association, 2005.

Graham, Brian, Gregory John Ashworth, and John E. Tunbridge. "The Uses and Abuses of Heritage." 26–37 in *Heritage, Museums and Galleries: An Introductory Reader*, ed. Gerard Corsane. London and New York: Routledge, 2005.

Guild, Ben. "Street Party Marks Opening of Steampunk Exhibition | Otago Daily Times Online News: Otago, South Island, New Zealand & International News." *Otago Daily Times*, 17 October 2011. www.odt.co.nz/regions/north-otago/182556/street-party-marks-opening-steampunk-exhibition (5 March 2012).

de la Haye, Amy. "Travellers' Boots, Body-Moulding, Rubber Fetish Clothes: Making Histories of Sub-Cultures." 143–151 in *Making Histories in Museums*, ed. Gaynor Kavanagh. London and New York: Leicester University Press, 1996.

Hein, Hilda. "Looking at Museums from a Feminist Perspective." 53–64 in *Gender, Sexuality and Museums: A Routledge Reader*, 1st ed., ed. Amy K. Levin. London: Routledge, 2010.

Holtorf, Cornelius. "Heritage Values in Contemporary Popular Culture." 43–54 in *Heritage Values in Contemporary Society*, ed. George S. Smith, Phyllis Mauch Messenger, and Hilary A. Soderland. Walnut Creek, Calif.: Left Coast Press, 2010.

Hooper-Greenhill, Eilean. *Museums and the Interpretation of Visual Culture*. Ed. E. Hooper-Greenhill and F. Kaplan. London and New York: Routledge, 2000.

Jeter, K. W. "Introduction: On Steampunk and 'Steampunk.'" In *Infernal Devices*. Kindle. Nottingham: Angry Robot, 2011.

KBSM. "The Greatest Steampunk Exhibition June 4th–August 29th—Kew Bridge Steam Museum, London." *Kew Bridge Steam Museum*, 26 May 2011. www.kbsm.org/news/2011–archive/224–the-greatest-steampunk-exhibition-june-4th-august-29th (25 January 2012).

———. "The Greatest Steampunk Exhibition: Publicity Leaflet." Kew Bridge Steam Museum, 2011.

Knell, Simon J. "Altered Values: Searching for a New Collecting." 1–46 in *Museums and the Future of Collecting*, ed. Simon J. Knell. Aldershot, UK: Ashgate Publishing, 2004.

Kreps, Christina F. "Non-Western Models of Museums and Curation in Cross-Cultural Perspective." 457–472 in *A Companion to Museum Studies*, ed. Sharon Macdonald. Oxford and Malden, Mass.: Blackwell Publishing, 2006.

LCC. "Collections Online: Symington Collection of Corsetry, Foundation & Swimwear: Symington History, Part 1." *Leicestershire County Council Heritage Services*, n.d. http://museums.leics.gov.uk/collections-online/GetSingleCollection.do?collectionKey=68 (24 January 2012).

———. "Collections Online: Symington Collection of Corsetry, Foundation & Swimwear: Symington History, Part 2." *Leicestershire County Council Heritage Services*, n.d. http://museums.leics.gov.uk/collections-online/GetSingleCollection.do?collectionKey=68 (24 January 2012).

———. "New Age of Discovery—Events—Snibston—Leicestershire County Council," 2012. www.leics.gov.uk/discovery (11 February 2012).

MHS. "Broadsheet No. 9: Steampunk." Museum of the History of Science, 2009.

———. "Exhibition Programme for 'Steampunk.'" Museum of the History of Science, 2009.

———. "MHS—Museum of the History of Science, Oxford: History." *Museum of the History of Science*, 2011. www.mhs.ox.ac.uk/about/history (25 January 2012).

———. "MHS—Museum of the History of Science, Oxford: Steampunk." *Museum of the History of Science*, 2011. www.mhs.ox.ac.uk/exhibits/steampunk (25 January 2012).

Moskowitz, Gary. "What's with Steampunk?" 2010. www.moreintelligentlife.co.uk/content/lifestyle/gary-moskowitz/steampunk (11 February 2012).

Nevins, Jess. "Introduction: The 19th-Century Roots of Steampunk." 3–11 in *Steampunk*, ed. Ann VanderMeer and Jeff VanderMeer. San Francisco: Tachyon Publications, 2008.

Onion, Rebecca. "Reclaiming the Machine: An Introductory Look at Steampunk in Everyday Practice." *Neo-Victorian Studies* 1, no. 1 (2008): 138–163. www.neovictorianstudies.com.

Pearce, Susan M. "Collecting Reconsidered." 193–204 in *Interpreting Objects and Collections*, ed. Susan M. Pearce. Leicester Readers in Museum Studies. London and New York: Routledge, 1994.

Pho, Diana M. "Beyond Victoriana | A Multicultural Perspective on Steampunk," n.d. http://beyondvictoriana.com (12 February 2012).

Prentice, Richard. "Heritage: A Key Sector in the 'New' Tourism." 243–256 in *Heritage, Museums and Galleries. An Introductory Reader*, ed. Gerard Corsane. London and New York: Routledge, 2005.

"Santa Claus Is Coming to Town" (*Arthur Christmas* version.) YouTube, 6 December 2011. www.youtube.comwatch?gl=GB&v=nAI_xI9wQnE (5 March 2012).

Smith, Laurajane. *Uses of Heritage*. London and New York: Routledge, 2006.

"Steampunk Art Exhibition 2008—YouTube." YouTube, 2008. www.youtube.comwatch?v=Piw9X-O5jsw&feature=related (12 February 2012).

"Steampunk Festival—Non-Profit Organization—Waltham, MA | Facebook." *Facebook.com*, n.d. www.facebook.comCRMISteampunkFestival (5 March 2012).

Steen, Anna. "Samdok: Tools to Make the World Visible." 196–203 in *Museums and the Future of Collecting*, ed. Simon J. Knell. Aldershot, UK: Ashgate Publishing, 2004.

Strongman, Jay. *Steampunk: The Art of Victorian Futurism*. London: Korero Books, 2011.

"The Steampunk Opium Wars—Untold London." *Untold London*, 2012. http://untoldlondon.org.uk/events/entry/the_steampunk_opium_wars (5 March 2012).

"The Steampunktoberfest Ball." *The Period Events and Entertainments Re-Creation Society, Inc.*, n.d. www.peers.org/steampunk.html (5 March 2012).

Tinker, Thadeus. "Major Tinker's Emporium—Steampunk in Great Britain," n.d. http://tinkers-emporium.synthasite.com (10 February 2012).

tridecalogism. "The Negative Side of Steampunk Going Mainstream." *Manbehindthecurtain*, 7 February 2012. http://manbehindthecurtain.ie/2012/02/07/the-negative-side-of-steampunk-going-mainstream (5 March 2012).

University of the Arts, London. "Universal Leonardo: Leonardo Da Vinci Online › Exhibitions List," 2012. www.universalleonardo.org/exhibitions.php (12 February 2012).

V&A. "Wedding Fashion: Wedding of Mary Corey March and Christopher Paul Saari," 2010. www.vam.ac.uk/things-to-do/wedding-fashion/546 (11 February 2012).

VanderMeer, Jeff, and S. J. Chambers. *The Steampunk Bible: An Illustrated Guide to the World of Imaginary Airships, Corsets and Goggles, Mad Scientists, and Strange Literature*. New York: Abrams Image, 2011.

de Vink, Jos. "Heteluchtmachines (Introduction to Jos de Vink's Work)," n.d. http://home.kpn.nl/gvink01/index.html (10 February 2012).

VSS. "The Victorian Steampunk Society," n.d. http://thevss.yolasite.com (25 January 2012).

Wallace, Terry. "Went the Day Well: Scripts, Glamour and Performance in War-Weekends." *International Journal of Heritage Studies* 13, no. 3 (2007): 200–223.

Warren, Philip. *Foundations of Fashion: The Symington Corsetry Collection, 1860–1990*. Leicester, UK: Leicestershire County Council, Museums, Arts and Records Service, 2001.

Watson, Sheila. "Museums and Their Communities." 1–23 in *Museums and Their Communities*, ed. Sheila Watson. Leicester Readers in Museum Studies. London: Routledge, 2007.

Weil, Stephen. "The Museum and the Public." 32–46 in *Museums and Their Communities*, ed. Sheila Watson. Leicester Readers in Museum Studies. London: Routledge, 2007.

Wenger, Etienne. *Communities of Practice: Learning, Meaning, and Identity*. Cambridge: Cambridge University Press, 1998.

———. "Communities of Practice: A Brief Introduction." *Communities of Practice*, 2006. www.ewenger.comtheory/index.htm (12 February 2012).

West, Susie. "Introduction." 1–6 in *Understanding Heritage in Practice*, ed. Susie West. Understanding Global Heritage. Manchester and Milton Keynes: Manchester University Press in association with the Open University, 2010.

Wilkins, Amy C. *Wannabes, Goths and Christians: The Boundaries of Sex, Style, and Status*. Chicago: University of Chicago Press, 2008.

Ship of dreams. *Copyright Jody Steel*

Steampunk:
Looking at the Evidence

Jeff VanderMeer

If you're reading this afterword, you hardly need me to tell you what steam-punk is or where it might be going—you have had excellent guides through the tangled back corridors of this perplexingly complex form of retrofuturism. What I may be able to do is provide a wider scope to what you have just read, however, in part because while I have documented and studied steampunk, I don't write it that often and I don't self-identify as a steampunk. This is by way of saying, my view is an overview from the outside looking in, and trying to get at the whole of it. While that may seem like common sense, one reason that a book like this one is of value is that it comes from a view-point of accurate information. The fact is that steampunk often feels as if it is undefinable simply because the explosion in its popularity has led to the promulgation of inaccuracy.

Much of what we see about steampunk is in the form of received ideas—someone reads something about it and then he blogs, or someone reads a couple of books, and maybe not the best ones, and she's got a sense of what the subgenre is and isn't from a small sample. It's an easy target because the term itself may conjure up for some escapism and perhaps a false romanticism for a bygone age. But steampunk is more complicated than that, as you must know by now. One of its precursors, H. G. Wells, was a socialist and wrote anti-imperial novels and socially aware novels as well. Another precursor, Michael Moorcock, wrote his *Nomads of the Time Stream* series specifically as a comment on the ills of the empire. Jumping forward to the creation of the term by K. W. Jeter in 1987, you have Jeter's own *Infernal Devices*, which satirizes and comments on the Victorian era right there at the start—it isn't a love song to Victoriana.

The pulse then gets thready for a while despite the adrenaline rush of books by Tim Powers, James Blaylock, and Messrs. Gibson and Sterling, which means that in part steampunk has survived so long because it's been on life support from time to time. It rises from the dead due to steampunk fashion and music in the 1990s and some steampunk aesthetic expressed in movies and comics. Then the maker movement fashions a heart for it through creation of actual steampunk-inspired machines, which feeds back into all of the rest of the subculture. In addition, *SteamPunk Magazine*, properly anarchist and green in focus, provides an edge for the field to aspire to politically—a soul, so to speak. In this environment of growing pop culture appeal meshed with political/social interest, steampunk becomes popular in part because it contains multitudes.

There's a certain movement that then builds, a forward momentum, that in a way mimics the "generative force" described by Cynthia J. Miller in her chapter on the airship, a forward momentum that as she puts it "mobilizes and transforms—animates, reconstructs, and renews." This is how "marvels surge, flip, roll, and hum": the subculture reanimates the impulse to create steampunk fiction, the fiction energizes the subculture, and websites like Beyond Victoriana plot a course for steampunk that includes a response to imperialism and other issues from the point of view of the colonized, creating agency and discourse through new channels.

As alluded to by Amy Sue Bix, many steampunks seek to reject the conformity of the modern, soulless, featureless design of technology—and all that implies. "Love the machine, hate the factory," part of the title of Sally-Anne Huxtable's contribution, sums it up rather nicely. Steampunks offer DIY solutions to the damage caused by industrialization. This isn't simply an impulse to whitewash the bad parts of the Victorian era—it is instead a progressive impulse to reclaim the dead past in a positive and affirmative way. And as Mike Perschon points out in his chapter, this is entirely in keeping with the progressive strands of Victoriana itself.

Adding further relevance and ideas, steampunk enclaves in Brazil, France, and elsewhere become visible to US/UK audiences through the Internet, fostering further cross-pollination within the subgenre. This next wave is also largely dominated by women, including Gail Carriger, Cherie Priest, Karin Lowachee, and Ekaterina Sedia, and has begun to move away from being purely Victorian or English in setting or culture. In another generation, the true energy behind steampunk may have moved away from Anglo settings and perspectives altogether.

And all of this creates an atmosphere for publishers in which the term *steampunk* sells books. Whenever a term can sell books, it naturally creates fragmentation, contamination, and mutation of the term in question, which is why thinking of steampunk as a kind of umbrella or an aesthetic rather than a movement is more useful. (This naturally has created some friction between gatekeepers and those who hold radically different ideas of what steampunk is in their heads, but some amount of head-butting during transition periods is inevitable.)

Fragmentation, contamination, and mutation are not necessarily bad things. In the case of steampunk, in the future the popularity of the term will mean that fluffy, escapist books are published, but also that much stronger, more literary, more diverse books are published as well—and Trojan horses: books that look fluffy and escapist but are anything but. Steampunk is rapidly creating a safe haven for very, very interesting material that might not otherwise enter the world through commercial publishers, or even through indie publishers—not to mention the amazing amount of short fiction, which runs the usual gamut from crap to amazing. It is creating a space for progressive alt-histories that are acts of reclamation. There is feminist steampunk, international steampunk, and multicultural steampunk in ever-growing numbers. And as ever, the fact that it is spread out through fashion, music, fiction, making, and so much more means it is much easier for something like steampunk to last even longer.

Index

312 ～ Index

Holmes, Meredith, 71, 85
Holub, Miroslav, 132
"home-made zoo," xx, 92. *See also*
    Professor Elemental
Homebrew Computer Club, 246
Homonculus (1986), xv
Hoover Dam, 241, 257
"The Huge Hunter, or The Steam Man
    of the Prairies" (1868), 147, 159n2,
    162
Hugo (film, 2011), 135
"Human Powered" (2011), 54, 60n65,
    73, 86
humor, 25, 30, 97, 109, 126, 136, 148,
    193–199, 205, 225, 243, 284
Hunt, Stephen, 3, 10, 11, 14, 17n37, 18
Hunt Museum (Limerick, Ireland), 278
Hutcheon, Linda, 44–45, 58n16, 202,
    206n58, 209
Huxtable, Sally-Anne, xxii, 213–233,
    300
hybridity. *See* steampunk

"Icarus compound," 57
iceberg, 105, 109, 110–114, 116, 158
icepunk, 106, 121n40, 122
identity, 53, 93, 219, 293n73, 297;
    gender and, 25, 50, 57, 219, 303;
    genre, x, xxvii, 148, 185–186;
    heritage used to define, 273–274,
    281; hidden, 53, 93; steampunk
    fans' construction of, xxii, 185–186,
    188–193, 284
ideology, 159n6, 161, 166, 172; gender
    and, 30, 33, 38n52, 39, 44, 58n6,
    82n38, 84; of style, xxv, 45, 62,
    80n5, 84, 206n60, 207; steampunk
    defined by, x, xx, 66, 80n5, 174,
    185–187, 191, 196, 200–202,
    204n28, 206n60, 209, 218, 228
"ideoplasm," 66
imagination, xv, xxi–xxiii, 22, 77, 145,
    146, 153, 156, 268; erotic, 52, 53,

67; historical, 38n45, 41, 173–174,
    178, 202, 228; public, xix, 4, 36,
    150, 152, 248n17, 251; role in
    steampunk world-building, 9, 11, 22,
    23, 36, 119, 167, 170, 173–174, 216,
    218, 287; works of Verne, 126–127,
    139, 141n37
imperialism, 5, 17n46, 51, 77, 110,
    147–148, 177, 179, 193–194, 200,
    214, 259, 299–300
The Impossible Voyage (stage production,
    1882), 136
"In the Deep of Time" (1897), 22,
    37n7, 39
India, 146, 240
The Indifference Engine (album, 2010),
    91–93, 95, 97–98, 101
industrialization, xxv, 127, 131, 181n27,
    182, 207, 248n12, 249n38, 251, 252,
    256, 268n2, 292n48, 294; defining
    role in steampunk, xxii, 67, 173,
    191, 277, 287; impact on aesthetics,
    239–245; social aspects, xviii, 6–8,
    10, 12, 15n9, 35, 137, 259, 300
"infernal devices," 50, 54, 84, 161n28,
    162
Infernal Devices (1987), 66, 80n4, 85,
    288, 295, 299
"Infernal Machine" (2011), 75, 86
The Innocent's Progress (2010), 25, 40,
    87
innovation, xvi, 118, 156, 159, 222,
    244, 250n38, 253, 261, 267, 287
Institute of Incoherent Geography, 136
Internet, 77, 82n33, 83, 173, 187, 190,
    213–214, 227, 229, 232, 300. *See also*
    names of specific sites
intertexuality, 161n32, 167, 172, 175,
    177, 178, 181n29n32, 182
invention (as process), 94, 117, 157,
    162, 237, 244, 248n8, 263, 285
inventions, xv, xvii, xxi, 7, 12, 95, 99,
    117–118, 126, 127, 129, 131–132,

About the Editors,
Contributors, and Artists

Editors

Cynthia J. Miller is a cultural anthropologist, specializing in popular culture and visual media. She serves as director of communication for the Center for the Study of Film and History as well as scholar-in-residence at Emerson College. Cynthia's writing has appeared in a wide range of journals and anthologies, including *Post Script*, the *Journal of Popular Film and Television*, and *Film & History*. She is the editor of *Too Bold for the Box Office: The Mockumentary, From Big Screen to Small* (Scarecrow Press); *Cadets, Rangers, and Junior Space Men: Televised "Rocketman" Series of the 1950s and Their Fans*; and *Undead in the West: Vampires, Zombies, Mummies and Ghosts on the Cinematic Frontier* (Scarecrow Press), the latter two coedited with A. Bowdoin Van Riper. Cynthia is also film review editor for the journal *Film & History* and series editor for Scarecrow Press's *Film and History* book series.

Julie Anne Taddeo is visiting associate professor of history at the University of Maryland, where she specializes in Victorian and twentieth-century culture and gender studies. She is the author of *Lytton Strachey and the Search for Modern Sexual Identity* (2002), the editor of *Catherine Cookson Country: On the Borders of Legitimacy, Fiction, and History* (2012), and the coeditor (with Ken Dvorak) of *The Tube Has Spoken: Reality TV and History* (2009). She has published articles on such topics as British modernism, sexuality, and popular culture in *Journal of the History of Sexuality*; *Journal of Popular Culture*, *Film & History*; and *Clues: A Journal of Detection*.

Contributors

Jeanette Atkinson works as a distance learning associate tutor in the School of Museum Studies, University of Leicester, UK, and is copyeditor and member of the editorial board of *museum & society*. She holds a PhD in museum studies from the University of Leicester (funded by an Arts and Humanities Research Council award) and is author of "Engagement and Performance: Created Identities in Steampunk, Cosplay and Reenactment" in *The Cultural Moment in Tourism* (2012). She is currently working on a monograph for Ashgate Publishing titled *Education, Values and Ethics in International Heritage: Learning to Respect*. Jeanette previously worked as a heritage practitioner in various public institutions in the United Kingdom, including the Victoria and Albert Museum, and in New Zealand at the National Library of New Zealand. She has also worked in private conservation practices in London and Cambridge, UK, and in Wellington, New Zealand.

Suzanne Barber is a dual PhD student within the Folklore and Ethnomusicology and Anthropology departments at Indiana University, Bloomington. She has her MA in folk studies from Western Kentucky University, where she completed a thesis on the Society for Creative Anachronism. Her BA is in English from California State University East Bay. She has one publication, titled "Negotiating a Shire: The Transformation of Local Values in the Society for Creative Anachronism," published in the *Folklore Forum*. Her research interests include environment and human animal relations in China, tourism, visual narratives, and ethnographic video production.

Amy Sue Bix is an associate professor in the History Department at Iowa State University and the director of Iowa State's Center for Historical Studies of Technology and Science. Her book *Inventing Ourselves Out of Jobs?: America's Debate over Technological Unemployment, 1929–1981* was published by Johns Hopkins University Press in 2000. She is also coauthor of *The Future Is Now: Science and Technology Policy in America Since 1950* (2007). Bix is currently finishing a book titled *"Girls Coming to Tech!": An Institutional, Intellectual, and Social History of Engineering Education for American Women*. Her most recent publications on other topics cover Depression-era American technology, as well as the history of women, tools, and home repair. Bix has also published on the history of breast cancer and AIDS research, history of eugenics, history of home economics, women and medicine, and post–World War II physics and engineering, among other subjects.

Ken Dvorak is the associate dean for academic support services and director of distance education for Northern New Mexico College, Española, New Mexico. He received a PhD in American culture studies from Bowling Green State University and is coeditor with Julie Anne Taddeo of *The Tube Has Spoken: Reality TV and History* (2009).

Erika Behrisch Elce teaches Victorian literature and science and literature at the Royal Military College of Canada, where she is an assistant professor in the Department of English. Her research interests lie mainly in nineteenth-century narratives of science and exploration and the discursive tensions between official mandates of expeditions and explorers' lived experiences in the field. Her book *As Affecting the Fate of My Absent Husband: Selected Letters of Lady Franklin Concerning the Search for the Lost Franklin Expedition, 1848–1860* was published in 2009.

Matt Hale is a dual PhD student within the Folklore and Ethnomusicology and Communication and Culture departments at Indiana University. He earned his BA in anthropology and MA in folk studies from Western Kentucky University. He is the recipient of numerous academic awards, the most recent of which include the Warren Roberts Prize for Best Student Paper in Folk Art from the American Folklore Society and the Richard Dorson Paper Prize from the Folklore Institute at Indiana University. His research interests include visual anthropology and ethnographic film production, material culture, verbal art, American popular and participatory cultures, embodiment, and sensory ethnography. He has one publication, titled "Shaping Theory, Bending Method, Tapping [New] Media," published in *Folklore Forum*. He is currently finalizing a series of articles focusing on steampunk fashion, art, and performance from ethnographic fieldwork conducted at Dragon*Con in Atlanta, Georgia, since 2010.

Sally-Anne Huxtable is a lecturer in art and design history at Northumbria University in the UK. Huxtable has also undertaken work for a number of museums including Tate Britain, the Courtauld Institute of Art, the Museo Nacional del Prado, the Museo de Arte de Ponce, and the De Morgan Centre, as well as lecturing at the University of Bristol. Recent and forthcoming publications include *Catalogue of the British Collection at Museo de Arte, Ponce* (2012); "'Art and Money, or the Story of the Room:' Whistler, the Peacock Room and the Artist as Magus," in Lee Glazer and Linda Merrill (eds.), *Palaces of Art: Whistler and the Art Worlds of Aestheticism* (2012); "Order and Disarray: Two Watercolours by Frederick Walker," in *Life, Legend Landscape: Victorian Drawings and Watercolours* (2011); and "Re-Reading the Green Dining Room," in Jason Edwards and Imogen Hart (eds.), *Rethinking the Interior c. 1867–1896* (2010). She is currently working on a monograph on Aestheticism and interiority titled *Inward Worlds: Aestheticism and Its Interiors, 1848 to 1900.*

Dru Pagliassotti is a fiction editor and writer whose works include the award-winning steampunk romance novel *Clockwork Heart* (2008) and the steampunk short stories "Terminus" with Jo Gerrard (2009, *Magic & Mechanica*), "The Manufactory" (2009, *Beneath Ceaseless Skies*), "Code of Blood" (2011, *Corsets & Clockwork*), and "The Ghost in the Machine" (2012, *The Mammoth Book of Ghost Romance*). She is also a professor of communication at California Lutheran University, where she researches the rise and growing popularity of boys' love manga and male/male romance fiction in the United States. She coedited *Boys' Love Manga: Essays on the Sexual Ambiguity and Cross-Cultural Fandom of the Genre* (2010) and is currently coediting a special boys' love issue of the *Journal of Graphic Novels and Comics.*

Mike Perschon is finishing up his dissertation on steampunk literature for his PhD at the University of Alberta in Edmonton, Alberta, in the Great White North of Canada. He has been an independent musician, a Mennonite minister, a freelance writer, and a jeans salesman but is currently feeling like he's "finally arrived," instructing English at Grant MacEwan University. Mike publishes regularly on speculative fiction at Tor.com and in a number of fanzines, academic journals, and his blogs, including steampunkscholar.com.

Diana M. Pho received her MA in performance studies at New York University and works as an activist, blogger, and founding editor of the award-winning blog Beyond Victoriana (beyondvictoriana.com), which focuses on multicultural steampunk and retrofuturism. Diana has also traveled the country as a professional convention speaker about social justice issues at science fiction, steampunk, and anime conventions under the stage name Ay-leen the Peacemaker. Her published work can be found in *SteamPunk Magazine—The First Years: Issues #1–7* (2011) and in the academic anthology *Fashion Talks: Undressing the Power of Style* (SUNY Press, 2012). Additionally, she has been interviewed about steampunk and its evolving subculture for many media outlets, including BBC America, the Science Channel, and HGTV; the websites Tor.com and Racialicious; and the books *The Steampunk Bible* (2011), *Steampunk: Reloaded* (2010), and *The WisCon Chronicles*, Vol. 5 (2010). Diana currently resides in New York City.

Jamieson Ridenhour is a scholar of Victorian Gothic literature at the University of Mary in Bismarck, North Dakota, where he serves as chair of Language and Literature. He is the editor of the Valancourt edition of Sheridan Le Fanu's 1872 vampire novella *Carmilla*, as well as a novelist and filmmaker. His published academic essays include work on Charles Dickens, Iris Murdoch, and Sheridan Le Fanu.

Catherine Siemann has a PhD in nineteenth-century British literature from Columbia University, as well as a JD from New York University. She is currently an adjunct assistant professor at Cooper Union and John Jay College, CUNY, both in New York City. Her article "Curiouser and Curiouser: Law in the *Alice* Books" is forthcoming in *Law & Literature*, and her essay "Darkness Falls on the Endless Summer: Buffy as Gidget for the Fin de Siècle" appeared in *Fighting the Forces: What's at Stake in Buffy the Vampire Slayer*, ed. Rhonda V. Wilcox and David Lavery (Rowman & Littlefield, 2002). She is working on projects on Lewis Carroll, Charles Dickens, and China Miéville, as well as a book-length project on steampunk.

John C. Tibbetts is an associate professor of film and media studies at the University of Kansas. His most recent publications are the forthcoming *Douglas Fairbanks and the Choreography of Hope* and *Peter Weir: Interviews*, both for Mississippi University Press. His other published books include *The Gothic Imagination* (2011), *Robert Schumann: A Chorus of Voices* (2010), and *All My Loving? The Films of Tony Palmer* (2009). Other books include *The American Theatrical Film* (1985), *Dvorak in America* (1993), *Encyclopedia of Novels into Film* (2002), and *Composers in the Movies* (2005). His articles on film, literature, painting, theater, and music have appeared in *Journal of the Fantastic in the Arts*, *Film Comment*, *Opera News*, *Historical Journal of Film Radio and Television*, and *Literature/Film Quarterly*. He has worked as a broadcaster for National Public Radio, the Christian Science Monitor Radio

Network, Voice of America, and CBS television. Both of his radio series, *The World of Robert Schumann* and *Piano Portraits*, have been heard worldwide on the WFMT broadcast network and National Public Radio. He was recently awarded the 2008 Kansas Governor's "Arts in Education" Award. His hobbies include playing piano for silent films and illustrating his own books and articles.

A. Bowdoin Van Riper is an independent scholar whose work focuses on the history of modern science and technology, images of science and technology in popular culture, and historical memory on film. His work has appeared in *Film & History*, *New Scientist*, *Journal of Popular Film and Television*, and collections such as *Icons of Evolution* (ed. Brian Regal, 2008), *Sounds of the Future* (ed. Mathew J. Bartowiak, 2009), and *Too Bold for the Box Office* (ed. Cynthia J. Miller, 2012). He is the author, most recently, of *A Biographical Encyclopedia of Scientists and Inventors in American Film and TV Since 1930* (2011), and coeditor, with Cynthia J. Miller, of the forthcoming collections *1950s "Rocketman" TV Series and Their Fans: Cadets, Rangers, and Junior Spacemen* (2012) and *Undead in the West: Vampires, Mummies, Zombies and Ghosts on the Cinematic Frontier* (Scarecrow, 2012).

Jeff VanderMeer's fiction has been published in over twenty countries. His books, including the best-selling *City of Saints & Madmen* and *Finch*, have recently made the year's best lists of the *Wall Street Journal*, the *Washington Post*, and the *San Francisco Chronicle*. VanderMeer's surreal, often fantastical, fiction has won two World Fantasy Awards and an NEA-funded Florida Individual Writers' Fellowship and Travel Grant, along with being a finalist for the Hugo Award, Nebula Award, and many others. He regularly reviews books for the *New York Times Book Review*, *Los Angeles Times Book Review*, and the *Washington Post*, while his short fiction has appeared in Conjunctions, Black Clock, Arc, and Tor.com, among others. With his wife, Ann, the Hugo Award–winning editor of *Weird Tales*, he has edited such iconic anthologies as *Steampunk*, *Steampunk Reloaded*, *The Weird*, *The New Weird*, *The Thackery T. Lambshead Pocket Guide to Eccentric & Discredited Diseases*, and *The Thackery T. Lambshead Cabinet of Curiosities*. He is the author of the definitive *Steampunk Bible*. VanderMeer is the assistant director for the unique teen SF/fantasy writing camp Shared Worlds, based at Wofford College. He lives in Tallahassee, Florida.

The future will be built of iron, brass, and dreams. *Copyright Jody Steel*

Artists

Brian Kesinger has been fortunate to wear many hats within the animation industry. His artistic travels have led him to his current position as a story artist at Walt Disney animation studios. He is inspired by the amazing work of his friends and coworkers as well as an eagerness to learn. He hopes to share his learning experiences with readers and perhaps offer some inspiration as a way of giving back to the community of artists who have given so much to him. His work may be found at www.bkartonline.com.

Ashley Norfleet is an artist with a strong background in illustration. She creates vivid illustrative scenes that tell a story or depict an idea. The foundation of her work is within the initial concept; the uniqueness of the idea is the driving force behind every piece. Bold color schemes and meticulous rendering are pleasing to the eye, and the use of these tools entices the audience, subsequently holding their attention. After this, they can begin to process the concept behind the work. It is within this principle she seeks to evoke thought, plant ideas, and broadcast powerful messages that force the surrender of attention within the mind of the viewer. "The little cloud that could" is a piece created with her father in mind, a crafty and resourceful man with many gifts. He has reminded her repeatedly throughout her life—if there is a desire or a need for the nonexistent or the unimaginable, then it's up to you to create it yourself. Ashley's work may be found at www .bossladydesign.com.

Jody Steel is currently studying film production at Emerson College and draws her motivation from her family, peers, and professors. Ever since she was a child, she has used her artistic abilities to express herself. Whether she was drawing at home or during class, those around her began to take notice of her artistic endeavors and commissioned her to create a variety of work. Jody's work ranges from paintings and illustrations to tattoo designs and graphics. While she is specifically studying production design and art direction for film, she intends to work as a freelance artist in many other media; so when asked to create steampunk illustrations, she seized the opportunity. Because of this work, she hopes to be involved with the steampunk community again in the future.

Steamir &

A Steampunk Anthology

Edited by
Julie Anne Taddeo
Cynthia J. Miller

ROWMAN & LITTLEFIELD
Lanham • Boulder • New York • Toronto • Plymouth, UK

Publi by Rowman & Littlefield
4501 es Boulevard, Suite 200, Lanham, Maryland 20706
www man.com

10 hombury Road, Plymouth PL6 7PP, United Kingdom

British Library Cataloguing in Publication Information Available

Library of Congress Cataloging-in-Publication Data

The hardback edition of this book was previously catalogued by the Library of Congress
as follows:

Steaming into a Victorian future : a steampunk anthology / edited by Julie Anne
Taddeo, Cynthia J. Miller.
     p. cm.
  Includes bibliographical references and index.
  ISBN 978-0-8108-8586-8 (cloth : alk. paper) — ISBN 978-0-8108-8587-5 (ebook)
1. Steampunk fiction—History and criticism. 2. Steampunk culture. I. Taddeo, Julie
Anne. II. Miller, Cynthia J., 1958-
  PN3448.S73S74 2013
  809.3'8766—dc23   2012024041

ISBN: 978-0-8108-8586-8 (cloth : alk. paper)
ISBN: 978-0-8108-9315-3 (paper : alk. paper)
ISBN: 978-0-8108-8587-5 (ebook)

In honor of steampunk's
Rebels, Idealists, Explorers, and Visionaries,
from artisans to airship pirates,
and all those who inspire them